Shojo Beat

Skip·Beat!

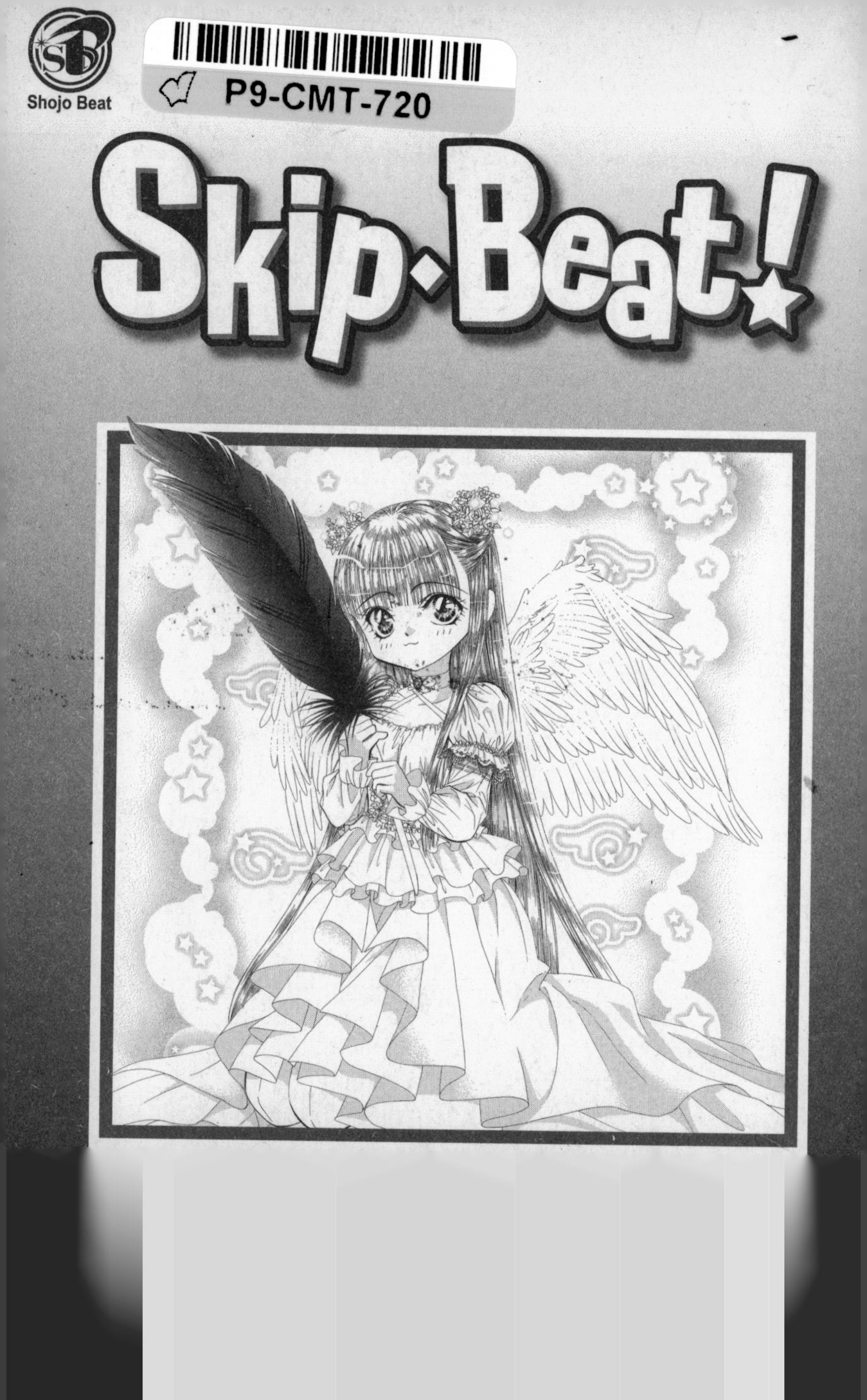

Skip·Beat!

Volume 7

CONTENTS

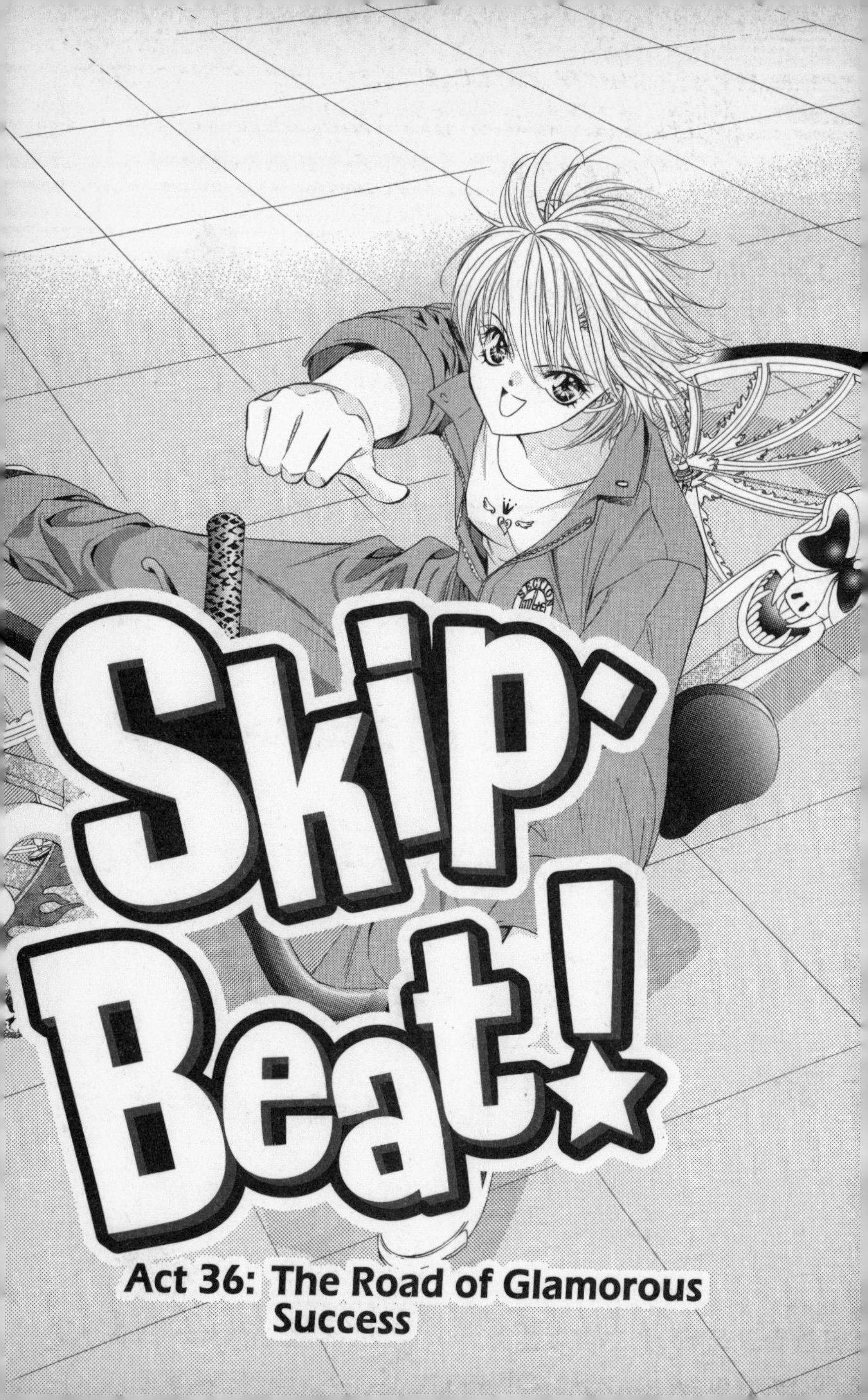
Skip Beat!

Act 36: The Road of Glamorous Success

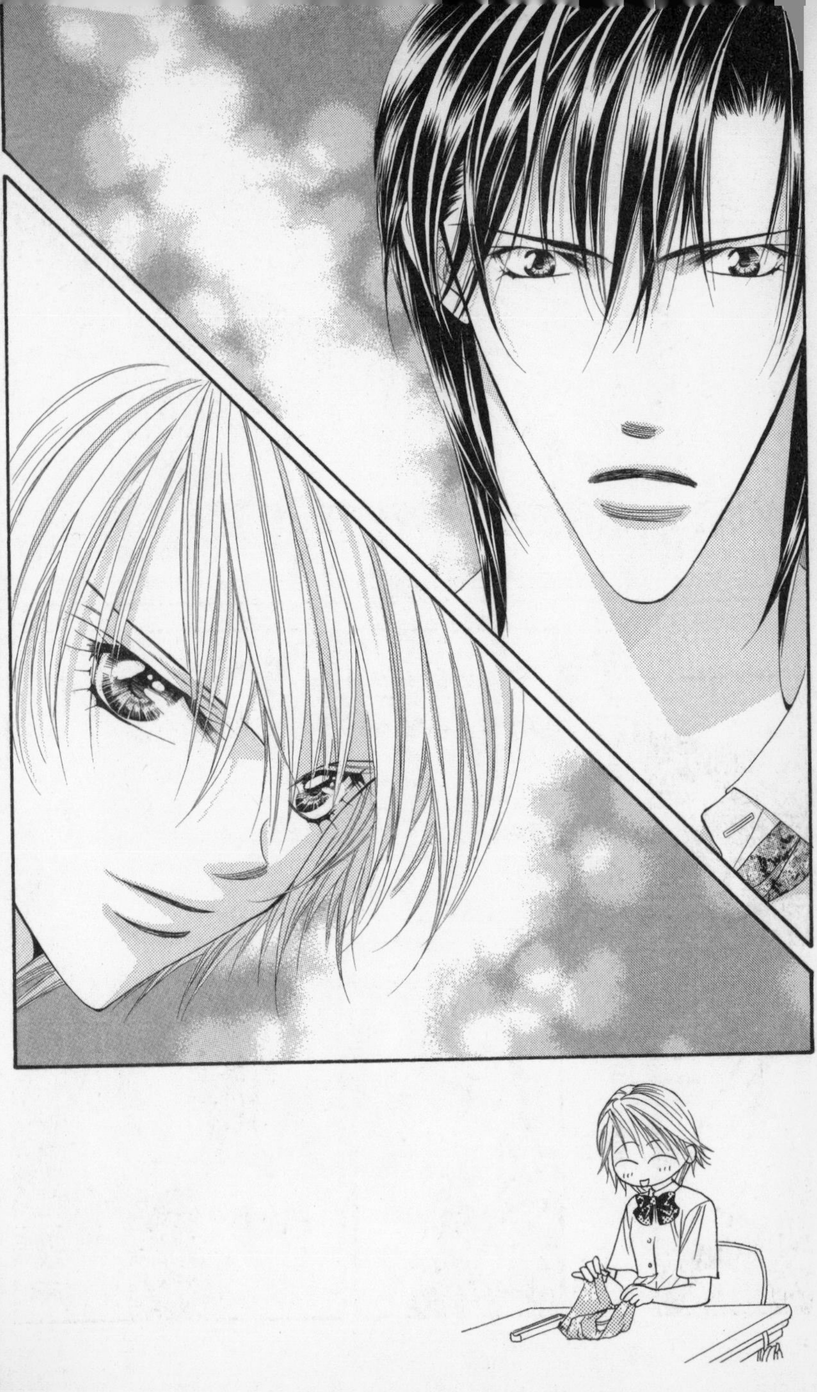

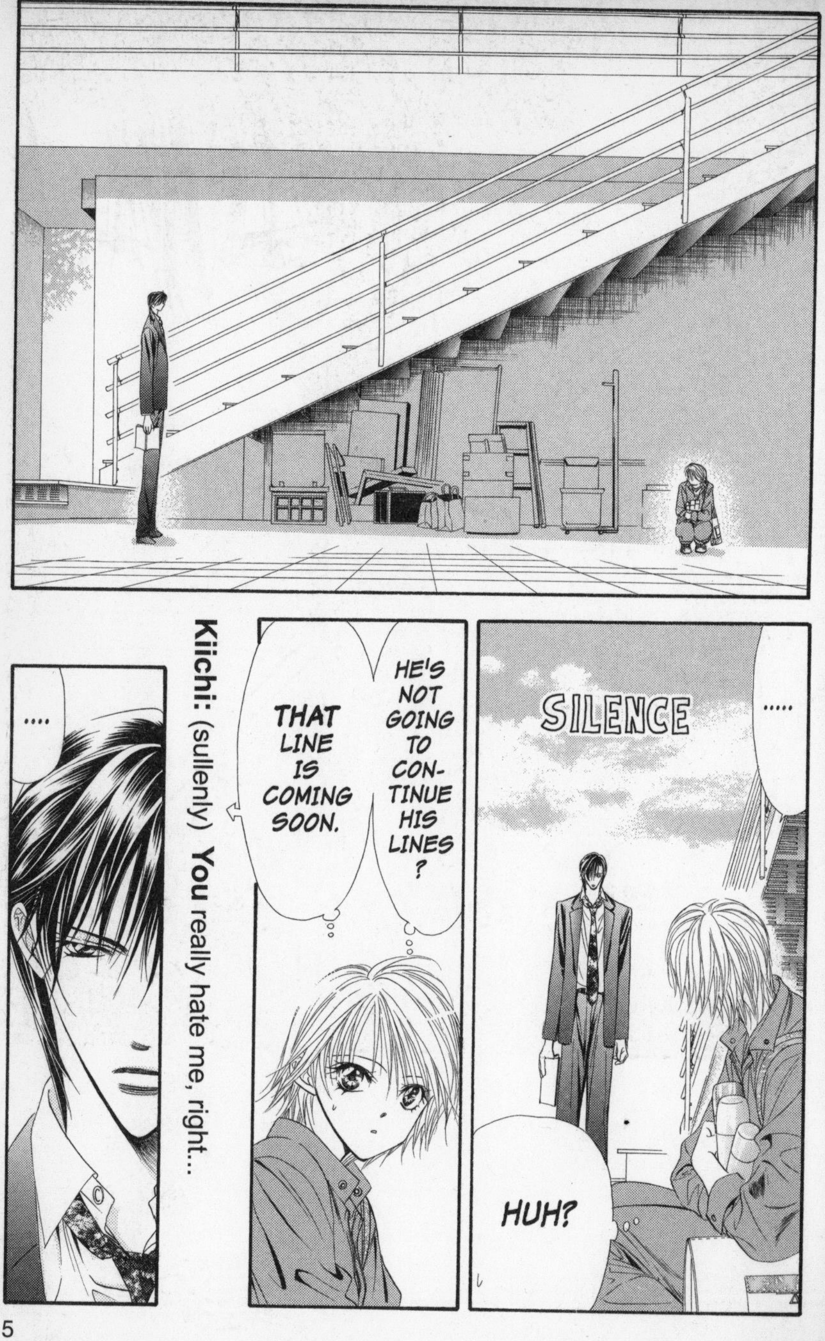
SILENCE
.....
HUH?
HE'S NOT GOING TO CONTINUE HIS LINES?
THAT LINE IS COMING SOON.
Kiichi: (sullenly) You really hate me, right...
....

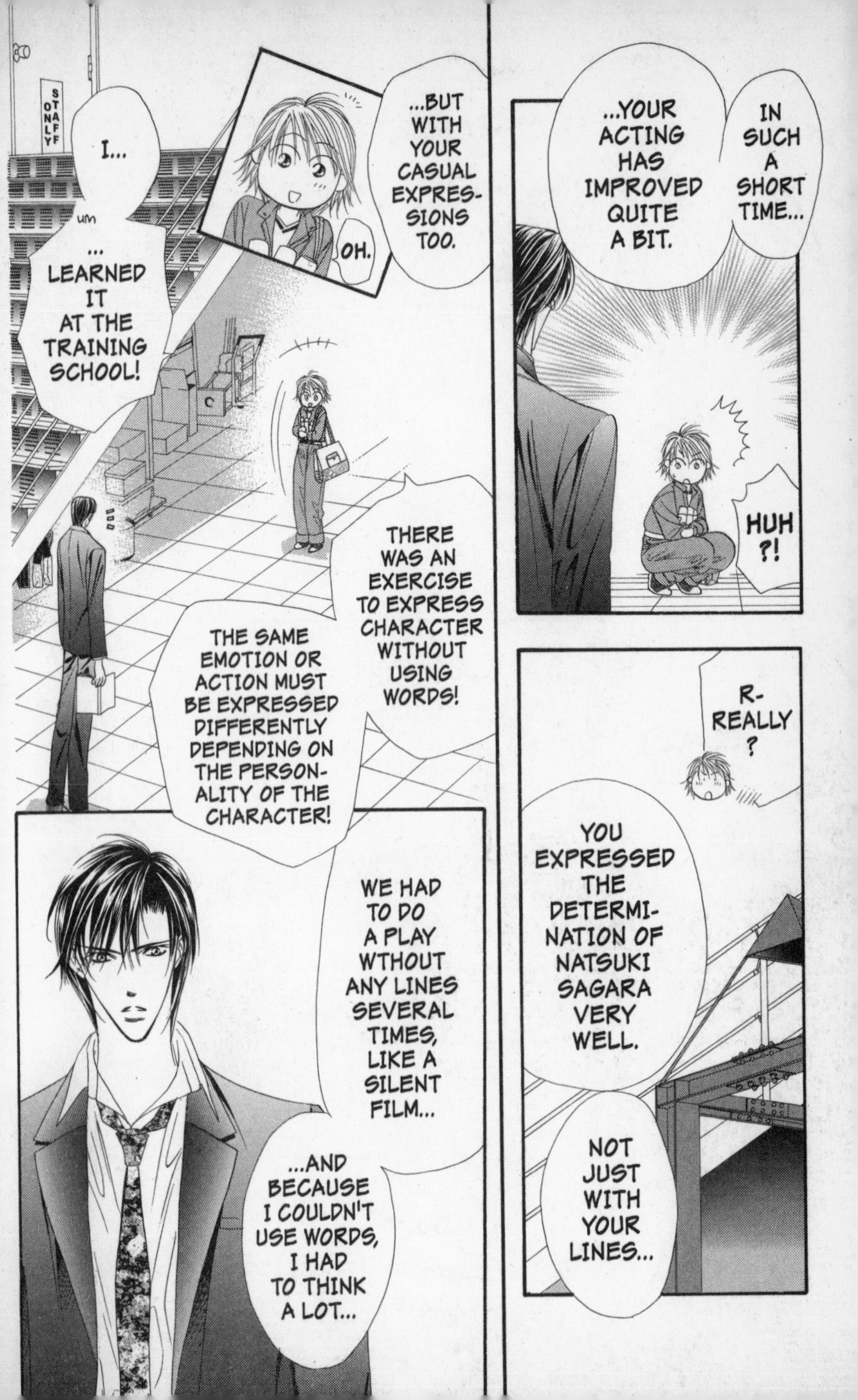
IN SUCH A SHORT TIME...
...YOUR ACTING HAS IMPROVED QUITE A BIT.
HUH?!
R-REALLY?
YOU EXPRESSED THE DETERMINATION OF NATSUKI SAGARA VERY WELL.
NOT JUST WITH YOUR LINES...
...BUT WITH YOUR CASUAL EXPRESSIONS TOO.
OH.
STAFF ONLY
I...
um
... LEARNED IT AT THE TRAINING SCHOOL!
THERE WAS AN EXERCISE TO EXPRESS CHARACTER WITHOUT USING WORDS!
THE SAME EMOTION OR ACTION MUST BE EXPRESSED DIFFERENTLY DEPENDING ON THE PERSONALITY OF THE CHARACTER!
WE HAD TO DO A PLAY WTHOUT ANY LINES SEVERAL TIMES, LIKE A SILENT FILM...
...AND BECAUSE I COULDN'T USE WORDS, I HAD TO THINK A LOT...

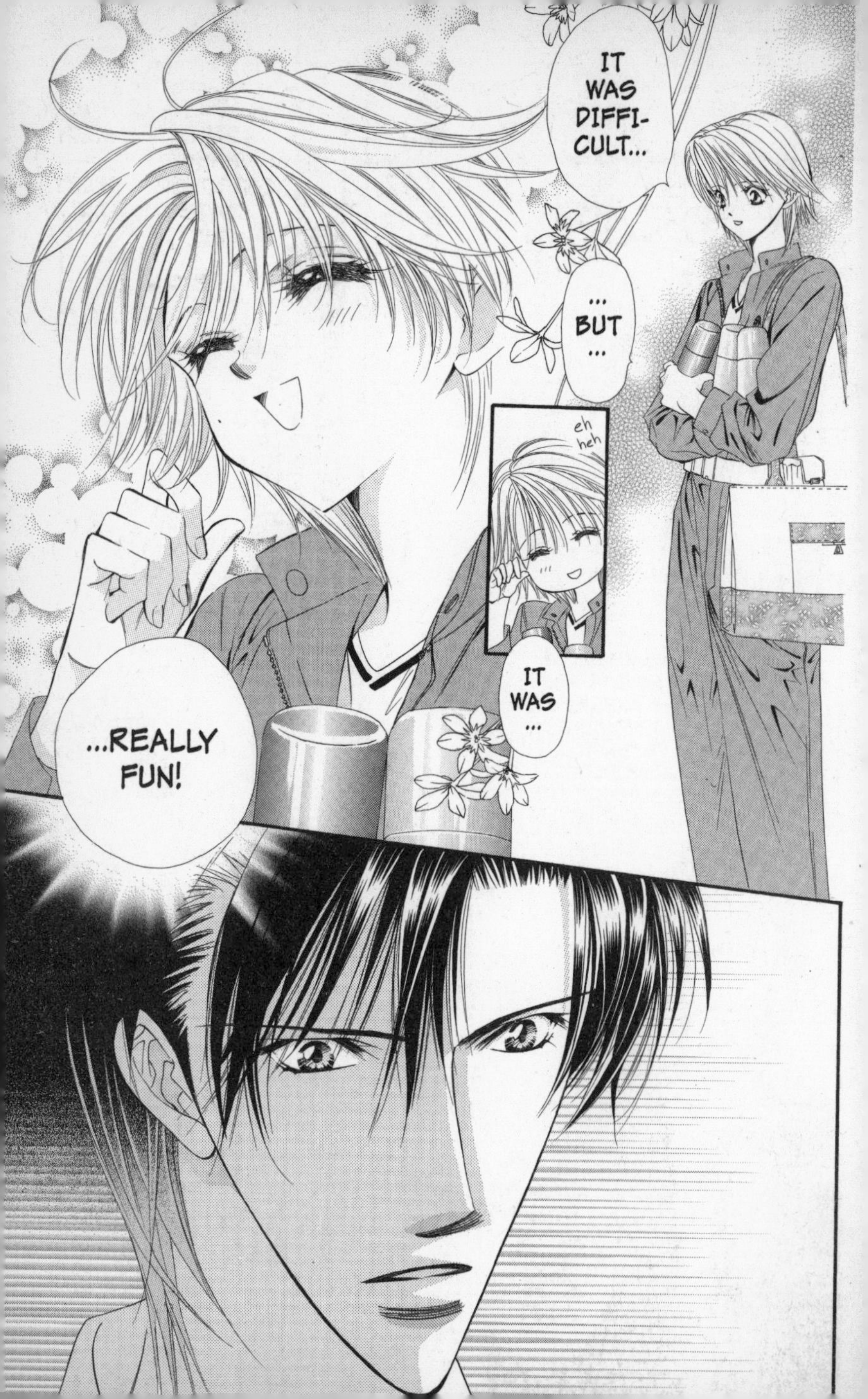
IT WAS DIFFI-CULT...
...BUT...
eh heh
IT WAS...
...REALLY FUN!

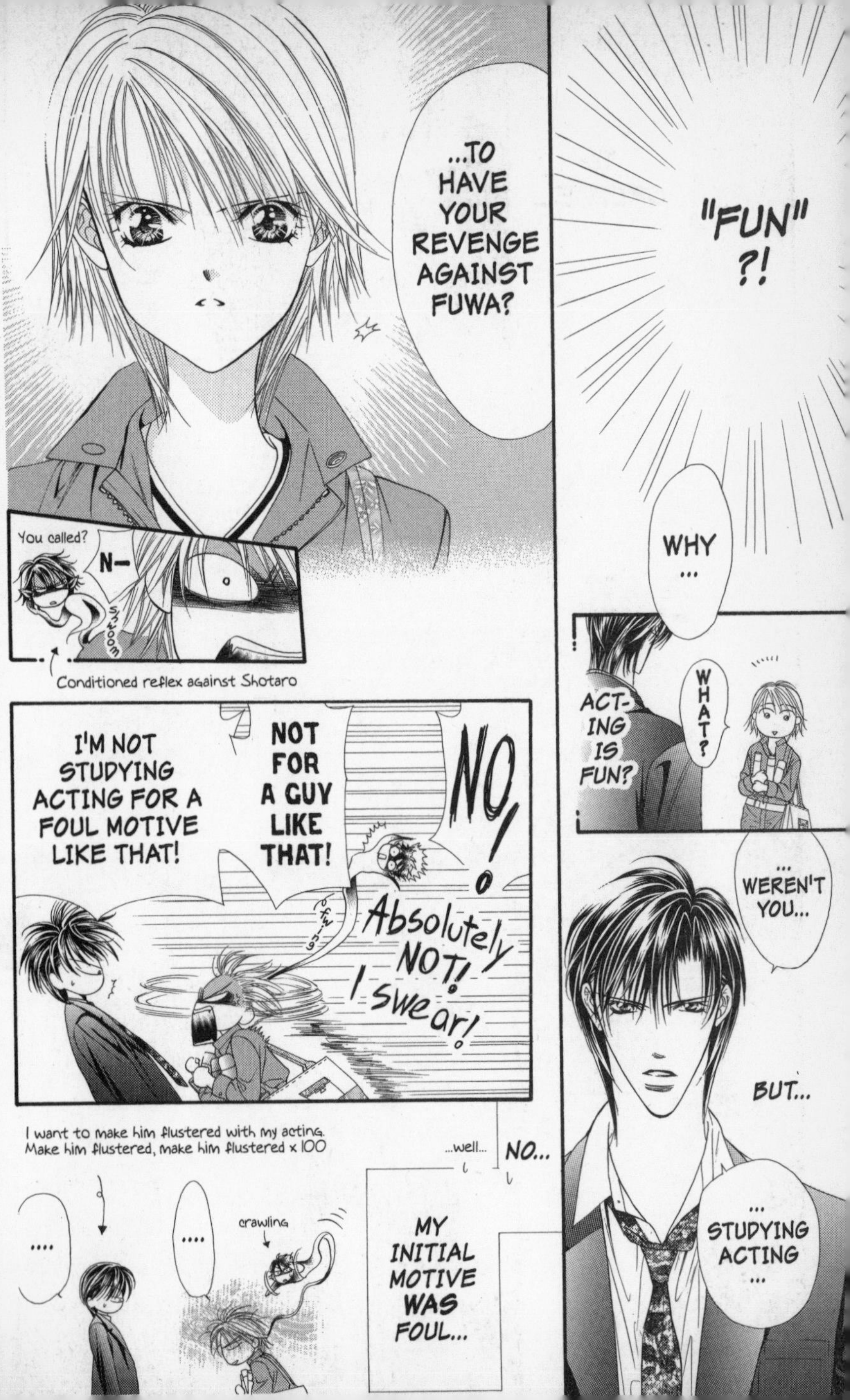
"FUN" ?!
WHY ...
WHAT?
ACT-ING IS FUN?
... WEREN'T YOU...
BUT...
... STUDYING ACTING ...
...TO HAVE YOUR REVENGE AGAINST FUWA?
N—
You called?
SWOOM
Conditioned reflex against Shotaro
NO!
Absolutely NOT! I swear!
NOT FOR A GUY LIKE THAT!
I'M NOT STUDYING ACTING FOR A FOUL MOTIVE LIKE THAT!
fwing
I want to make him flustered with my acting.
Make him flustered, make him flustered x 100
NO...
...well...
MY INITIAL MOTIVE WAS FOUL...
....
crawling
....

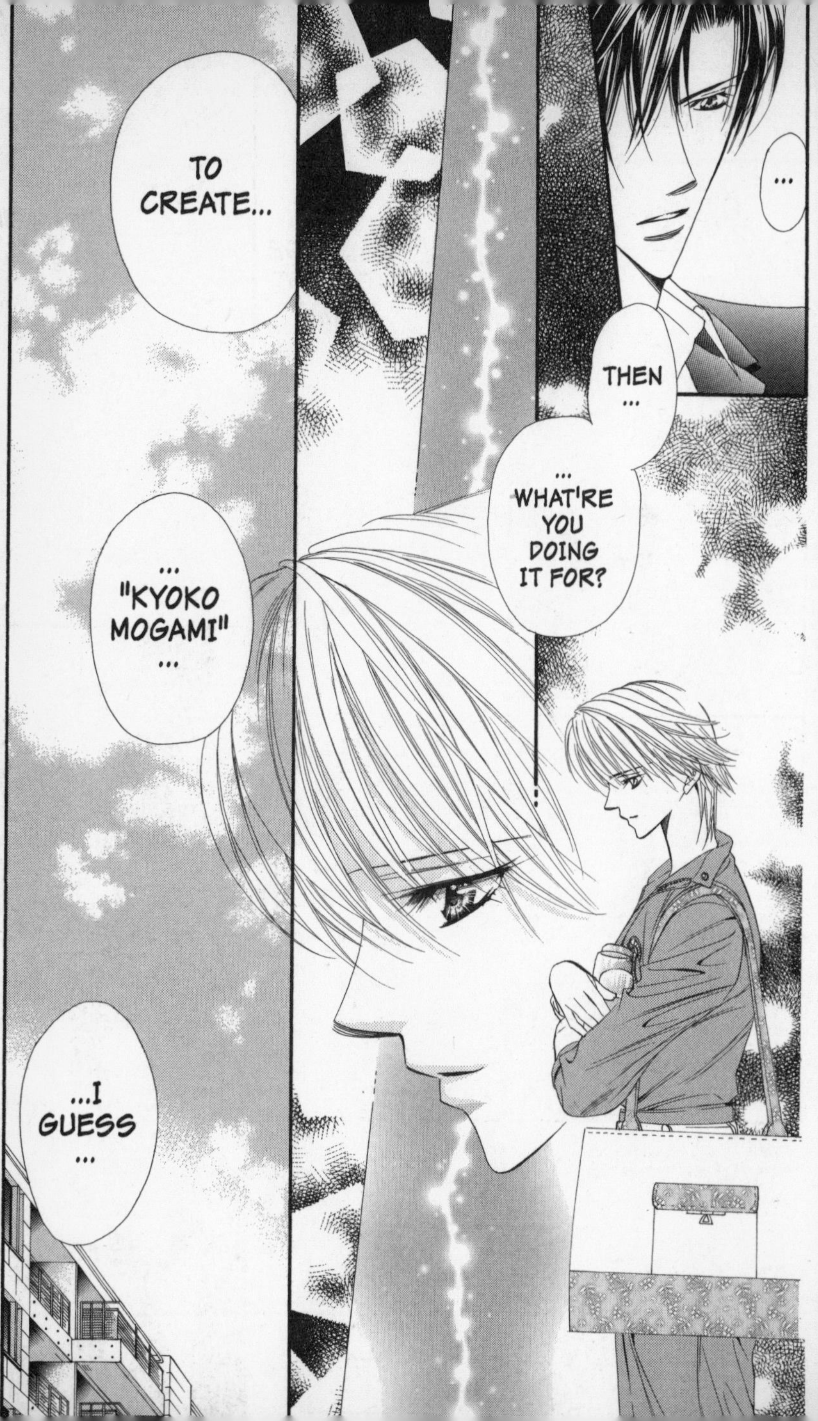
...
THEN ...
... WHAT'RE YOU DOING IT FOR?
TO CREATE...
... "KYOKO MOGAMI" ...
...I GUESS ...

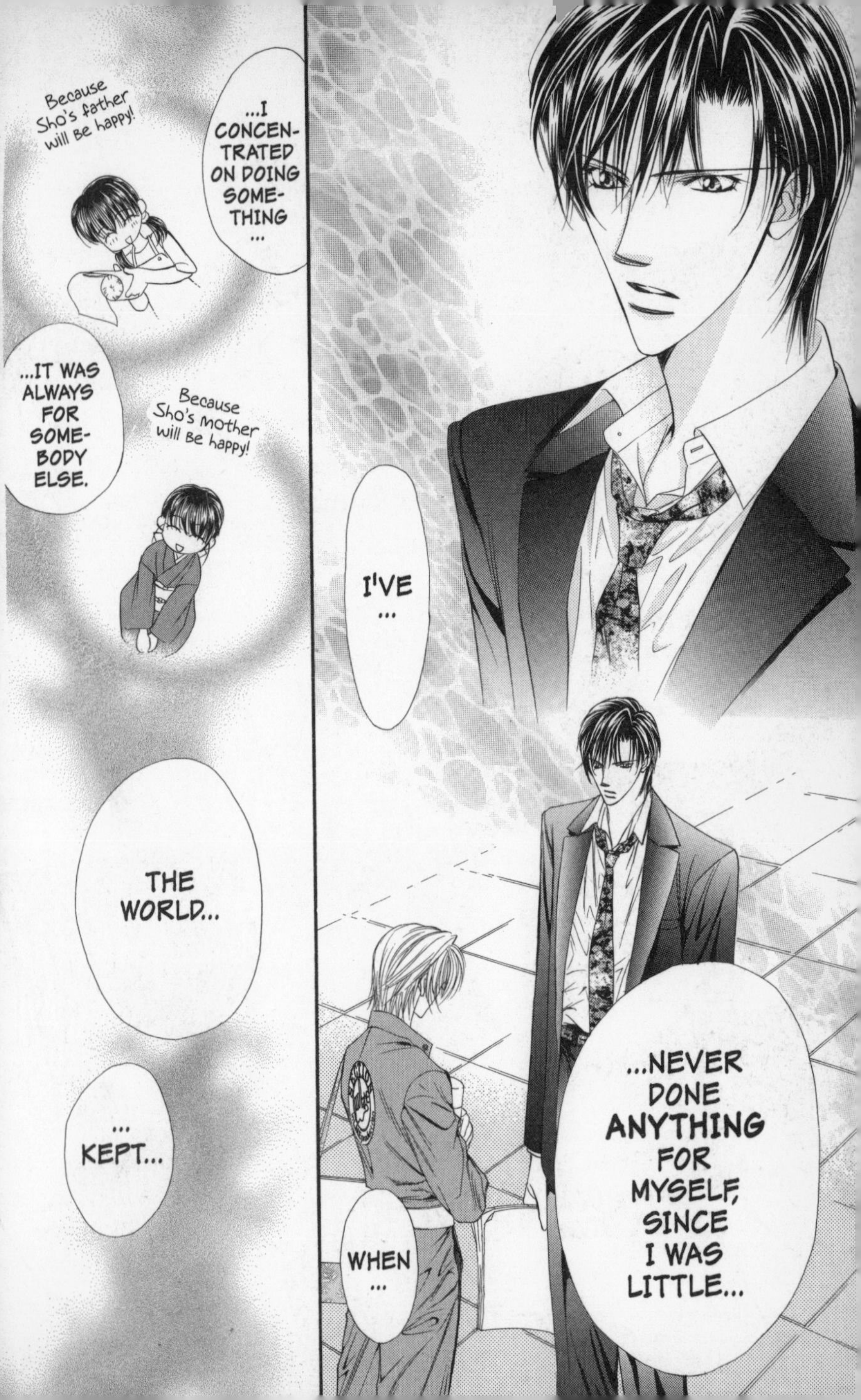
I'VE ...
...NEVER DONE ANYTHING FOR MYSELF, SINCE I WAS LITTLE...
WHEN ...
...I CONCENTRATED ON DOING SOMETHING ...
Because Sho's father will be happy!
...IT WAS ALWAYS FOR SOMEBODY ELSE.
Because Sho's mother will be happy!
THE WORLD...
... KEPT...

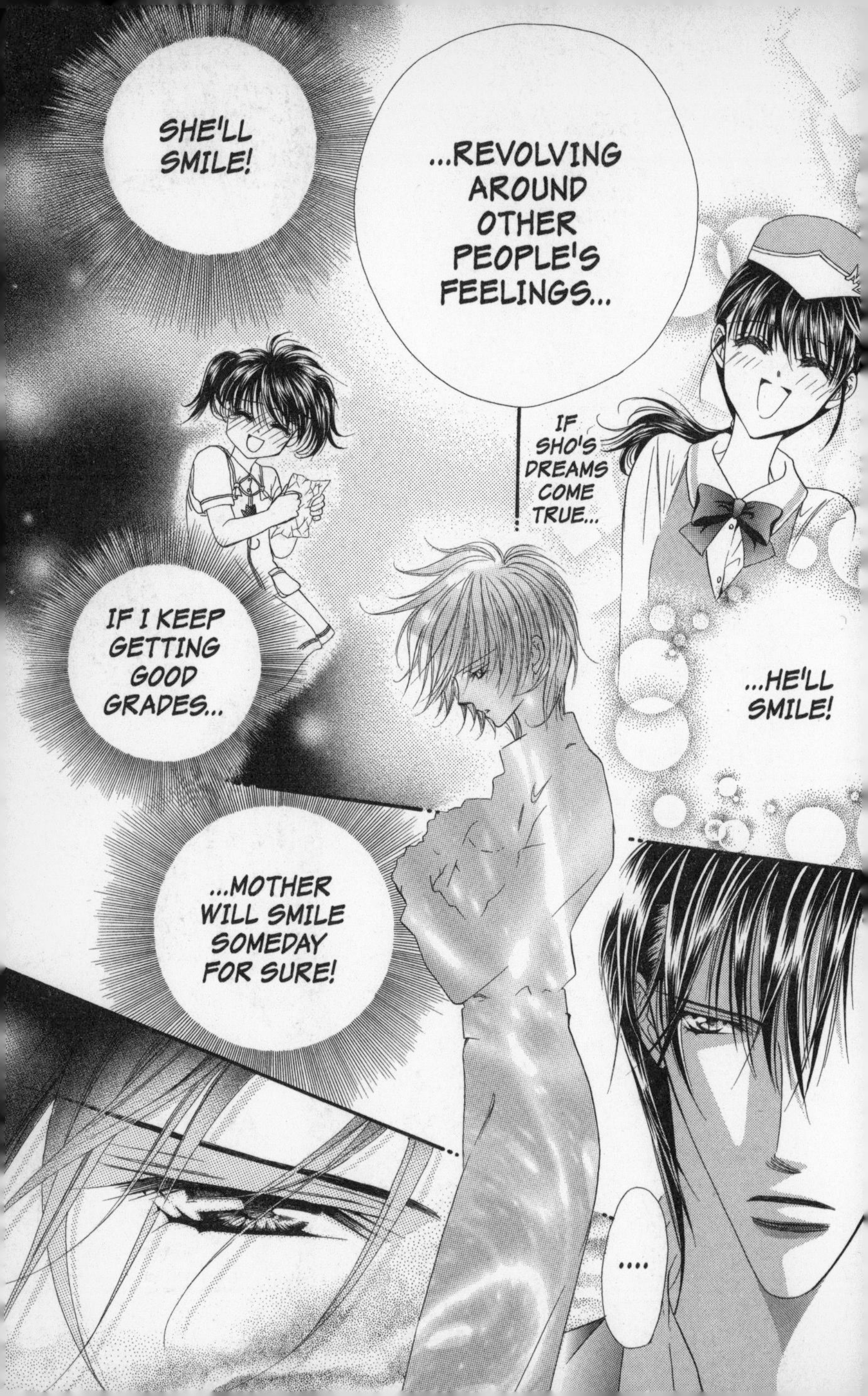
...REVOLVING AROUND OTHER PEOPLE'S FEELINGS...
SHE'LL SMILE!
IF SHO'S DREAMS COME TRUE...
...HE'LL SMILE!
IF I KEEP GETTING GOOD GRADES...
...MOTHER WILL SMILE SOMEDAY FOR SURE!
....

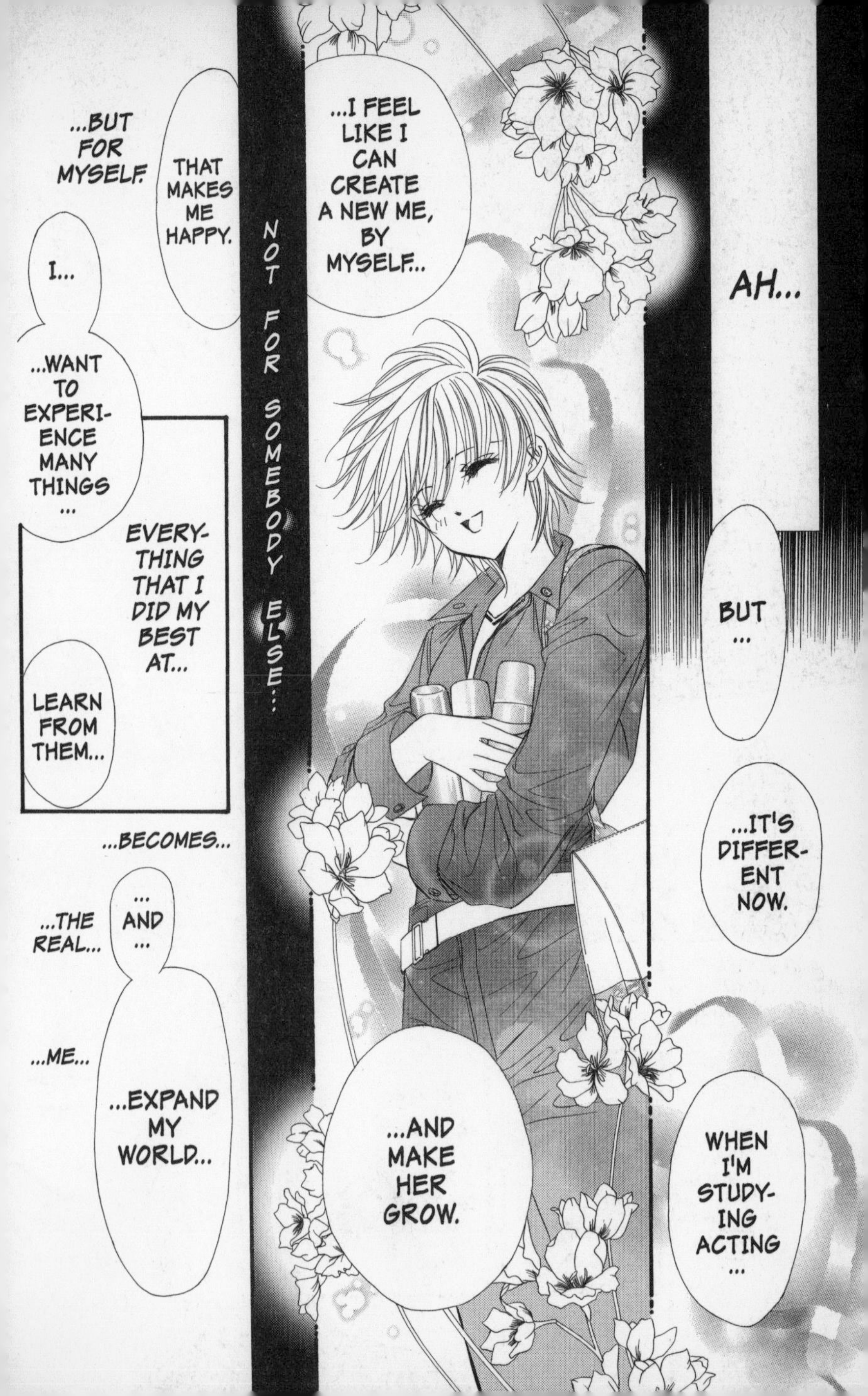
AH...
BUT ...
...IT'S DIFFERENT NOW.
WHEN I'M STUDYING ACTING ...
...I FEEL LIKE I CAN CREATE A NEW ME, BY MYSELF...
NOT FOR SOMEBODY ELSE...
...AND MAKE HER GROW.
THAT MAKES ME HAPPY.
...BUT FOR MYSELF.
I...
...WANT TO EXPERIENCE MANY THINGS ...
EVERYTHING THAT I DID MY BEST AT...
LEARN FROM THEM...
...BECOMES...
... AND ...
...THE REAL...
...ME...
...EXPAND MY WORLD...

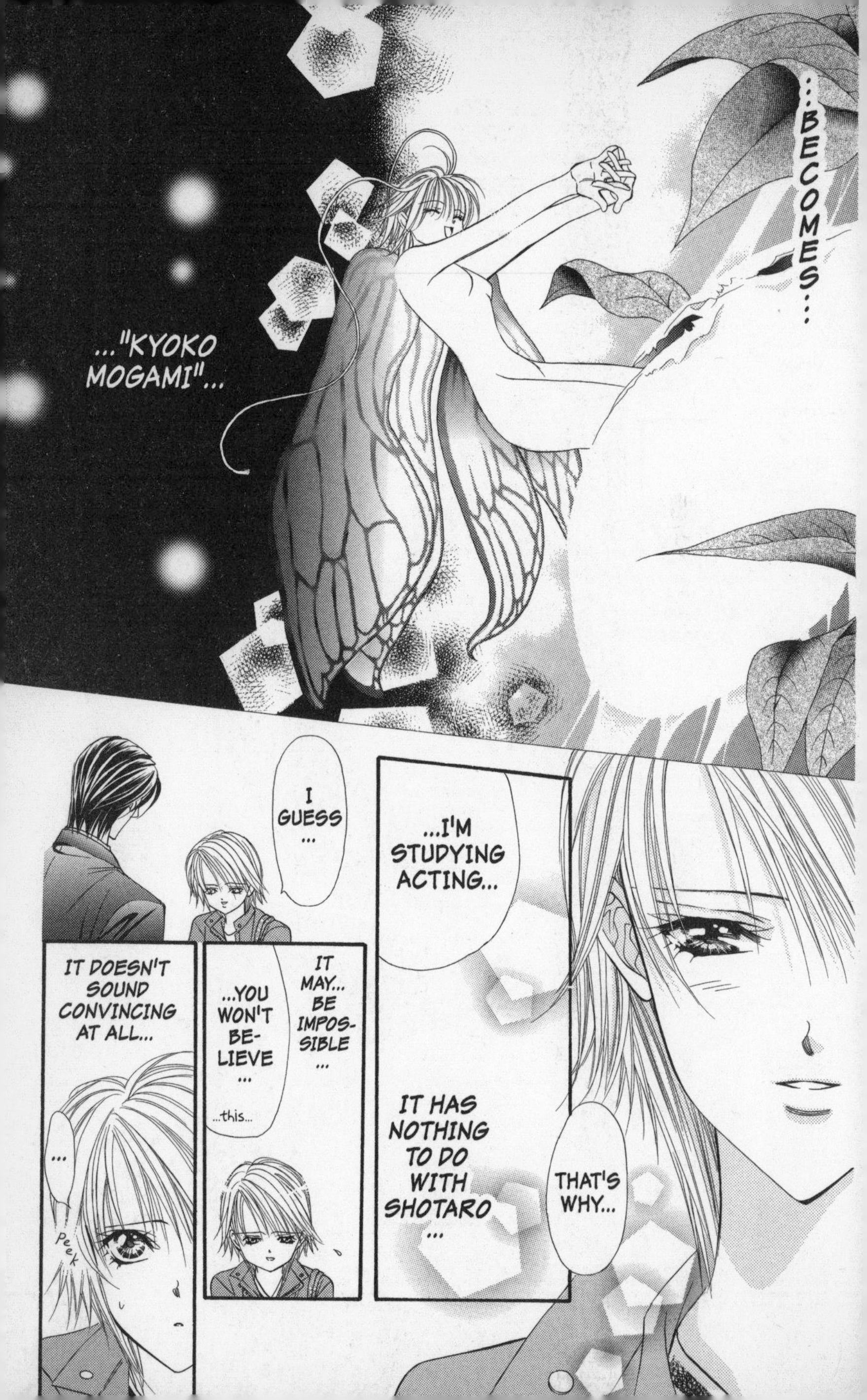
...BECOMES...
..."KYOKO MOGAMI"...
THAT'S WHY...
...I'M STUDYING ACTING...
IT HAS NOTHING TO DO WITH SHOTARO...
I GUESS...
IT MAY... BE IMPOSSIBLE...
...YOU WON'T BELIEVE...
...this...
IT DOESN'T SOUND CONVINCING AT ALL...
...
Peek

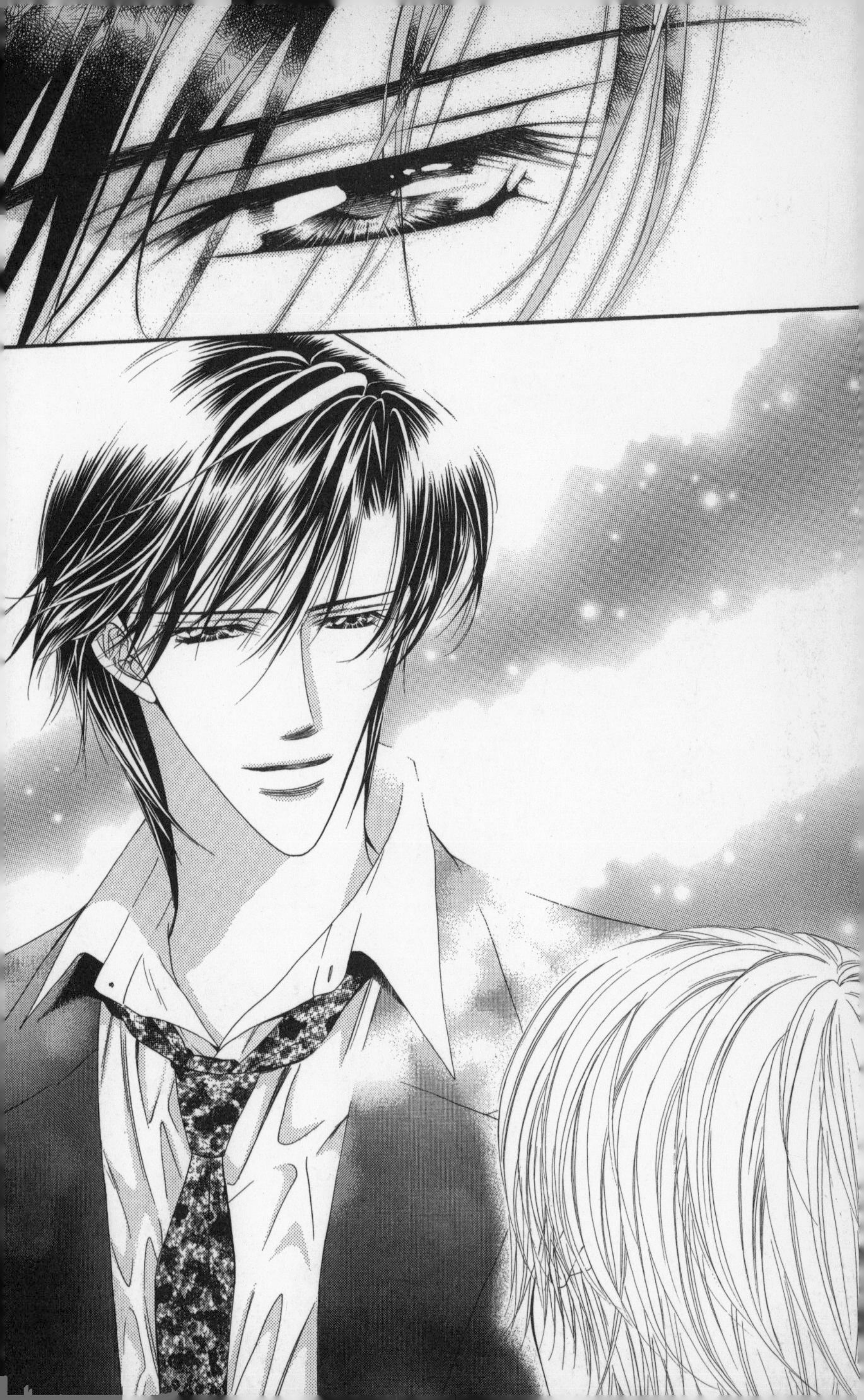

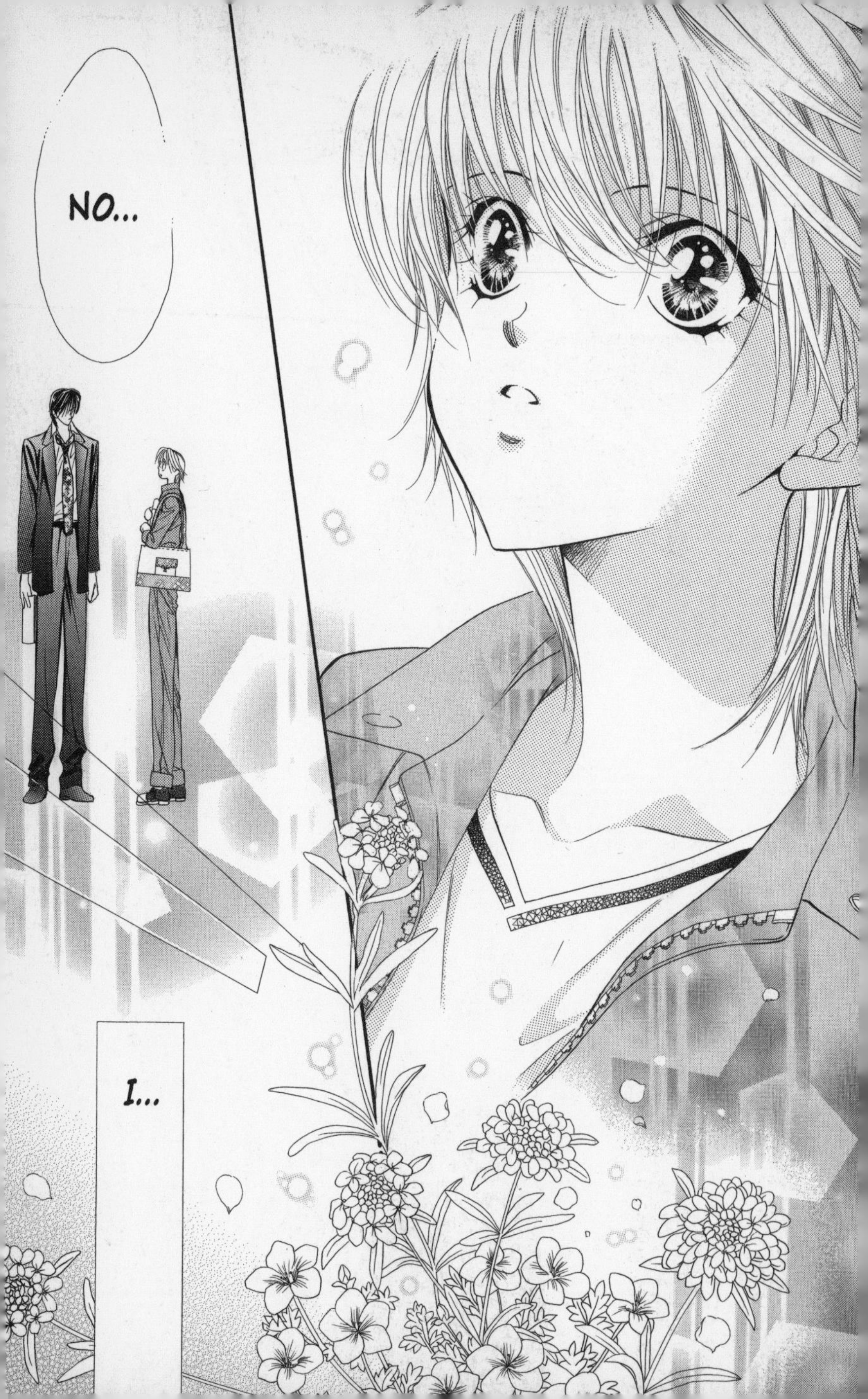
NO...
I...

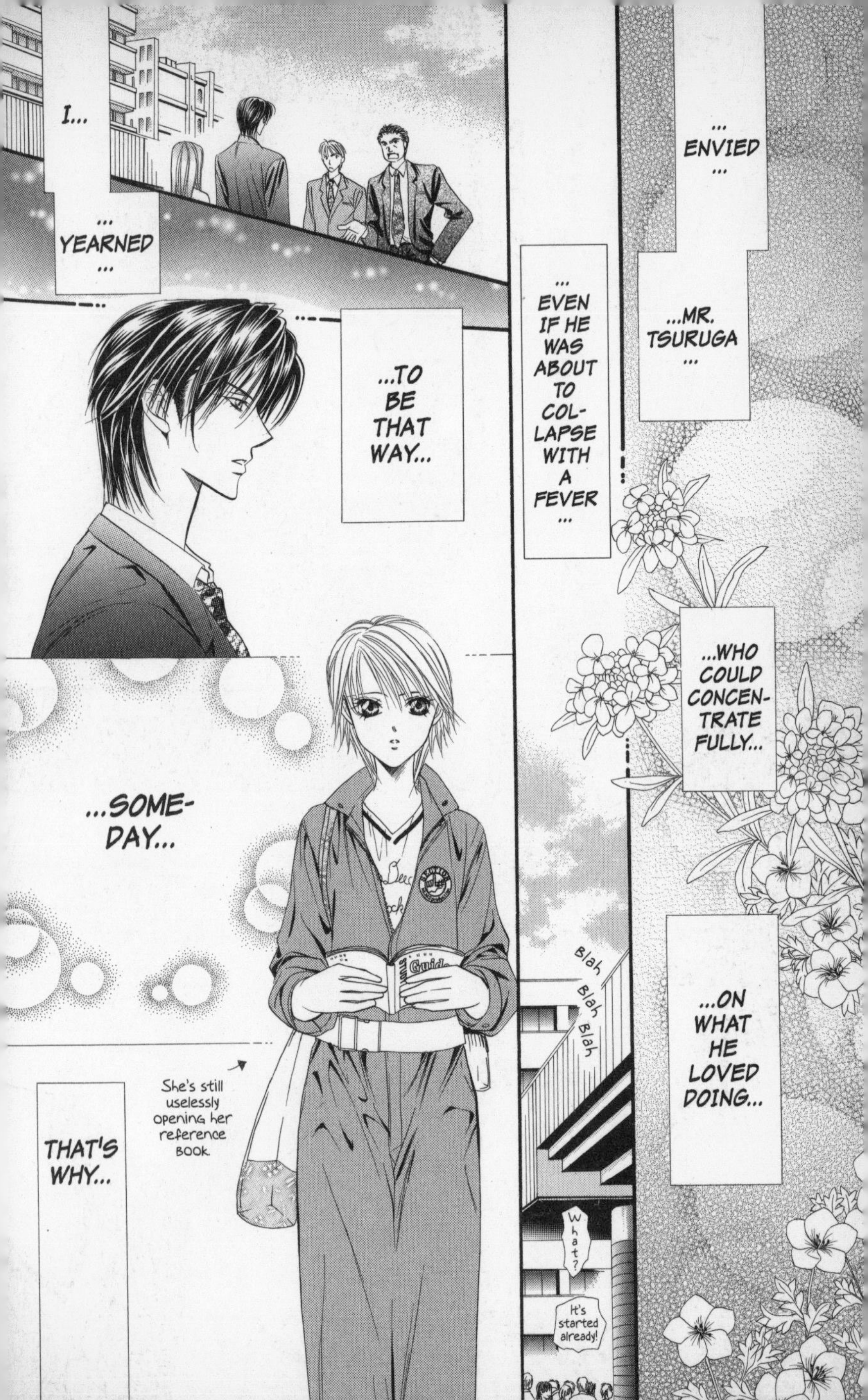

...ENVIED...
...MR. TSURUGA...
...EVEN IF HE WAS ABOUT TO COL-LAPSE WITH A FEVER...
...WHO COULD CONCEN-TRATE FULLY...
...ON WHAT HE LOVED DOING...
Blah Blah Blah
What?
It's started already!
I...
...YEARNED...
...TO BE THAT WAY...
...SOME-DAY...
She's still uselessly opening her reference book.
THAT'S WHY...

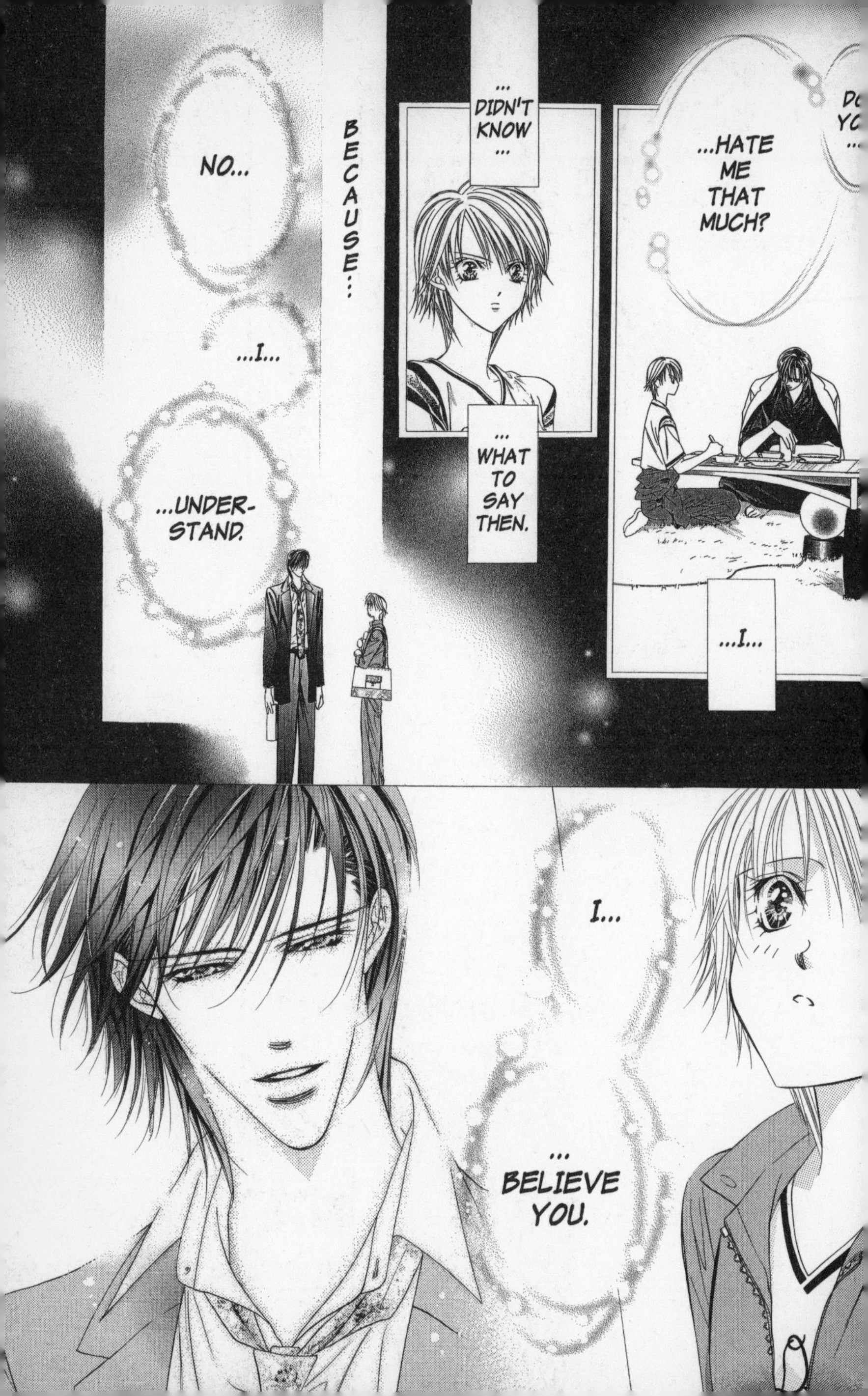
...HATE ME THAT MUCH?
...I...
...DIDN'T KNOW...
...WHAT TO SAY THEN.
BECAUSE...
NO...
...I...
...UNDER-STAND.
I...
...BELIEVE YOU.

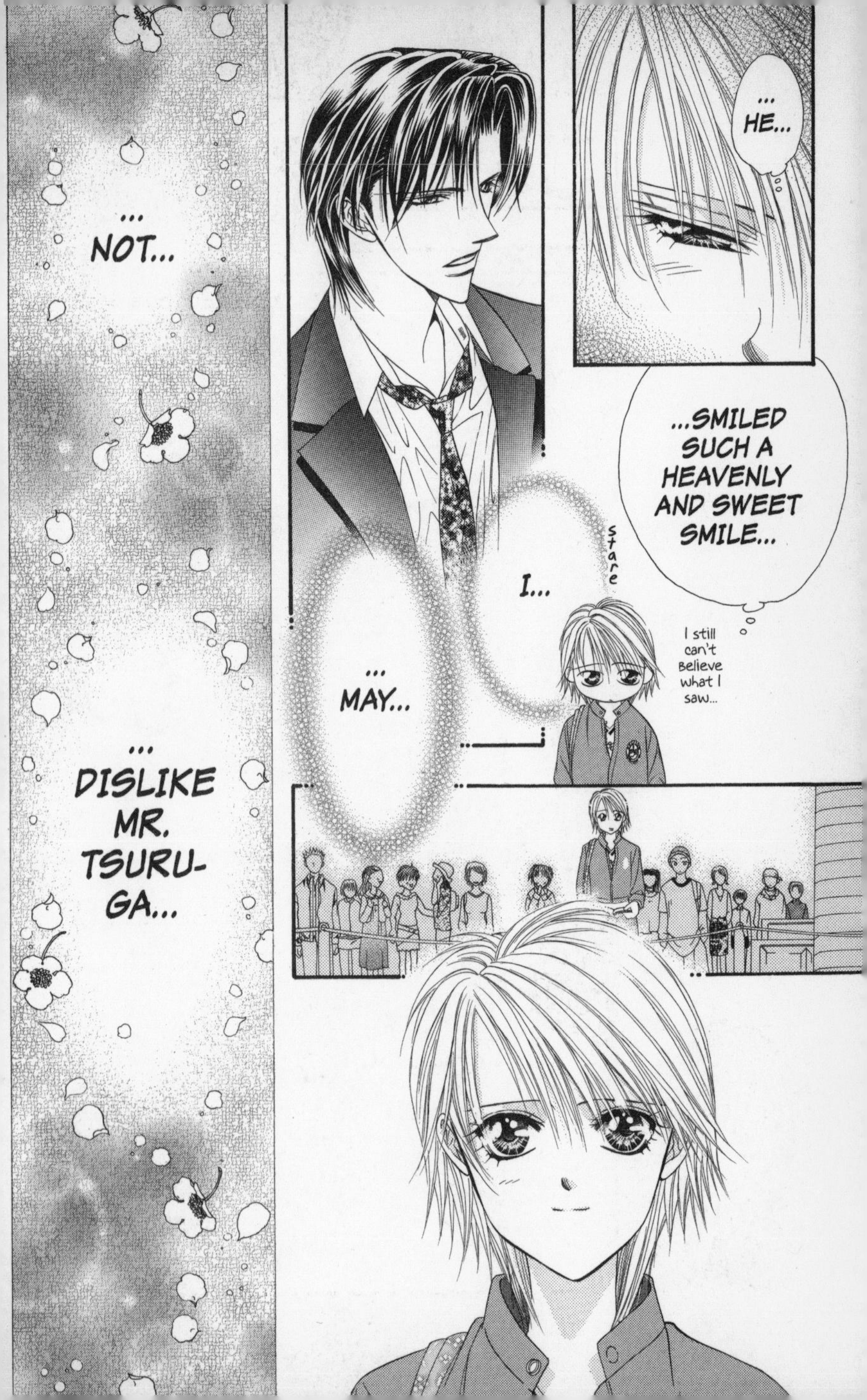
...HE...
...SMILED SUCH A HEAVENLY AND SWEET SMILE...
stare
I still can't believe what I saw...
I...
...MAY...
...NOT...
...DISLIKE MR. TSURU-GA...

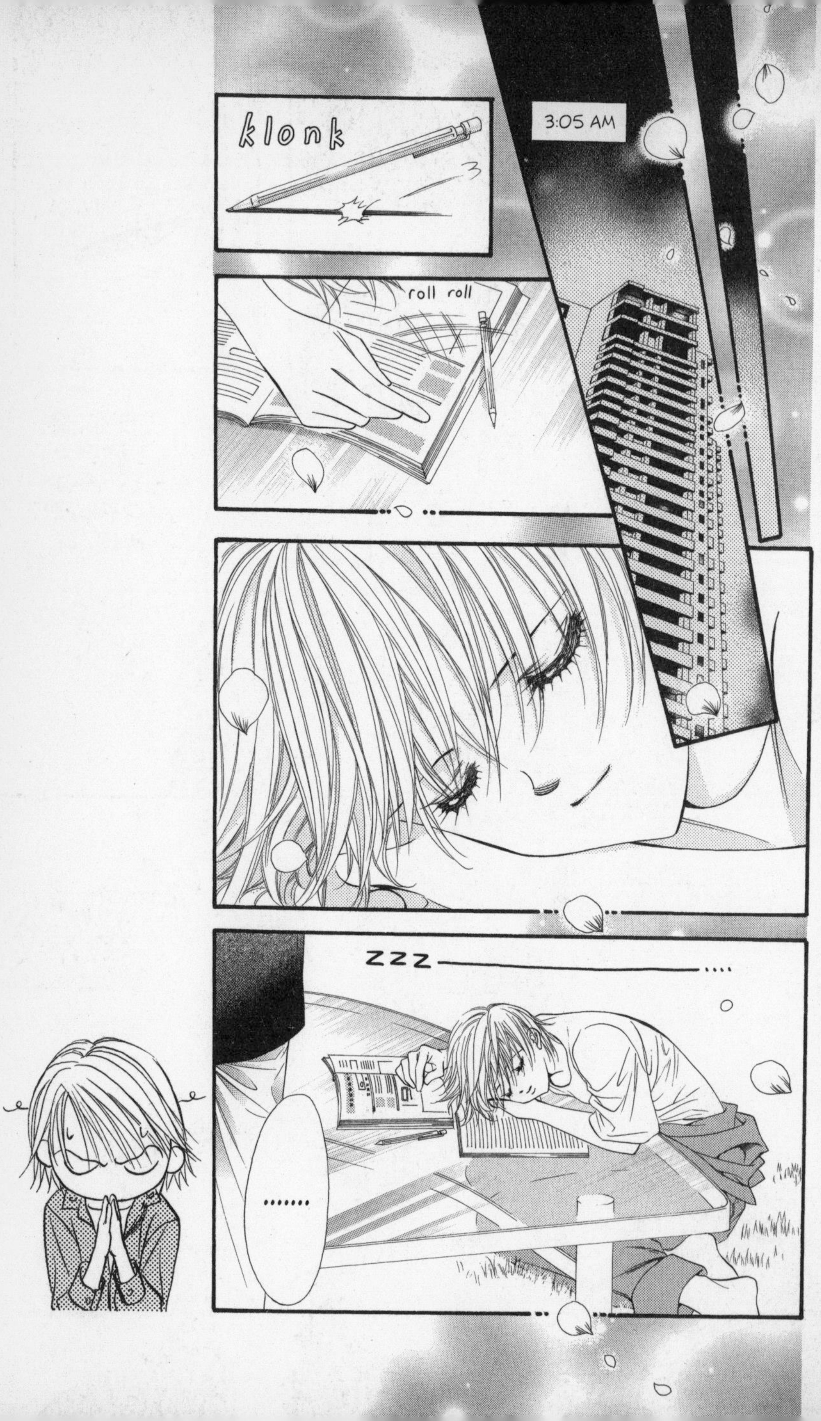
3:05 AM
klonk
roll roll
zzz——....
....

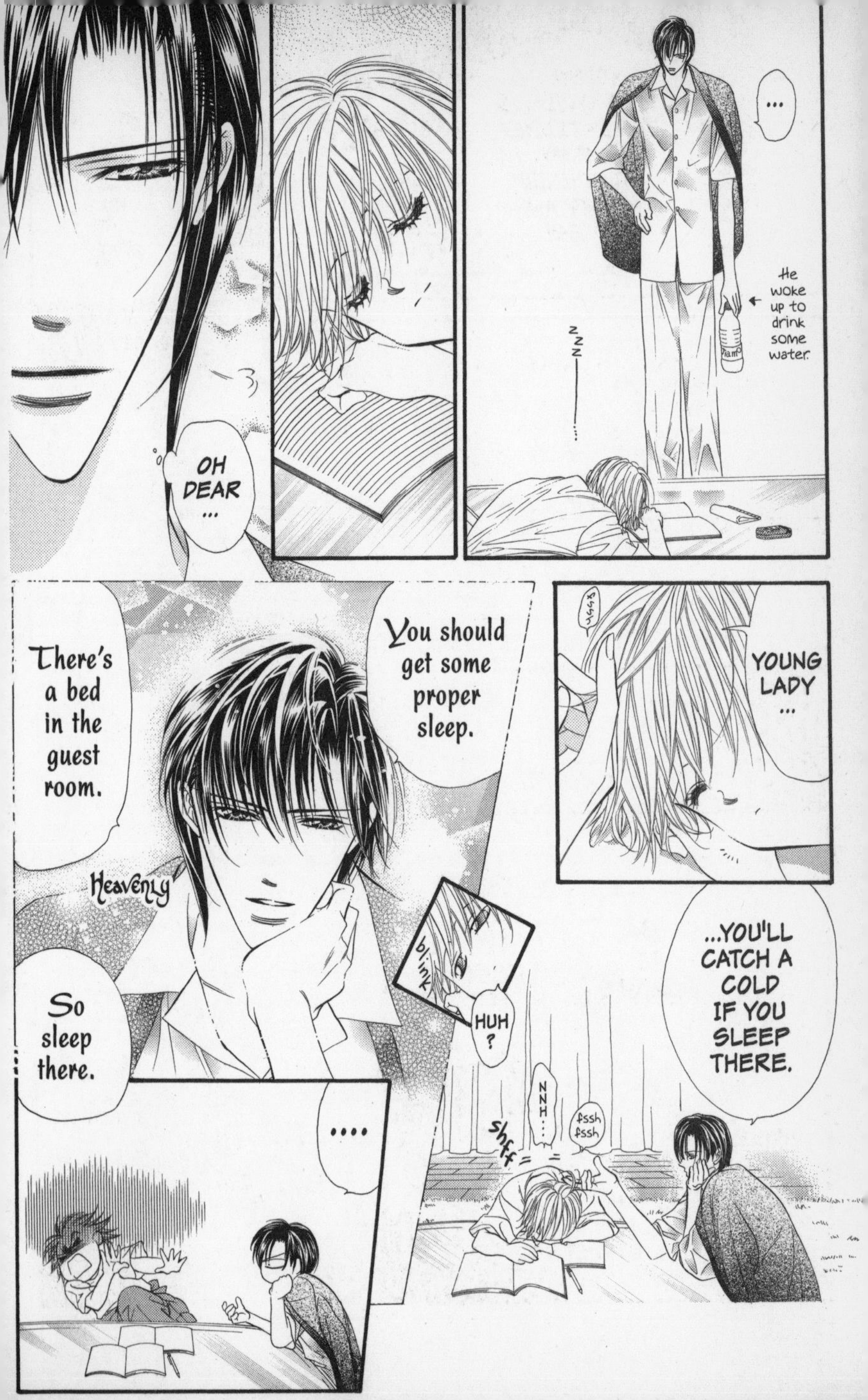
...
He woke up to drink some water.
ZZZ——......
OH DEAR ...
fssh
YOUNG LADY ...
...YOU'LL CATCH A COLD IF YOU SLEEP THERE.
NNH...
fssh fssh
shff
blink
HUH?
You should get some proper sleep.
There's a bed in the guest room.
Heavenly
So sleep there.
....

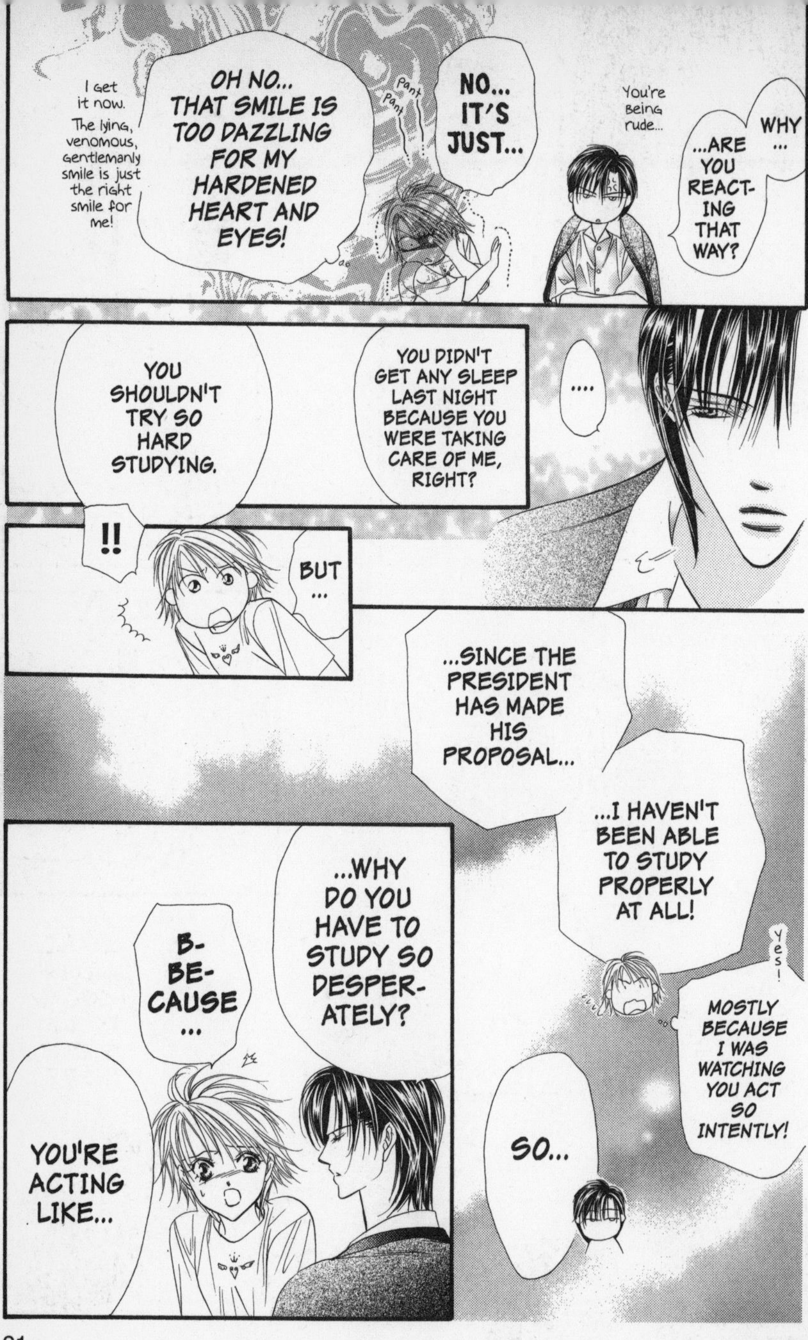
WHY...
...ARE YOU REACT-ING THAT WAY?
You're being rude...
NO... IT'S JUST...
Pant Pant
OH NO... THAT SMILE IS TOO DAZZLING FOR MY HARDENED HEART AND EYES!
I get it now. The lying, venomous, gentlemanly smile is just the right smile for me!
....
YOU DIDN'T GET ANY SLEEP LAST NIGHT BECAUSE YOU WERE TAKING CARE OF ME, RIGHT?
YOU SHOULDN'T TRY SO HARD STUDYING.
!!
BUT...
...SINCE THE PRESIDENT HAS MADE HIS PROPOSAL...
...I HAVEN'T BEEN ABLE TO STUDY PROPERLY AT ALL!
Yes!
MOSTLY BECAUSE I WAS WATCHING YOU ACT SO INTENTLY!
SO...
...WHY DO YOU HAVE TO STUDY SO DESPER-ATELY?
B-BE-CAUSE...
YOU'RE ACTING LIKE...

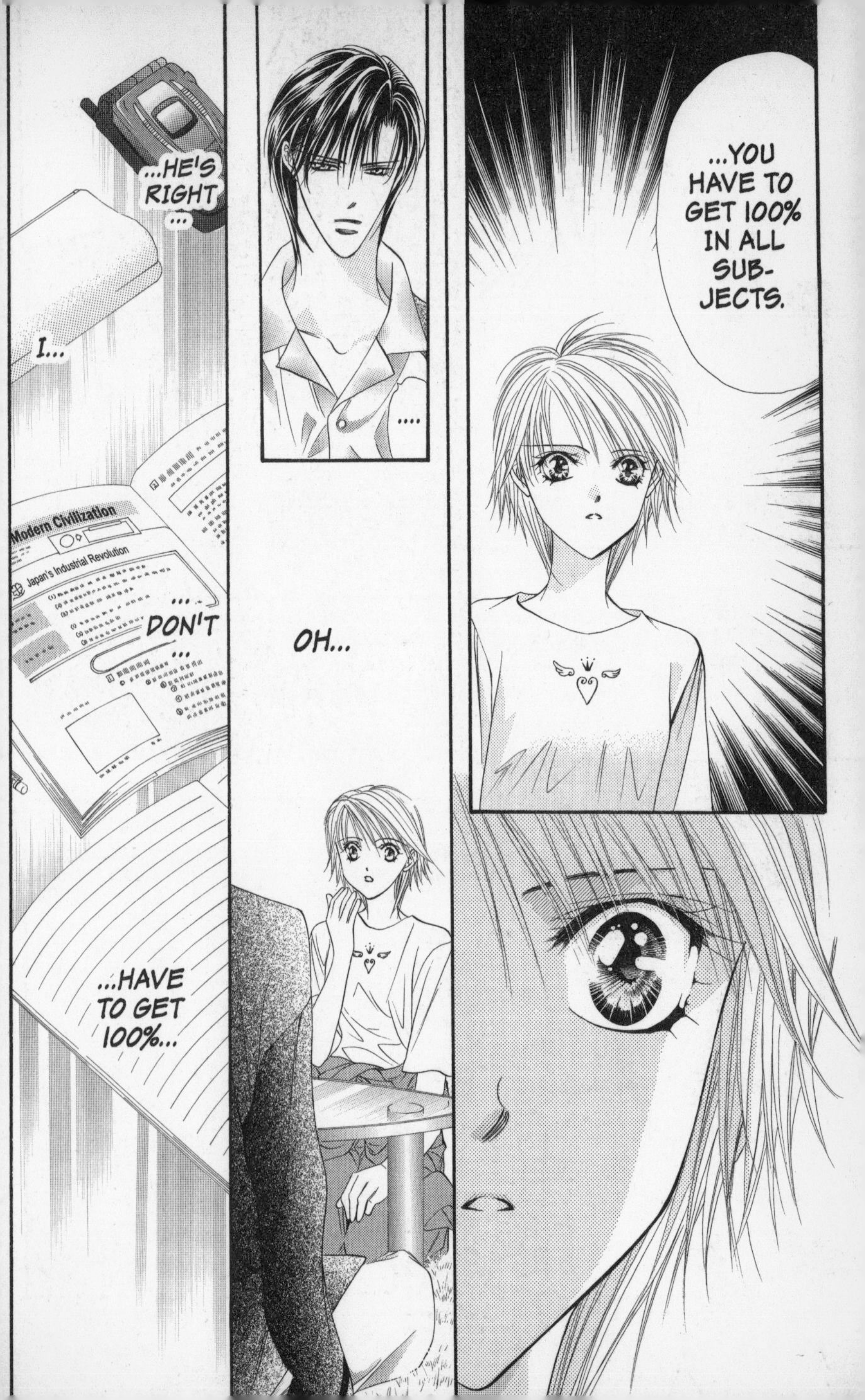
...YOU HAVE TO GET 100% IN ALL SUB-JECTS.
....
OH...
...HE'S RIGHT ...
I...
Modern Civilization
Japan's Industrial Revolution
... DON'T ...
...HAVE TO GET 100%...

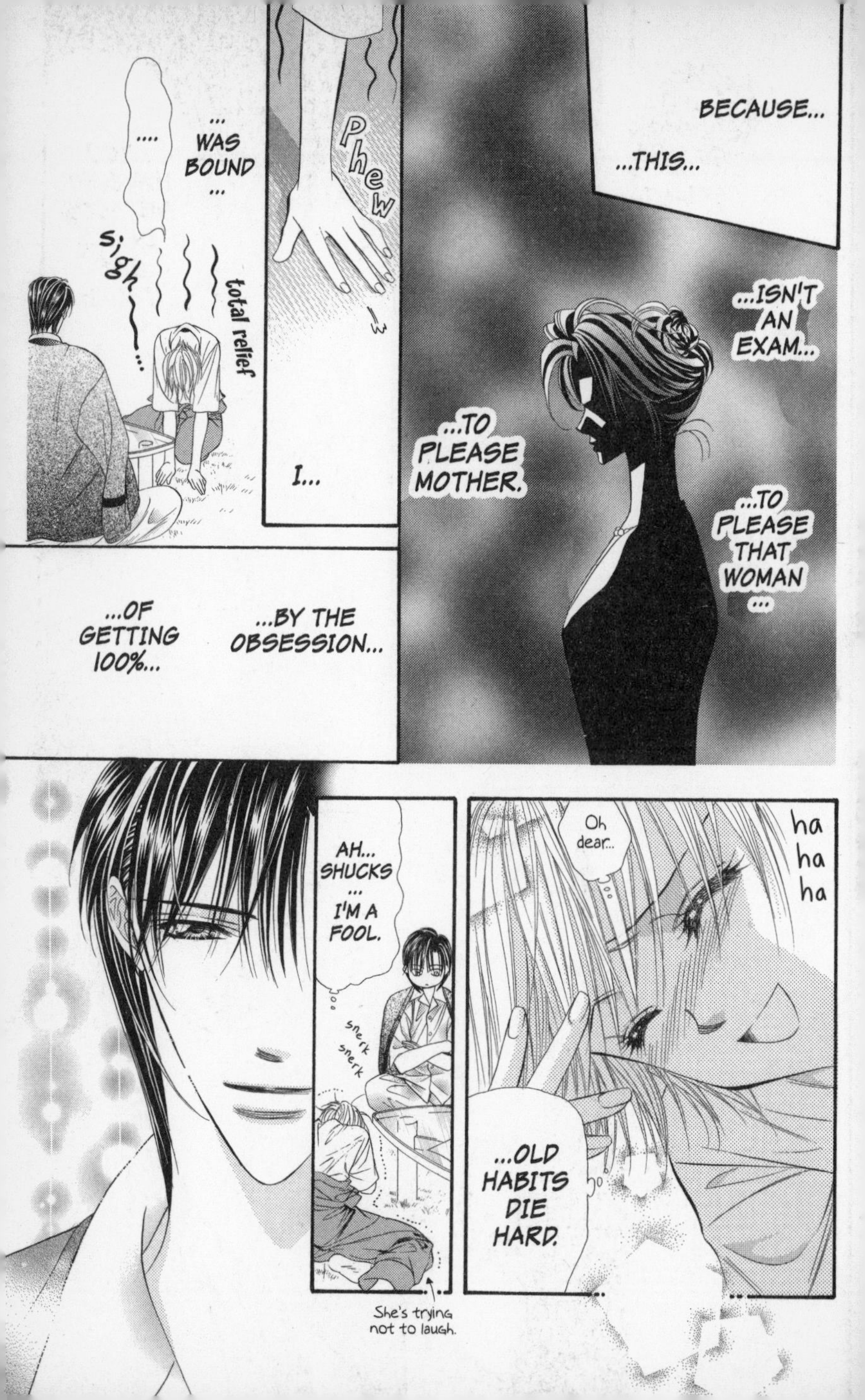

BECAUSE...
...THIS...
...ISN'T AN EXAM...
...TO PLEASE THAT WOMAN...
...TO PLEASE MOTHER.
Phew
I...
...WAS BOUND...
....
sigh
total relief
...BY THE OBSESSION...
...OF GETTING 100%...
ha ha ha
Oh dear...
...OLD HABITS DIE HARD.
AH... SHUCKS... I'M A FOOL.
snerk snerk
She's trying not to laugh.

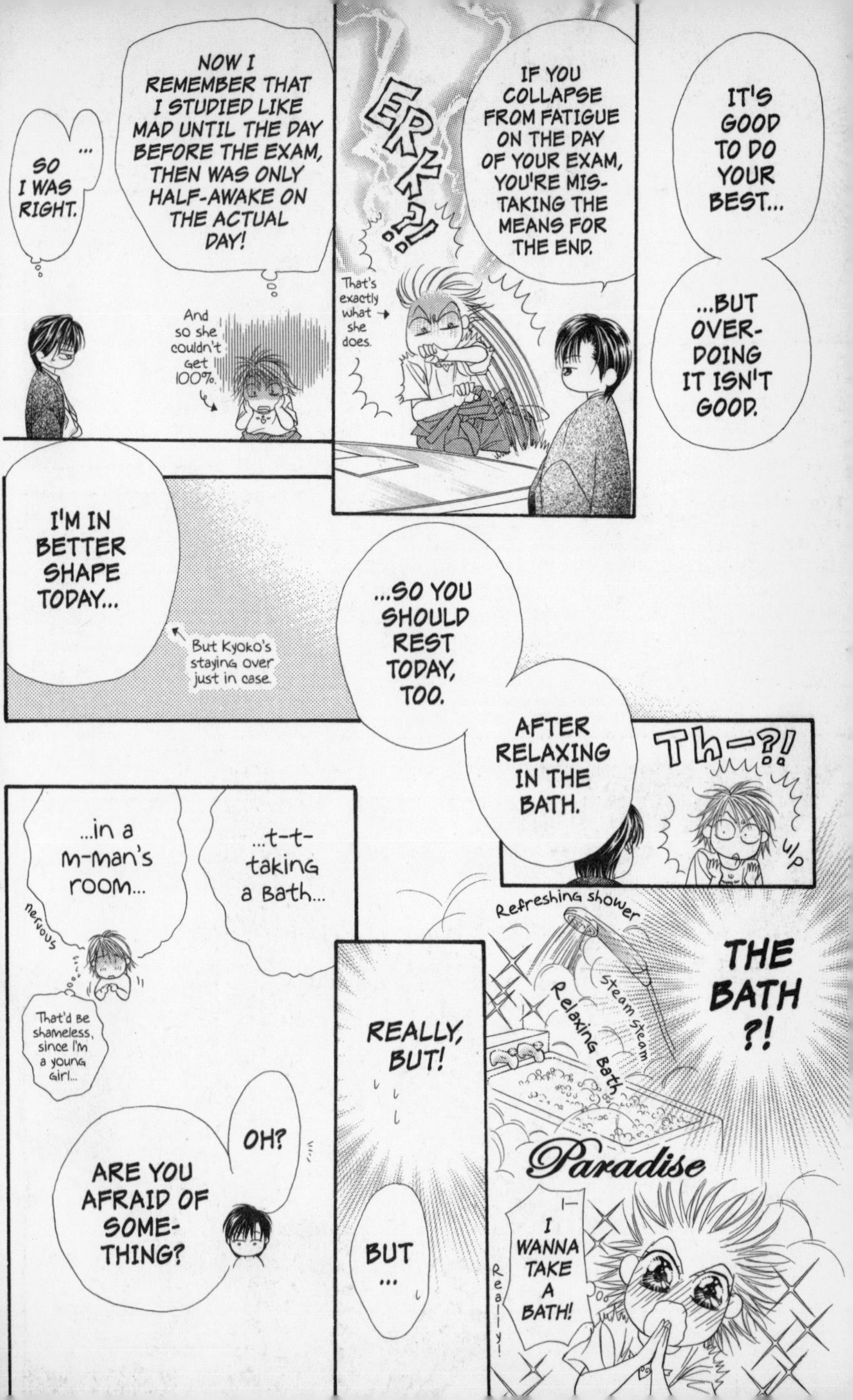
IT'S GOOD TO DO YOUR BEST...
...BUT OVER-DOING IT ISN'T GOOD.
IF YOU COLLAPSE FROM FATIGUE ON THE DAY OF YOUR EXAM, YOU'RE MIS-TAKING THE MEANS FOR THE END.
ERK?!
That's exactly what she does.
NOW I REMEMBER THAT I STUDIED LIKE MAD UNTIL THE DAY BEFORE THE EXAM, THEN WAS ONLY HALF-AWAKE ON THE ACTUAL DAY!
... SO I WAS RIGHT.
And so she couldn't get 100%.
I'M IN BETTER SHAPE TODAY...
But Kyoko's staying over just in case.
...SO YOU SHOULD REST TODAY, TOO.
AFTER RELAXING IN THE BATH.
Th-?!
THE BATH?!
Refreshing shower
Steam steam
Relaxing Bath
Paradise
I-I WANNA TAKE A BATH!
Really!
REALLY, BUT!
BUT ...
...t-t-taking a Bath...
...in a m-man's room...
nervous
That'd be shameless, since I'm a young girl...
OH?
ARE YOU AFRAID OF SOME-THING?

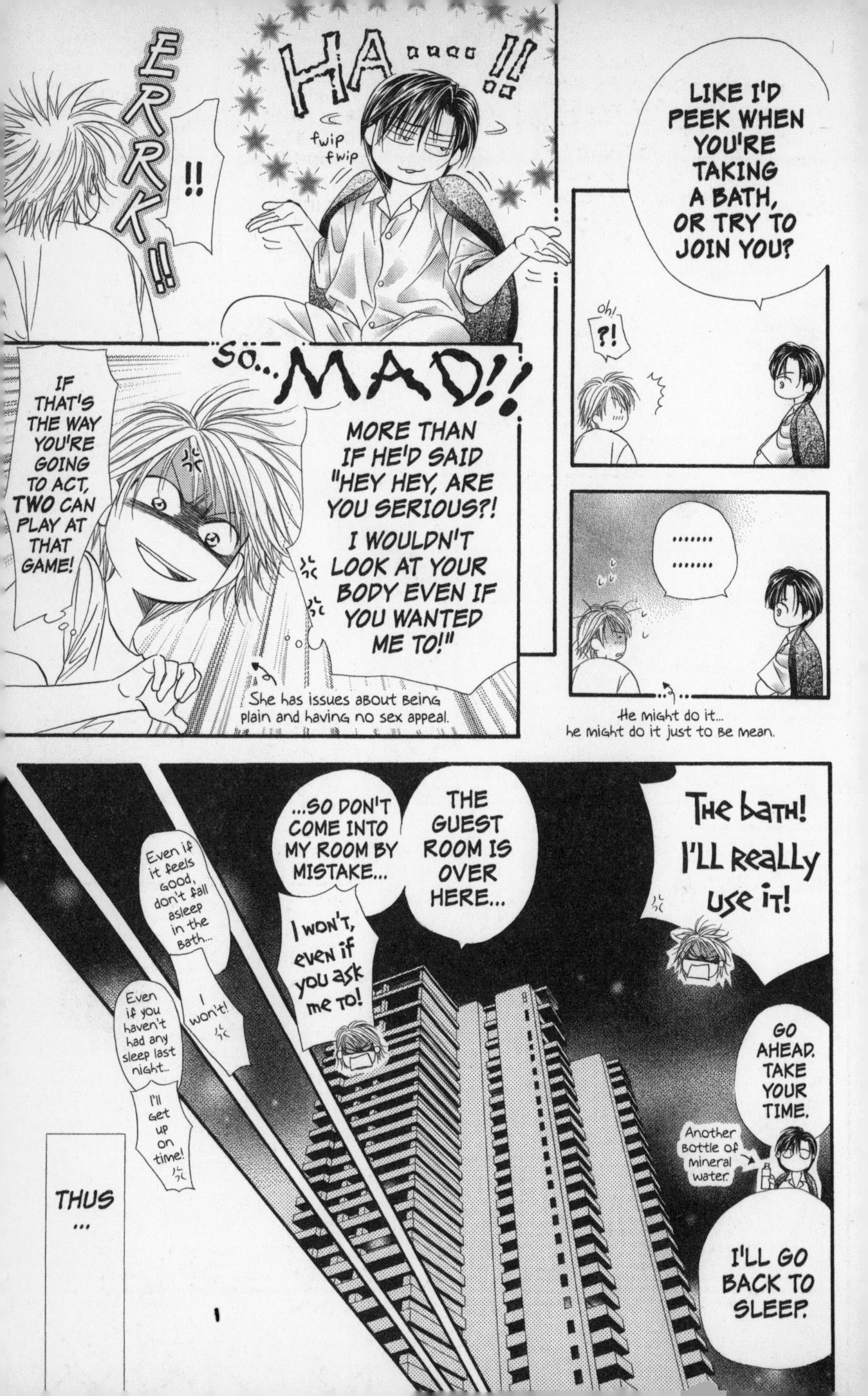
LIKE I'D PEEK WHEN YOU'RE TAKING A BATH, OR TRY TO JOIN YOU?
Oh!
?!
......
......
He might do it... he might do it just to be mean.
HA....!!
fwip fwip
ERRK!!
!!
SO...MAD!!
MORE THAN IF HE'D SAID "HEY HEY, ARE YOU SERIOUS?! I WOULDN'T LOOK AT YOUR BODY EVEN IF YOU WANTED ME TO!"
IF THAT'S THE WAY YOU'RE GOING TO ACT, TWO CAN PLAY AT THAT GAME!
She has issues about being plain and having no sex appeal.
The bath! I'll really use it!
GO AHEAD. TAKE YOUR TIME.
Another bottle of mineral water.
I'LL GO BACK TO SLEEP.
THE GUEST ROOM IS OVER HERE...
...SO DON'T COME INTO MY ROOM BY MISTAKE...
I won't, even if you ask me to!
Even if it feels good, don't fall asleep in the bath...
I won't!
Even if you haven't had any sleep last night...
I'll get up on time!
THUS...

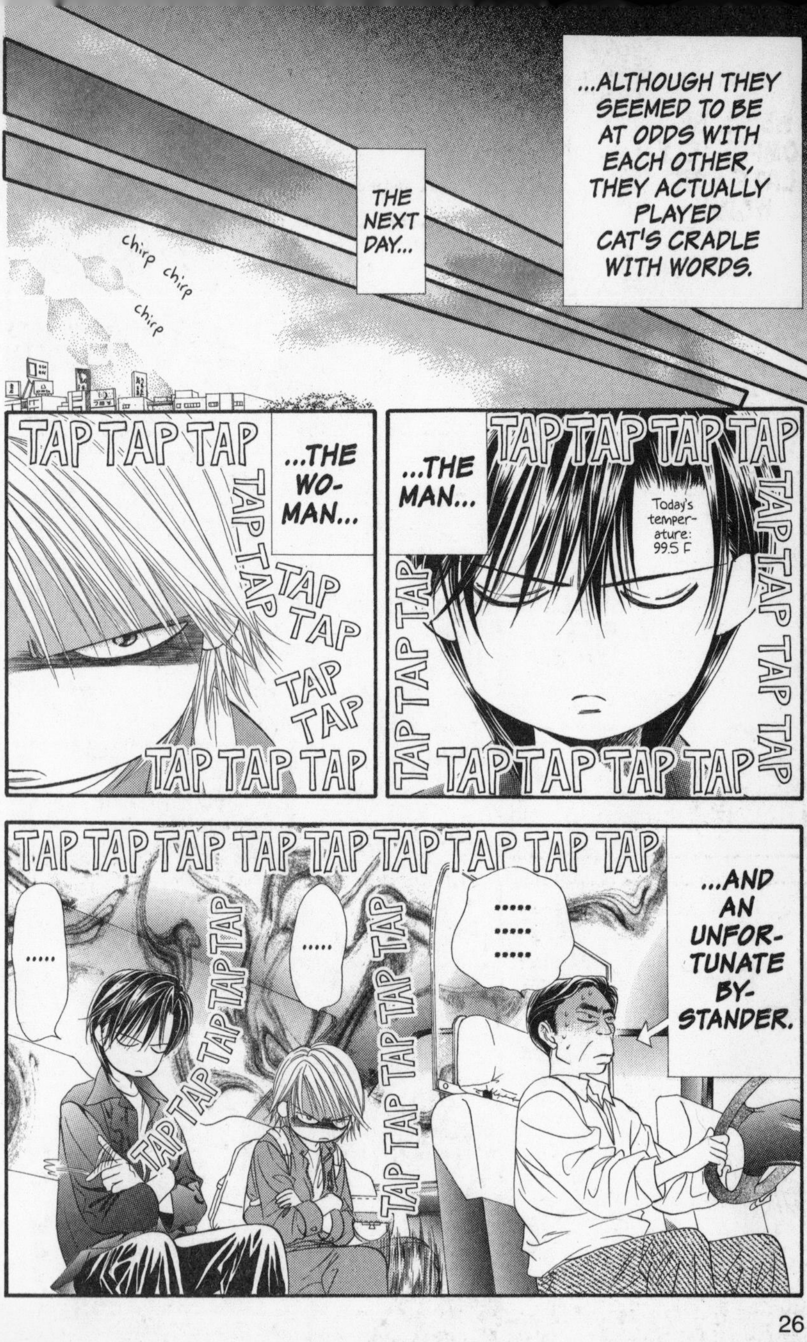
...ALTHOUGH THEY SEEMED TO BE AT ODDS WITH EACH OTHER, THEY ACTUALLY PLAYED CAT'S CRADLE WITH WORDS.
THE NEXT DAY...
chirp chirp
chirp
...THE MAN...
TAP TAP TAP TAP
Today's temper-ature: 99.5 F
TAP TAP TAP TAP
TAP TAP TAP TAP
TAP TAP TAP TAP
...THE WO-MAN...
TAP TAP TAP
TAP TAP
TAP TAP
TAP TAP
TAP TAP TAP
...AND AN UNFOR-TUNATE BY-STANDER.
TAP TAP TAP TAP TAP TAP TAP TAP TAP
.....
.....
.....
TAP TAP TAP TAP
.....
TAP TAP TAP TAP TAP TAP
.....

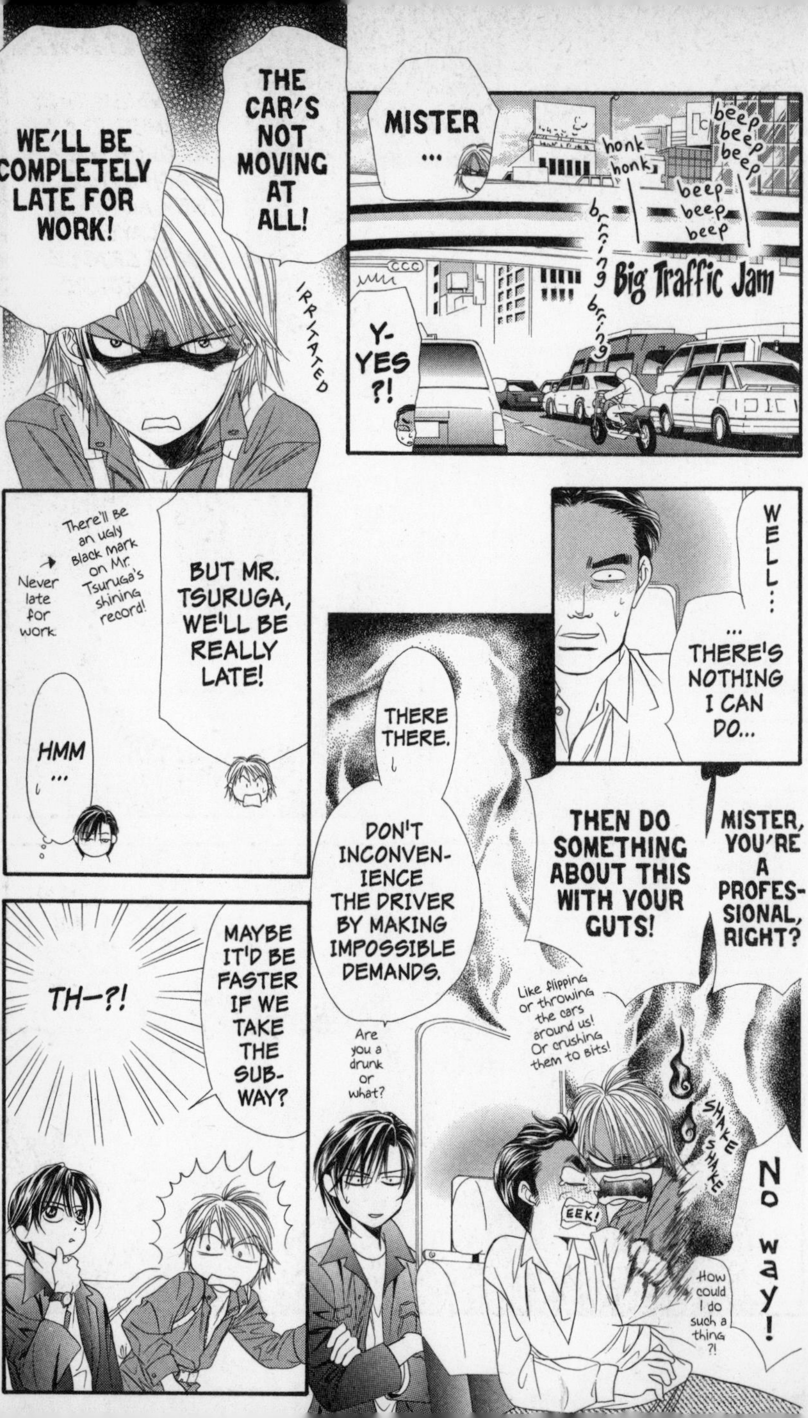
beep beep beep
MISTER ...
honk honk
beep beep beep
brring brring
Big Traffic Jam
Y-YES?!
THE CAR'S NOT MOVING AT ALL!
WE'LL BE COMPLETELY LATE FOR WORK!
IRRITATED
WELL...
... THERE'S NOTHING I CAN DO...
BUT MR. TSURUGA, WE'LL BE REALLY LATE!
There'll be an ugly Black Mark on Mr. Tsuruga's shining record!
Never late for work
HMM ...
MISTER, YOU'RE A PROFESSIONAL, RIGHT?
THEN DO SOMETHING ABOUT THIS WITH YOUR GUTS!
THERE THERE.
DON'T INCONVENIENCE THE DRIVER BY MAKING IMPOSSIBLE DEMANDS.
Like flipping or throwing the cars around us! Or crushing them to bits!
Are you a drunk or what?
SHAKE SHAKE
EEK!
No way!
How could I do such a thing?!
MAYBE IT'D BE FASTER IF WE TAKE THE SUBWAY?
TH-?!

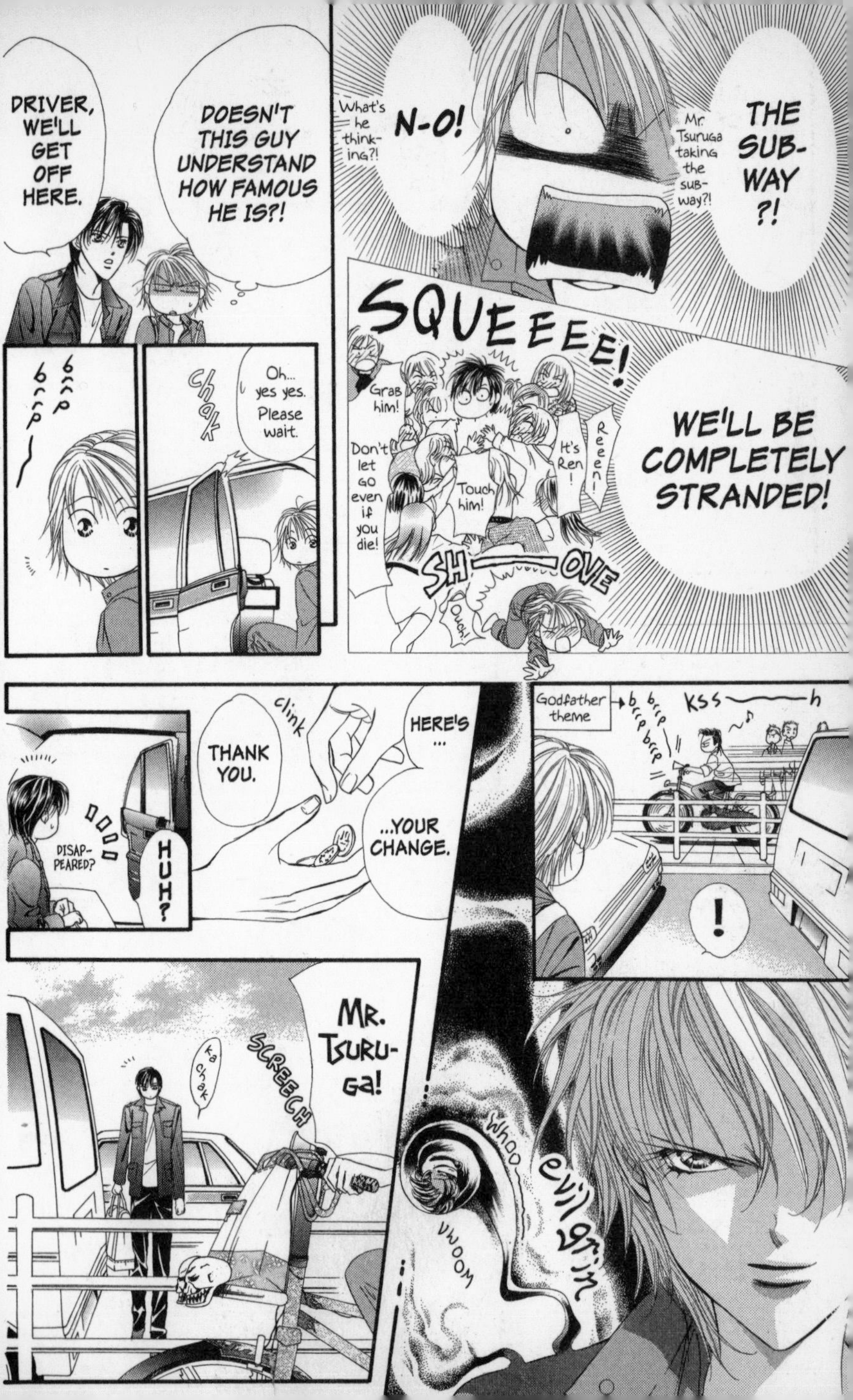
THE SUBWAY?!
Mr. Tsuruga taking the subway?!
N-O!
What's he thinking?!
SQUEEEEE!
WE'LL BE COMPLETELY STRANDED!
Reeen!
It's Ren!
Touch him!
Grab him!
Don't let go even if you die!
SH——OVE
Ouch!
DOESN'T THIS GUY UNDERSTAND HOW FAMOUS HE IS?!
DRIVER, WE'LL GET OFF HERE.
Oh... yes yes. Please wait.
chak
brrp brrp
Godfather theme
brrp brrp brrp brrp
KSS———h
!
HERE'S ...
...YOUR CHANGE.
clink
THANK YOU.
HUH?
DISAPPEARED?
whoo
evil grin
vwoom
MR. TSURUGA!
SCREECH
ka chak

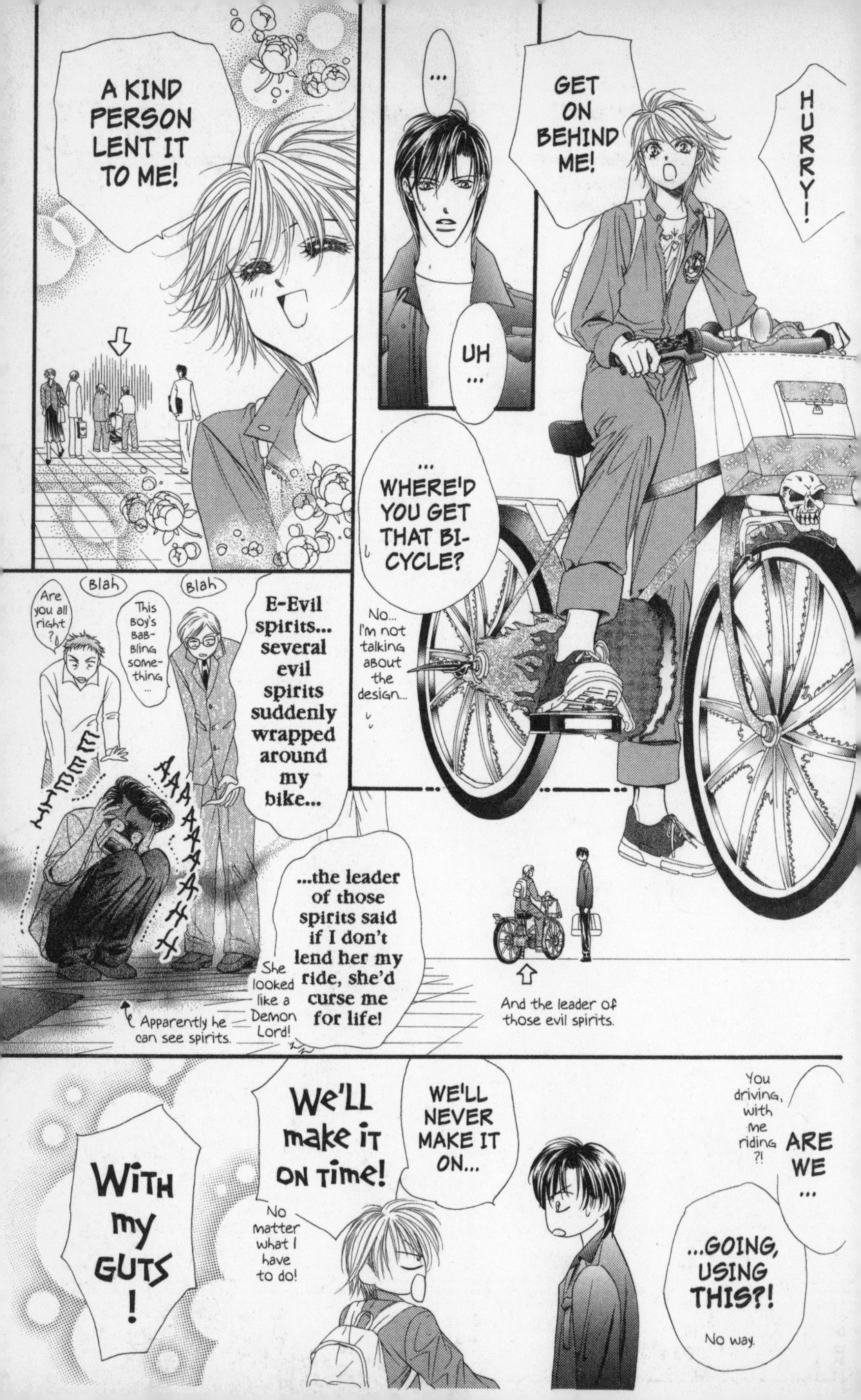
HURRY!
GET ON BEHIND ME!
...
UH...
...WHERE'D YOU GET THAT BI-CYCLE?
No... I'm not talking about the design...
A KIND PERSON LENT IT TO ME!
E-Evil spirits... several evil spirits suddenly wrapped around my bike...
...the leader of those spirits said if I don't lend her my ride, she'd curse me for life!
She looked like a Demon Lord!
Blah
This boy's babbling something...
Blah
Are you all right?
AAAAAAAHHH
EEEEHHH
Apparently he can see spirits.
And the leader of those evil spirits.
ARE WE...
You driving, with me riding?!
...GOING, USING THIS?!
No way.
WE'LL NEVER MAKE IT ON...
We'LL make it on time!
No matter what I have to do!
WITH my GUTS!

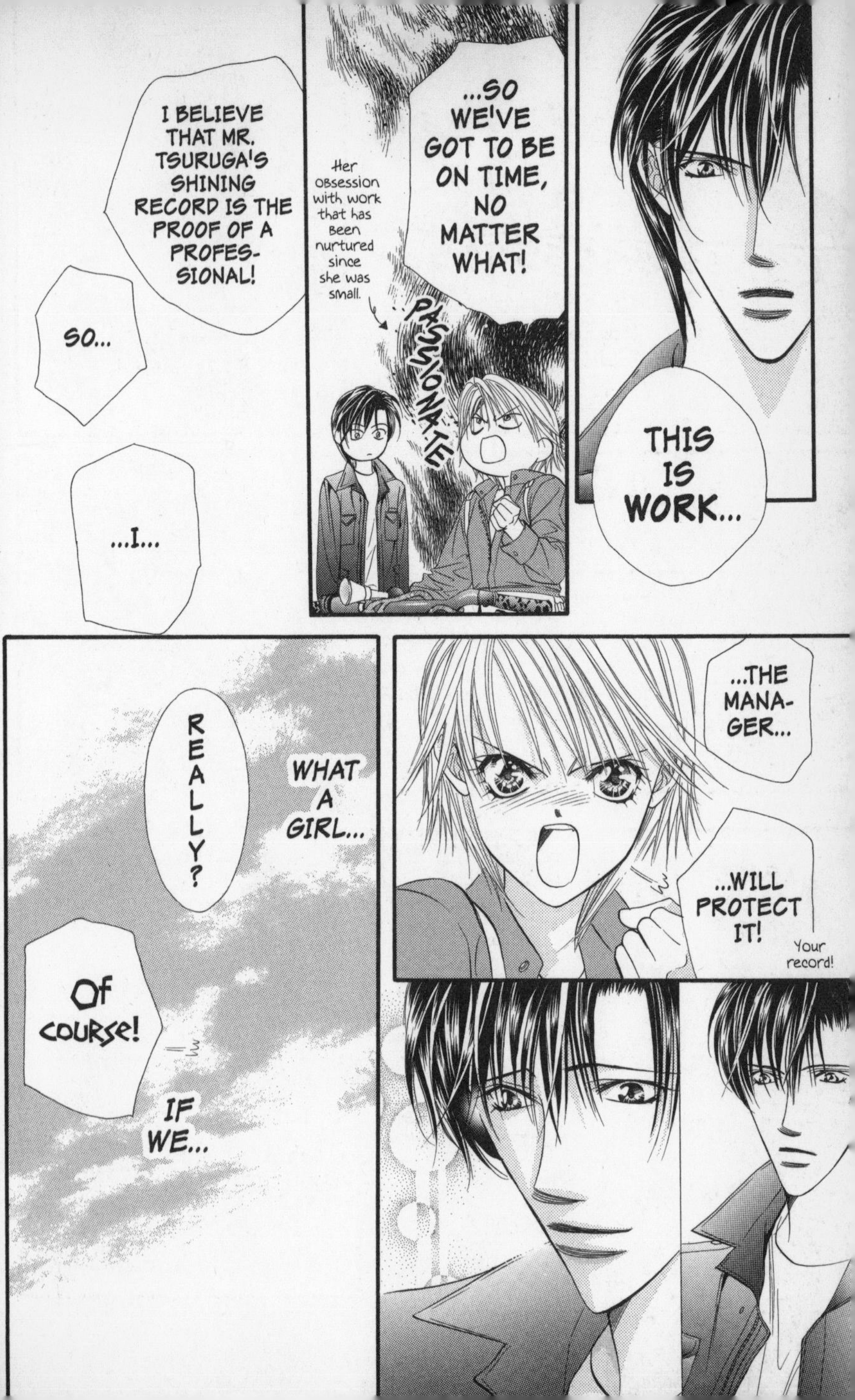
THIS IS WORK...
...SO WE'VE GOT TO BE ON TIME, NO MATTER WHAT!
Her obsession with work that has Been nurtured since she was small.
PASSIONATE
I BELIEVE THAT MR. TSURUGA'S SHINING RECORD IS THE PROOF OF A PROFESSIONAL!
SO...
...I...
...THE MANAGER...
...WILL PROTECT IT!
Your record!
REALLY?
WHAT A GIRL...
Of course!
IF WE...

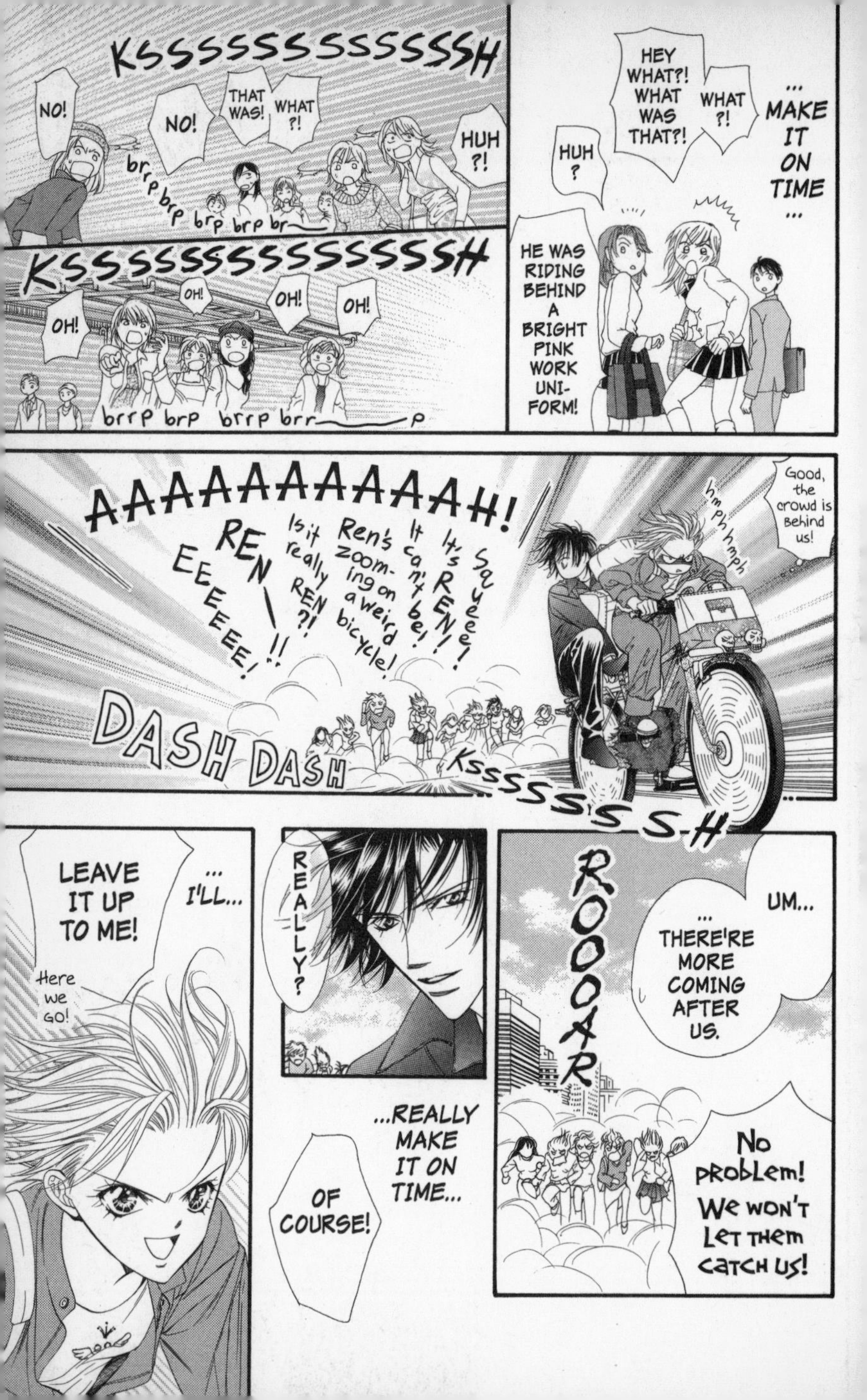
... MAKE IT ON TIME ...
WHAT ?!
HEY WHAT?! WHAT WAS THAT?!
HUH ?
HE WAS RIDING BEHIND A BRIGHT PINK WORK UNIFORM!
KSSSSSSSSSSSSSH
HUH ?!
WHAT ?!
THAT WAS!
NO!
NO!
brrp brp brp brp br—
KSSSSSSSSSSSSSSH
OH!
OH!
OH!
OH!
brrp brp brrp brr——p
Good, the crowd is behind us!
hmph hmph
AAAAAAAAAAAH!
Squeeee!
It's REN!
It can't be!
Ren's zooming on a weird bicycle!
Is it really REN ?!
REN—!!
EEEEEEE!
DASH DASH
KSSSSSSSH
UM...
... THERE'RE MORE COMING AFTER US.
ROOOAR
No problem! We won't let them catch us!
REALLY?
...REALLY MAKE IT ON TIME...
OF COURSE!
... I'LL...
LEAVE IT UP TO ME!
Here we GO!

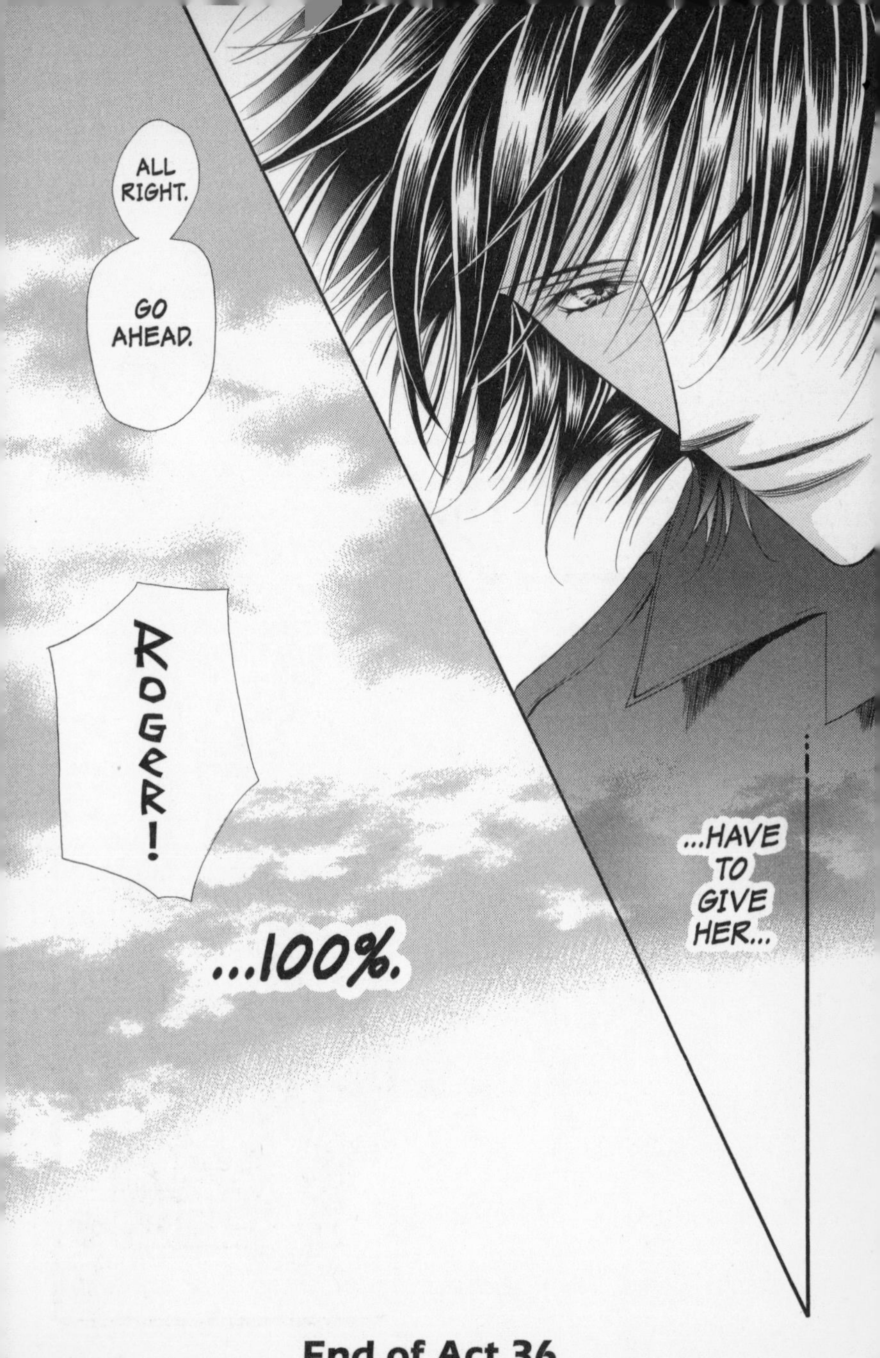
ALL RIGHT.
GO AHEAD.
ROGER!
...HAVE TO GIVE HER...
...100%.

End of Act 36

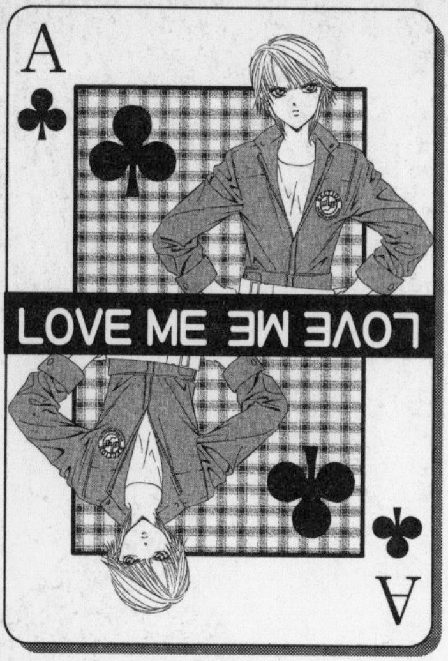
A
LOVE ME
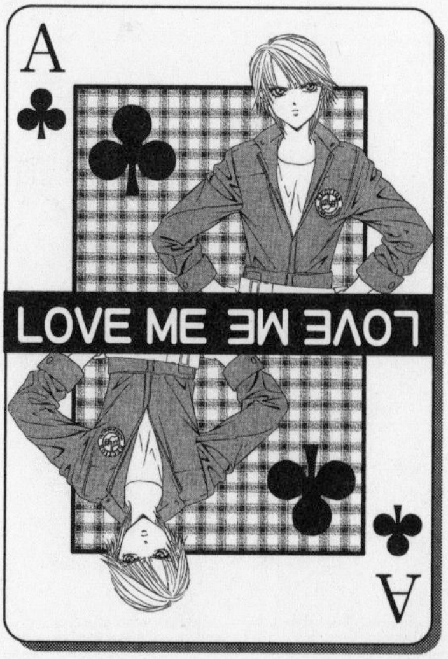
A
LOVE ME

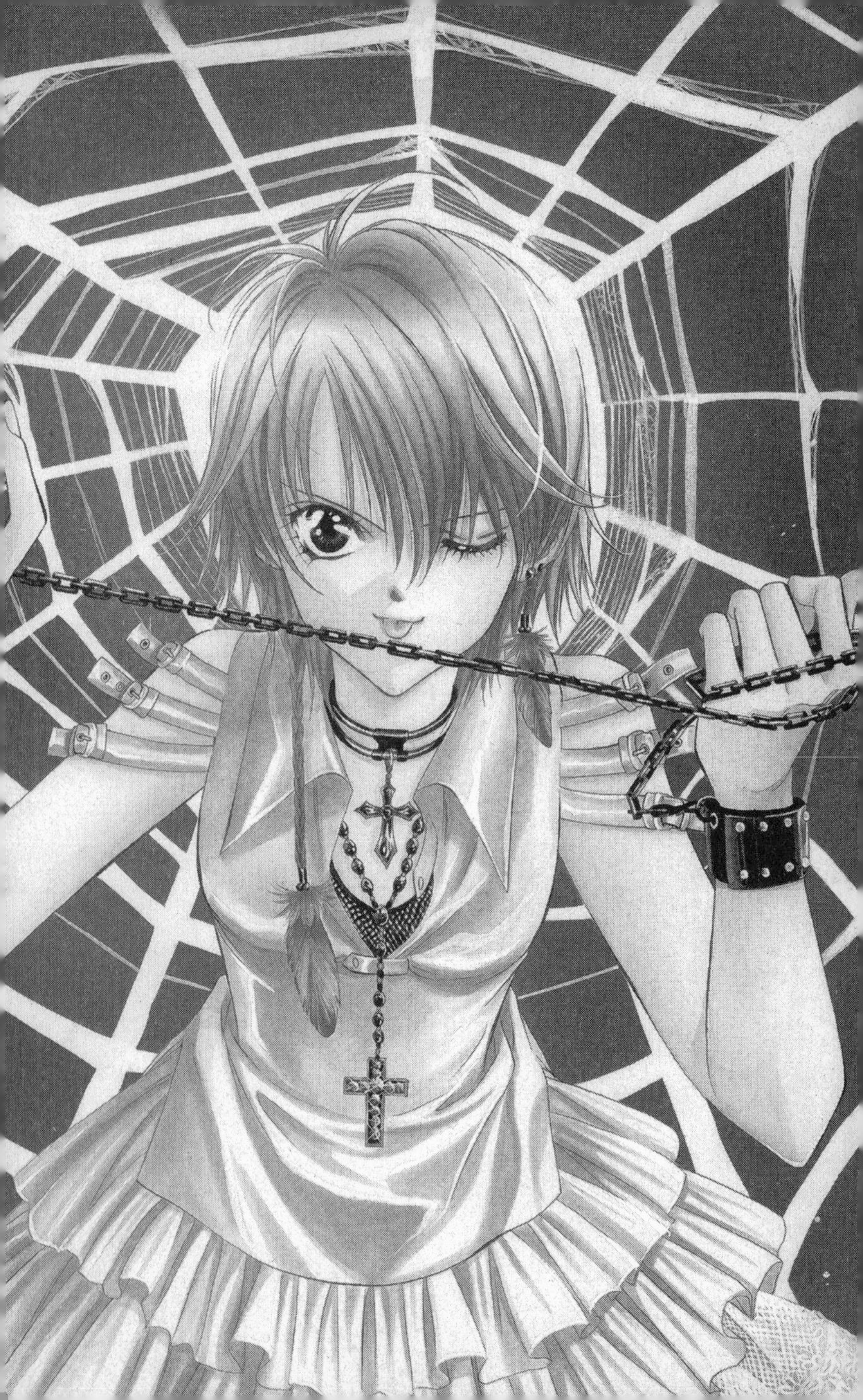

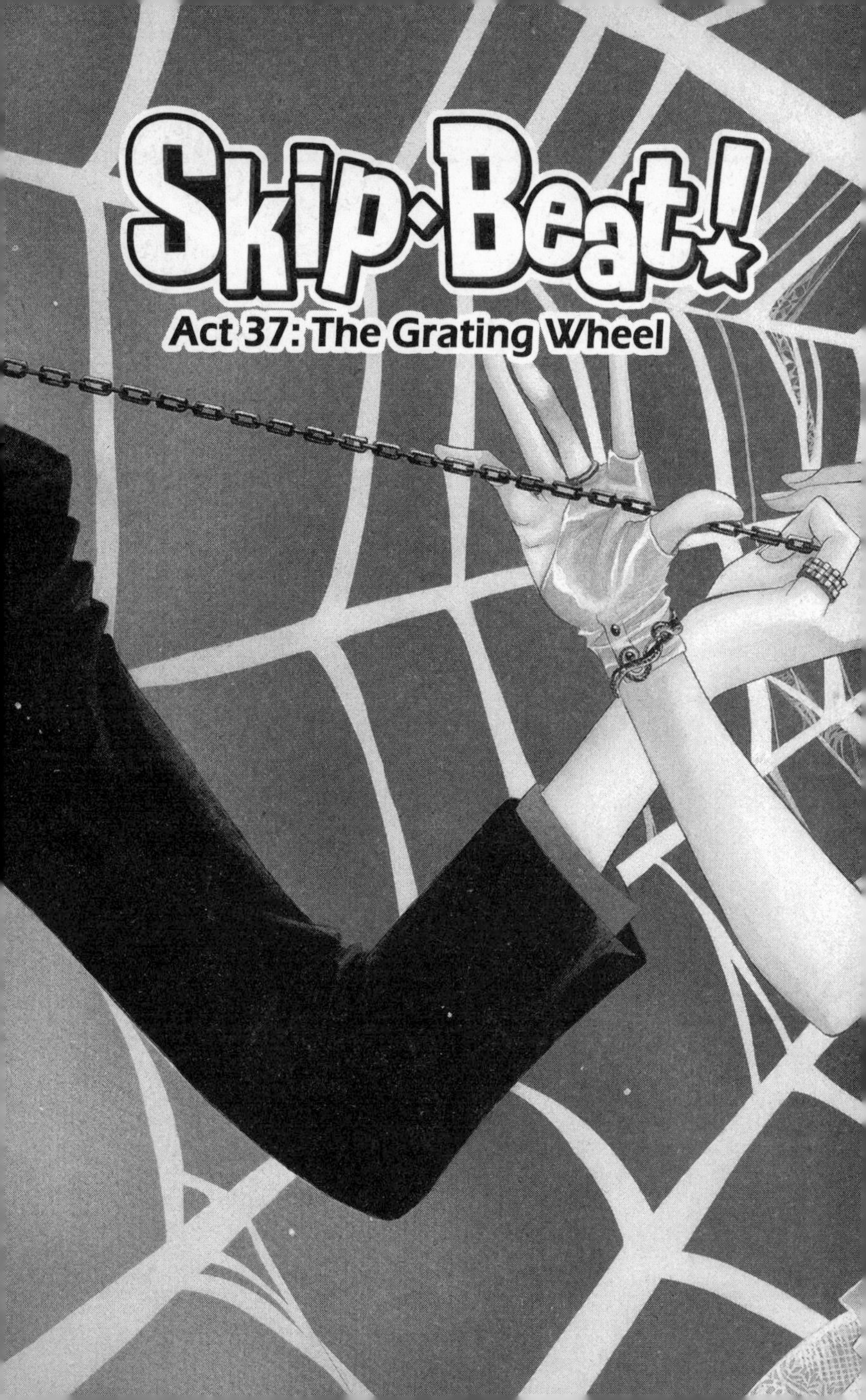
Skip·Beat!
Act 37: The Grating Wheel

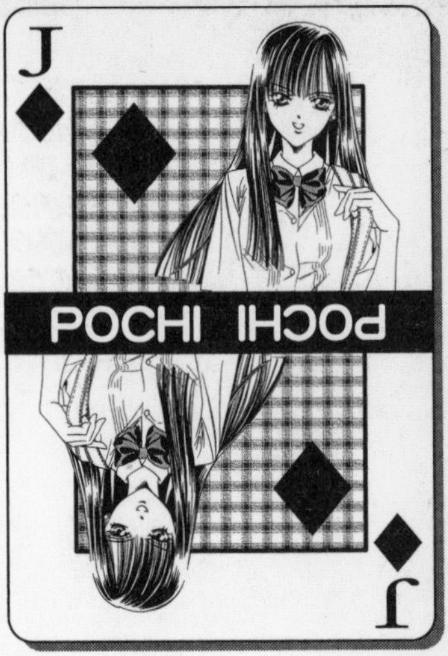
J
POCHI
POCHI
J

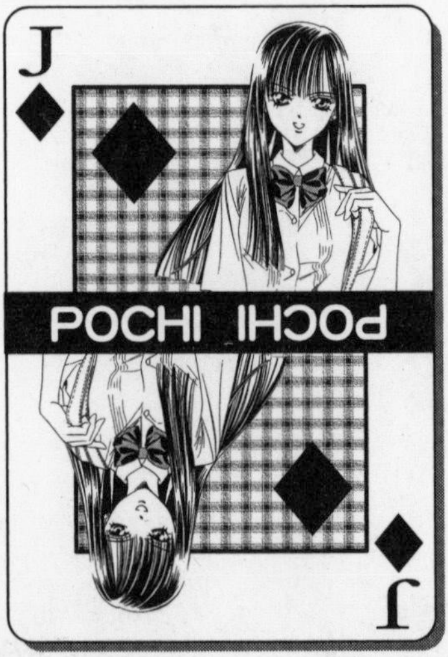
J
POCHI
POCHI
J

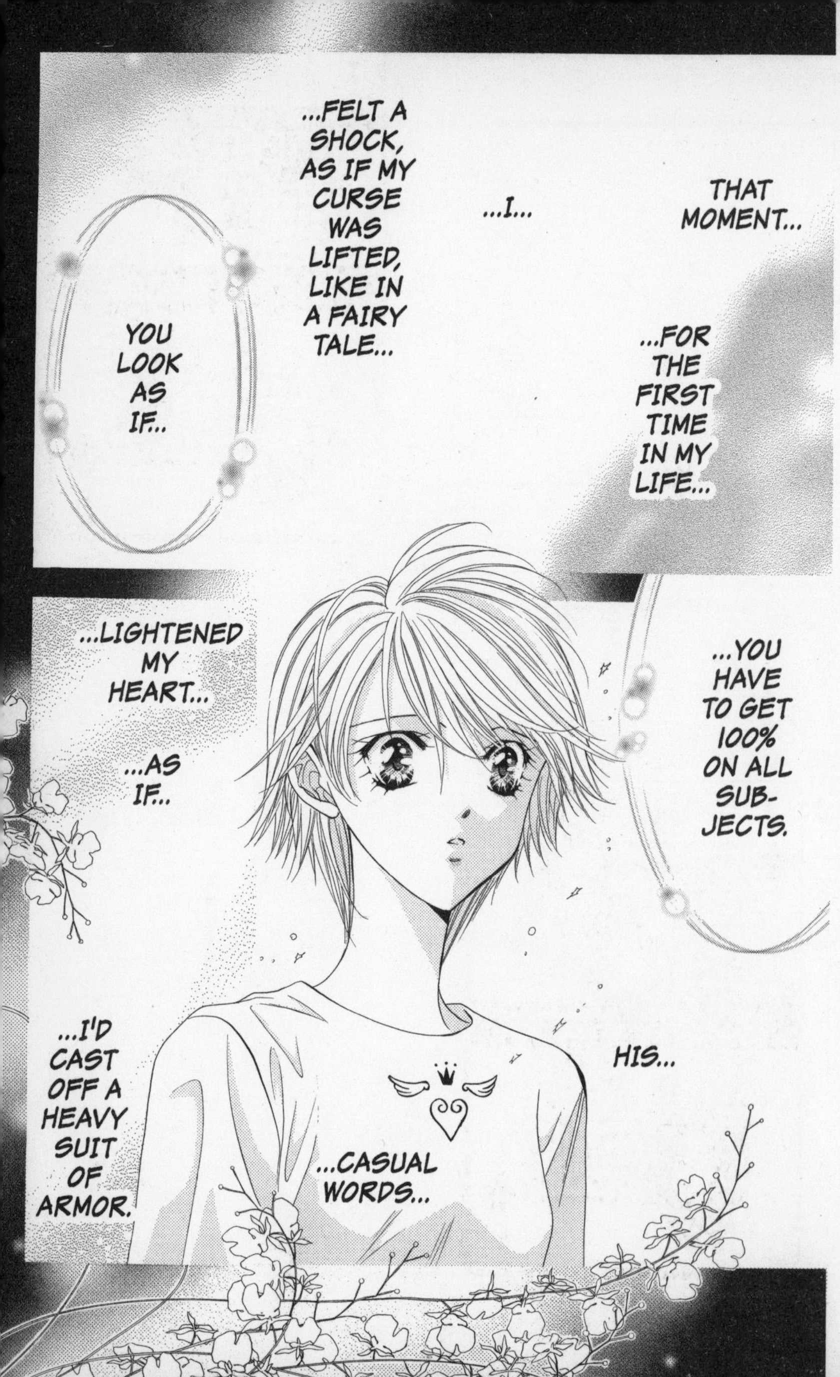
THAT MOMENT...
...FOR THE FIRST TIME IN MY LIFE...
...I...
...FELT A SHOCK, AS IF MY CURSE WAS LIFTED, LIKE IN A FAIRY TALE...
YOU LOOK AS IF...
...YOU HAVE TO GET 100% ON ALL SUB-JECTS.
HIS...
...CASUAL WORDS...
...LIGHTENED MY HEART...
...AS IF...
...I'D CAST OFF A HEAVY SUIT OF ARMOR.

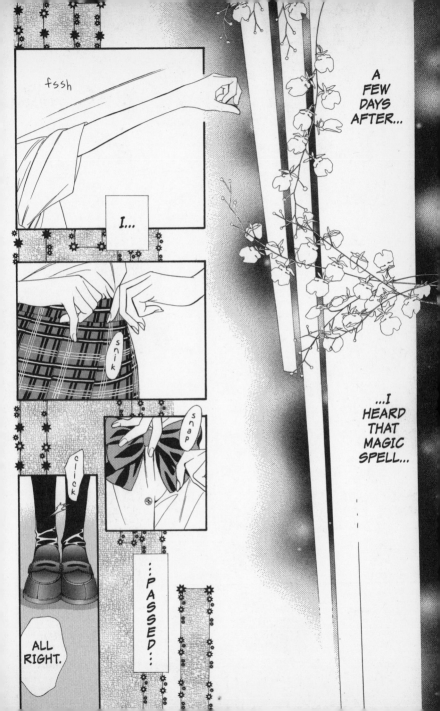

fssh

I...

snik

snap

click

A FEW DAYS AFTER...

...I HEARD THAT MAGIC SPELL...

...PASSED...

ALL RIGHT.

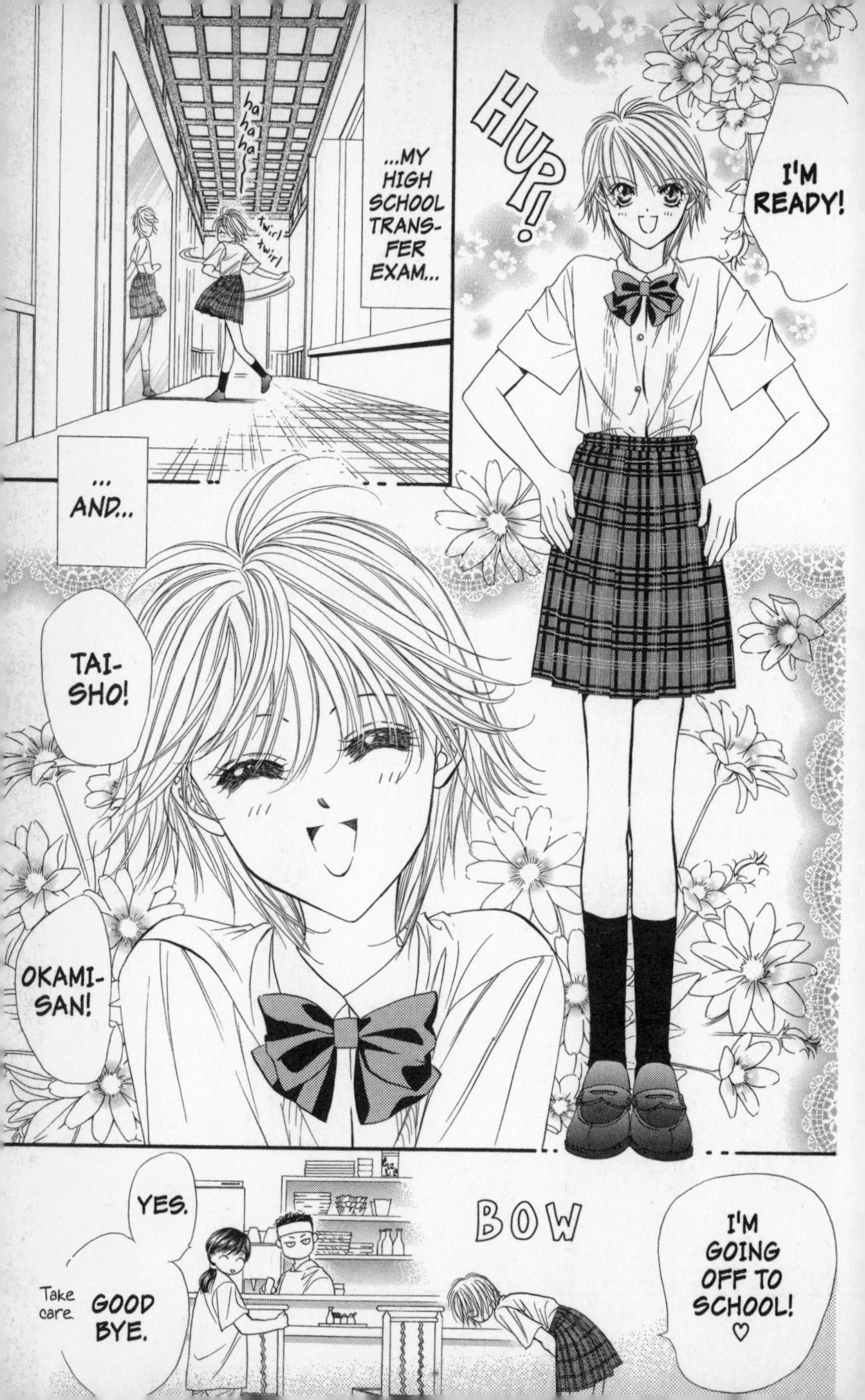
HUP!
I'M READY!
...MY HIGH SCHOOL TRANSFER EXAM...
ha ha ha~
twirl twirl
... AND...
TAI-SHO!
OKAMI-SAN!
I'M GOING OFF TO SCHOOL! ♡
BOW
YES.
GOOD BYE.
Take care.

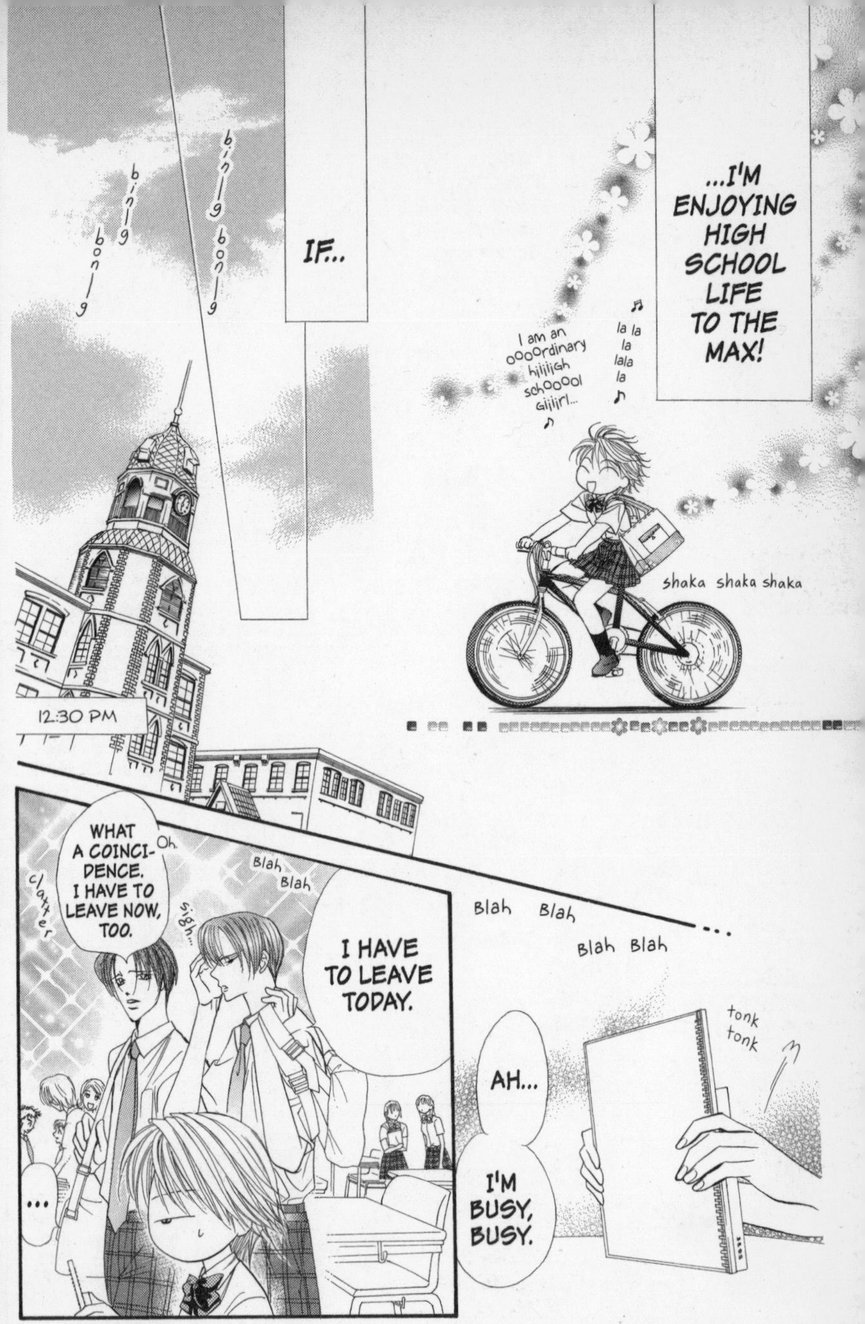

...I'M ENJOYING HIGH SCHOOL LIFE TO THE MAX!
la la la lala la
I am an ooooordinary hiiiiigh schooool Giiiirl...
shaka shaka shaka
IF...
bing bong
bing bong
12:30 PM
tonk tonk
AH...
I'M BUSY, BUSY.
Blah Blah
Blah Blah
...
I HAVE TO LEAVE TODAY.
Blah Blah
Oh.
WHAT A COINCIDENCE. I HAVE TO LEAVE NOW, TOO.
sigh...
clatter
...

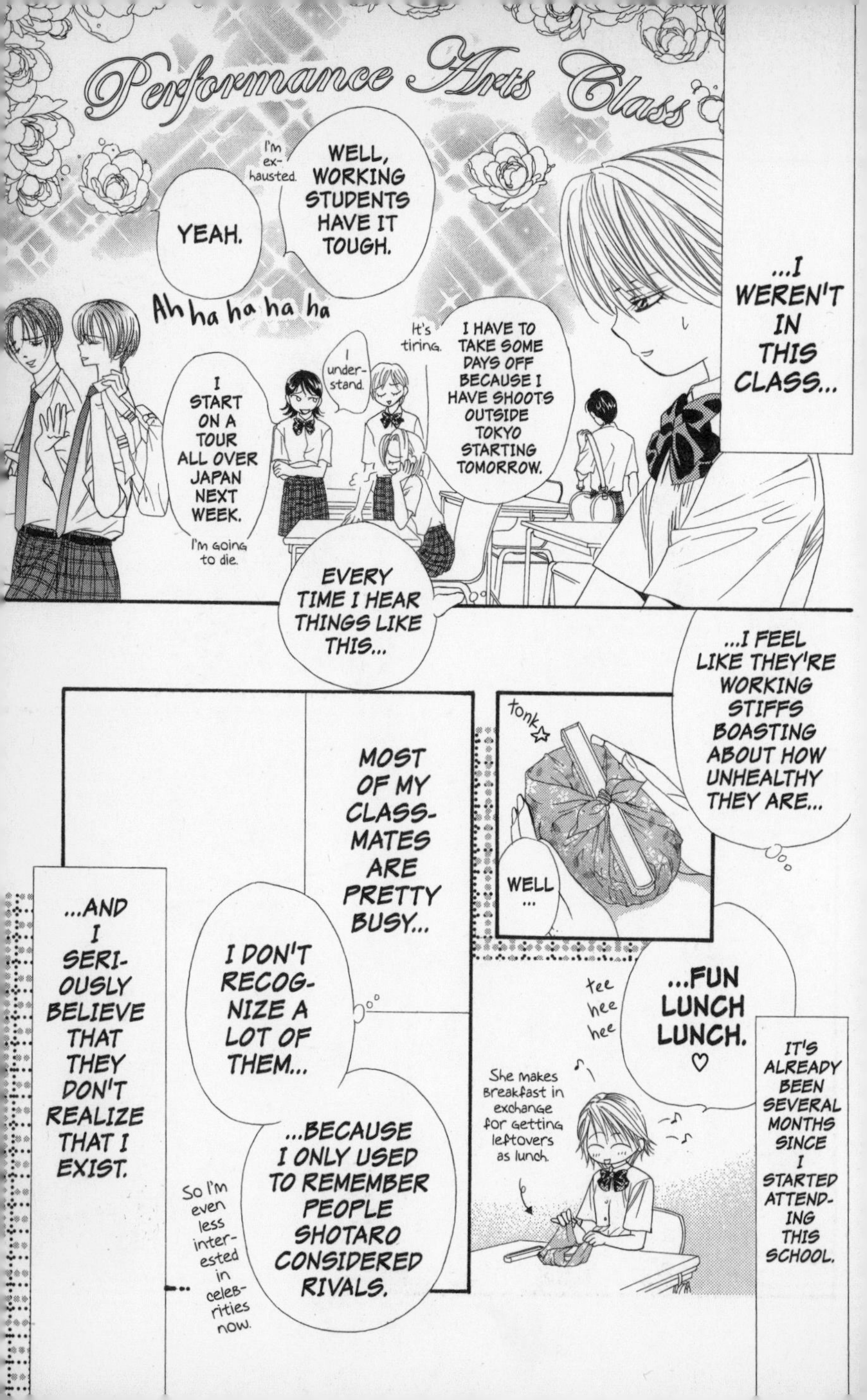

Performance Arts Class
...I WEREN'T IN THIS CLASS...
WELL, WORKING STUDENTS HAVE IT TOUGH.
I'm exhausted.
YEAH.
I HAVE TO TAKE SOME DAYS OFF BECAUSE I HAVE SHOOTS OUTSIDE TOKYO STARTING TOMORROW.
It's tiring.
I understand.
Ah ha ha ha ha
I START ON A TOUR ALL OVER JAPAN NEXT WEEK.
I'm going to die.
EVERY TIME I HEAR THINGS LIKE THIS...
...I FEEL LIKE THEY'RE WORKING STIFFS BOASTING ABOUT HOW UNHEALTHY THEY ARE...
tonk☆
WELL...
IT'S ALREADY BEEN SEVERAL MONTHS SINCE I STARTED ATTENDING THIS SCHOOL.
...FUN LUNCH LUNCH.♡
tee hee hee
She makes breakfast in exchange for getting leftovers as lunch.
MOST OF MY CLASSMATES ARE PRETTY BUSY...
I DON'T RECOGNIZE A LOT OF THEM...
...BECAUSE I ONLY USED TO REMEMBER PEOPLE SHOTARO CONSIDERED RIVALS.
So I'm even less interested in celebrities now.
...AND I SERIOUSLY BELIEVE THAT THEY DON'T REALIZE THAT I EXIST.

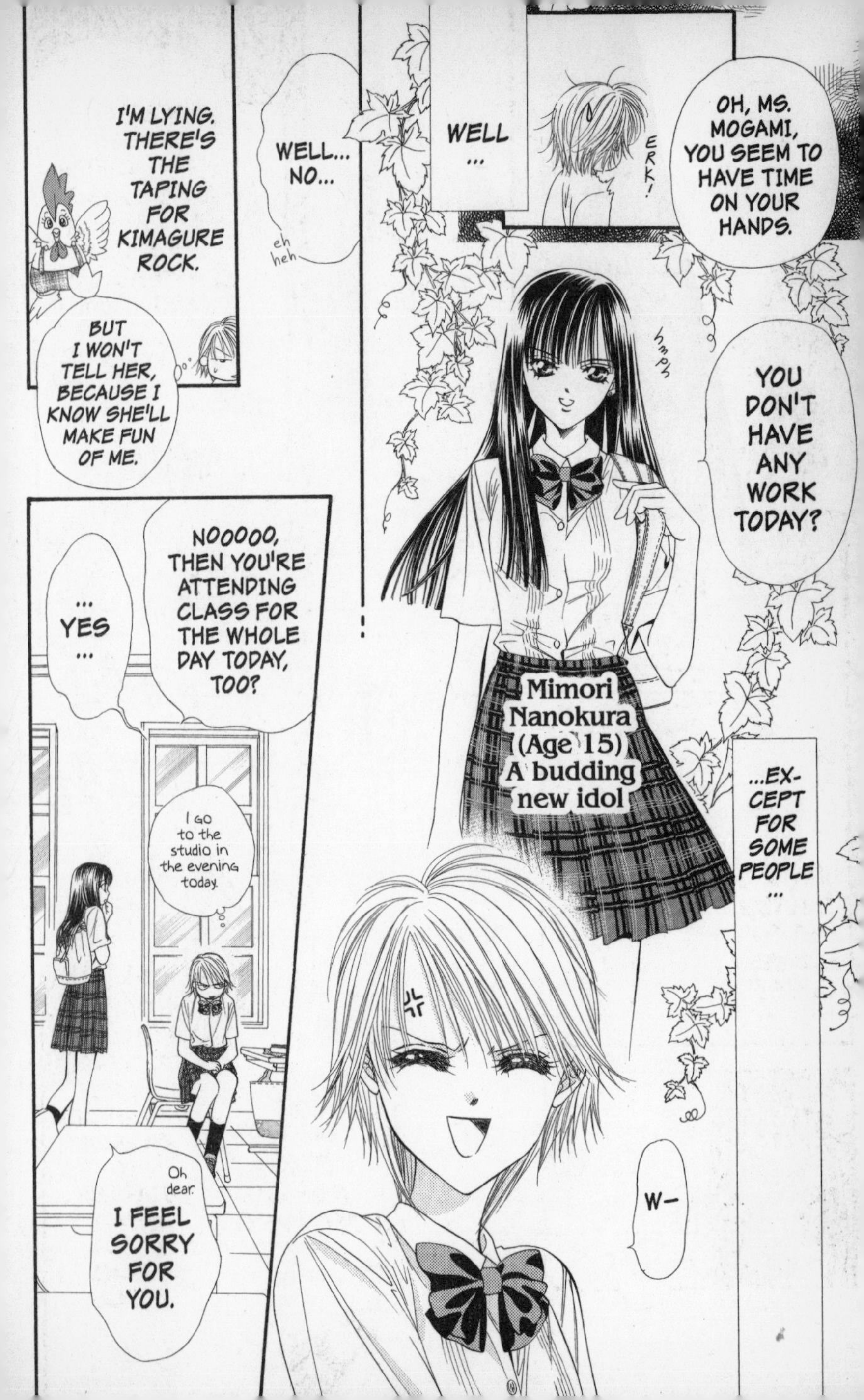
OH, MS. MOGAMI, YOU SEEM TO HAVE TIME ON YOUR HANDS.
ERK!
WELL ...
hmph
YOU DON'T HAVE ANY WORK TODAY?
Mimori Nanokura (Age 15) A budding new idol
...EX-CEPT FOR SOME PEOPLE ...
W–
WELL... NO...
eh heh
I'M LYING. THERE'S THE TAPING FOR KIMAGURE ROCK.
BUT I WON'T TELL HER, BECAUSE I KNOW SHE'LL MAKE FUN OF ME.
NOOOOO, THEN YOU'RE ATTENDING CLASS FOR THE WHOLE DAY TODAY, TOO?
... YES ...
I go to the studio in the evening today.
Oh dear.
I FEEL SORRY FOR YOU.

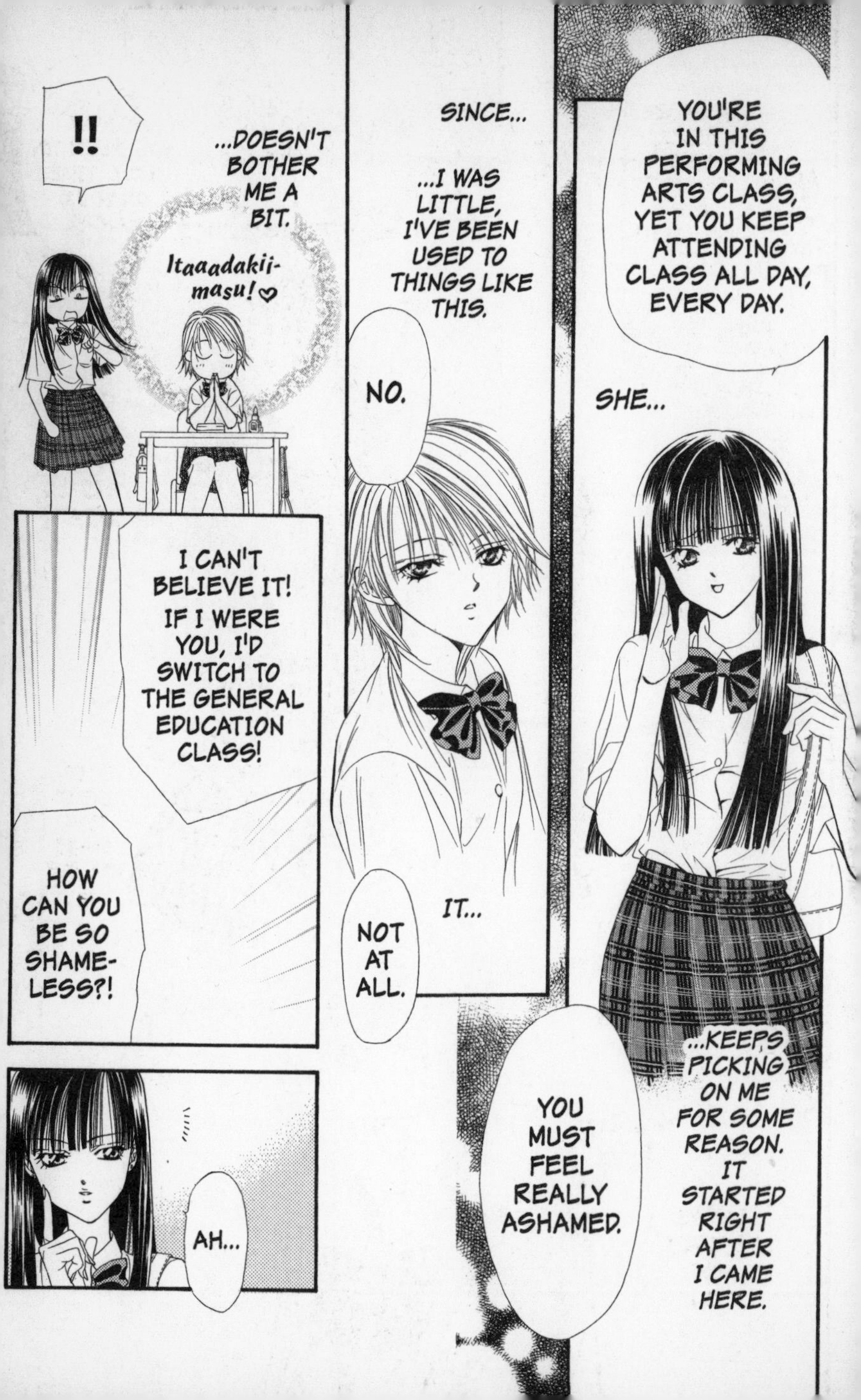
YOU'RE IN THIS PERFORMING ARTS CLASS, YET YOU KEEP ATTENDING CLASS ALL DAY, EVERY DAY.
SHE...
...KEEPS PICKING ON ME FOR SOME REASON. IT STARTED RIGHT AFTER I CAME HERE.
YOU MUST FEEL REALLY ASHAMED.
SINCE...
...I WAS LITTLE, I'VE BEEN USED TO THINGS LIKE THIS.
NO.
IT...
NOT AT ALL.
...DOESN'T BOTHER ME A BIT.
!!
Itaaadakii-masu! ♡
I CAN'T BELIEVE IT! IF I WERE YOU, I'D SWITCH TO THE GENERAL EDUCATION CLASS!
HOW CAN YOU BE SO SHAME-LESS?!
AH...

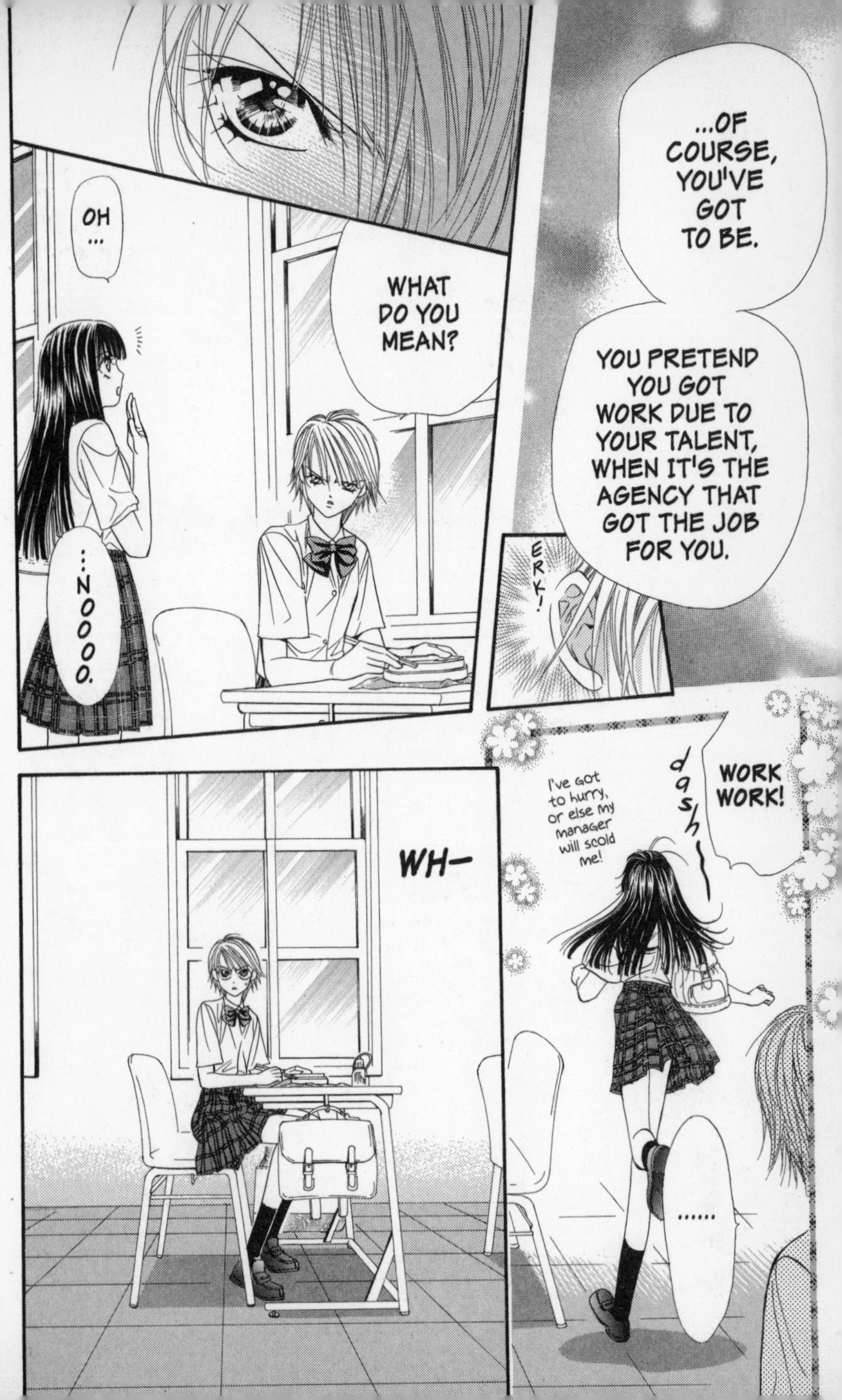
OH ...
WHAT DO YOU MEAN?
...NOOOO.
...OF COURSE, YOU'VE GOT TO BE.
YOU PRETEND YOU GOT WORK DUE TO YOUR TALENT, WHEN IT'S THE AGENCY THAT GOT THE JOB FOR YOU.
ERK!
WORK WORK!
dash
I've got to hurry, or else my manager will scold me!
......
WH-

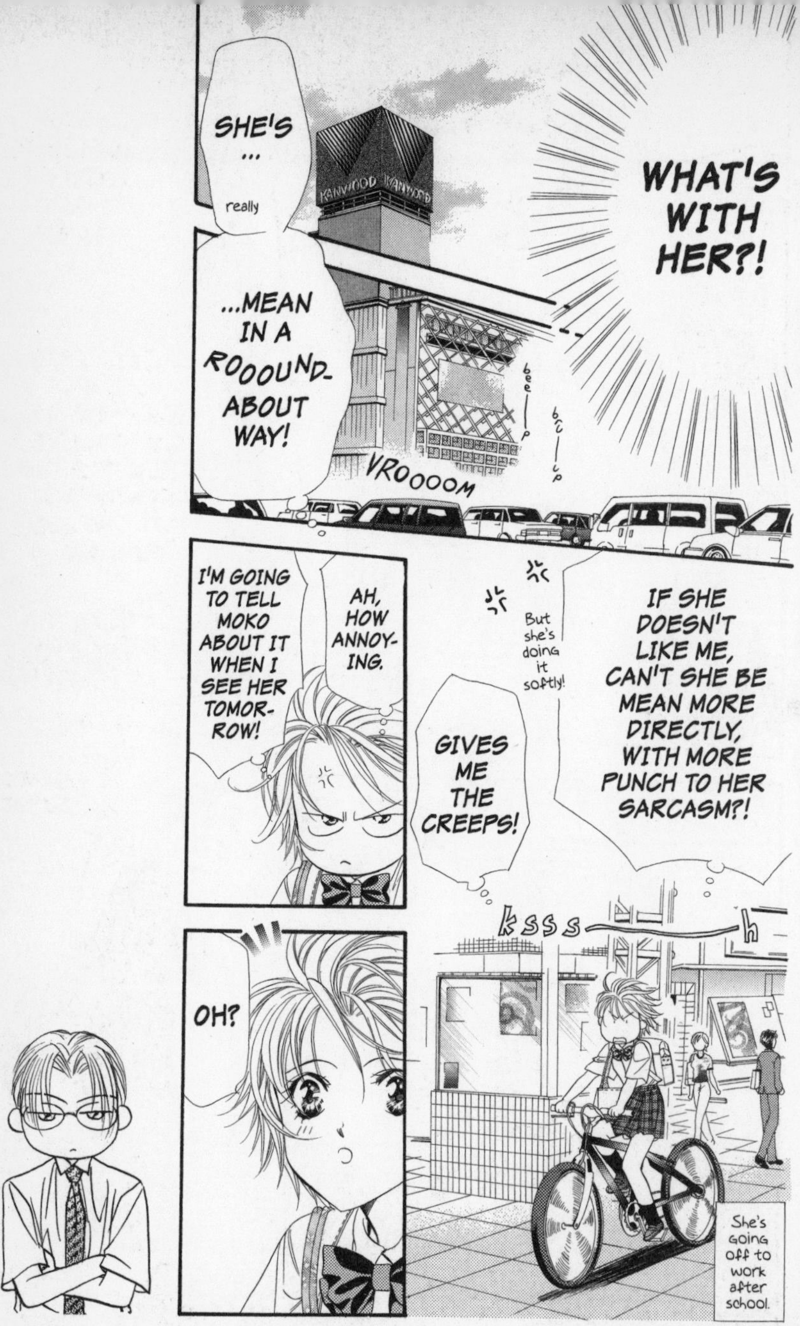
SHE'S ... really
...MEAN IN A ROOOUND-ABOUT WAY!
WHAT'S WITH HER?!
bee—p
brr—p
VROOOOM
IF SHE DOESN'T LIKE ME, CAN'T SHE BE MEAN MORE DIRECTLY, WITH MORE PUNCH TO HER SARCASM?!
But she's doing it softly!
GIVES ME THE CREEPS!
AH, HOW ANNOY-ING.
I'M GOING TO TELL MOKO ABOUT IT WHEN I SEE HER TOMOR-ROW!
ksss—h
She's going off to work after school.
OH?

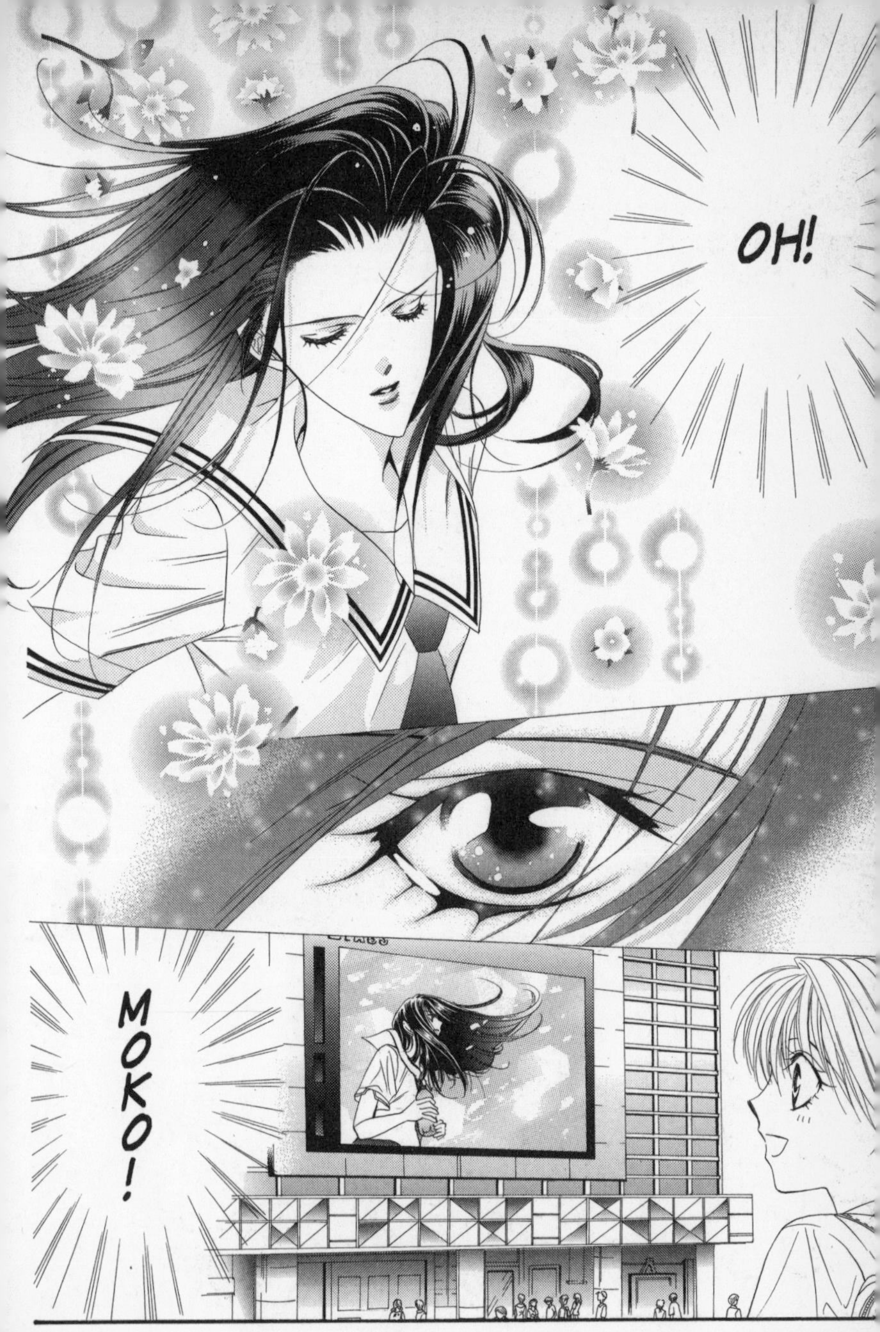
OH!
MOKO!

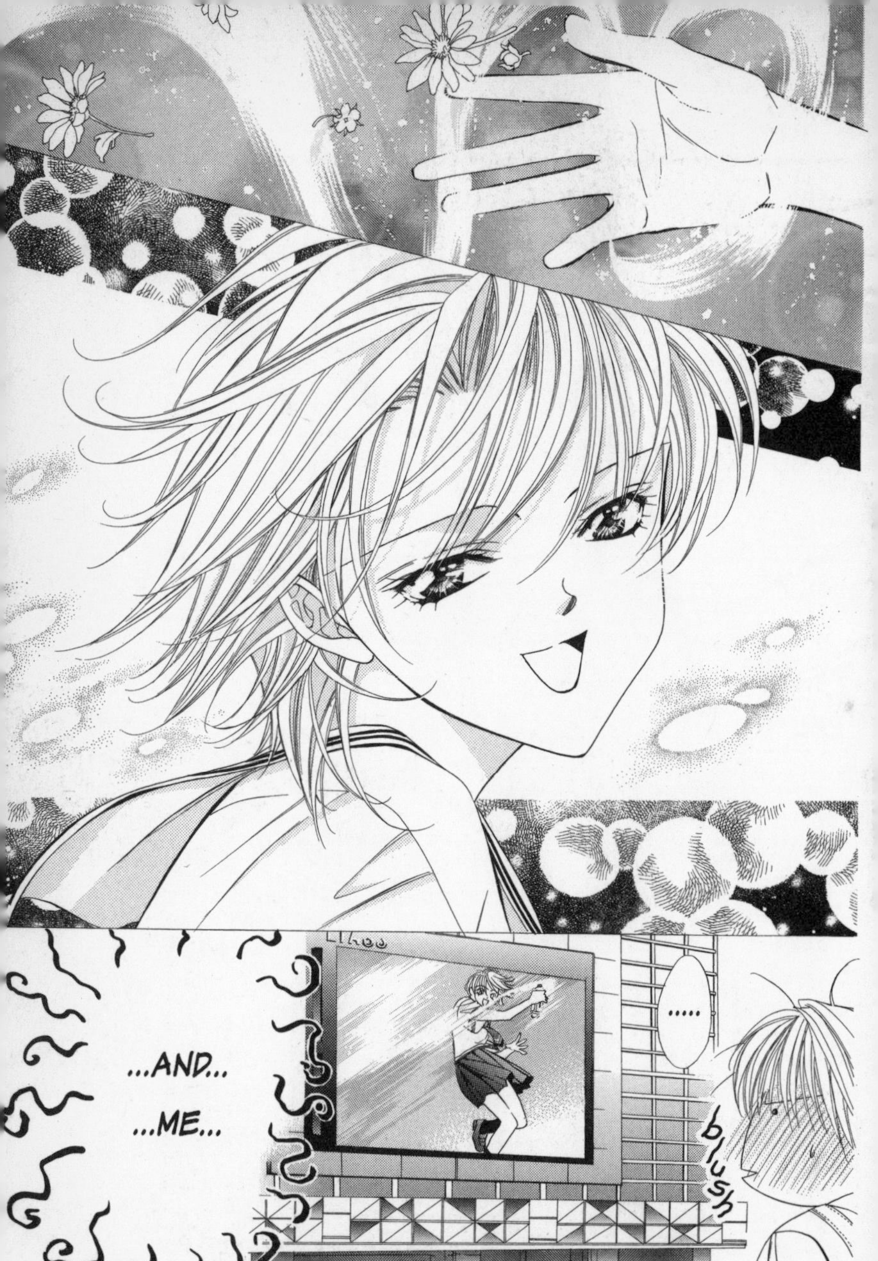
.....
blush
...AND...
...ME...

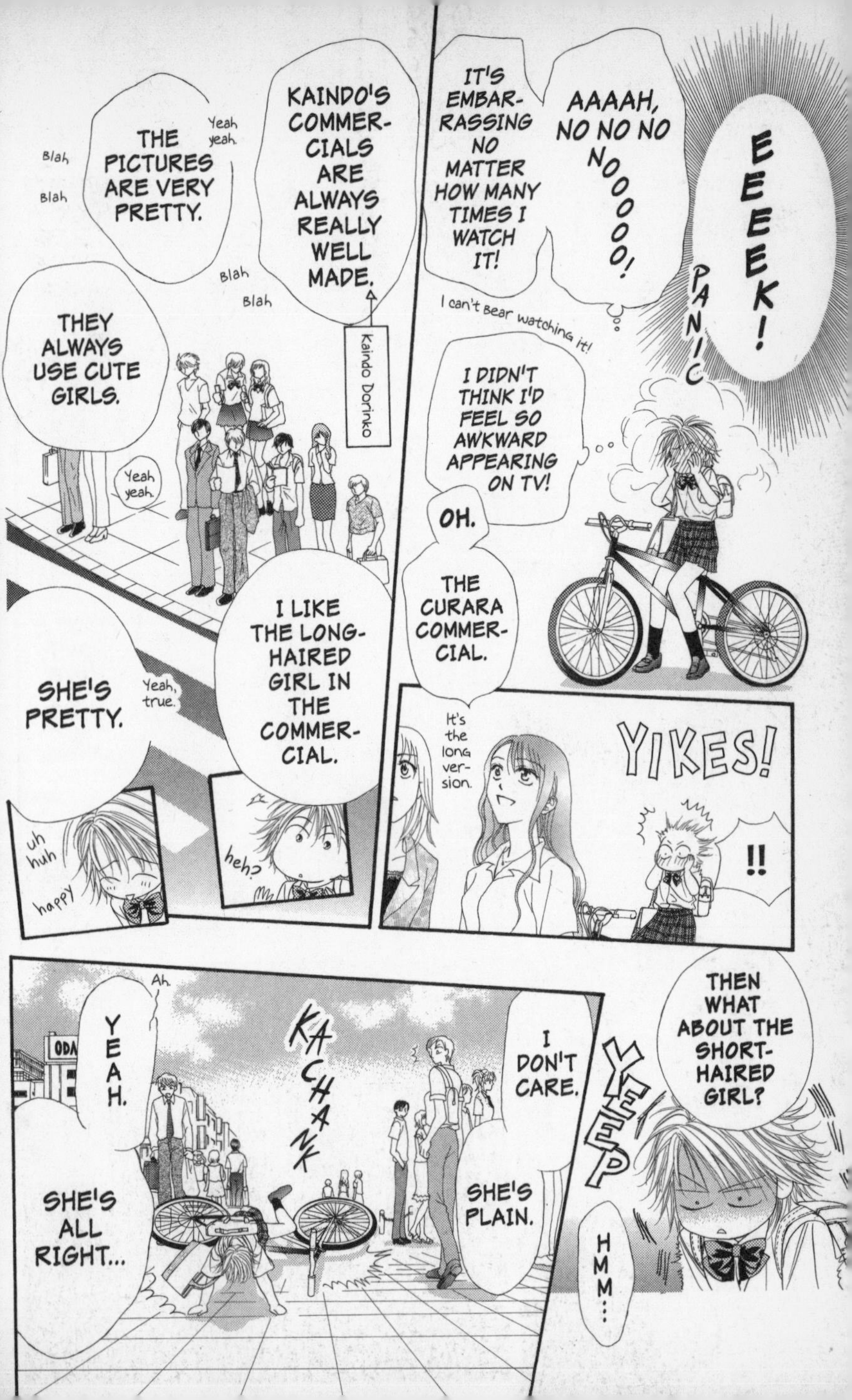
AAAAH, NO NO NO NOOOOOO!
IT'S EMBARRASSING NO MATTER HOW MANY TIMES I WATCH IT!
EEEEK!
PANIC
I can't Bear watching it!
I DIDN'T THINK I'D FEEL SO AWKWARD APPEARING ON TV!
OH.
THE CURARA COMMERCIAL.
KAINDO'S COMMERCIALS ARE ALWAYS REALLY WELL MADE.
Kaindo Dorinko
Yeah yeah.
THE PICTURES ARE VERY PRETTY.
Blah
Blah
Blah
Blah
THEY ALWAYS USE CUTE GIRLS.
Yeah yeah.
I LIKE THE LONG-HAIRED GIRL IN THE COMMERCIAL.
Yeah, true.
SHE'S PRETTY.
YIKES!
!!
It's the long version.
heh?
uh huh
happy
THEN WHAT ABOUT THE SHORT-HAIRED GIRL?
YEEP
HMM...
I DON'T CARE.
SHE'S PLAIN.
KACHANK
Ah.
YEAH.
SHE'S ALL RIGHT...

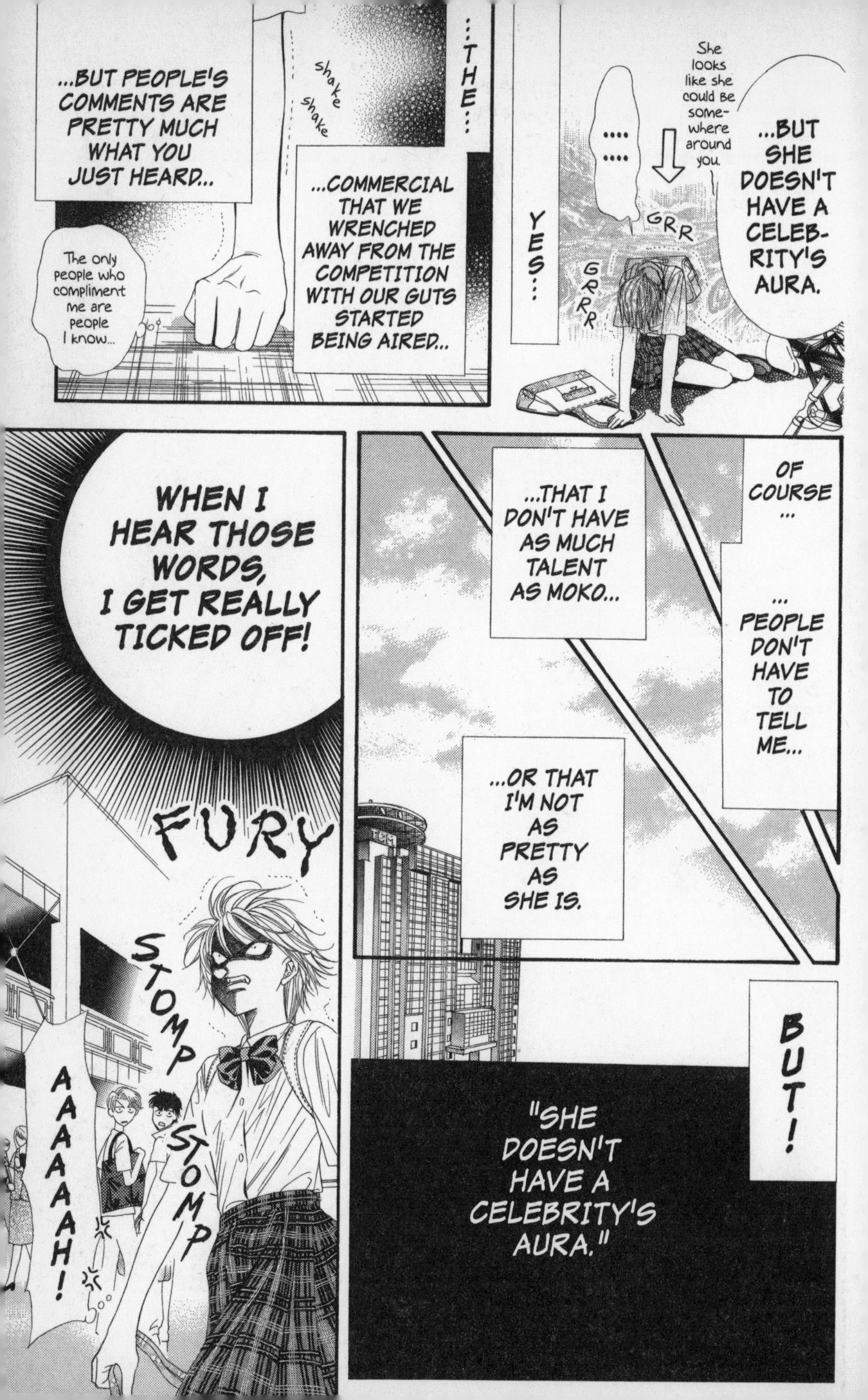
She looks like she could be somewhere around you.
...BUT SHE DOESN'T HAVE A CELEBRITY'S AURA.
....
....
GRR
GRRR
YES...
...THE...
shake shake
...COMMERCIAL THAT WE WRENCHED AWAY FROM THE COMPETITION WITH OUR GUTS STARTED BEING AIRED...
...BUT PEOPLE'S COMMENTS ARE PRETTY MUCH WHAT YOU JUST HEARD...
The only people who compliment me are people I know...
OF COURSE...
...PEOPLE DON'T HAVE TO TELL ME...
...THAT I DON'T HAVE AS MUCH TALENT AS MOKO...
...OR THAT I'M NOT AS PRETTY AS SHE IS.
BUT!
"SHE DOESN'T HAVE A CELEBRITY'S AURA."
WHEN I HEAR THOSE WORDS, I GET REALLY TICKED OFF!
FURY
STOMP
STOMP
AAAAAAAH!

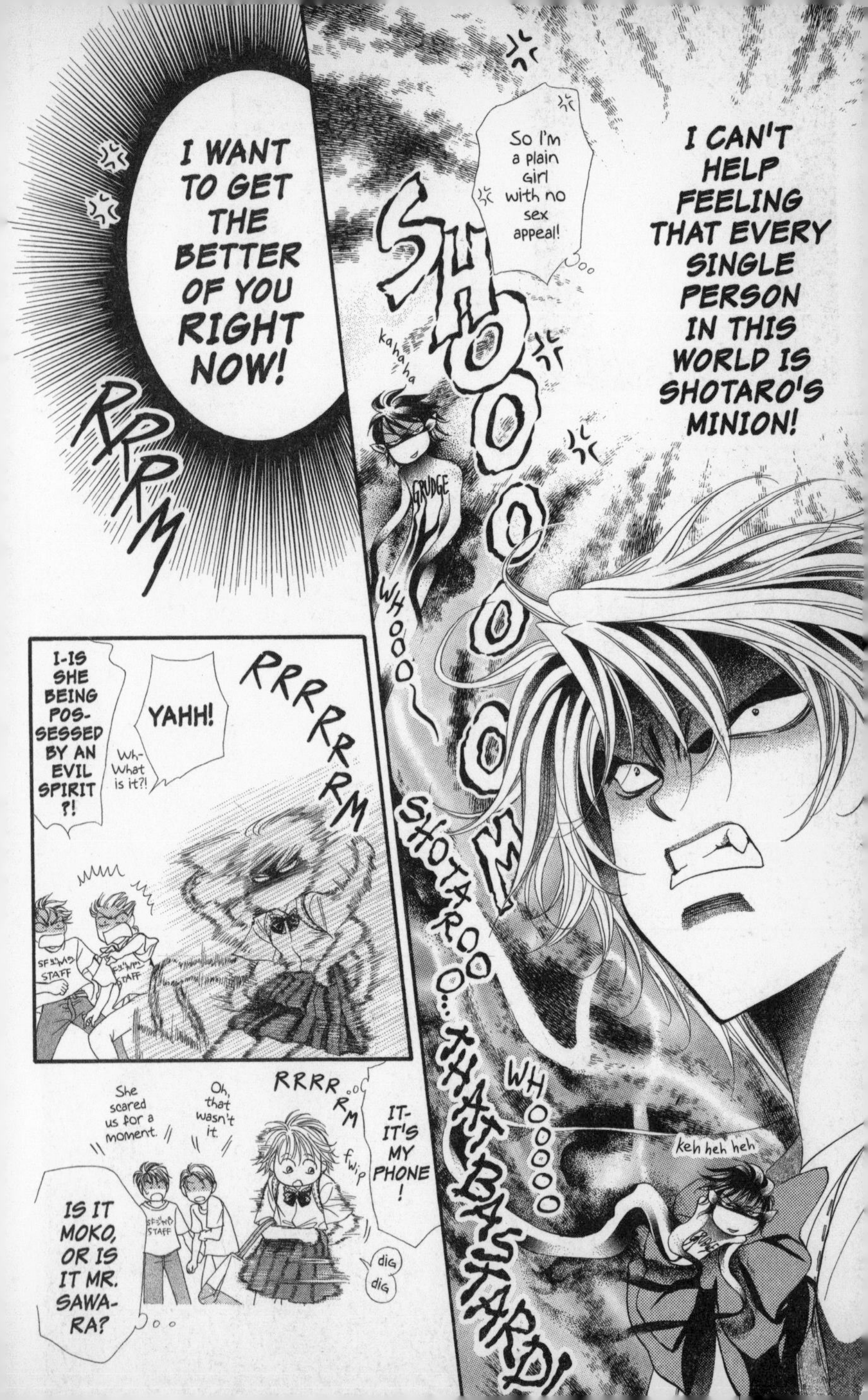
I CAN'T HELP FEELING THAT EVERY SINGLE PERSON IN THIS WORLD IS SHOTARO'S MINION!
So I'm a plain girl with no sex appeal!
SHOOOOOOOM
kahahaha
GRUDGE
WHOOO
SHOTAROO... THAT BASTARD!
WHOOOOOO
keh heh heh
I WANT TO GET THE BETTER OF YOU RIGHT NOW!
RRRM
RRRRRRRM
YAHH!
Wh-What is it?!
I-IS SHE BEING POS-SESSED BY AN EVIL SPIRIT?!
STAFF
STAFF
RRRRRM
IT-IT'S MY PHONE!
fwip
dig dig
Oh, that wasn't it.
She scared us for a moment.
STAFF
IS IT MOKO, OR IS IT MR. SAWA-RA?

NO CALLER-ID.
Beep
The agency gave her the cell phone ever since she substituted as Ren's manager.
IT MUST BE MR. SAWARA.
The agency usually calls with Caller ID off.
HELLO?
Hi.
You're slow to answer the phone, as usual.
WHA...
You're still...
...not used to it?
heh heh heh
WHA-WHA-WHA-WHA-WHA-WHA-WHA-WHA-?!
HOLD IT... TH-THIS VOICE...
And the way he's talking!
N-N-N-N-N-NO!
And ...

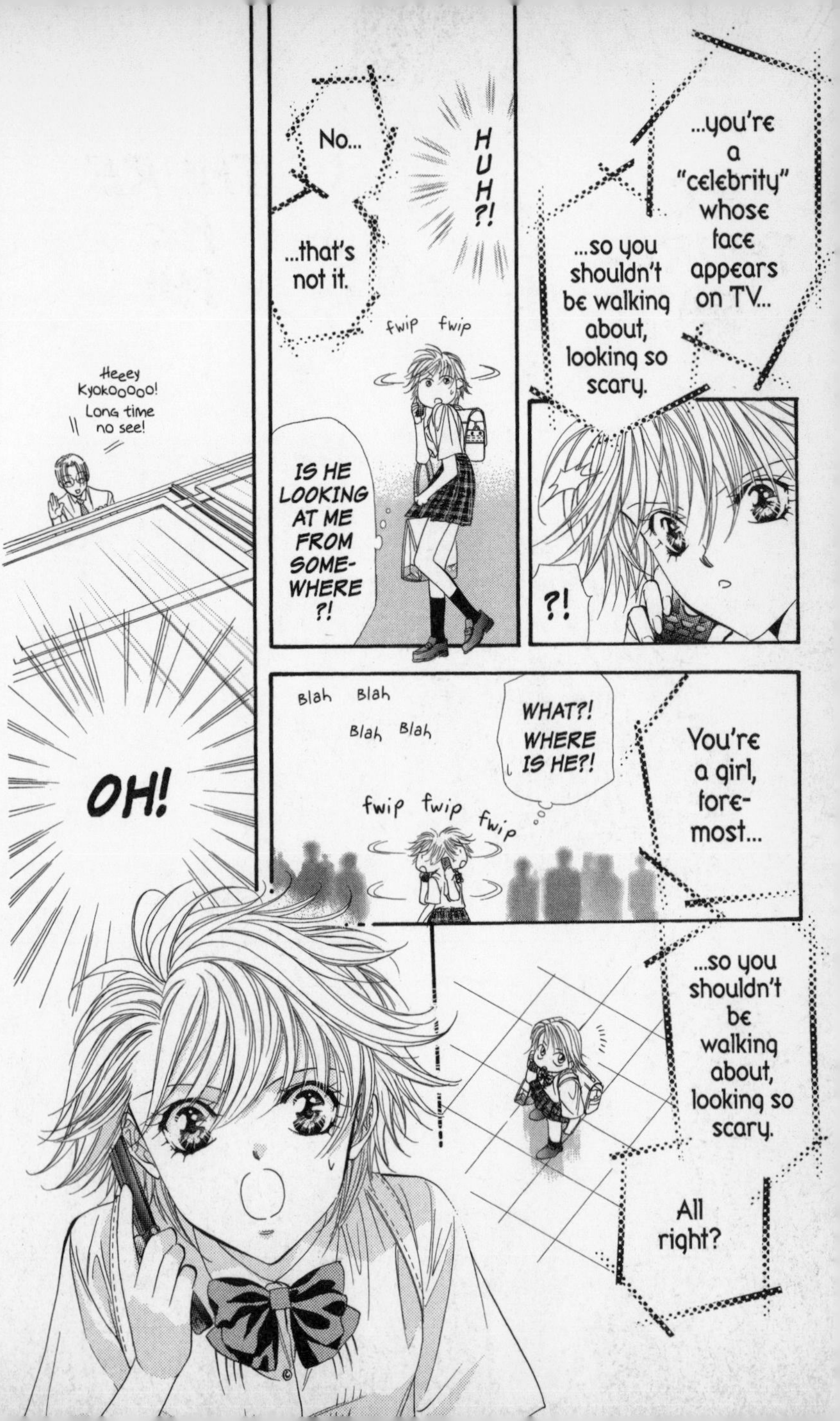

...you're a "celebrity" whose face appears on TV...
...so you shouldn't be walking about, looking so scary.
?!
No...
HUH?!
...that's not it.
fwip fwip
IS HE LOOKING AT ME FROM SOME-WHERE?!
You're a girl, fore-most...
WHAT?! WHERE IS HE?!
Blah Blah
Blah Blah
fwip fwip fwip
...so you shouldn't be walking about, looking so scary.
All right?
Heeey Kyokoooooo! Long time no see!
OH!

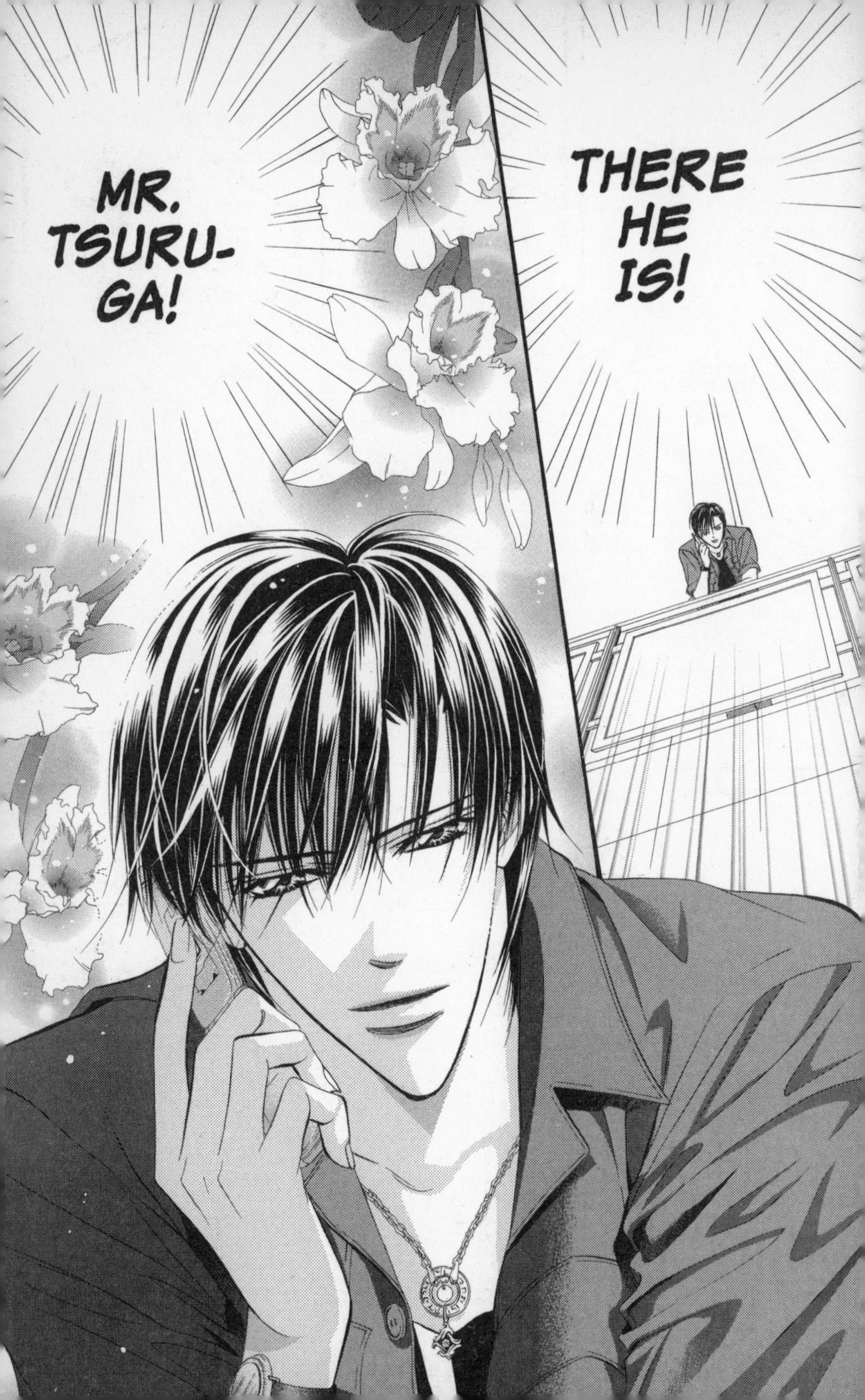
THERE HE IS!
MR. TSURU-GA!

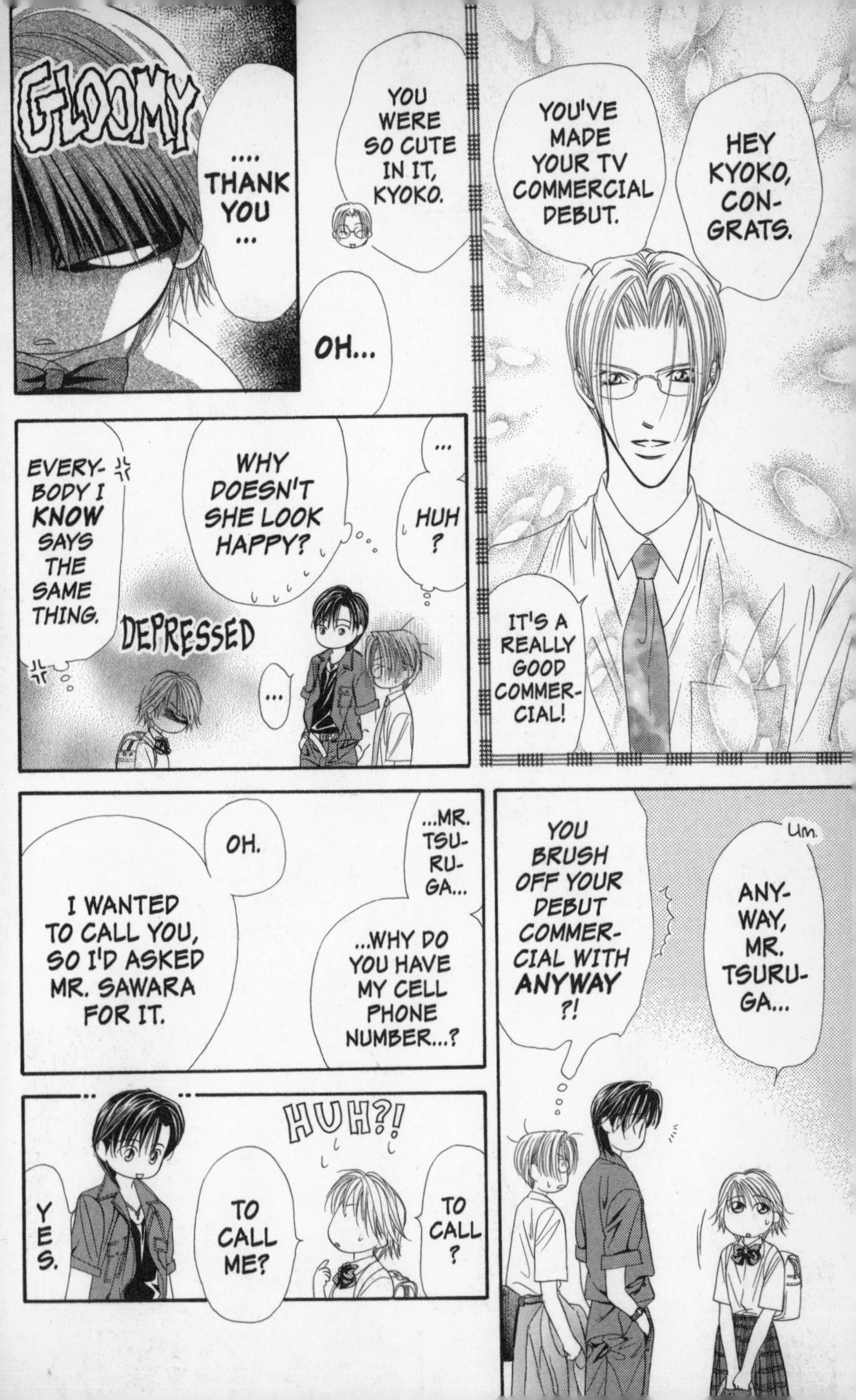
HEY KYOKO, CON-GRATS.
YOU'VE MADE YOUR TV COMMERCIAL DEBUT.
IT'S A REALLY GOOD COMMER-CIAL!
YOU WERE SO CUTE IN IT, KYOKO.
OH...
.... THANK YOU ...
GLOOMY
... HUH ?
WHY DOESN'T SHE LOOK HAPPY?
EVERY-BODY I KNOW SAYS THE SAME THING.
DEPRESSED
...
Um.
ANY-WAY, MR. TSURU-GA...
YOU BRUSH OFF YOUR DEBUT COMMER-CIAL WITH ANYWAY ?!
...MR. TSU-RU-GA...
...WHY DO YOU HAVE MY CELL PHONE NUMBER...?
OH.
I WANTED TO CALL YOU, SO I'D ASKED MR. SAWARA FOR IT.
HUH?!
TO CALL ?
TO CALL ME?
YES.

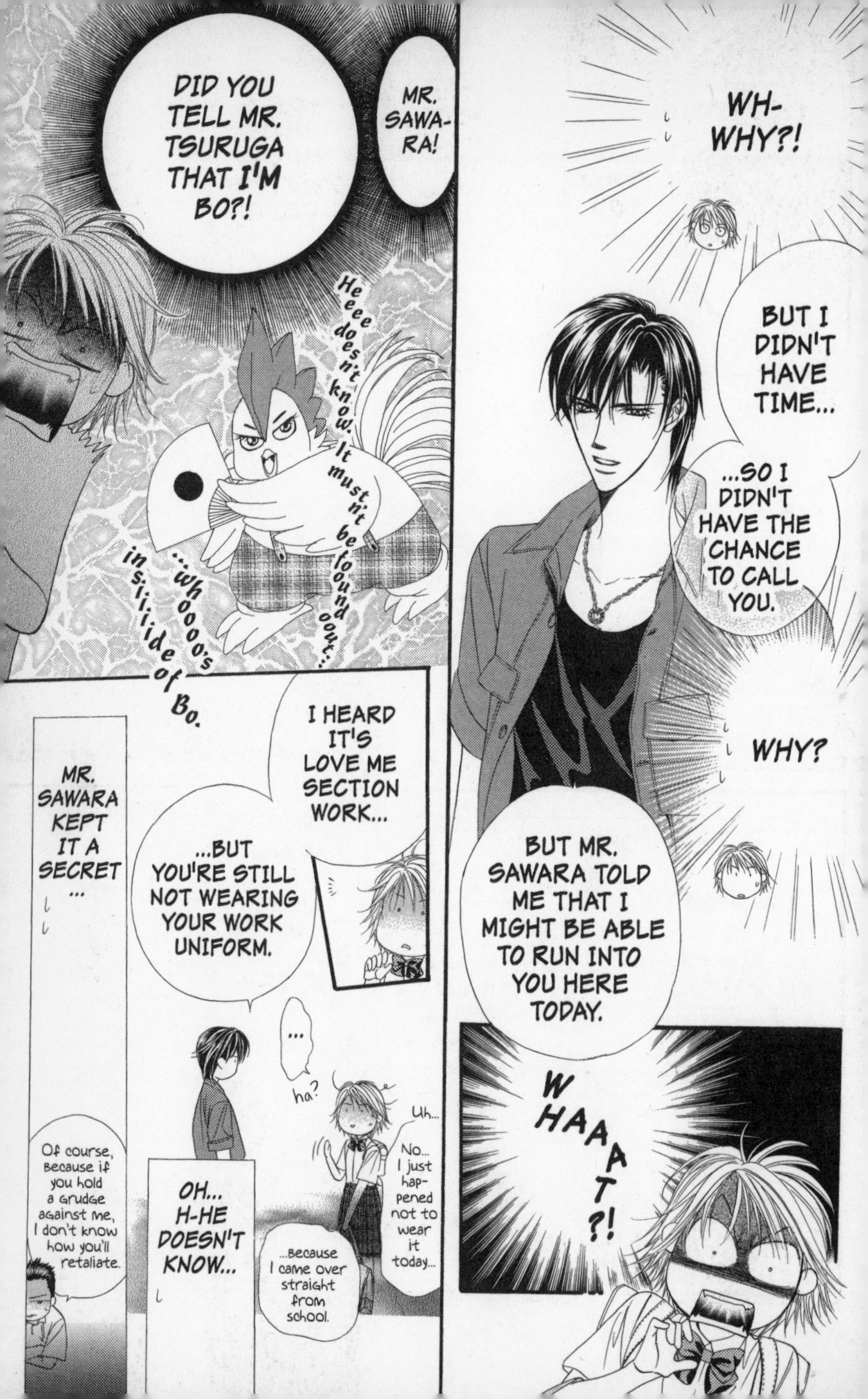
WH-WHY?!
BUT I DIDN'T HAVE TIME...
...SO I DIDN'T HAVE THE CHANCE TO CALL YOU.
WHY?
BUT MR. SAWARA TOLD ME THAT I MIGHT BE ABLE TO RUN INTO YOU HERE TODAY.
WHAAAT?!
MR. SAWA-RA!
DID YOU TELL MR. TSURUGA THAT I'M BO?!
Heeee doesn't know. It mustn't be found out...
...whoooo's insiiiide of Bo.
I HEARD IT'S LOVE ME SECTION WORK...
...BUT YOU'RE STILL NOT WEARING YOUR WORK UNIFORM.
MR. SAWARA KEPT IT A SECRET...
...
ha?
Uh...
No... I just hap-pened not to wear it today...
...Because I came over straight from school.
OH... H-HE DOESN'T KNOW...
Of course, Because if you hold a Grudge against me, I don't know how you'll retaliate.

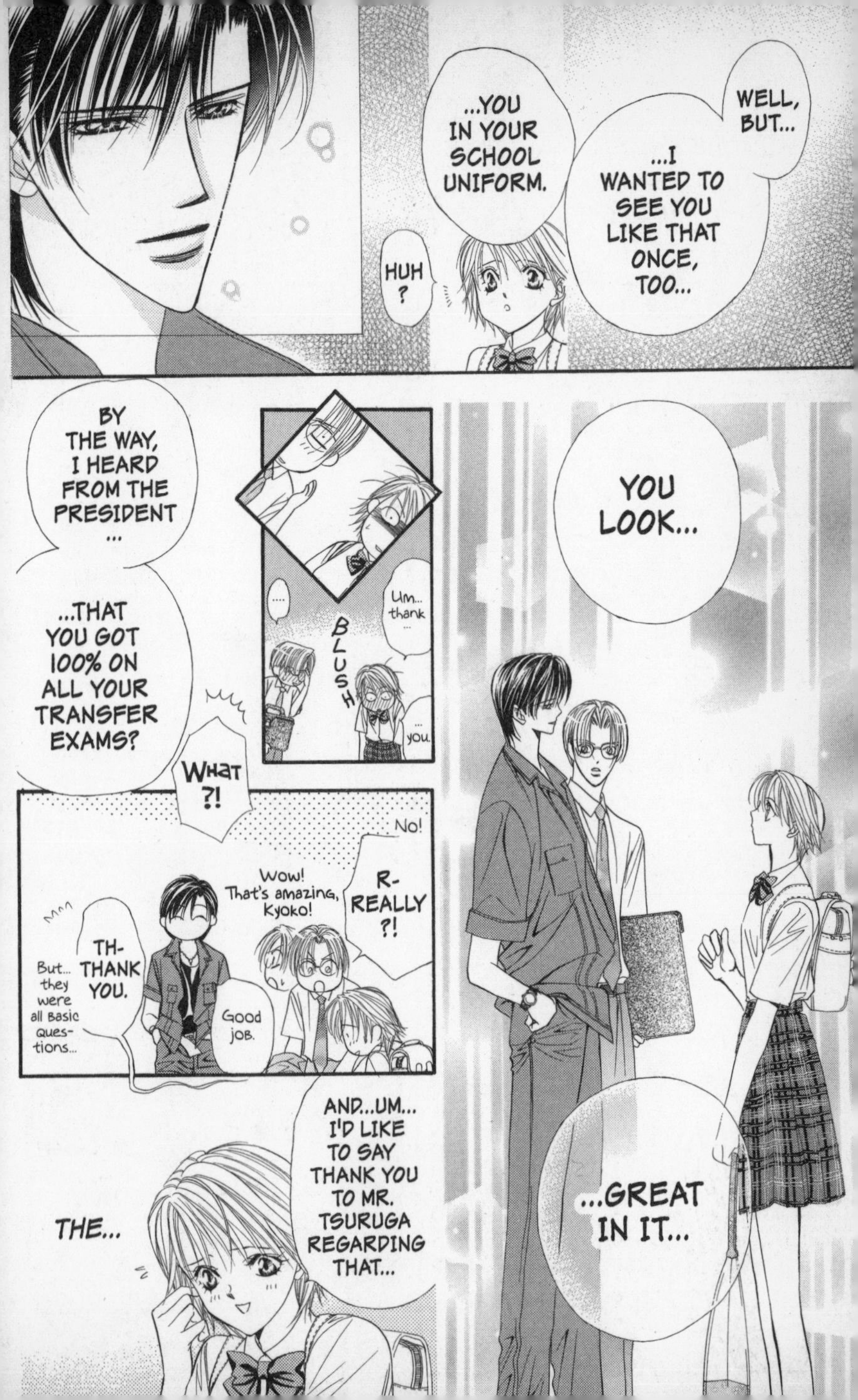
WELL, BUT...
...I WANTED TO SEE YOU LIKE THAT ONCE, TOO...
...YOU IN YOUR SCHOOL UNIFORM.
HUH?
YOU LOOK...
...GREAT IN IT...
....
Um... thank ...
BLUSH
... you.
BY THE WAY, I HEARD FROM THE PRESIDENT ...
...THAT YOU GOT 100% ON ALL YOUR TRANSFER EXAMS?
WHAT?!
No!
R-REALLY?!
Wow! That's amazing, Kyoko!
TH-THANK YOU.
But... they were all Basic ques-tions...
Good job.
AND...UM... I'D LIKE TO SAY THANK YOU TO MR. TSURUGA REGARDING THAT...
THE...

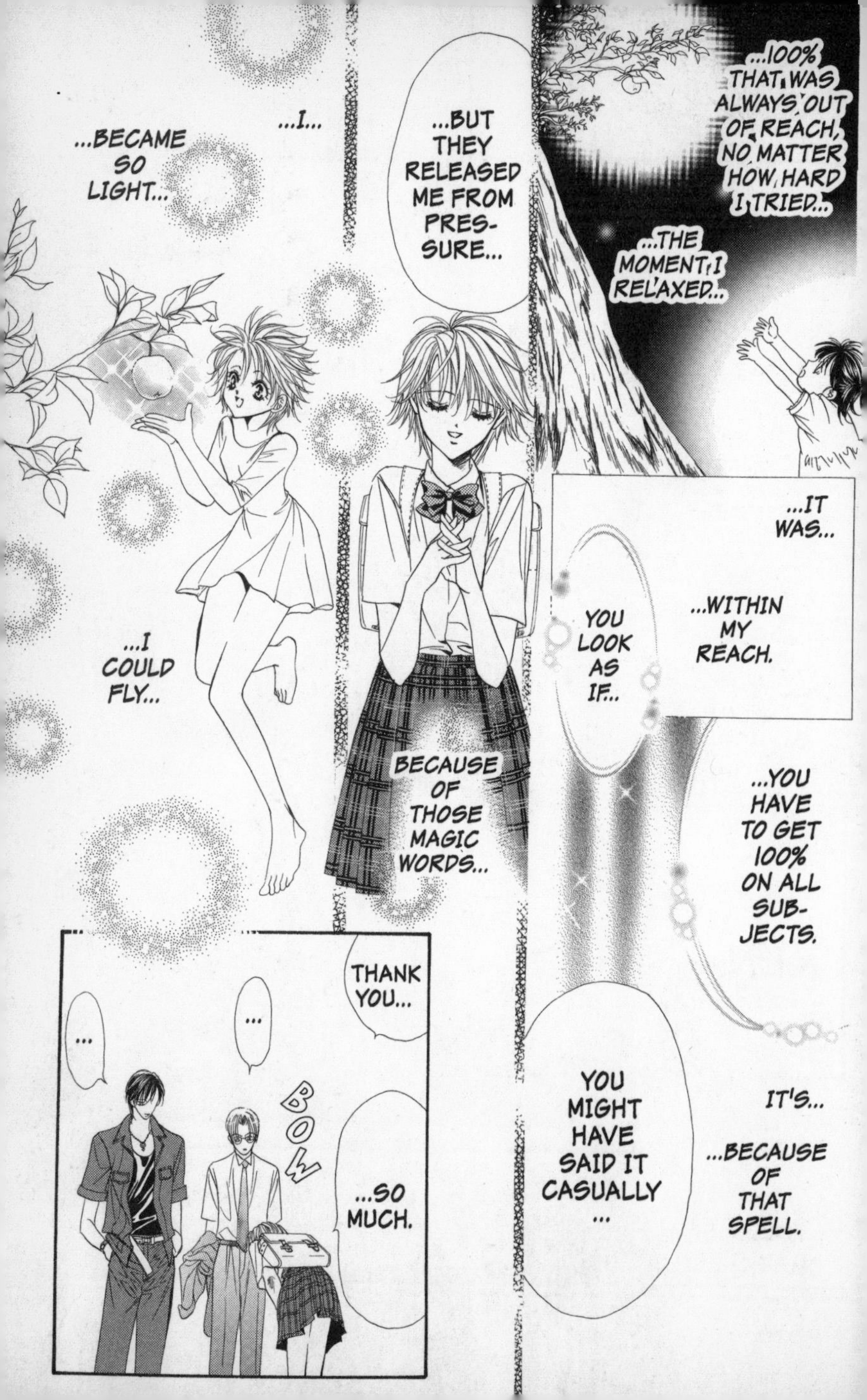
...100% THAT WAS ALWAYS OUT OF REACH, NO MATTER HOW HARD I TRIED...
...THE MOMENT I RELAXED...
...IT WAS...
...WITHIN MY REACH.
YOU LOOK AS IF...
...YOU HAVE TO GET 100% ON ALL SUBJECTS.
IT'S...
...BECAUSE OF THAT SPELL.
YOU MIGHT HAVE SAID IT CASUALLY...
...BUT THEY RELEASED ME FROM PRESSURE...
BECAUSE OF THOSE MAGIC WORDS...
...I...
...BECAME SO LIGHT...
...I COULD FLY...
THANK YOU...
...SO MUCH.
BOW
...
...

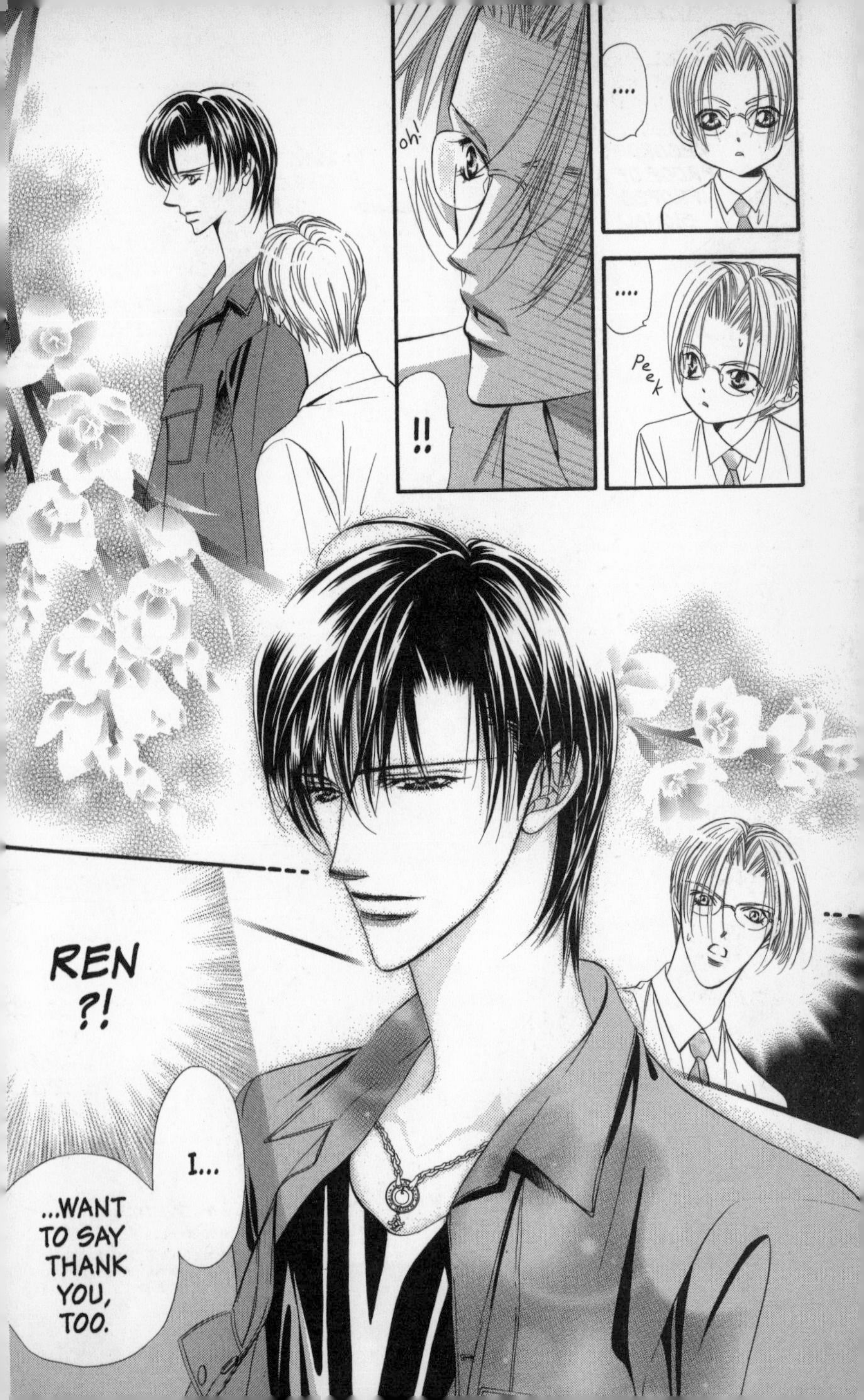
....
....
peek
oh!
!!
REN ?!
I...
...WANT TO SAY THANK YOU, TOO.

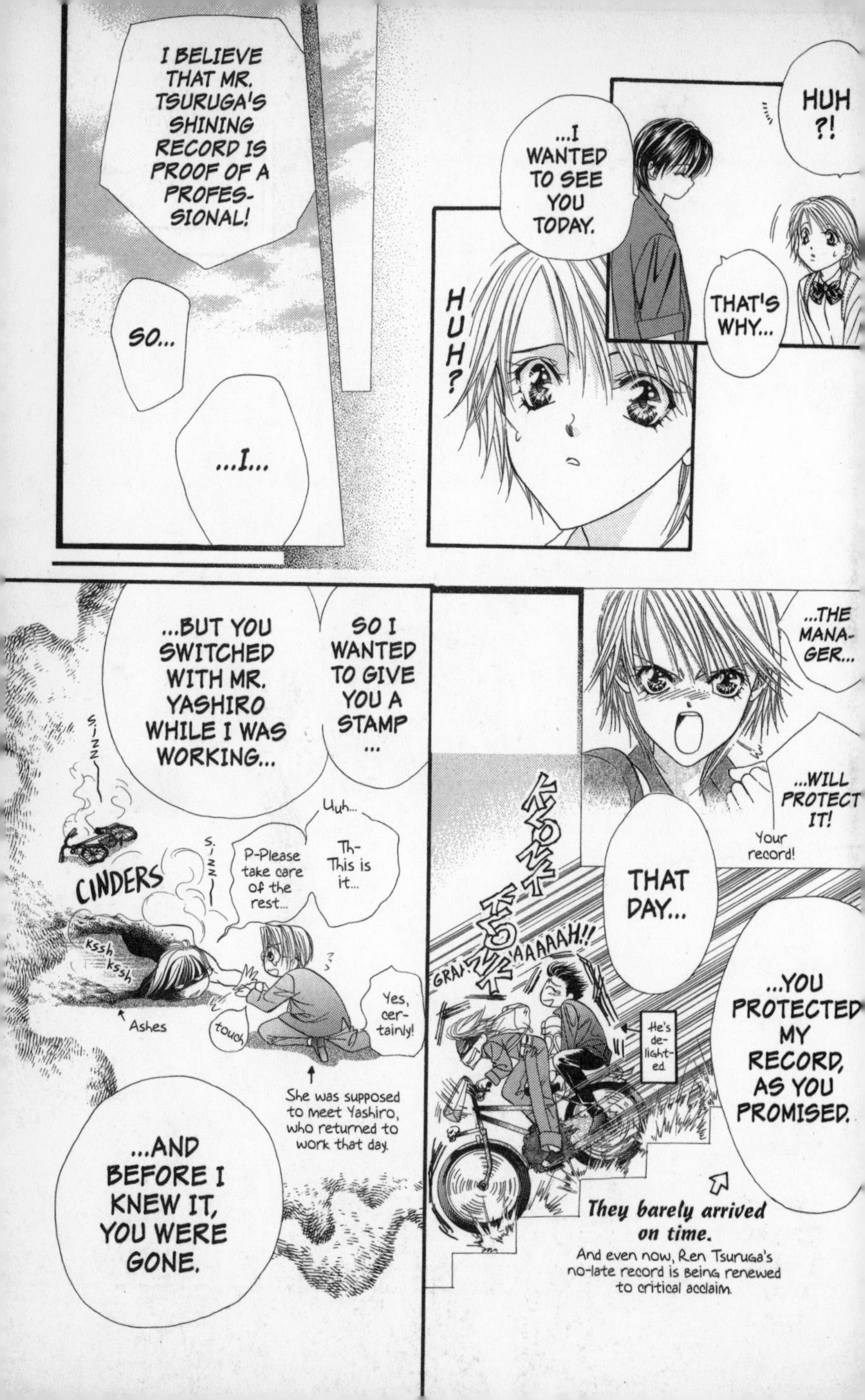
HUH ?!
THAT'S WHY...
...I WANTED TO SEE YOU TODAY.
HUH?
I BELIEVE THAT MR. TSURUGA'S SHINING RECORD IS PROOF OF A PROFES-SIONAL!
SO...
...I...
...THE MANA-GER...
...WILL PROTECT IT!
Your record!
THAT DAY...
...YOU PROTECTED MY RECORD, AS YOU PROMISED.
KONK
AAAAAH!!
GRA
He's de-light-ed.
They barely arrived on time.
And even now, Ren Tsuruga's no-late record is being renewed to critical acclaim.
SO I WANTED TO GIVE YOU A STAMP ...
...BUT YOU SWITCHED WITH MR. YASHIRO WHILE I WAS WORKING...
SIZZ
CINDERS
Uuh...
Th- This is it...
P-Please take care of the rest...
SIZZ
kssh kssh
Ashes
touch
Yes, cer-tainly!
She was supposed to meet Yashiro, who returned to work that day.
...AND BEFORE I KNEW IT, YOU WERE GONE.

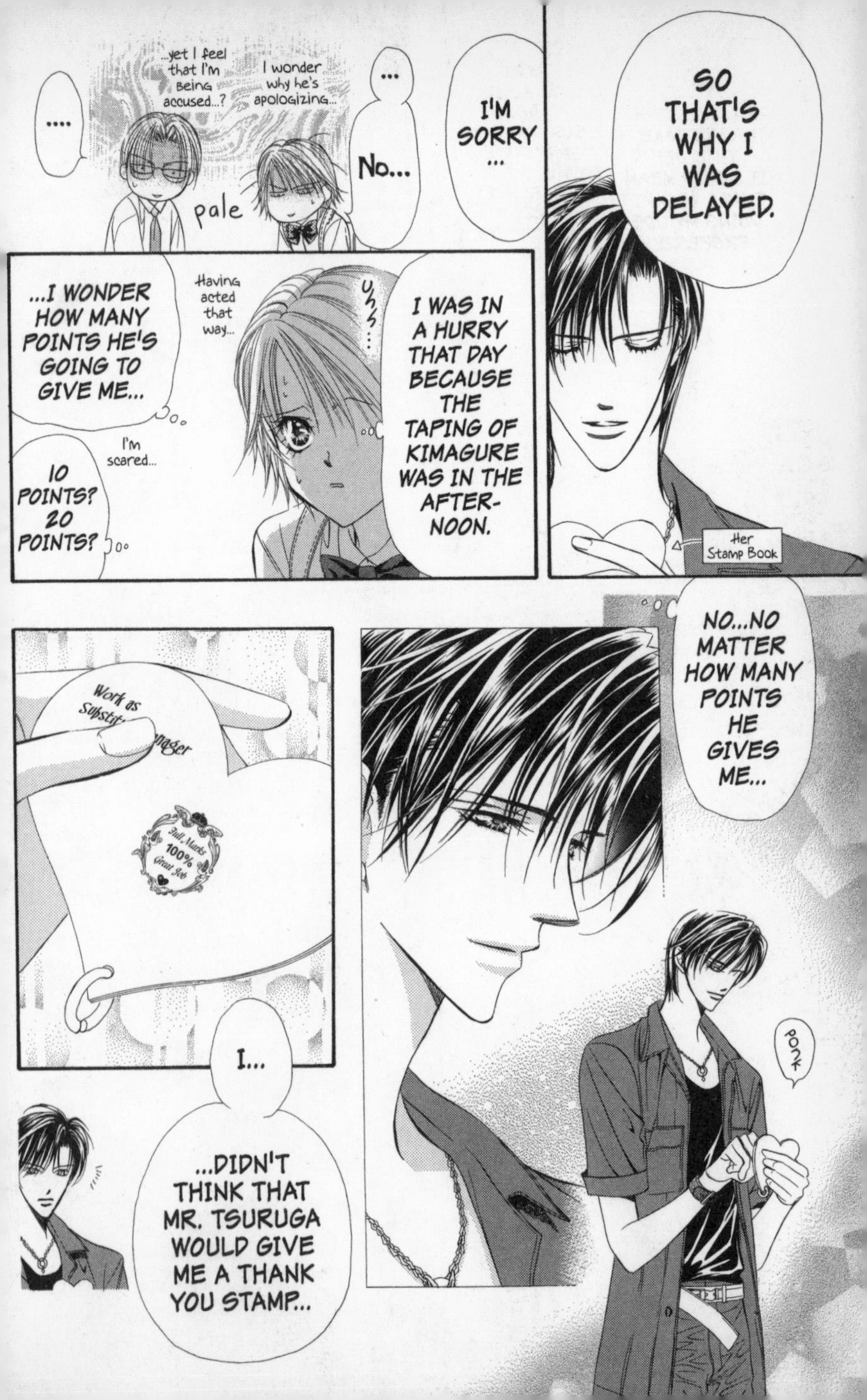
SO THAT'S WHY I WAS DELAYED.
Her Stamp Book
I'M SORRY ...
No...
...
I wonder why he's apologizing...
...yet I feel that I'm being accused...?
....
pale
I WAS IN A HURRY THAT DAY BECAUSE THE TAPING OF KIMAGURE WAS IN THE AFTER-NOON.
Having acted that way...
...I WONDER HOW MANY POINTS HE'S GOING TO GIVE ME...
I'm scared...
10 POINTS? 20 POINTS?
NO...NO MATTER HOW MANY POINTS HE GIVES ME...
PONK
Work as
Full Marks 100% Great Job
I...
...DIDN'T THINK THAT MR. TSURUGA WOULD GIVE ME A THANK YOU STAMP...

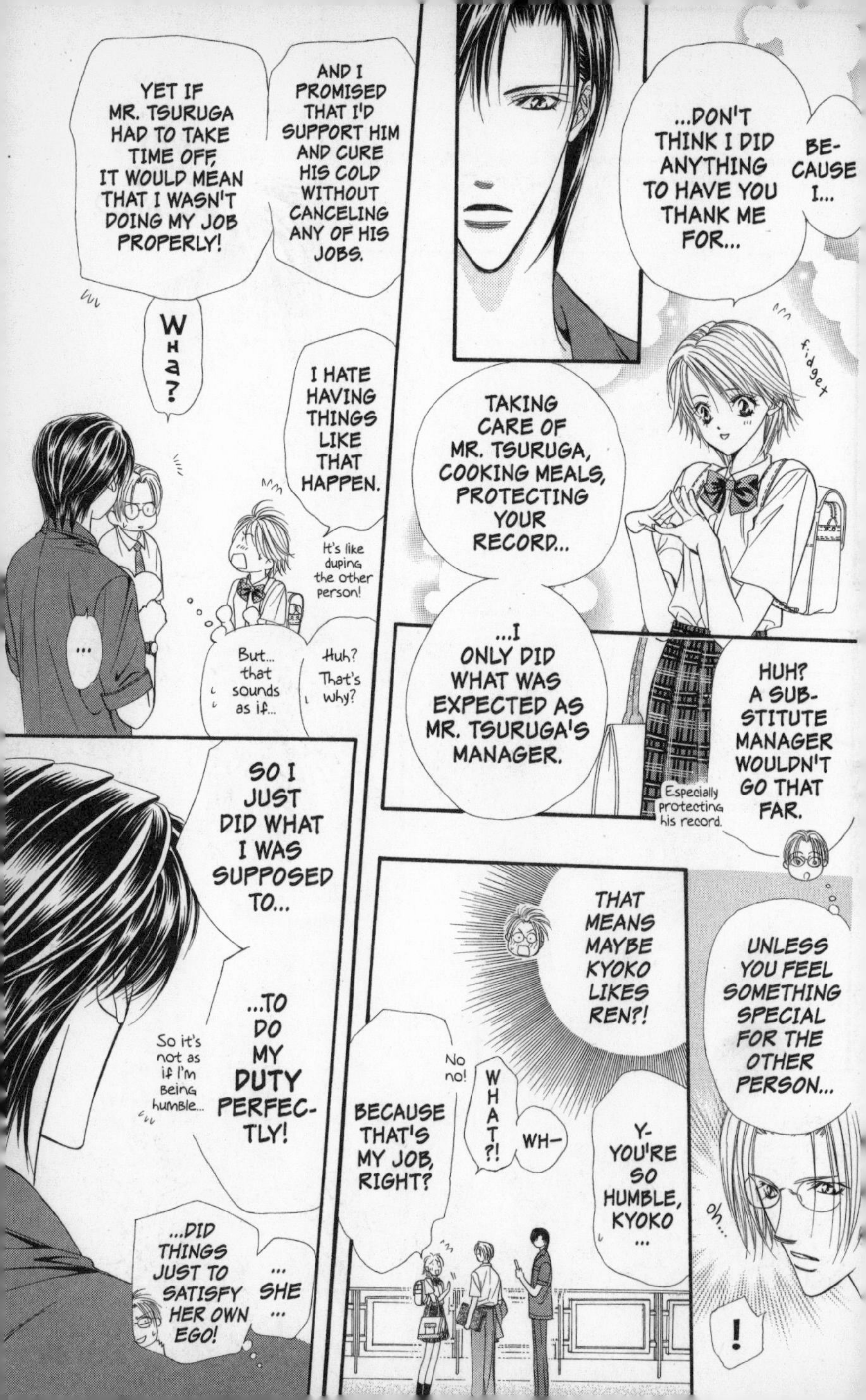
BE-CAUSE I...
...DON'T THINK I DID ANYTHING TO HAVE YOU THANK ME FOR...
fidget
TAKING CARE OF MR. TSURUGA, COOKING MEALS, PROTECTING YOUR RECORD...
...I ONLY DID WHAT WAS EXPECTED AS MR. TSURUGA'S MANAGER.
HUH? A SUB-STITUTE MANAGER WOULDN'T GO THAT FAR.
Especially protecting his record.
UNLESS YOU FEEL SOMETHING SPECIAL FOR THE OTHER PERSON...
oh...
!
THAT MEANS MAYBE KYOKO LIKES REN?!
Y- YOU'RE SO HUMBLE, KYOKO...
WH-
WHAT?!
No no!
BECAUSE THAT'S MY JOB, RIGHT?
AND I PROMISED THAT I'D SUPPORT HIM AND CURE HIS COLD WITHOUT CANCELING ANY OF HIS JOBS.
YET IF MR. TSURUGA HAD TO TAKE TIME OFF, IT WOULD MEAN THAT I WASN'T DOING MY JOB PROPERLY!
Wha?
I HATE HAVING THINGS LIKE THAT HAPPEN.
It's like duping the other person!
Huh? That's why?
But... that sounds as if...
...
SO I JUST DID WHAT I WAS SUPPOSED TO...
...TO DO MY DUTY PERFECTLY!
So it's not as if I'm being humble...
... SHE ...
...DID THINGS JUST TO SATISFY HER OWN EGO!

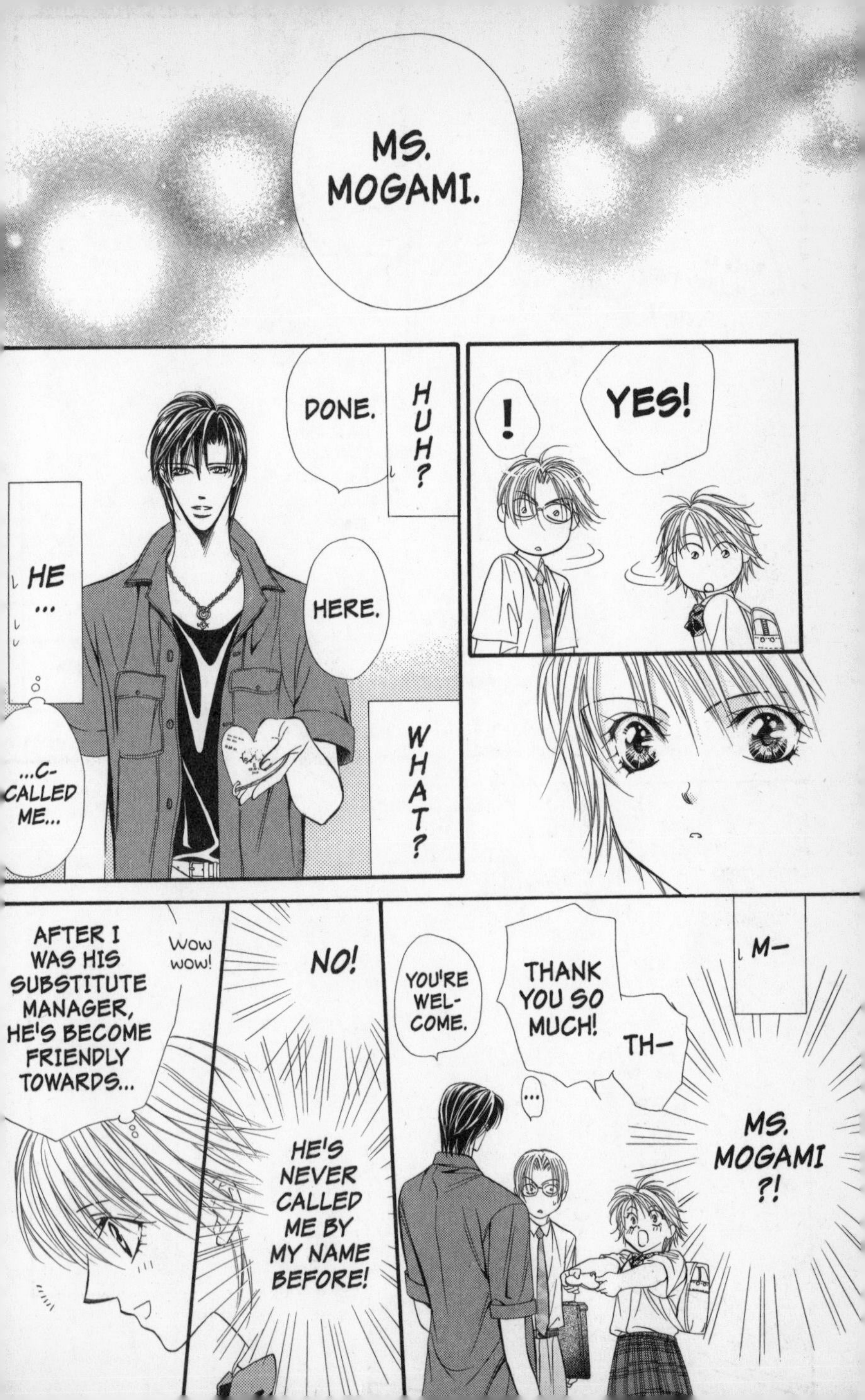
MS. MOGAMI.
YES!
!
HUH?
DONE.
WHAT?
HERE.
HE ...
...C-CALLED ME...
M—
THANK YOU SO MUCH!
TH—
YOU'RE WEL-COME.
...
MS. MOGAMI ?!
NO!
HE'S NEVER CALLED ME BY MY NAME BEFORE!
WOW WOW!
AFTER I WAS HIS SUBSTITUTE MANAGER, HE'S BECOME FRIENDLY TOWARDS...

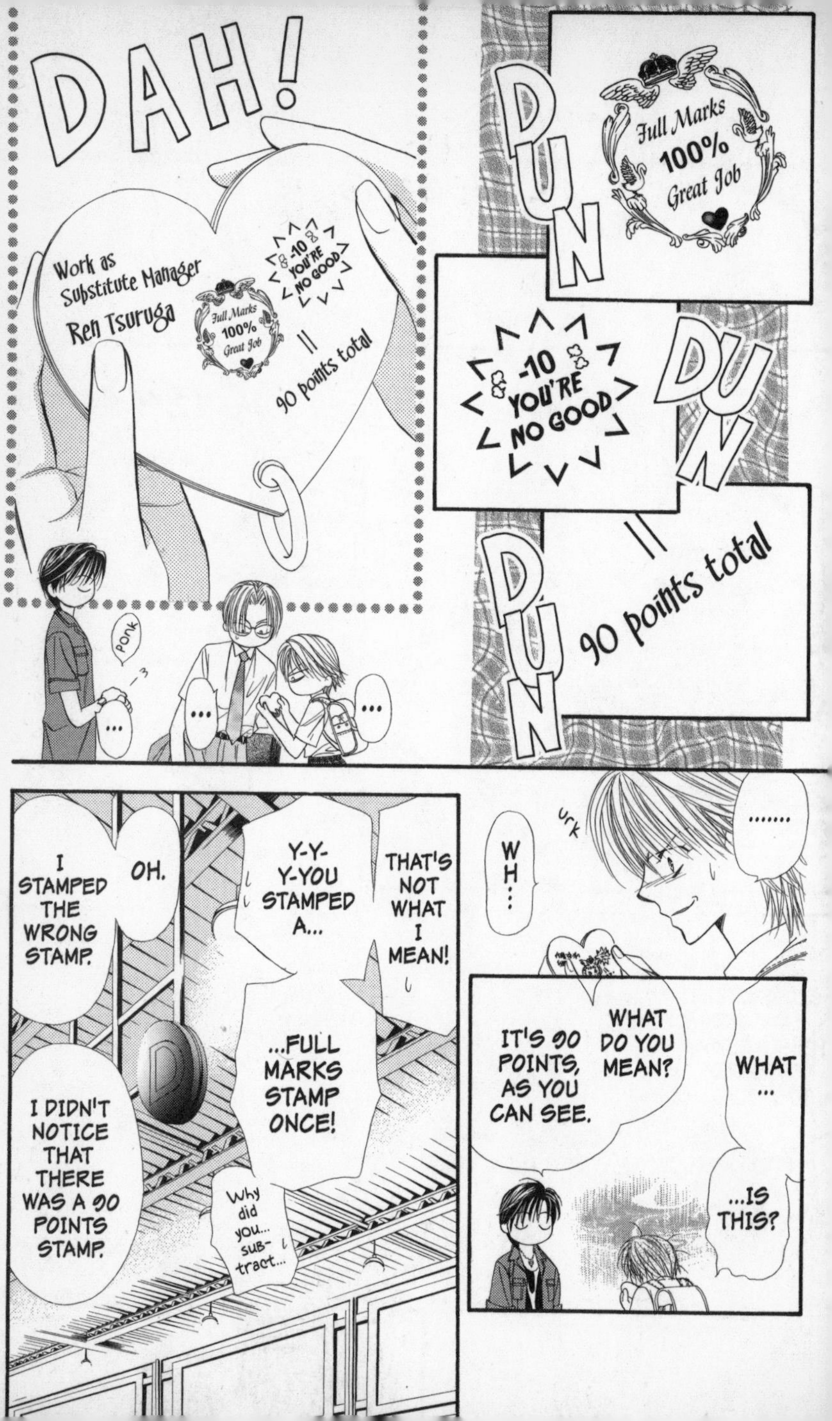
Full Marks 100% Great Job
DUN
-10 YOU'RE NO GOOD
DUN
= 90 points total
DUN
DAH!
Work as Substitute Manager Ren Tsuruga
Full Marks 100% Great Job
-10 YOU'RE NO GOOD
= 90 points total
ponk
...
...
...
....
urk
WH...
WHAT...
...IS THIS?
WHAT DO YOU MEAN?
IT'S 90 POINTS, AS YOU CAN SEE.
THAT'S NOT WHAT I MEAN!
Y-Y-Y-YOU STAMPED A...
...FULL MARKS STAMP ONCE!
OH.
I STAMPED THE WRONG STAMP.
I DIDN'T NOTICE THAT THERE WAS A 90 POINTS STAMP.
Why did you... sub-tract...

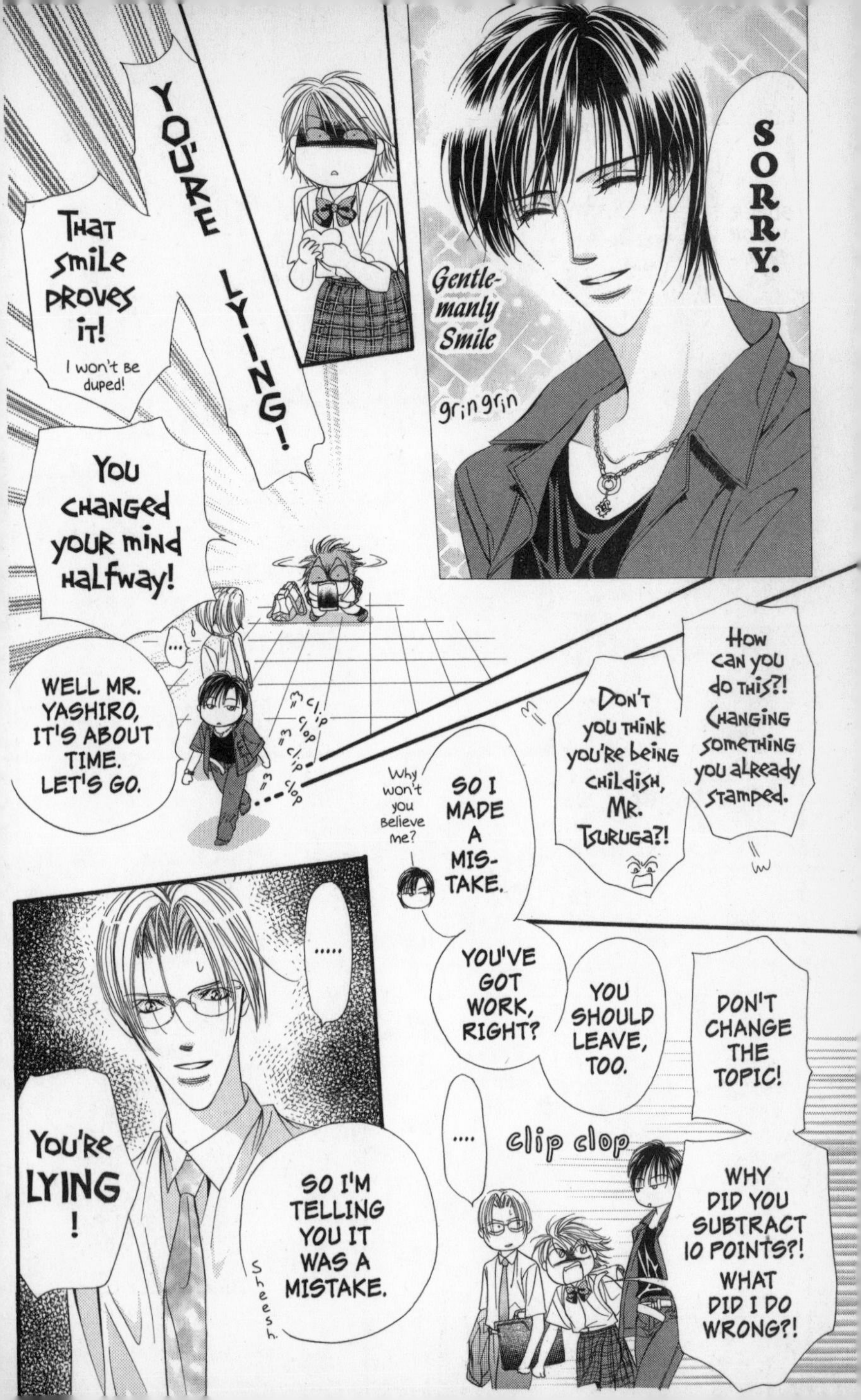
SORRY.
Gentle-manly Smile
gringrin
YOU'RE LYING!
That smile proves it!
I won't be duped!
You changed your mind halfway!
How can you do this?! Changing something you already stamped.
Don't you think you're being childish, Mr. Tsuruga?!
SO I MADE A MIS-TAKE.
Why won't you believe me?
....
WELL MR. YASHIRO, IT'S ABOUT TIME. LET'S GO.
clip clop clip clop clip clop
DON'T CHANGE THE TOPIC!
YOU SHOULD LEAVE, TOO.
YOU'VE GOT WORK, RIGHT?
clip clop
....
WHY DID YOU SUBTRACT 10 POINTS?! WHAT DID I DO WRONG?!
.....
You're LYING!
SO I'M TELLING YOU IT WAS A MISTAKE.
Sheesh.

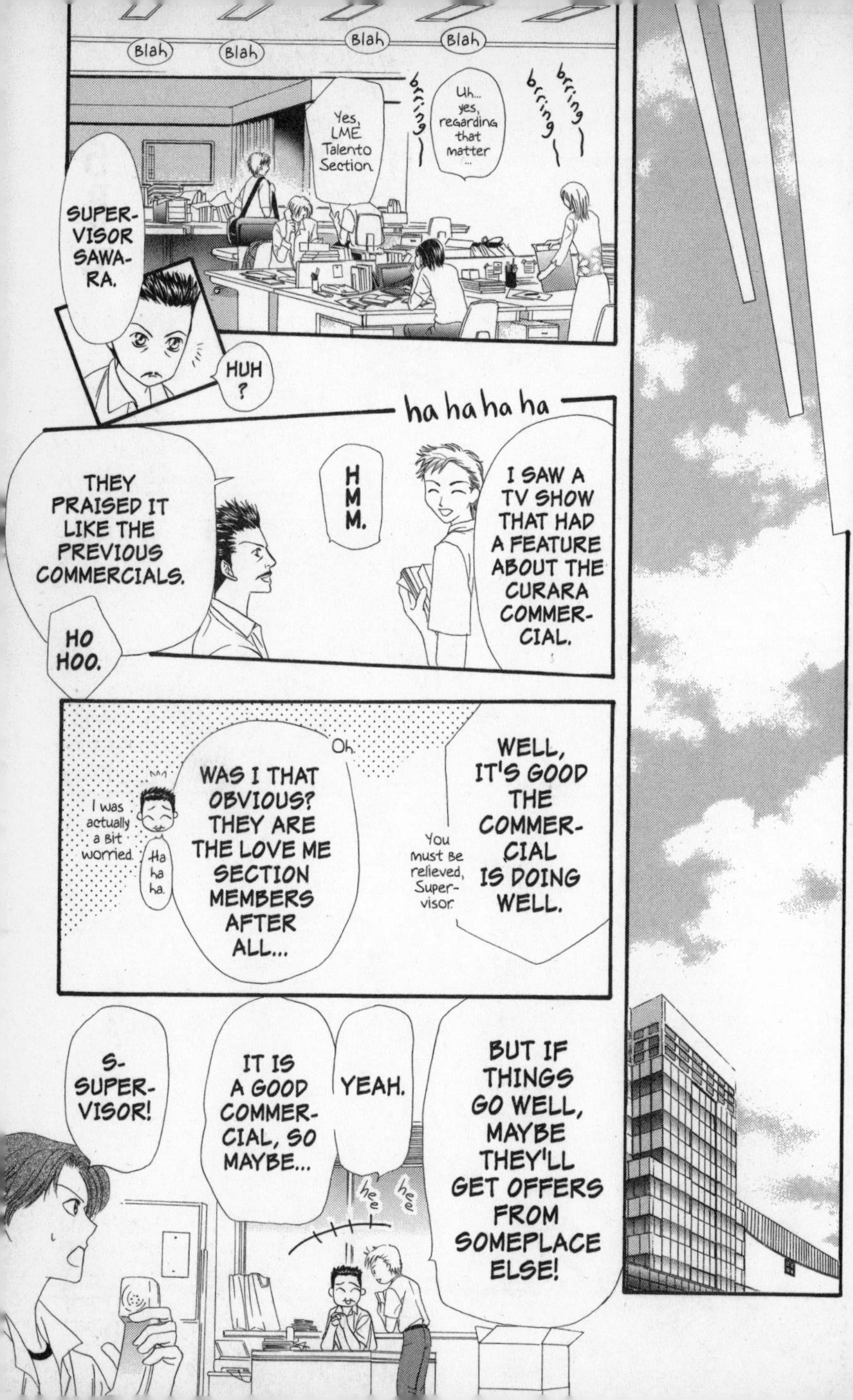
Blah
Blah
Blah
Blah
brring brring
Uh... yes, regarding that matter...
brring
Yes, LME Talento Section.
SUPER-VISOR SAWARA.
HUH?
ha ha ha ha
I SAW A TV SHOW THAT HAD A FEATURE ABOUT THE CURARA COMMER-CIAL.
HMM.
THEY PRAISED IT LIKE THE PREVIOUS COMMERCIALS.
HO HOO.
WELL, IT'S GOOD THE COMMER-CIAL IS DOING WELL.
You must be relieved, Super-visor.
Oh.
WAS I THAT OBVIOUS? THEY ARE THE LOVE ME SECTION MEMBERS AFTER ALL...
Ha ha ha.
I was actually a bit worried.
BUT IF THINGS GO WELL, MAYBE THEY'LL GET OFFERS FROM SOMEPLACE ELSE!
YEAH.
IT IS A GOOD COMMER-CIAL, SO MAYBE...
hee hee
S-SUPER-VISOR!

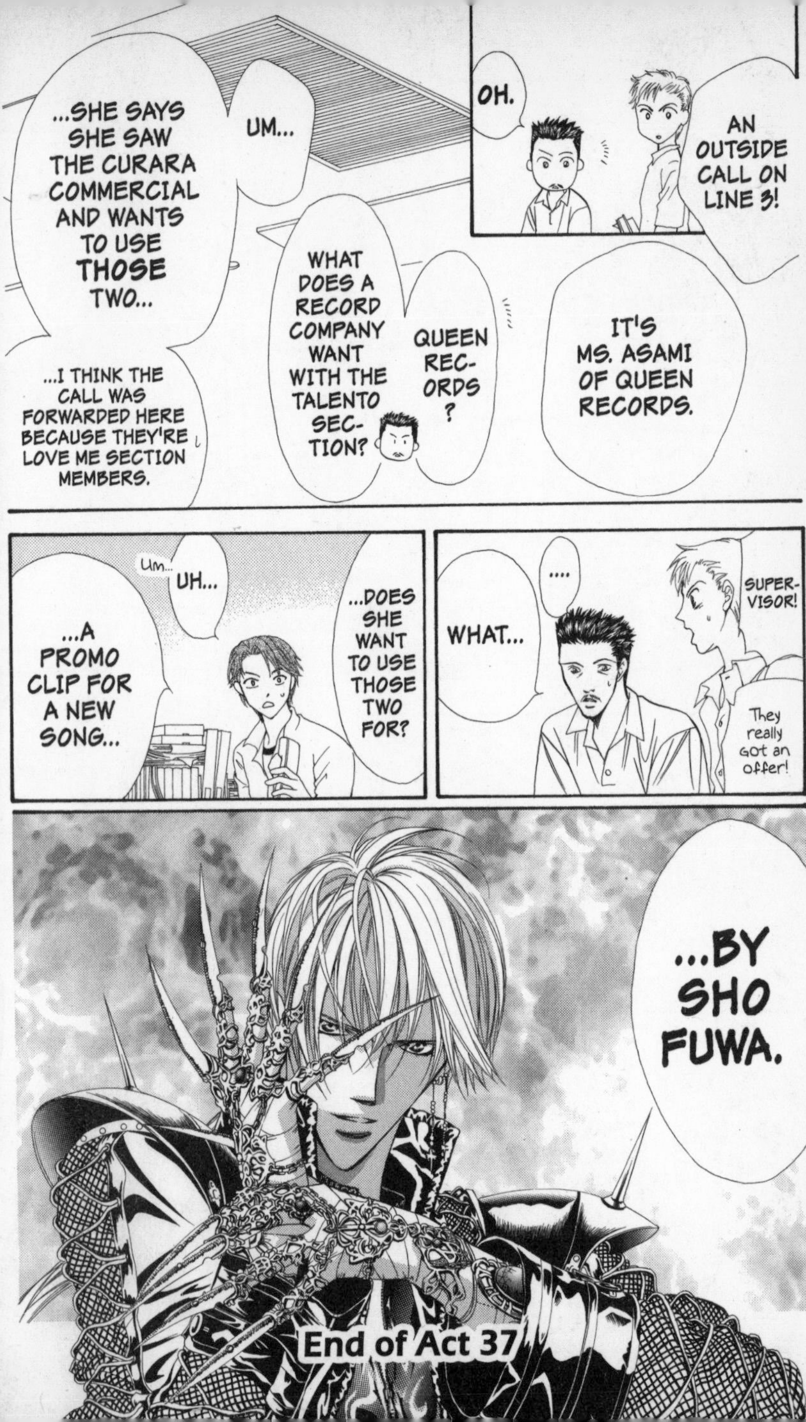
AN OUTSIDE CALL ON LINE 3!
OH.
IT'S MS. ASAMI OF QUEEN RECORDS.
QUEEN RECORDS?
WHAT DOES A RECORD COMPANY WANT WITH THE TALENTO SECTION?
UM...
...SHE SAYS SHE SAW THE CURARA COMMERCIAL AND WANTS TO USE THOSE TWO...
...I THINK THE CALL WAS FORWARDED HERE BECAUSE THEY'RE LOVE ME SECTION MEMBERS.
SUPERVISOR!
They really got an offer!
....
WHAT...
...DOES SHE WANT TO USE THOSE TWO FOR?
Um...
UH...
...A PROMO CLIP FOR A NEW SONG...
...BY SHO FUWA.
End of Act 37

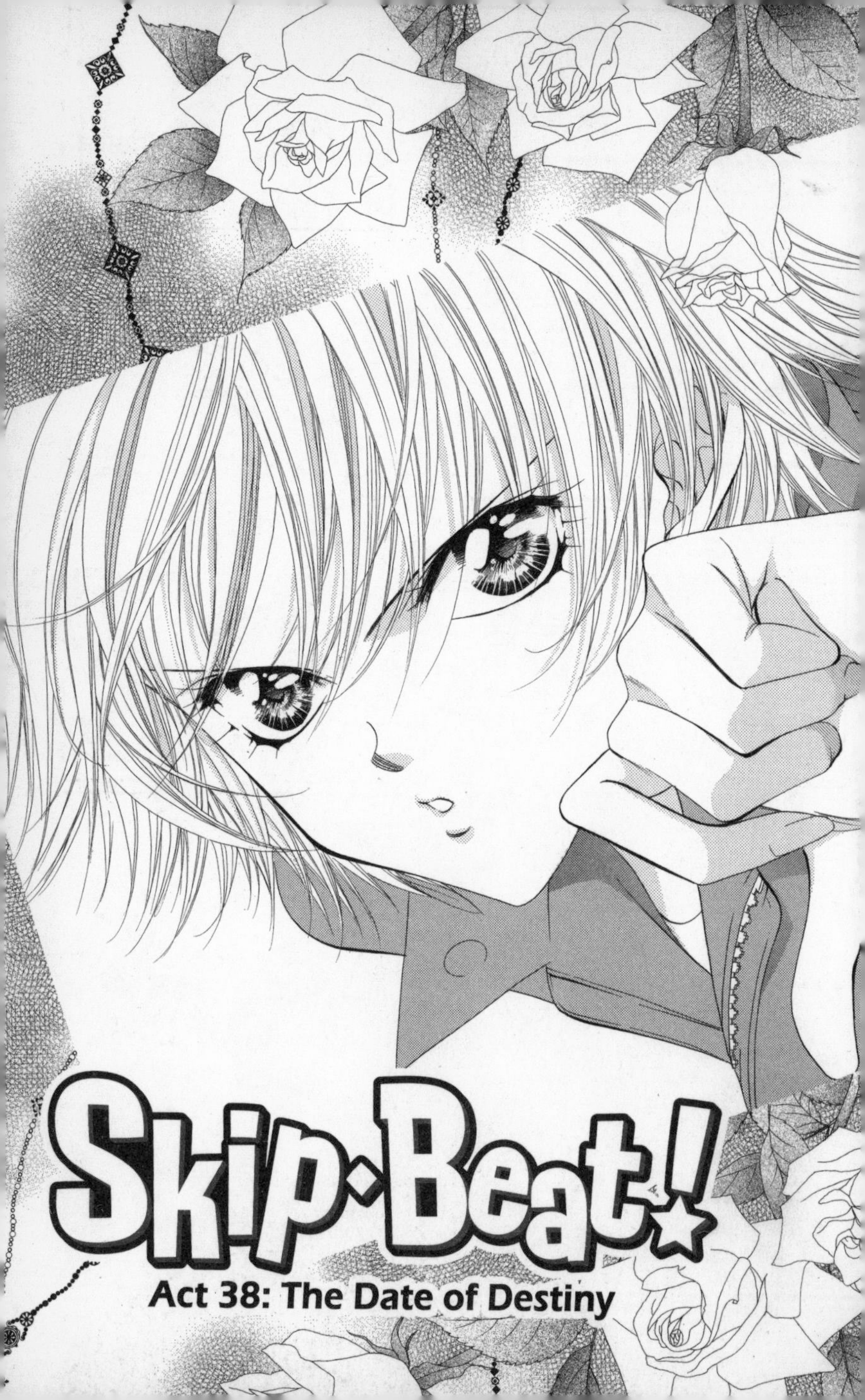
Skip·Beat!
Act 38: The Date of Destiny

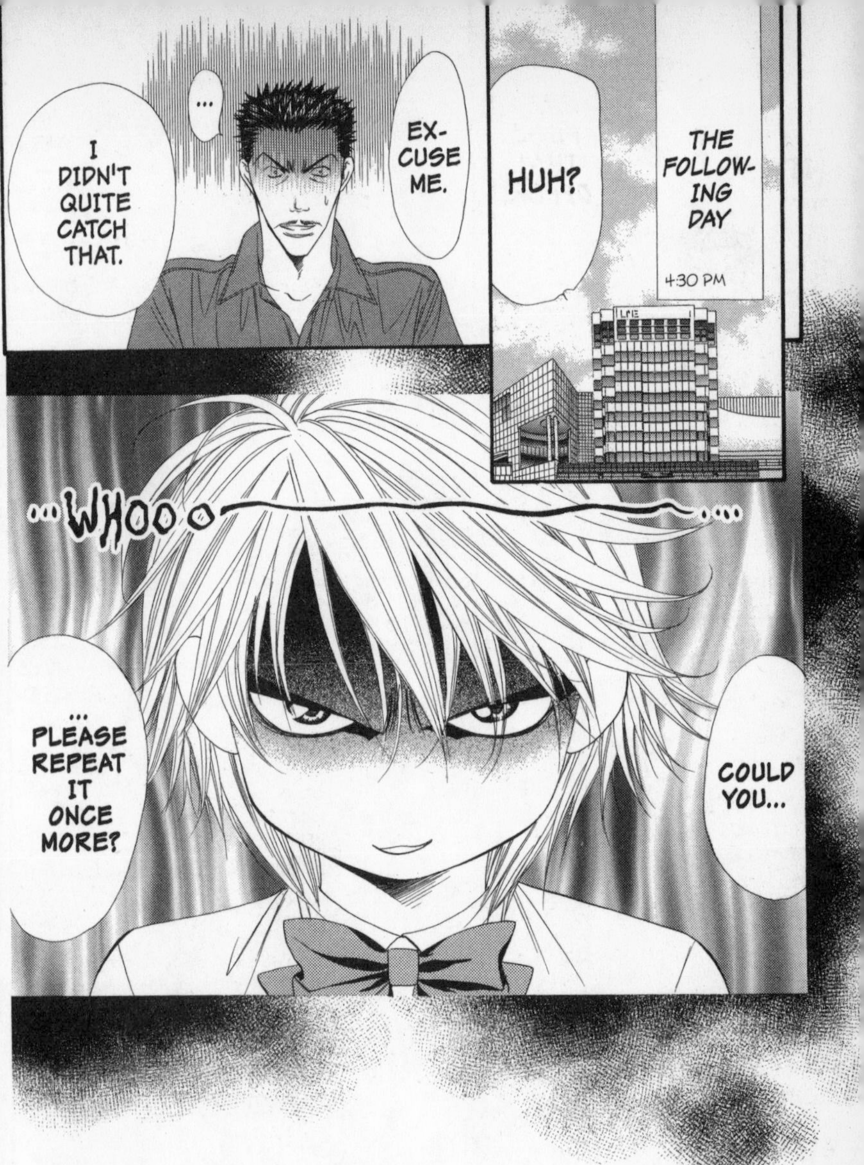
THE FOLLOWING DAY
4:30 PM
HUH?
EX-CUSE ME.
...
I DIDN'T QUITE CATCH THAT.
...WHOO...
COULD YOU...
...PLEASE REPEAT IT ONCE MORE?

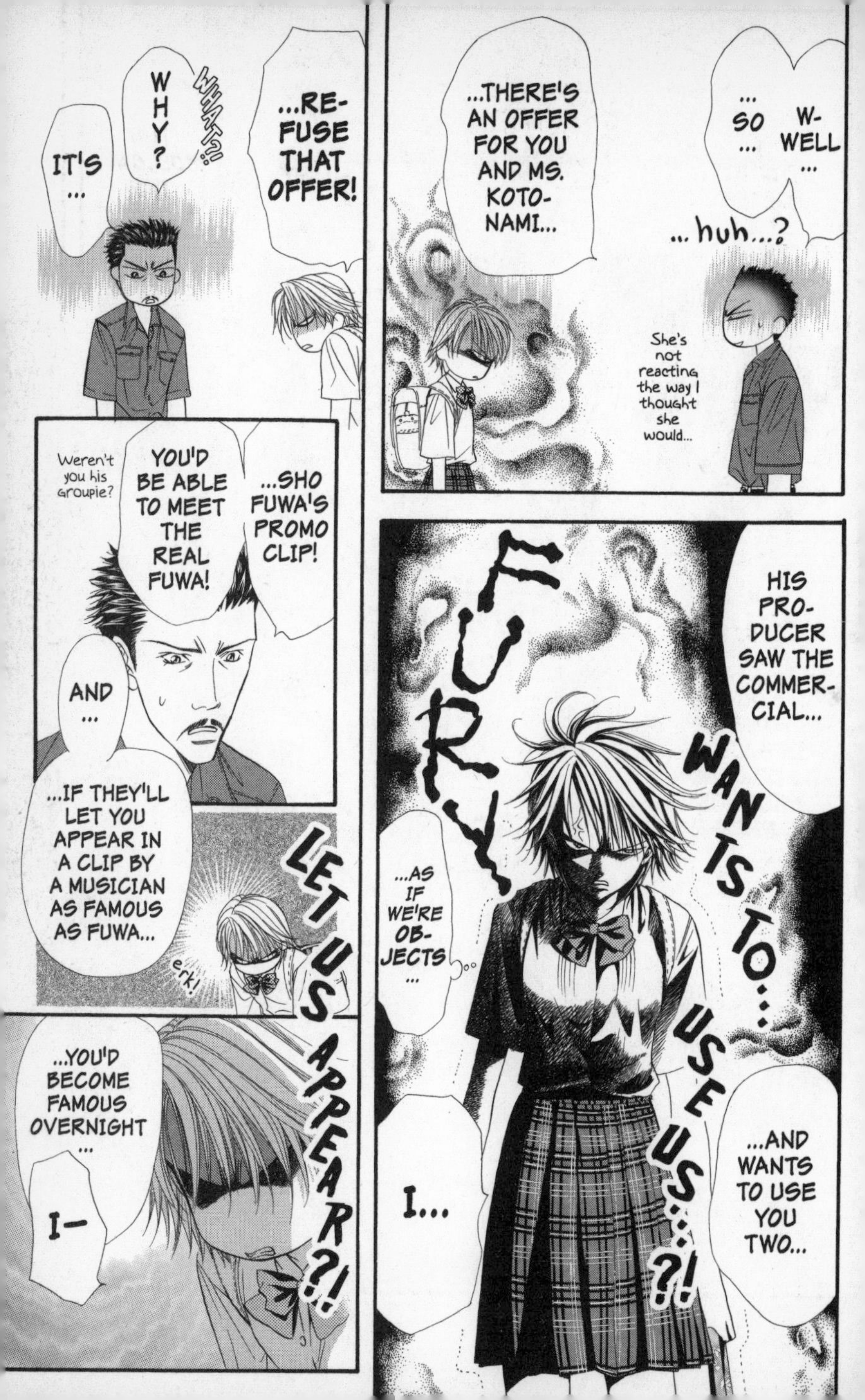
W-WELL...
...SO...
...huh...?
She's not reacting the way I thought she would...
...THERE'S AN OFFER FOR YOU AND MS. KOTONAMI...
HIS PRODUCER SAW THE COMMERCIAL...
...AND WANTS TO USE YOU TWO...
WANTS TO... USE US...?!
FURY
...AS IF WE'RE OBJECTS...
I...
...REFUSE THAT OFFER!
WHAT?!
WHY?
IT'S...
...SHO FUWA'S PROMO CLIP!
YOU'D BE ABLE TO MEET THE REAL FUWA!
Weren't you his groupie?
AND...
...IF THEY'LL LET YOU APPEAR IN A CLIP BY A MUSICIAN AS FAMOUS AS FUWA...
erk!
LET US APPEAR?!
...YOU'D BECOME FAMOUS OVERNIGHT...
I—

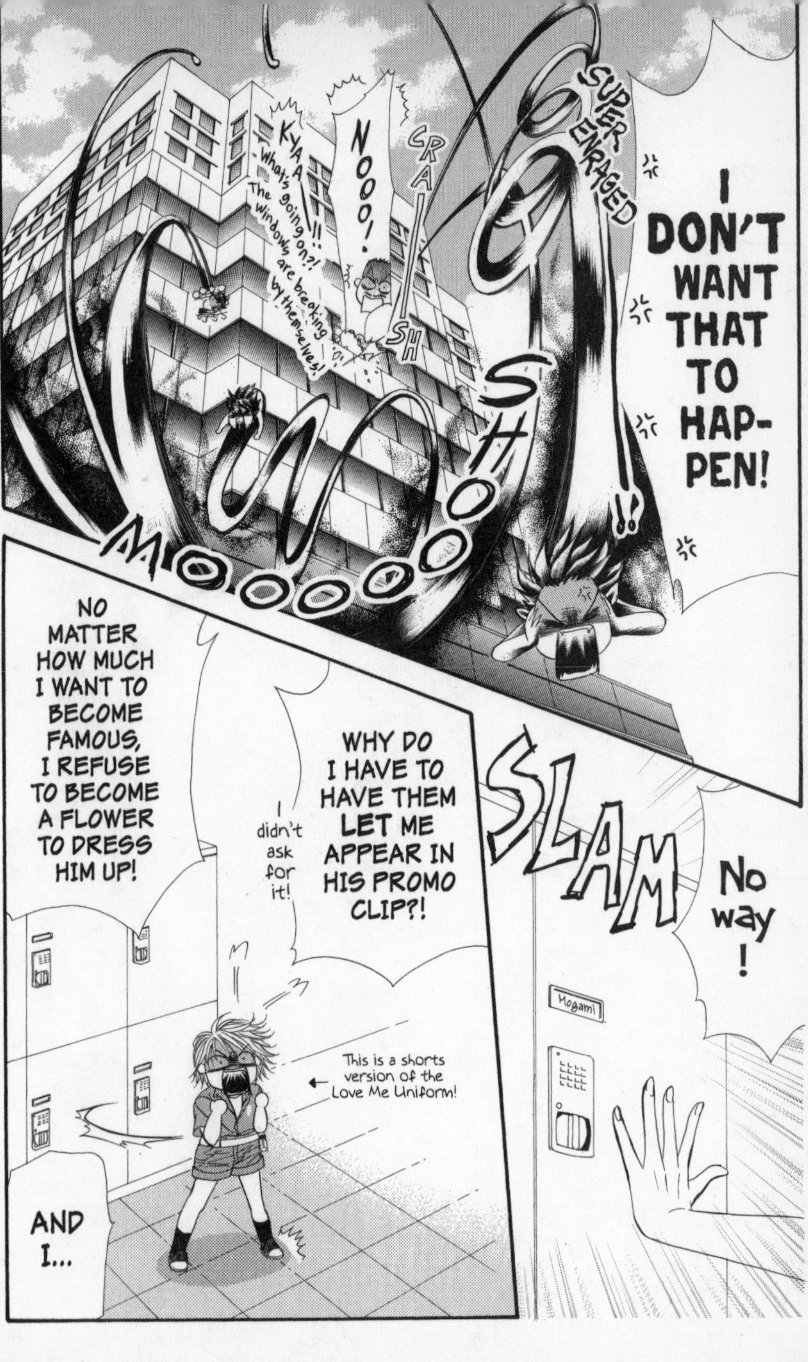
SUPER ENRAGED
I DON'T WANT THAT TO HAPPEN!
SHOOOOOOOM!!
CRAAASH
NOOOO!
KYAA!!
What's going on?! The windows are breaking by themselves!
No way!
SLAM
Mogami
WHY DO I HAVE TO HAVE THEM LET ME APPEAR IN HIS PROMO CLIP?!
I didn't ask for it!
NO MATTER HOW MUCH I WANT TO BECOME FAMOUS, I REFUSE TO BECOME A FLOWER TO DRESS HIM UP!
This is a shorts version of the Love Me Uniform!
AND I...

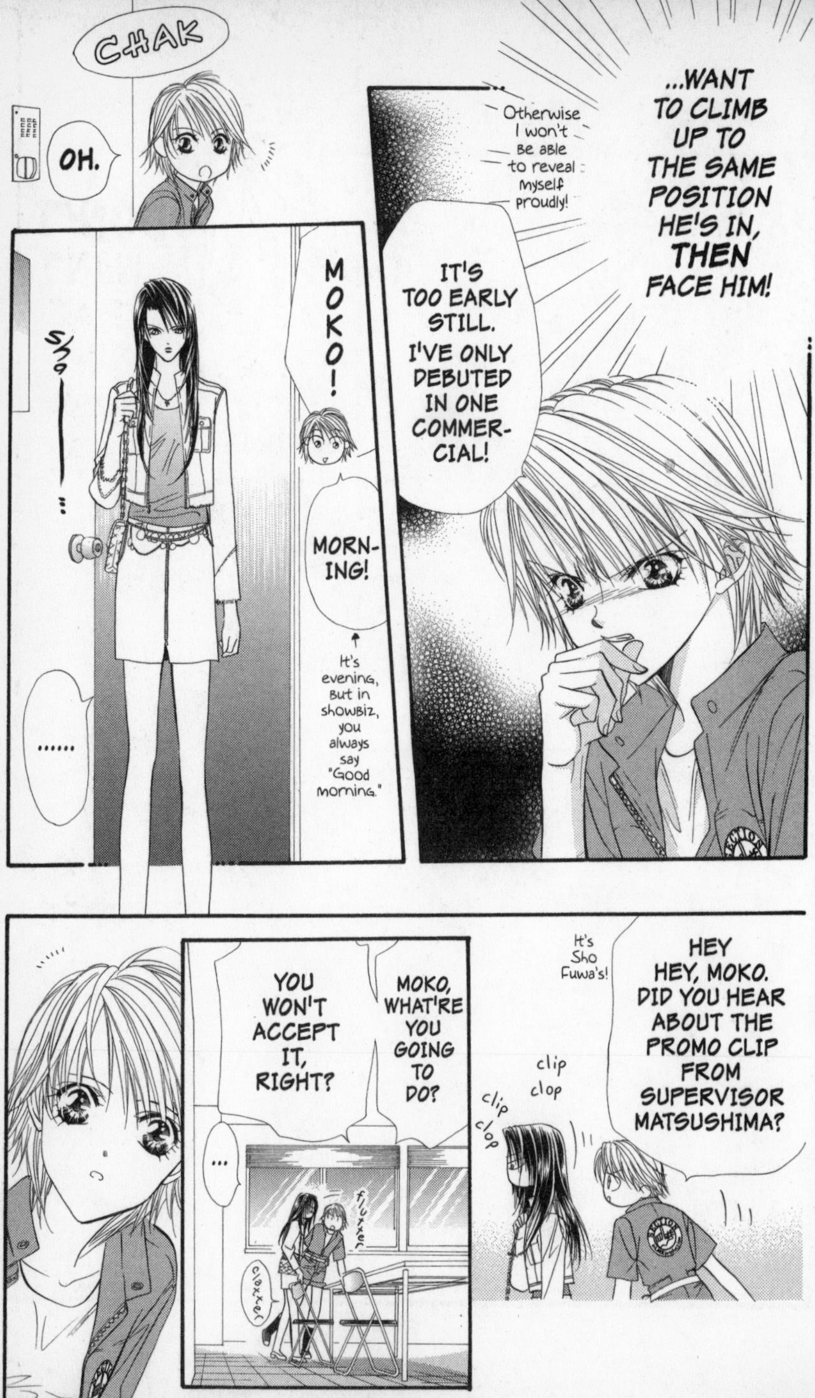
...WANT TO CLIMB UP TO THE SAME POSITION HE'S IN, THEN FACE HIM!
Otherwise I won't be able to reveal myself proudly!
IT'S TOO EARLY STILL. I'VE ONLY DEBUTED IN ONE COMMERCIAL!
CHAK
OH.
MOKO!
MORNING!
It's evening, but in showbiz, you always say "Good morning."
......
HEY HEY, MOKO. DID YOU HEAR ABOUT THE PROMO CLIP FROM SUPERVISOR MATSUSHIMA?
It's Sho Fuwa's!
clip clop
clip clop
MOKO, WHAT'RE YOU GOING TO DO?
YOU WON'T ACCEPT IT, RIGHT?
...
flutter
clatter

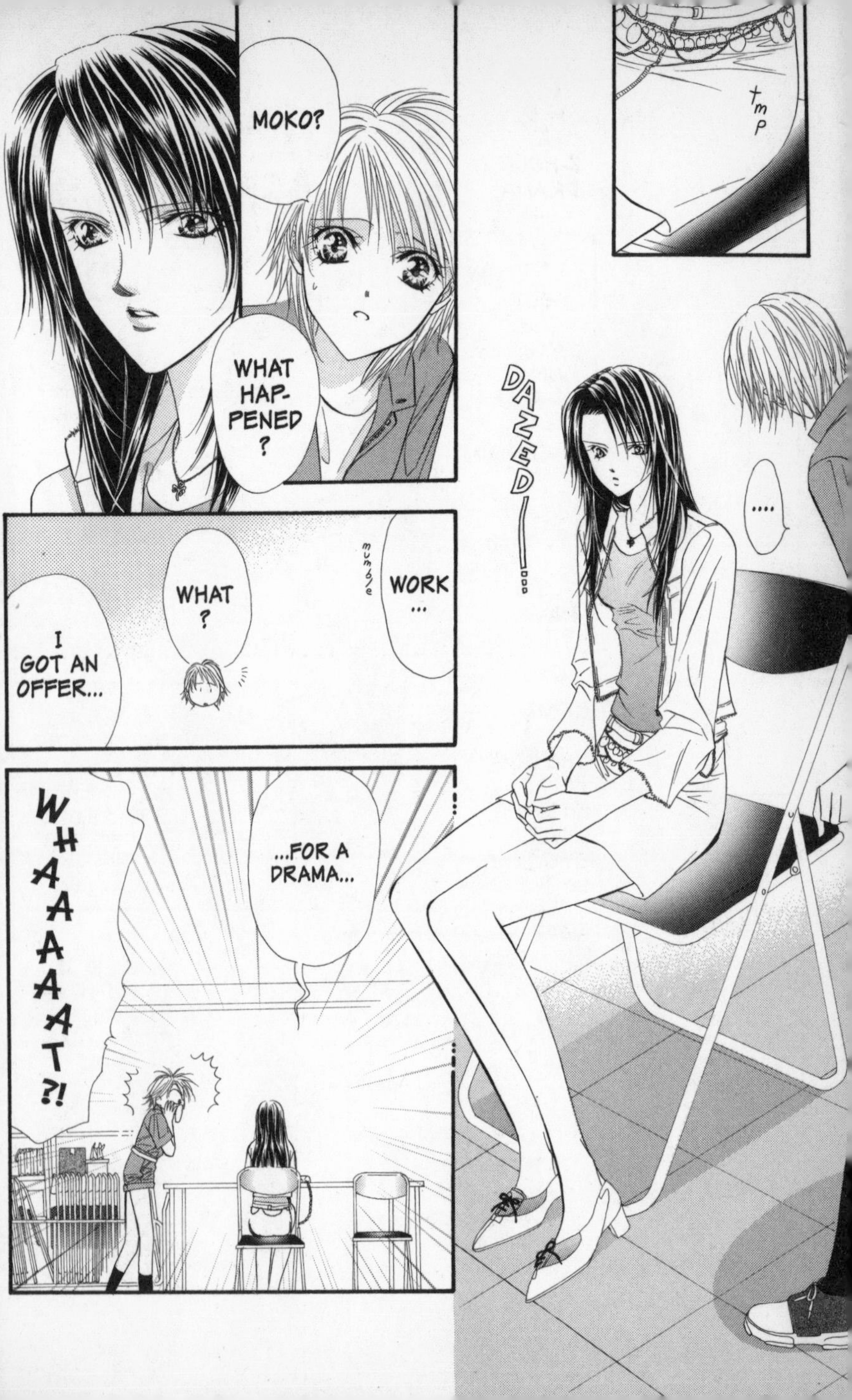
tmp
DAZED!!!
....
MOKO?
WHAT HAP-PENED?
WORK...
mumble
WHAT?
I GOT AN OFFER...
...FOR A DRAMA...
WHAAAAAAT?!

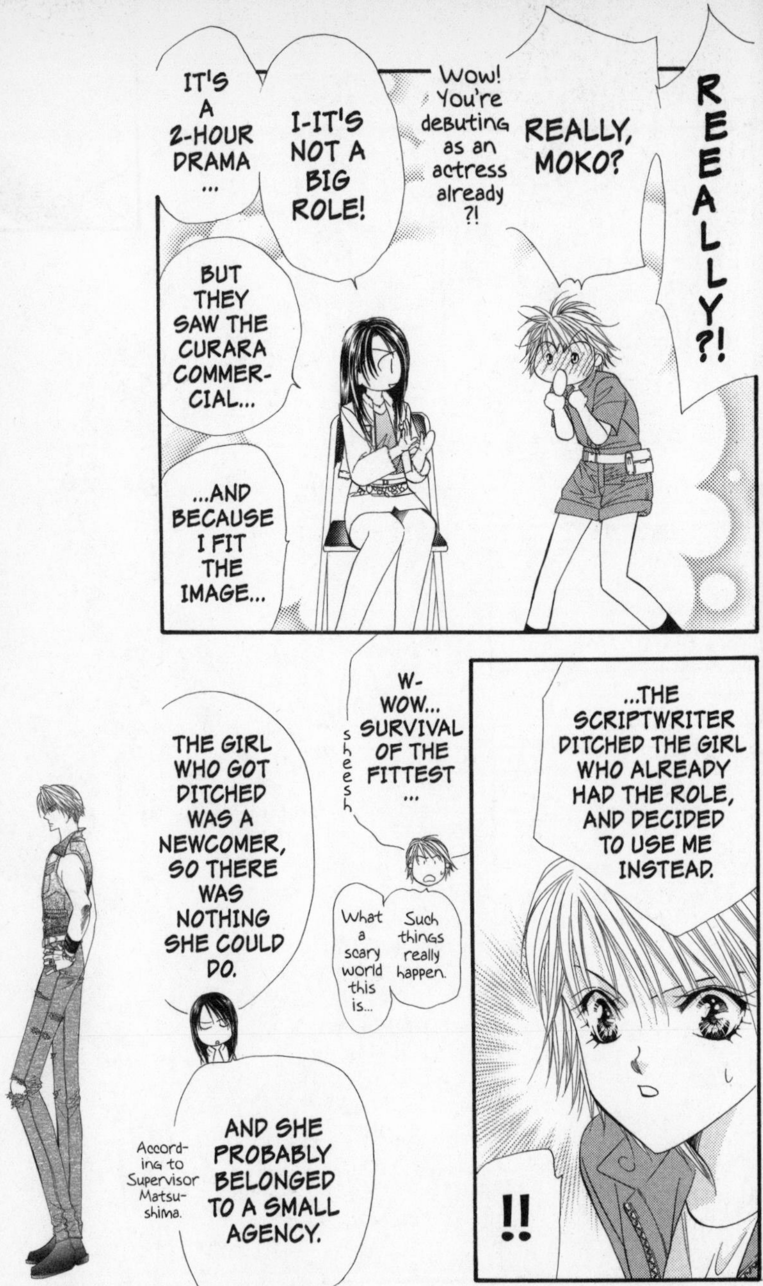
REEALLY?!
REALLY, MOKO?
Wow! You're debuting as an actress already?!
I-IT'S NOT A BIG ROLE!
IT'S A 2-HOUR DRAMA ...
BUT THEY SAW THE CURARA COMMERCIAL...
...AND BECAUSE I FIT THE IMAGE...
...THE SCRIPTWRITER DITCHED THE GIRL WHO ALREADY HAD THE ROLE, AND DECIDED TO USE ME INSTEAD.
!!
W-WOW... SURVIVAL OF THE FITTEST ...
sheesh
Such things really happen.
What a scary world this is...
THE GIRL WHO GOT DITCHED WAS A NEWCOMER, SO THERE WAS NOTHING SHE COULD DO.
AND SHE PROBABLY BELONGED TO A SMALL AGENCY.
According to Supervisor Matsushima.

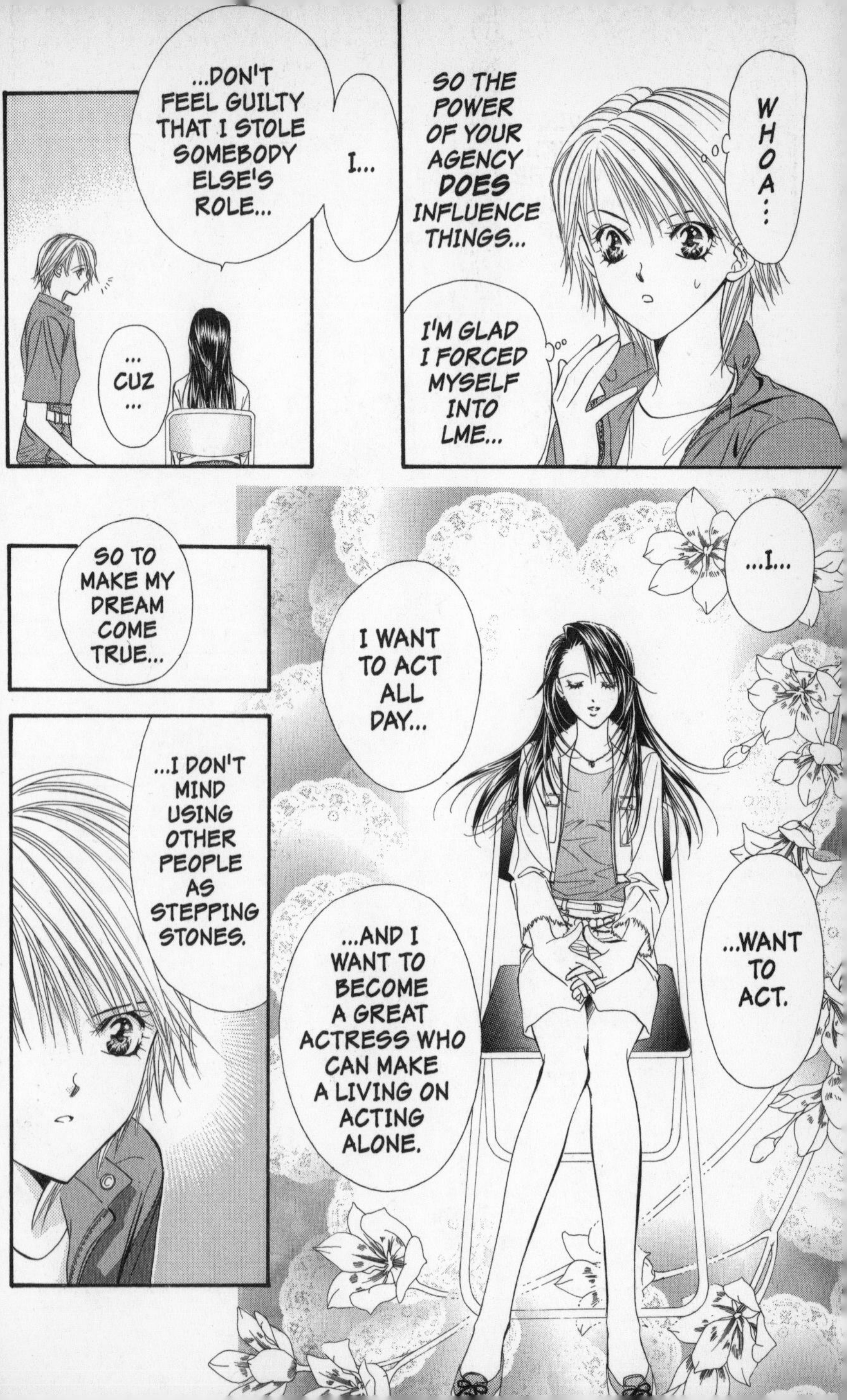
WHOA...
SO THE POWER OF YOUR AGENCY DOES INFLUENCE THINGS...
I'M GLAD I FORCED MYSELF INTO LME...
I...
...DON'T FEEL GUILTY THAT I STOLE SOMEBODY ELSE'S ROLE...
...CUZ...
...I...
...WANT TO ACT.
I WANT TO ACT ALL DAY...
...AND I WANT TO BECOME A GREAT ACTRESS WHO CAN MAKE A LIVING ON ACTING ALONE.
SO TO MAKE MY DREAM COME TRUE...
...I DON'T MIND USING OTHER PEOPLE AS STEPPING STONES.

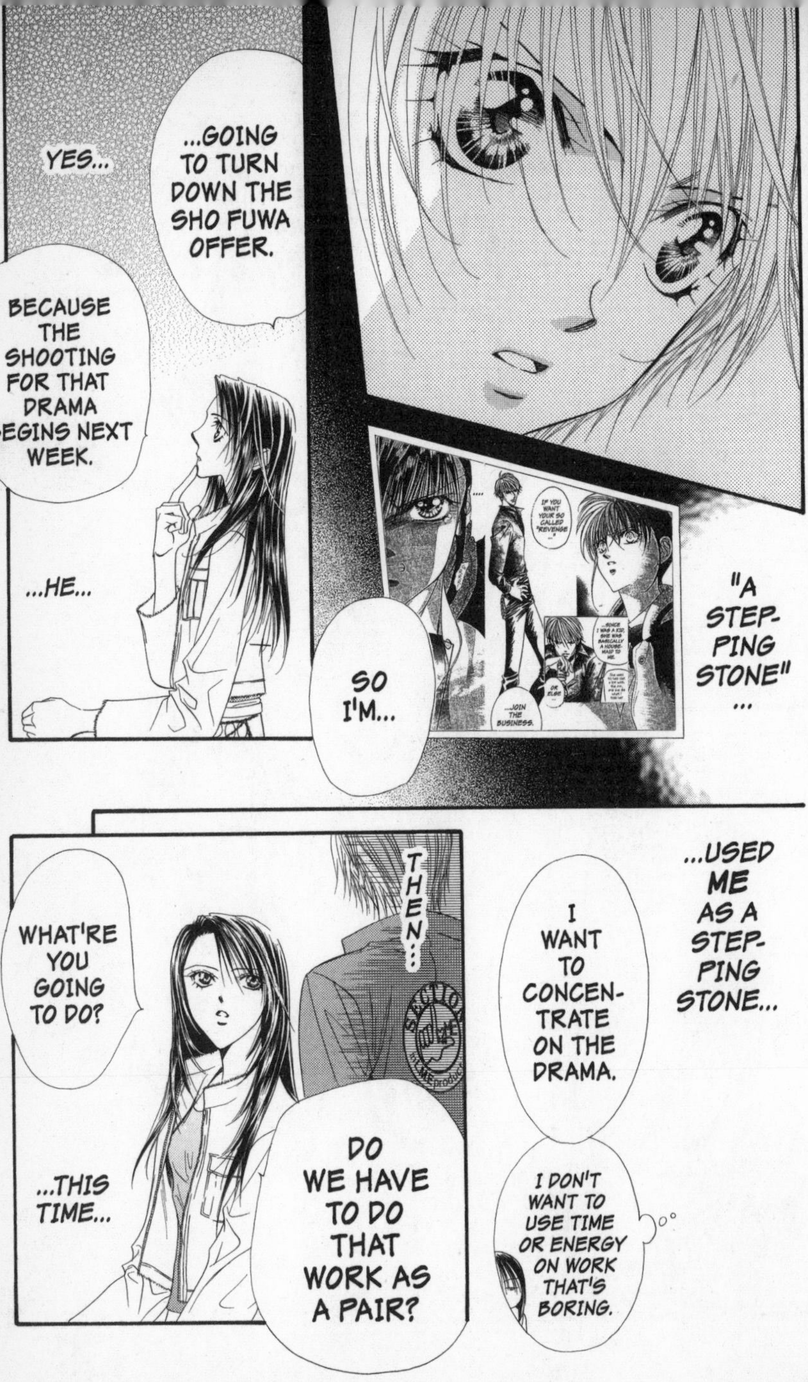
"A STEP-PING STONE"...
...
IF YOU WANT YOUR SO CALLED "REVENGE"...
...SINCE I WAS A KID, SHE WAS BASICALLY A HOUSE-MAID TO ME.
OR ELSE...
...JOIN THE BUSINESS.
SO I'M...
...GOING TO TURN DOWN THE SHO FUWA OFFER.
YES...
BECAUSE THE SHOOTING FOR THAT DRAMA BEGINS NEXT WEEK.
...HE...
...USED ME AS A STEP-PING STONE...
I WANT TO CONCEN-TRATE ON THE DRAMA.
I DON'T WANT TO USE TIME OR ENERGY ON WORK THAT'S BORING.
THEN...
DO WE HAVE TO DO THAT WORK AS A PAIR?
WHAT'RE YOU GOING TO DO?
...THIS TIME...

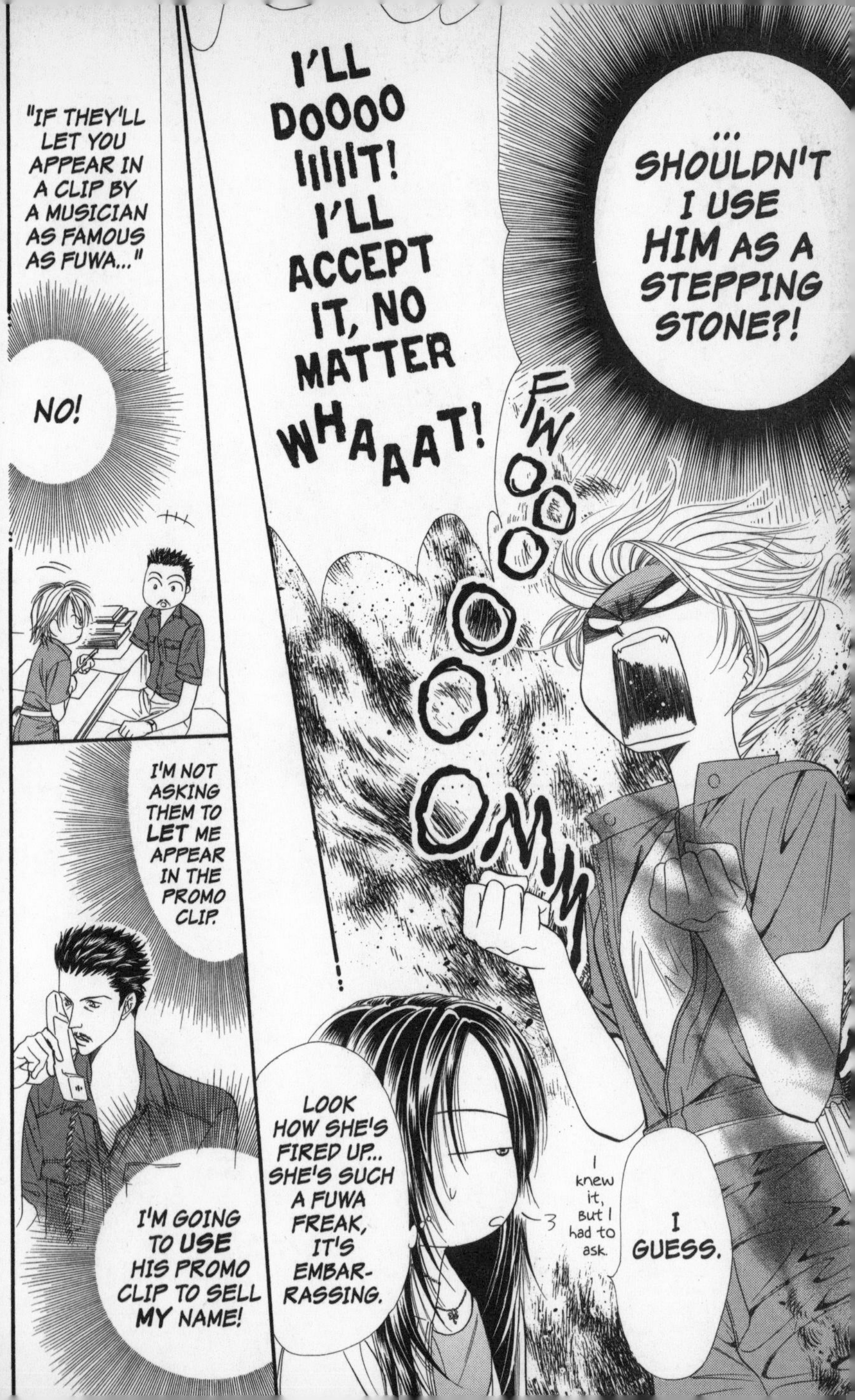
...SHOULDN'T I USE HIM AS A STEPPING STONE?!
I'LL DOOOO IIIIIIT! I'LL ACCEPT IT, NO MATTER WHAAAT!
FWOOOOOOMM
I GUESS.
I knew it, but I had to ask.
LOOK HOW SHE'S FIRED UP... SHE'S SUCH A FUWA FREAK, IT'S EMBARRASSING.
"IF THEY'LL LET YOU APPEAR IN A CLIP BY A MUSICIAN AS FAMOUS AS FUWA..."
NO!
I'M NOT ASKING THEM TO LET ME APPEAR IN THE PROMO CLIP.
I'M GOING TO USE HIS PROMO CLIP TO SELL MY NAME!

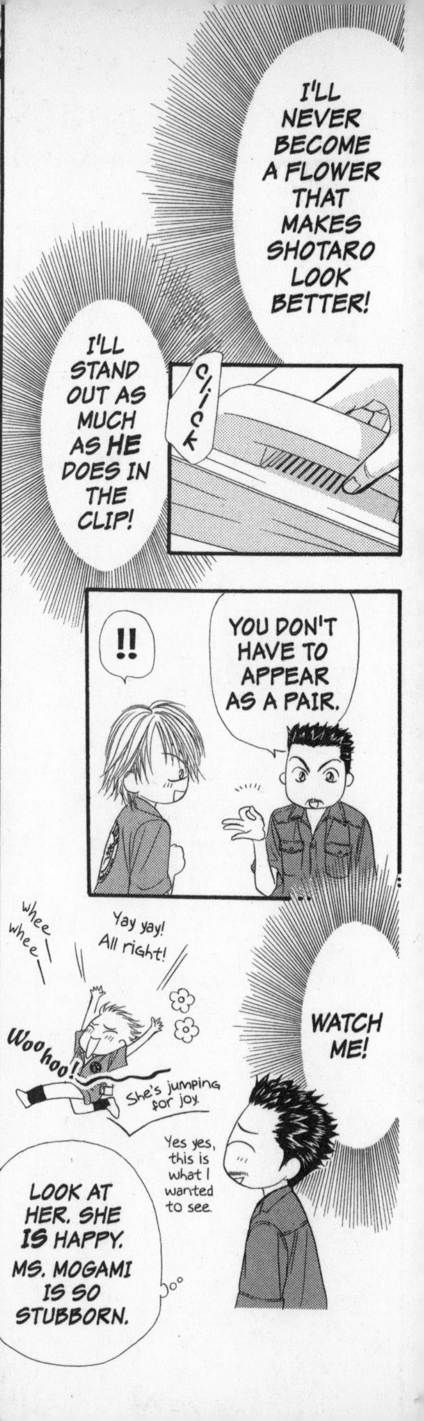
I'LL NEVER BECOME A FLOWER THAT MAKES SHOTARO LOOK BETTER!
CLICK
I'LL STAND OUT AS MUCH AS HE DOES IN THE CLIP!
YOU DON'T HAVE TO APPEAR AS A PAIR.
!!
WATCH ME!
Yes yes, this is what I wanted to see.
Yay yay! All right!
whee whee
Woohoo!
She's jumping for joy.
LOOK AT HER. SHE IS HAPPY. MS. MOGAMI IS SO STUBBORN.
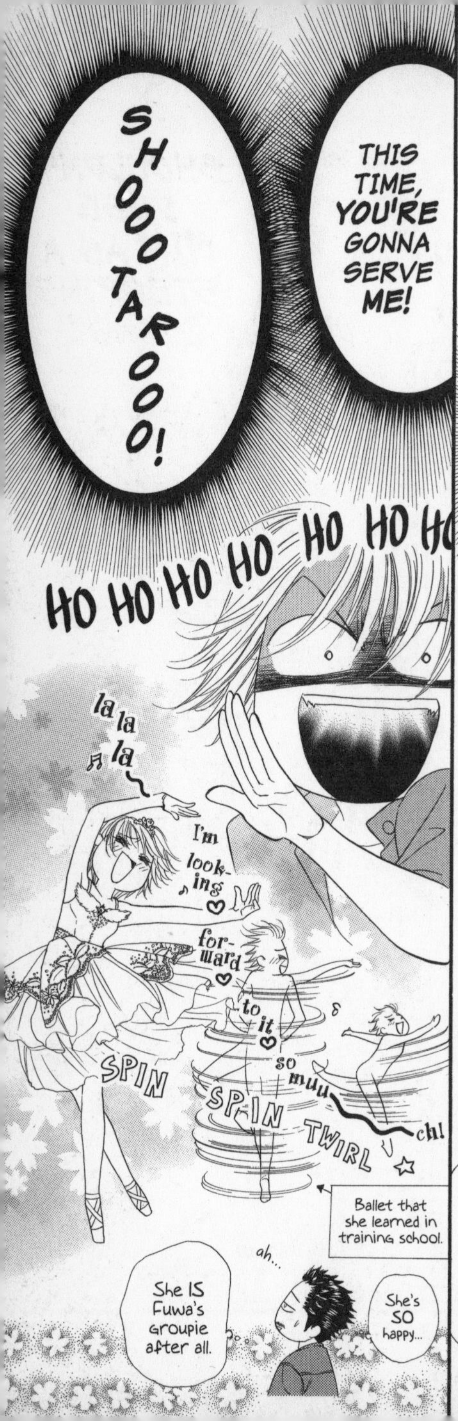
THIS TIME, YOU'RE GONNA SERVE ME!
SHOOOOTAROOOO!
HO HO HO HO HO HO HO
la la la
I'm looking forward to it so muuuch!
SPIN
SPIN
TWIRL
Ballet that she learned in training school.
She's SO happy...
ah...
She IS Fuwa's groupie after all.

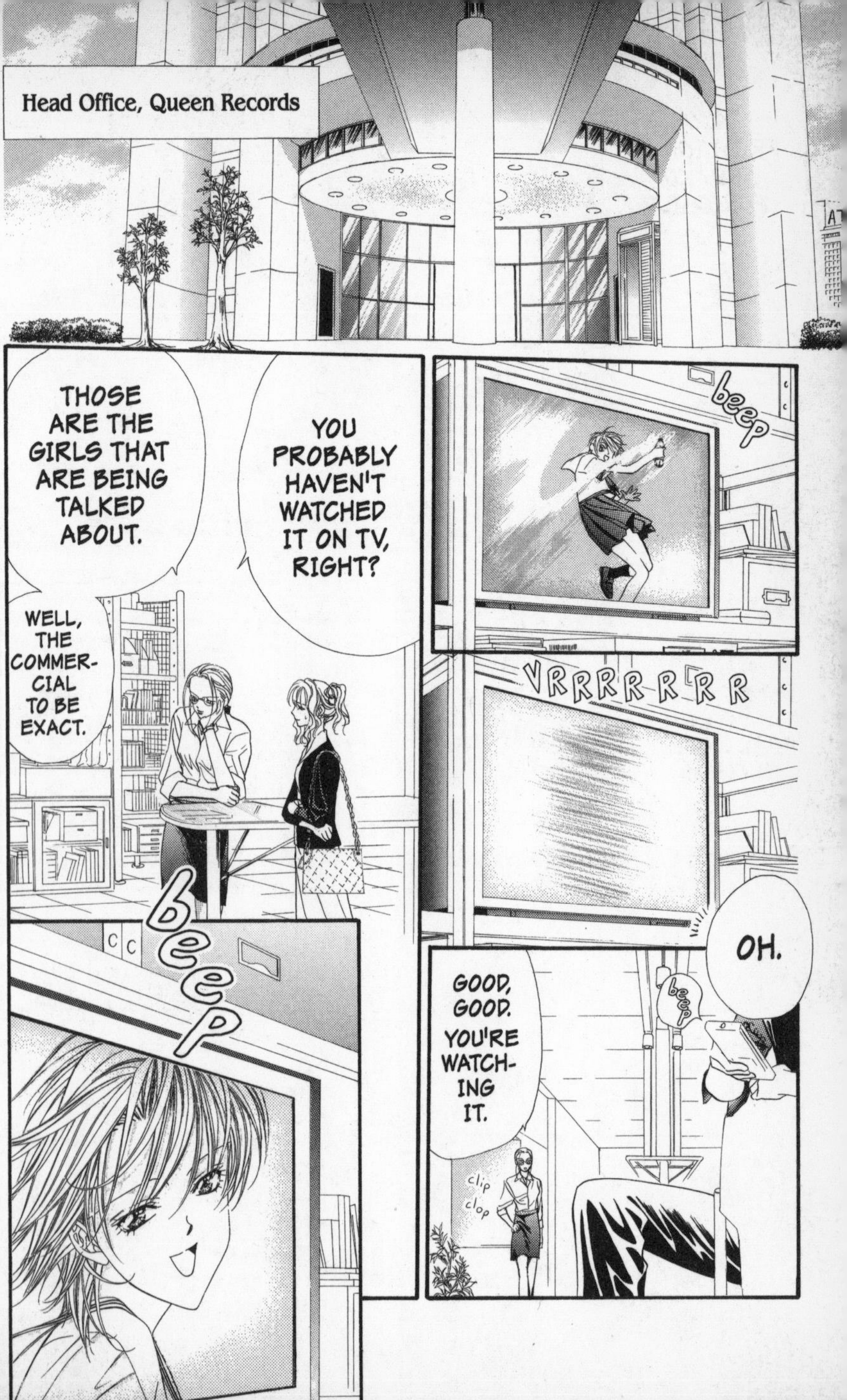
Head Office, Queen Records
beep
VRRRRRRR
YOU PROBABLY HAVEN'T WATCHED IT ON TV, RIGHT?
THOSE ARE THE GIRLS THAT ARE BEING TALKED ABOUT.
WELL, THE COMMERCIAL TO BE EXACT.
OH.
beep
GOOD, GOOD. YOU'RE WATCHING IT.
clip clop
beep

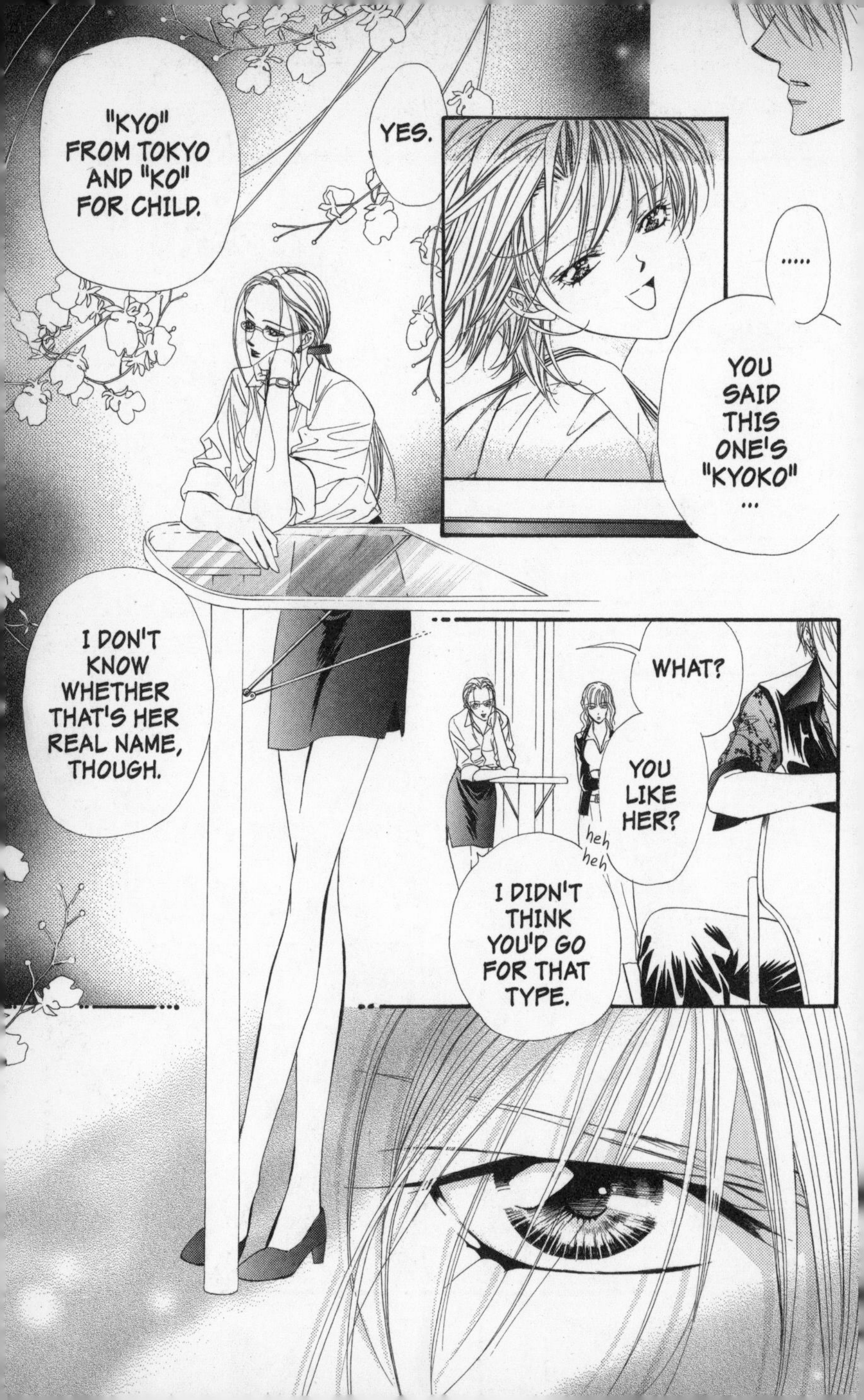
.....
YOU SAID THIS ONE'S "KYOKO" ...
YES.
"KYO" FROM TOKYO AND "KO" FOR CHILD.
I DON'T KNOW WHETHER THAT'S HER REAL NAME, THOUGH.
WHAT?
YOU LIKE HER?
heh heh
I DIDN'T THINK YOU'D GO FOR THAT TYPE.

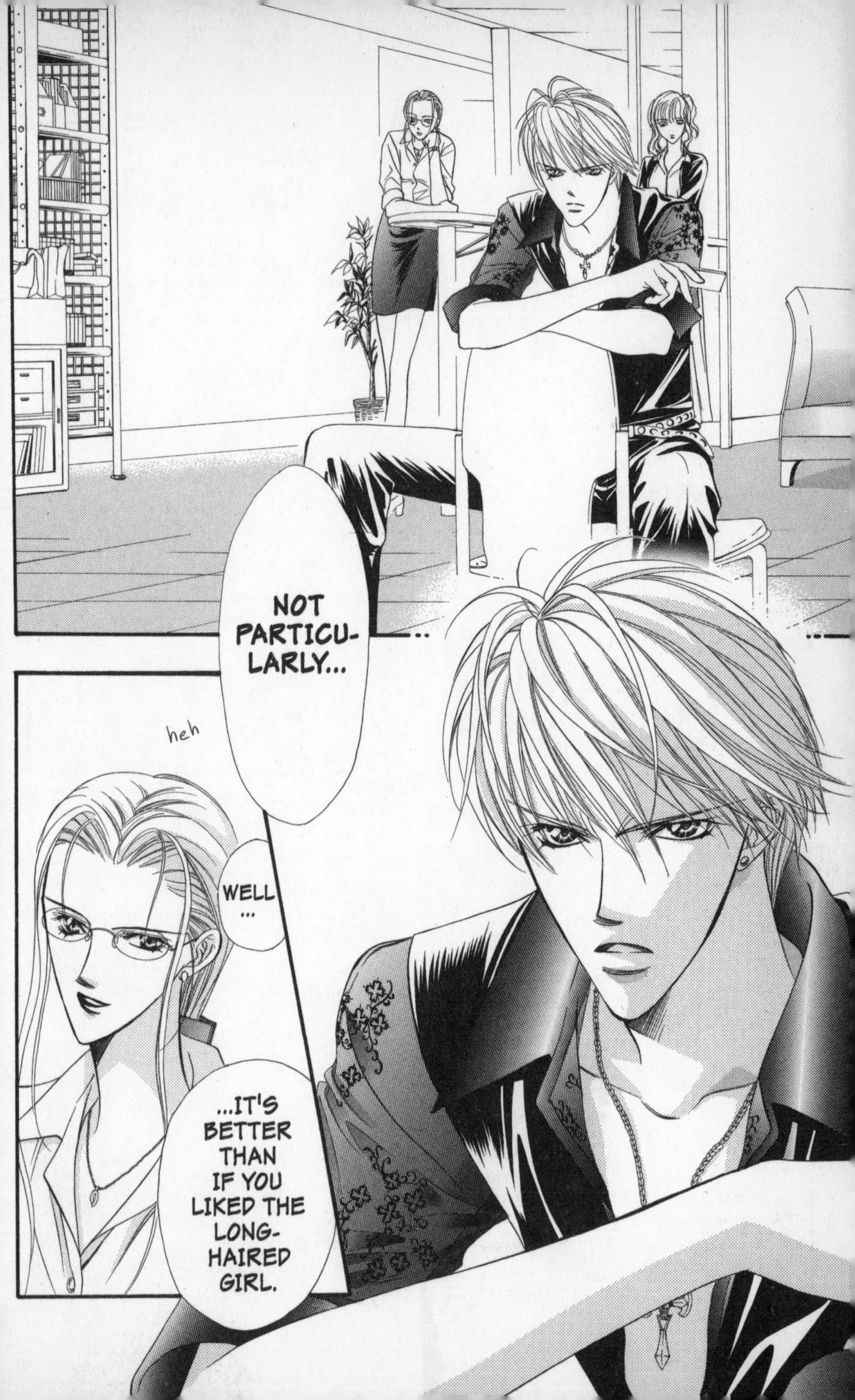
NOT PARTICU-LARLY...
heh
WELL...
...IT'S BETTER THAN IF YOU LIKED THE LONG-HAIRED GIRL.

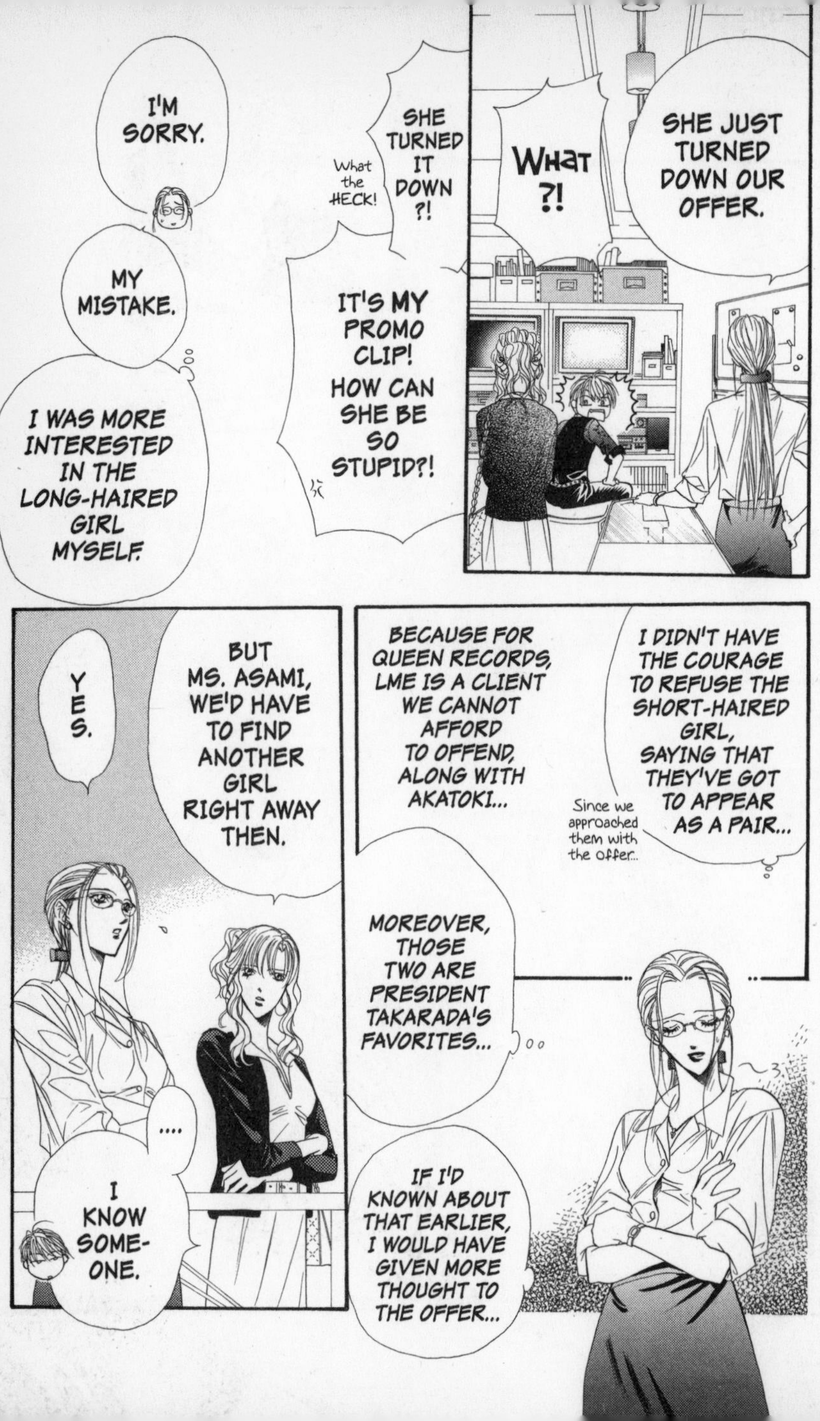
SHE JUST TURNED DOWN OUR OFFER.
WHAT?!
SHE TURNED IT DOWN?!
What the HECK!
IT'S MY PROMO CLIP! HOW CAN SHE BE SO STUPID?!
I'M SORRY.
MY MISTAKE.
I WAS MORE INTERESTED IN THE LONG-HAIRED GIRL MYSELF.
I DIDN'T HAVE THE COURAGE TO REFUSE THE SHORT-HAIRED GIRL, SAYING THAT THEY'VE GOT TO APPEAR AS A PAIR...
Since we approached them with the offer...
BECAUSE FOR QUEEN RECORDS, LME IS A CLIENT WE CANNOT AFFORD TO OFFEND, ALONG WITH AKATOKI...
MOREOVER, THOSE TWO ARE PRESIDENT TAKARADA'S FAVORITES...
IF I'D KNOWN ABOUT THAT EARLIER, I WOULD HAVE GIVEN MORE THOUGHT TO THE OFFER...
BUT MS. ASAMI, WE'D HAVE TO FIND ANOTHER GIRL RIGHT AWAY THEN.
YES.
....
I KNOW SOMEONE.

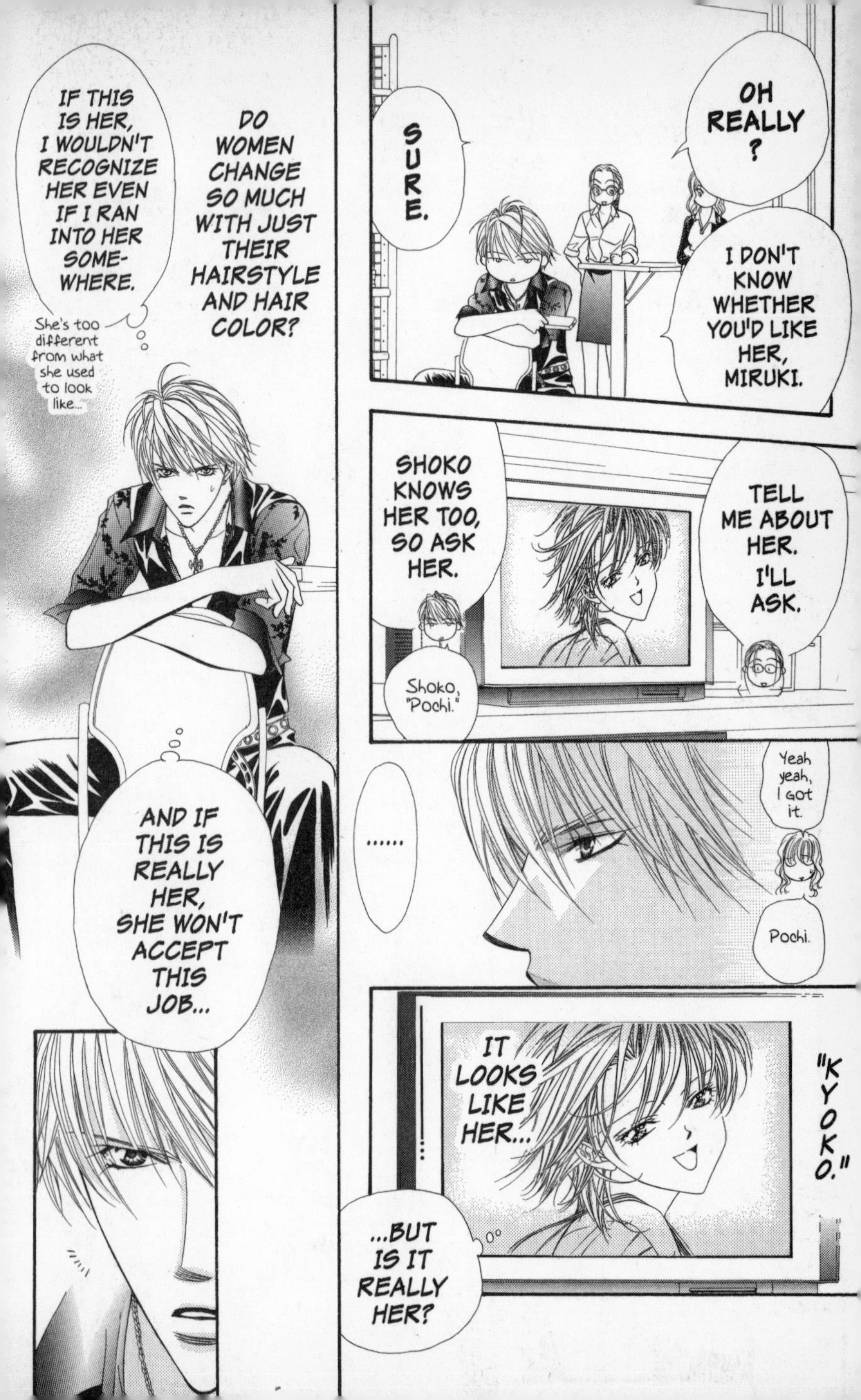
OH REALLY?
I DON'T KNOW WHETHER YOU'D LIKE HER, MIRUKI.
SURE.
TELL ME ABOUT HER.
I'LL ASK.
SHOKO KNOWS HER TOO, SO ASK HER.
Shoko, "Pochi."
Yeah yeah, I got it.
Pochi.
......
"KYOKO."
IT LOOKS LIKE HER...
...BUT IS IT REALLY HER?
DO WOMEN CHANGE SO MUCH WITH JUST THEIR HAIRSTYLE AND HAIR COLOR?
IF THIS IS HER, I WOULDN'T RECOGNIZE HER EVEN IF I RAN INTO HER SOMEWHERE.
She's too different from what she used to look like...
AND IF THIS IS REALLY HER, SHE WON'T ACCEPT THIS JOB...

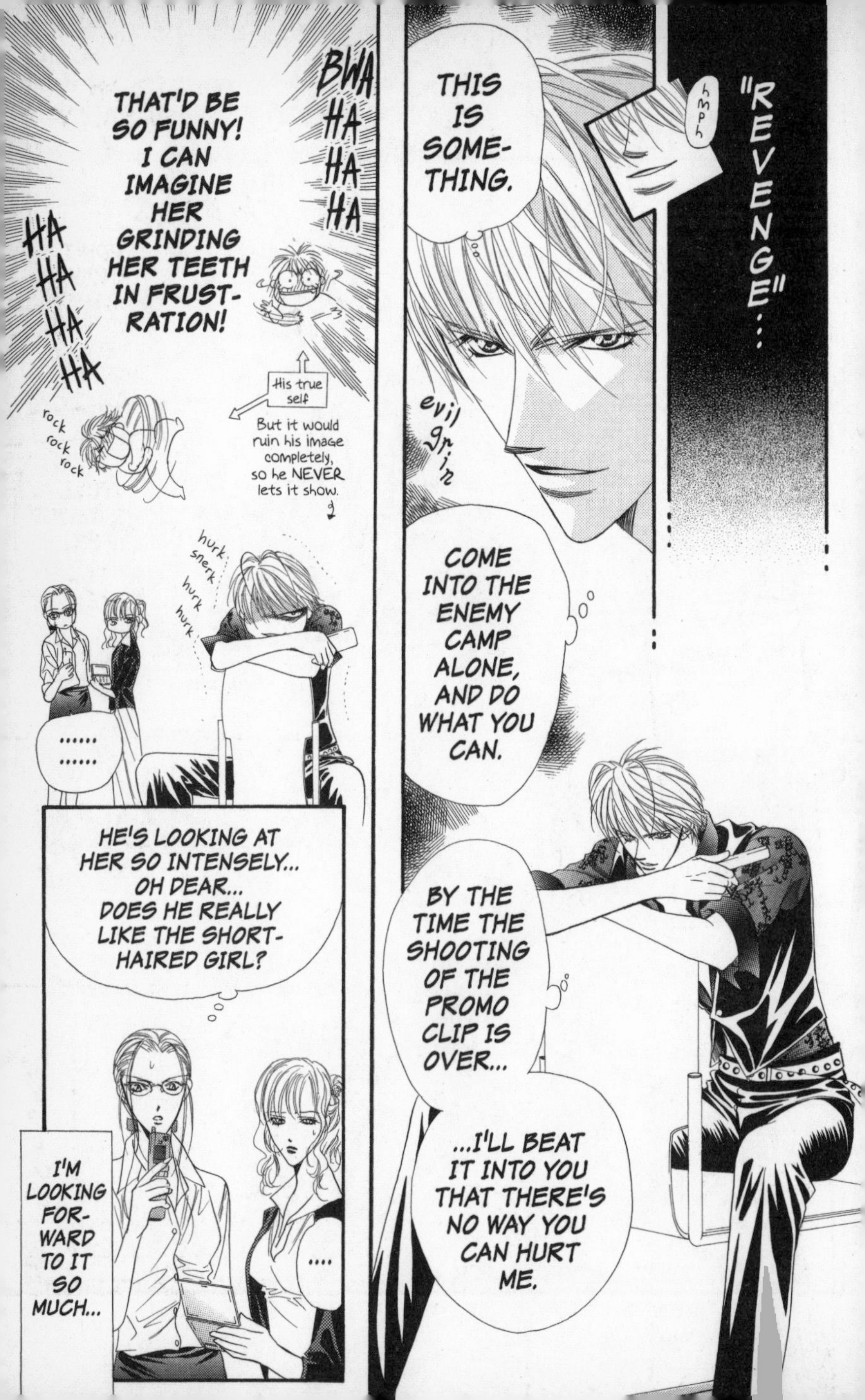
"REVENGE"...
hmph
THIS IS SOMETHING.
evil grin
COME INTO THE ENEMY CAMP ALONE, AND DO WHAT YOU CAN.
BY THE TIME THE SHOOTING OF THE PROMO CLIP IS OVER...
...I'LL BEAT IT INTO YOU THAT THERE'S NO WAY YOU CAN HURT ME.
BWA HA HA HA
THAT'D BE SO FUNNY! I CAN IMAGINE HER GRINDING HER TEETH IN FRUSTRATION!
HA HA HA HA
His true self
But it would ruin his image completely, so he NEVER lets it show.
rock rock rock
hurk snerk hurk hurk
....
HE'S LOOKING AT HER SO INTENSELY... OH DEAR... DOES HE REALLY LIKE THE SHORT-HAIRED GIRL?
I'M LOOKING FORWARD TO IT SO MUCH...
....

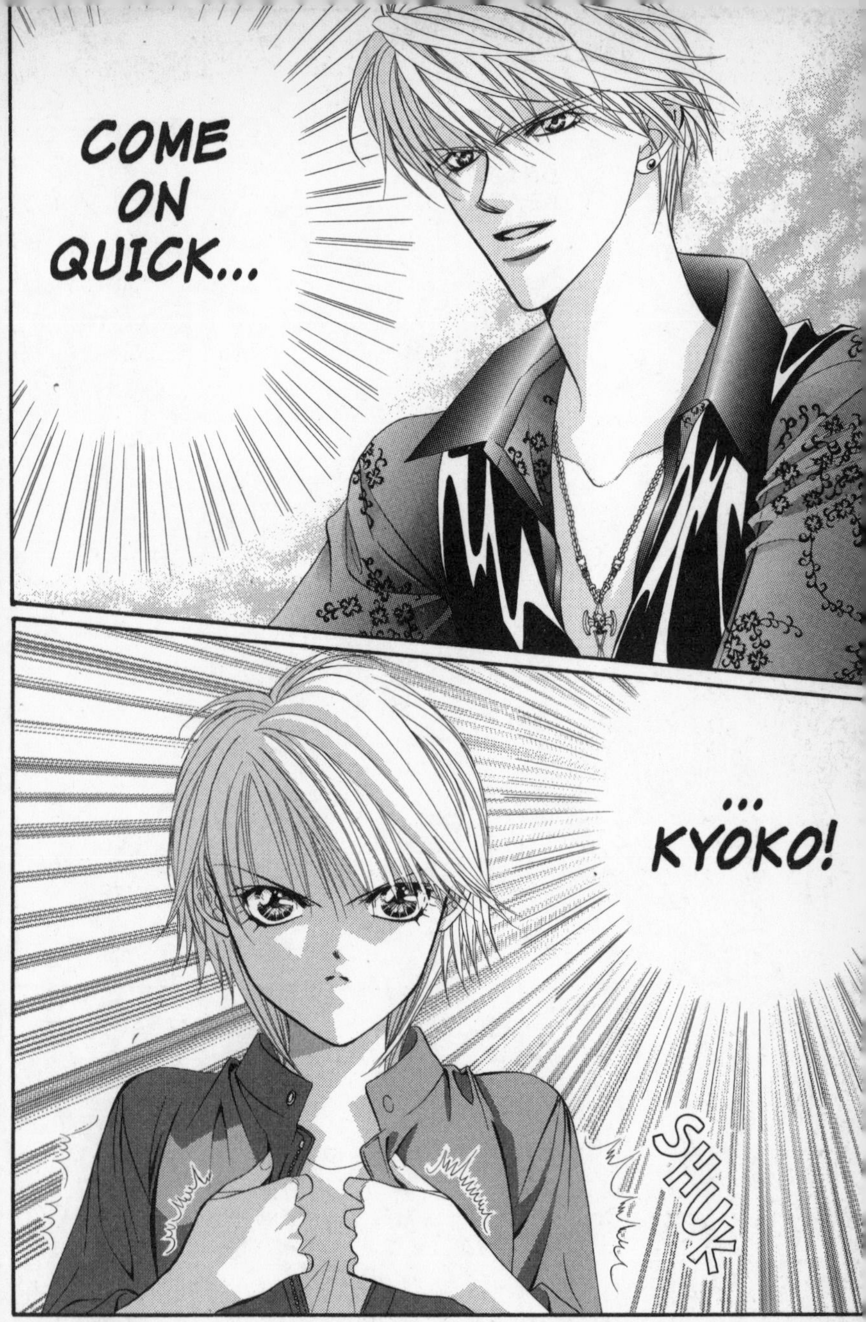
COME ON QUICK...
... KYOKO!
SHUK

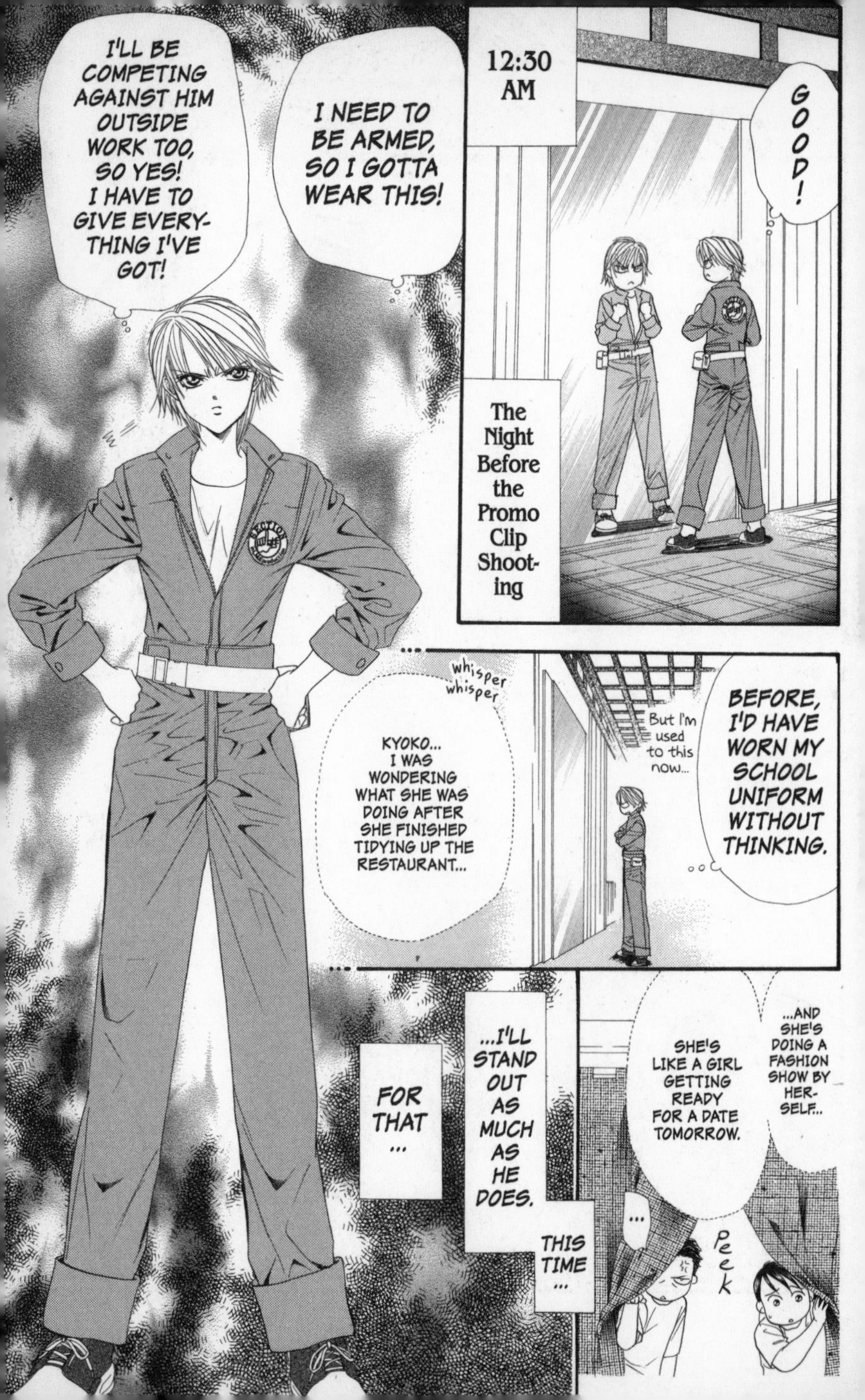
12:30 AM
The Night Before the Promo Clip Shooting
GOOD!
BEFORE, I'D HAVE WORN MY SCHOOL UNIFORM WITHOUT THINKING.
But I'm used to this now...
whisper whisper
KYOKO... I WAS WONDERING WHAT SHE WAS DOING AFTER SHE FINISHED TIDYING UP THE RESTAURANT...
SHE'S LIKE A GIRL GETTING READY FOR A DATE TOMORROW.
...AND SHE'S DOING A FASHION SHOW BY HER-SELF...
...
Peek
I NEED TO BE ARMED, SO I GOTTA WEAR THIS!
I'LL BE COMPETING AGAINST HIM OUTSIDE WORK TOO, SO YES! I HAVE TO GIVE EVERY-THING I'VE GOT!
...I'LL STAND OUT AS MUCH AS HE DOES.
THIS TIME...
FOR THAT...

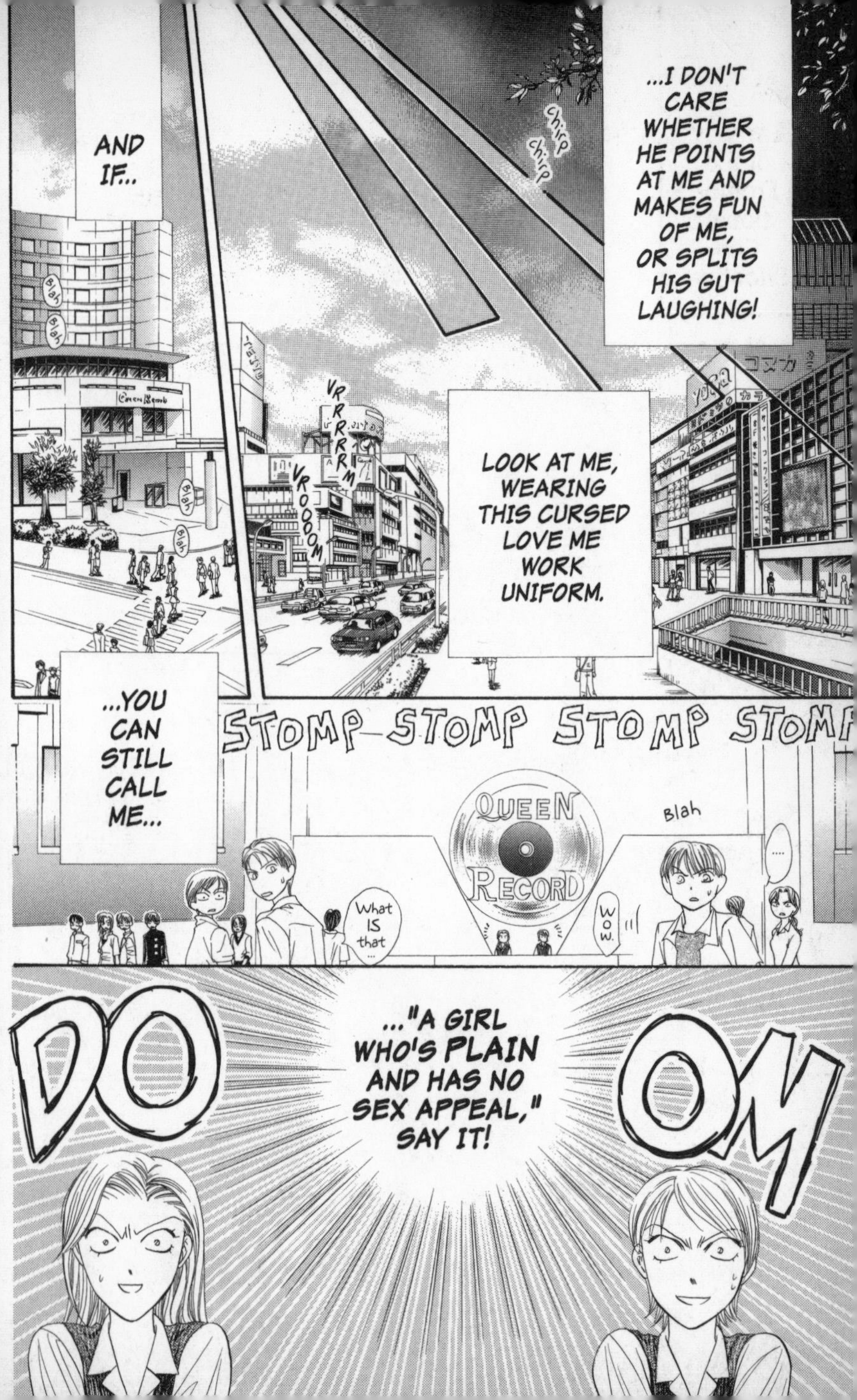
chirp
chirp
...I DON'T CARE WHETHER HE POINTS AT ME AND MAKES FUN OF ME, OR SPLITS HIS GUT LAUGHING!
VRRRRRM
VROOOOOM
LOOK AT ME, WEARING THIS CURSED LOVE ME WORK UNIFORM.
AND IF...
Blah
Blah
Blah
Blah
....
Blah
WOW.
What IS that ...
QUEEN RECORD
STOMP STOMP STOMP STOMP
...YOU CAN STILL CALL ME...
DOOM
..."A GIRL WHO'S PLAIN AND HAS NO SEX APPEAL," SAY IT!

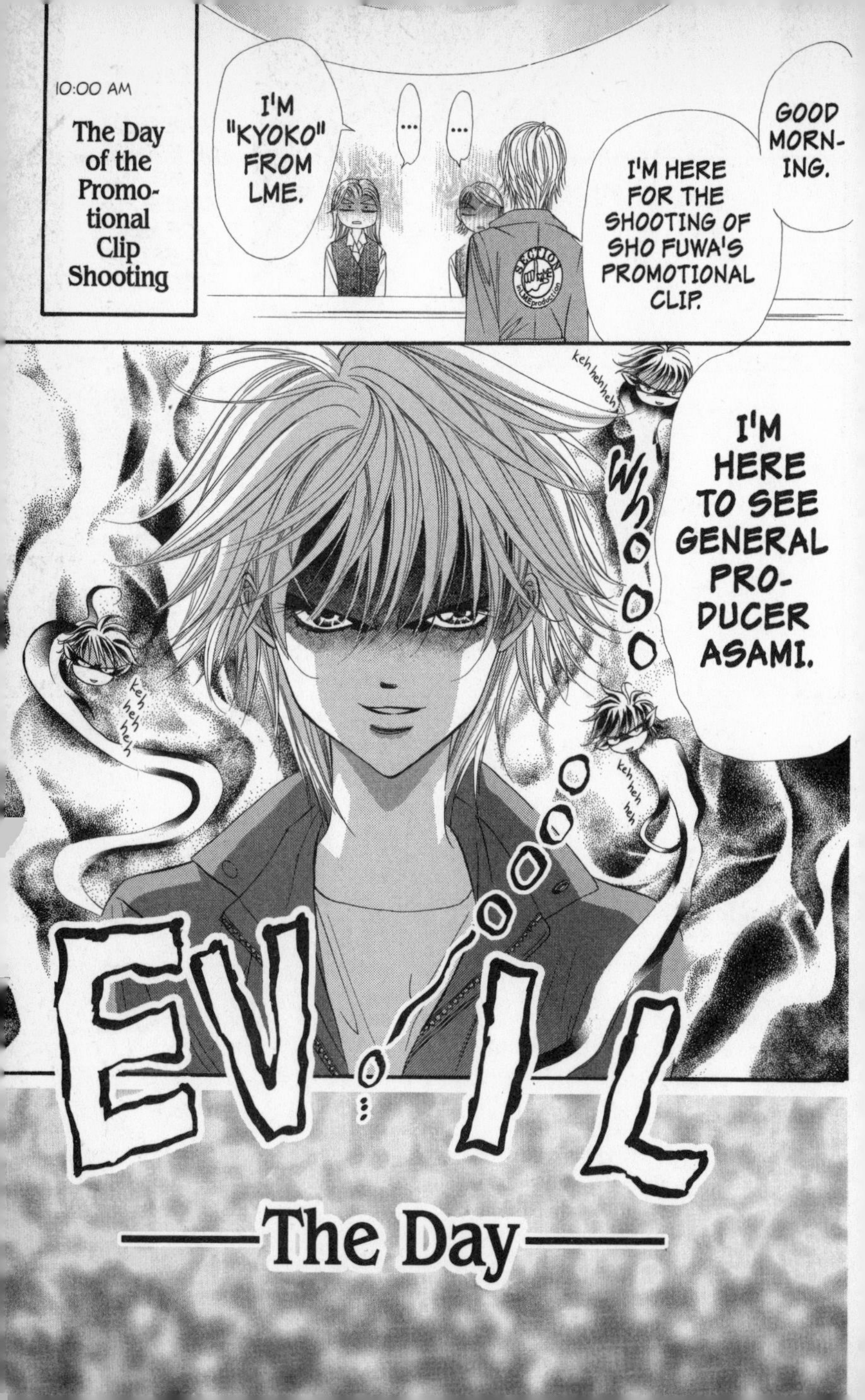
GOOD MORN-ING.
I'M HERE FOR THE SHOOTING OF SHO FUWA'S PROMOTIONAL CLIP.
...
...
I'M "KYOKO" FROM LME.
10:00 AM
The Day of the Promo-tional Clip Shooting
I'M HERE TO SEE GENERAL PRO-DUCER ASAMI.
keh heh heh
keh heh heh
keh heh heh
WHOOOOOOOOOOO
EV...IL
—The Day—

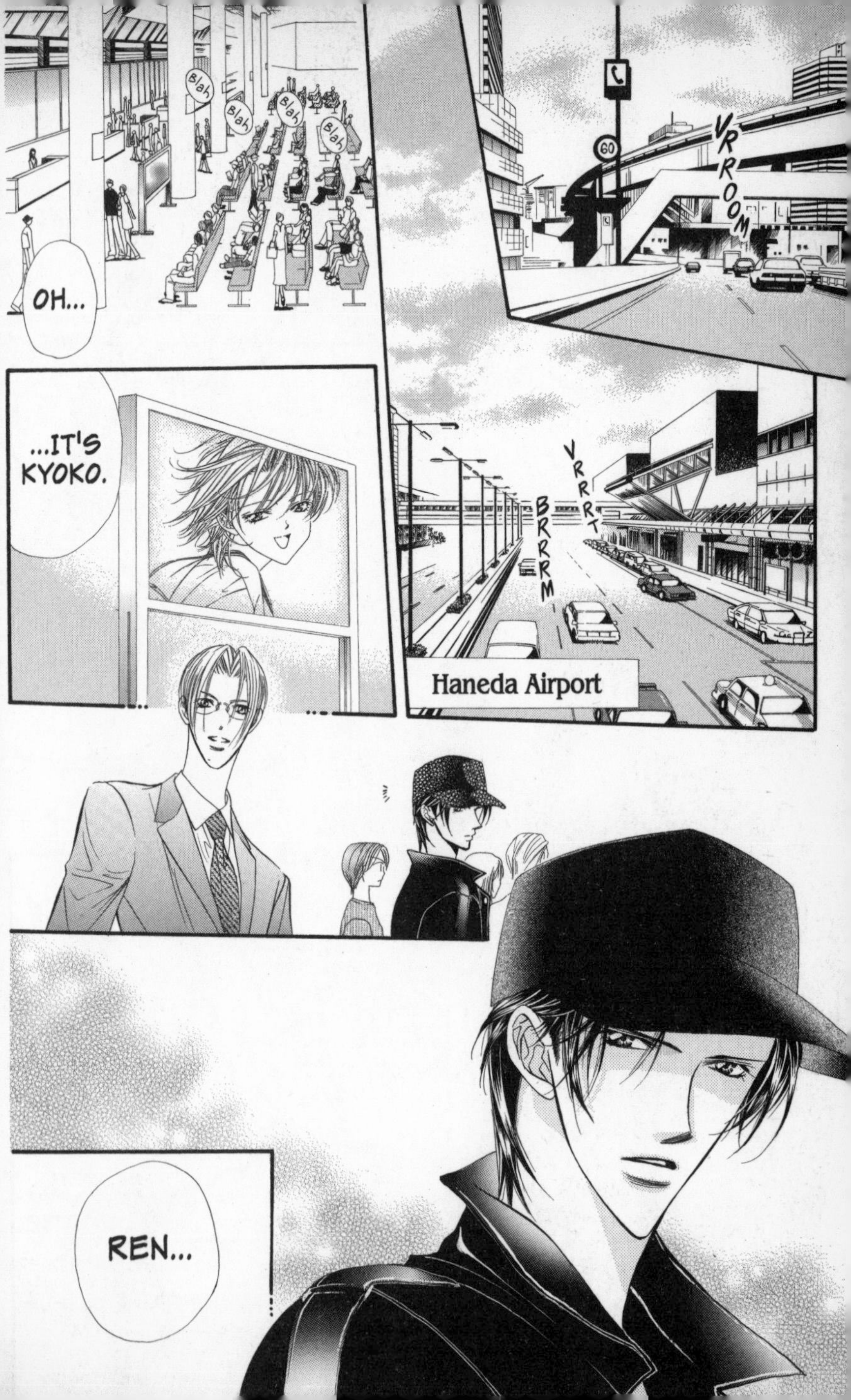
VRROOM
VRRRT
BRRRM
Haneda Airport
Blah
Blah
Blah
Blah
OH...
...IT'S KYOKO.
REN...

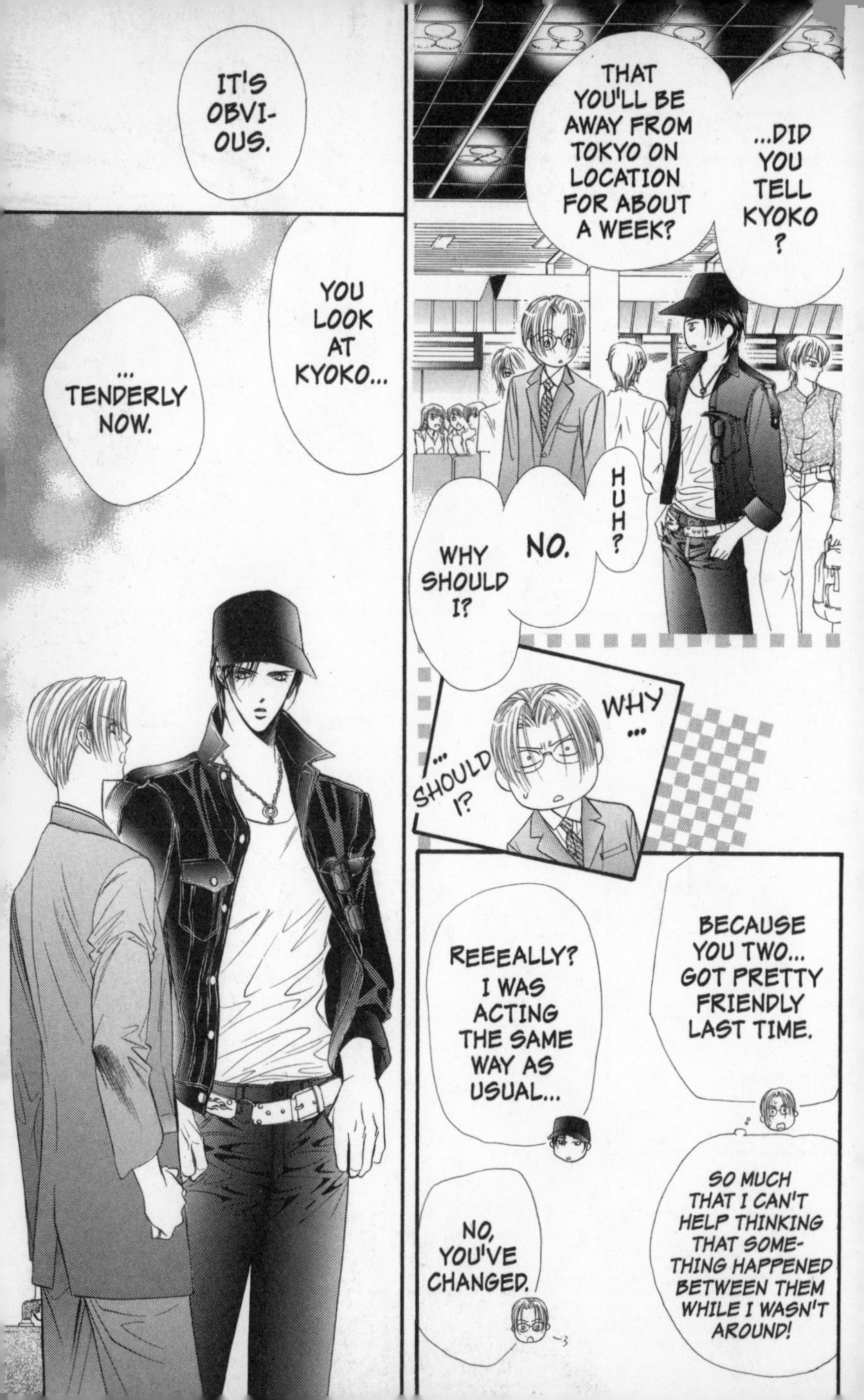
...DID YOU TELL KYOKO?
THAT YOU'LL BE AWAY FROM TOKYO ON LOCATION FOR ABOUT A WEEK?
HUH?
NO.
WHY SHOULD I?
WHY...
...SHOULD I?
BECAUSE YOU TWO... GOT PRETTY FRIENDLY LAST TIME.
REEEALLY? I WAS ACTING THE SAME WAY AS USUAL...
SO MUCH THAT I CAN'T HELP THINKING THAT SOME-THING HAPPENED BETWEEN THEM WHILE I WASN'T AROUND!
NO, YOU'VE CHANGED.
IT'S OBVI-OUS.
YOU LOOK AT KYOKO...
...TENDERLY NOW.

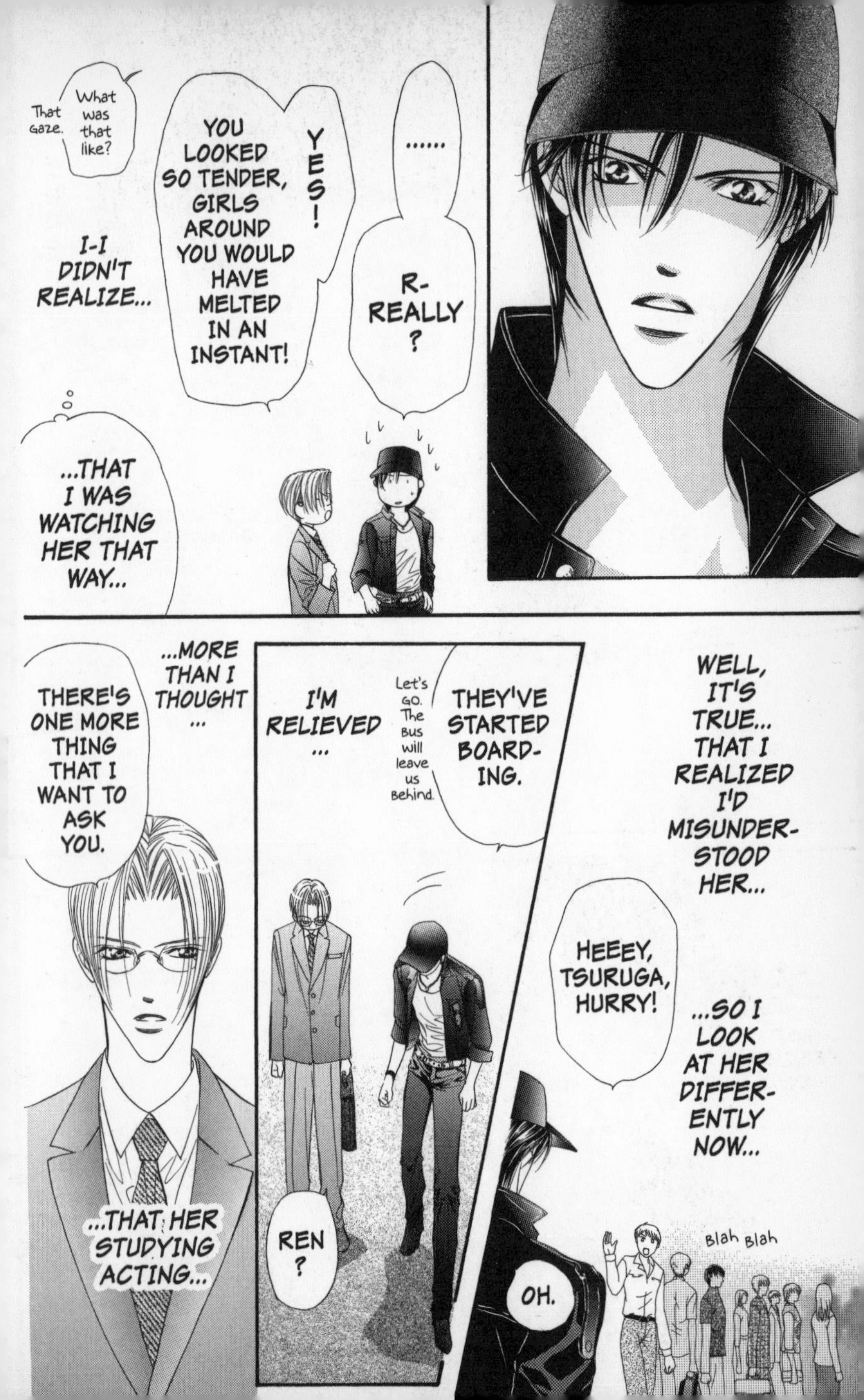
......
R-REALLY?
YES!
YOU LOOKED SO TENDER, GIRLS AROUND YOU WOULD HAVE MELTED IN AN INSTANT!
What was that like?
That Gaze.
I-I DIDN'T REALIZE...
...THAT I WAS WATCHING HER THAT WAY...
WELL, IT'S TRUE... THAT I REALIZED I'D MISUNDERSTOOD HER...
HEEEY, TSURUGA, HURRY!
...SO I LOOK AT HER DIFFERENTLY NOW...
Blah Blah
OH.
THEY'VE STARTED BOARDING.
Let's Go. The Bus will leave us Behind.
I'M RELIEVED...
REN?
...MORE THAN I THOUGHT...
THERE'S ONE MORE THING THAT I WANT TO ASK YOU.
...THAT HER STUDYING ACTING...

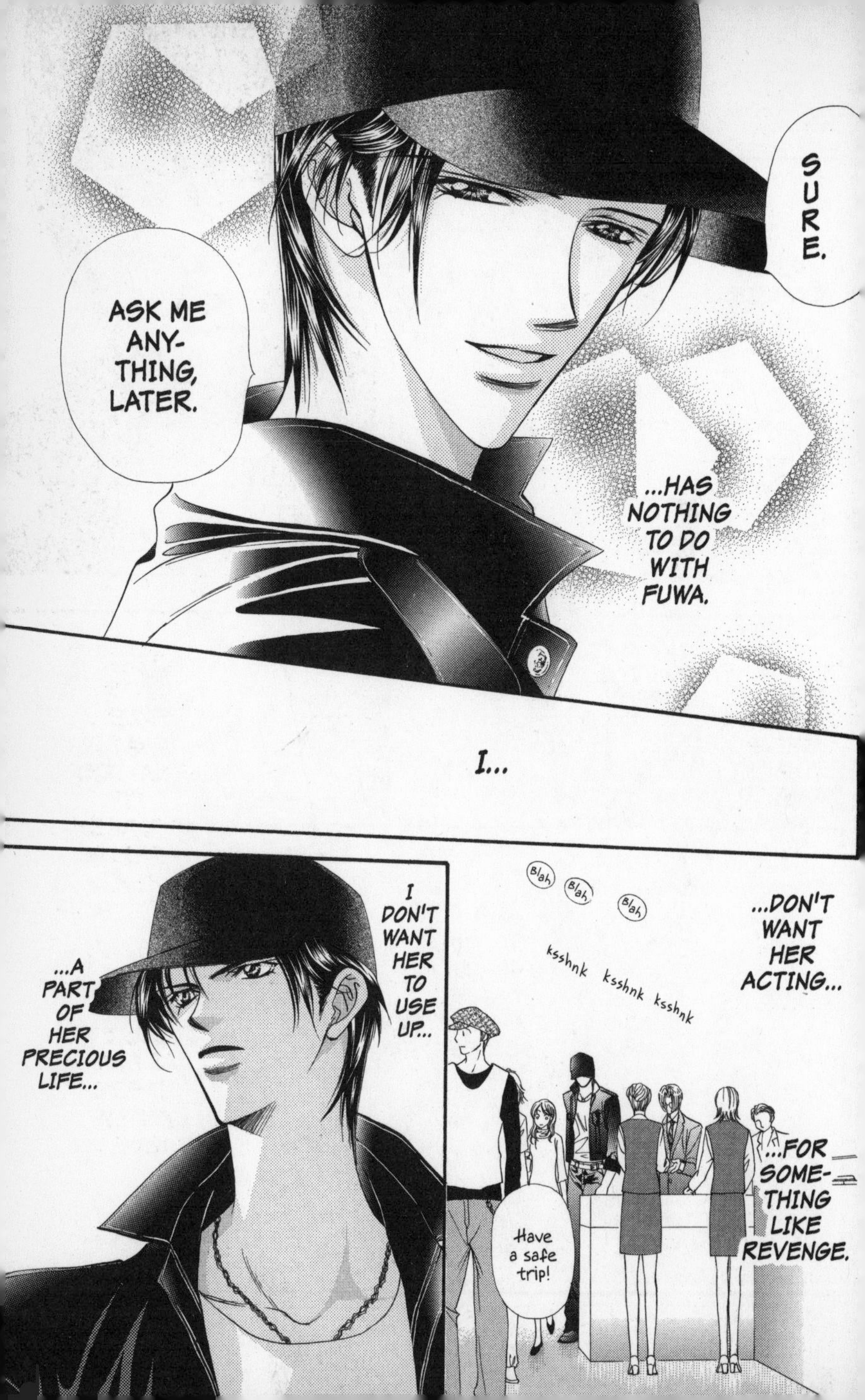
SURE.
ASK ME ANY-THING, LATER.
...HAS NOTHING TO DO WITH FUWA.
I...
...DON'T WANT HER ACTING...
Blah Blah Blah
ksshnk ksshnk ksshnk
Have a safe trip!
...FOR SOME-THING LIKE REVENGE.
I DON'T WANT HER TO USE UP...
...A PART OF HER PRECIOUS LIFE...

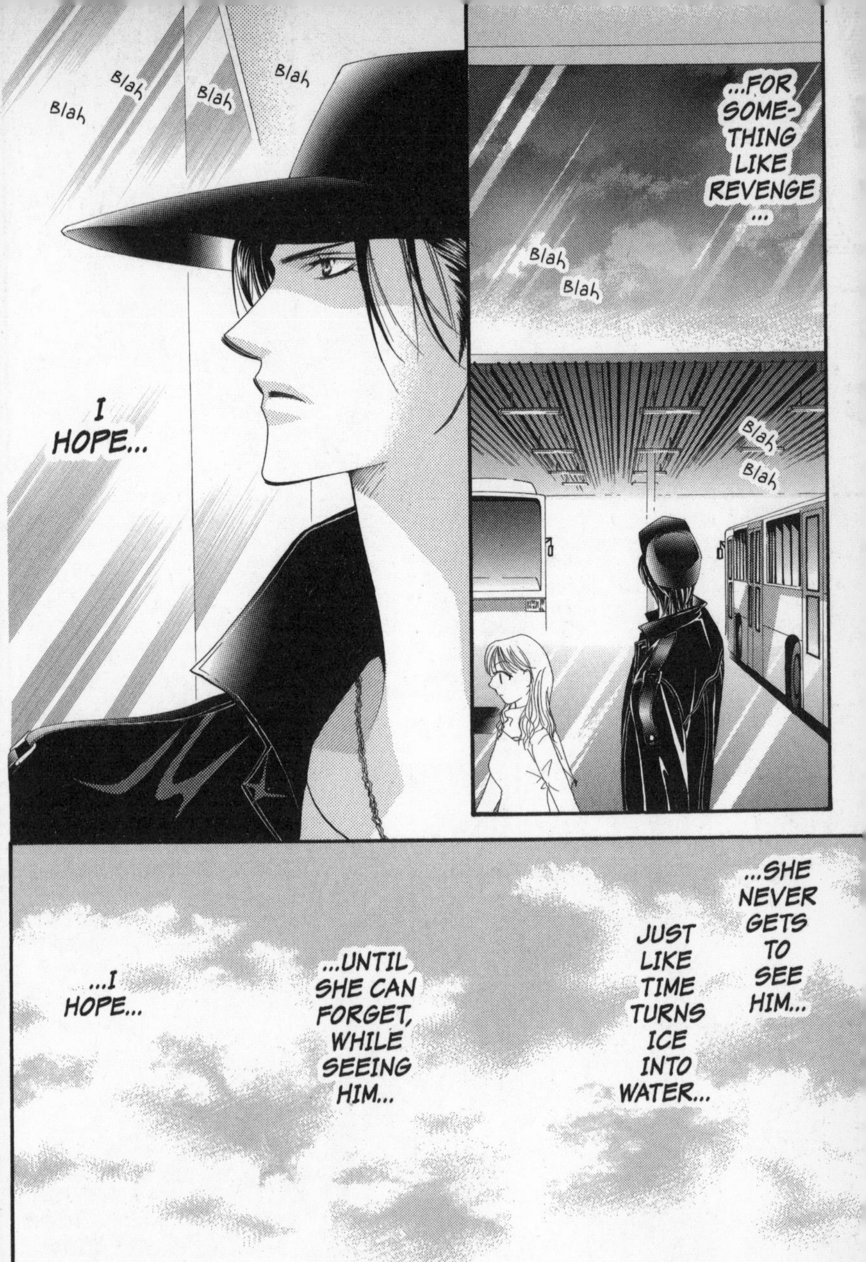
...FOR SOMETHING LIKE REVENGE...
Blah
Blah
Blah
Blah
Blah
Blah
Blah
Blah
I HOPE...
...SHE NEVER GETS TO SEE HIM...
JUST LIKE TIME TURNS ICE INTO WATER...
...UNTIL SHE CAN FORGET, WHILE SEEING HIM...
...I HOPE...

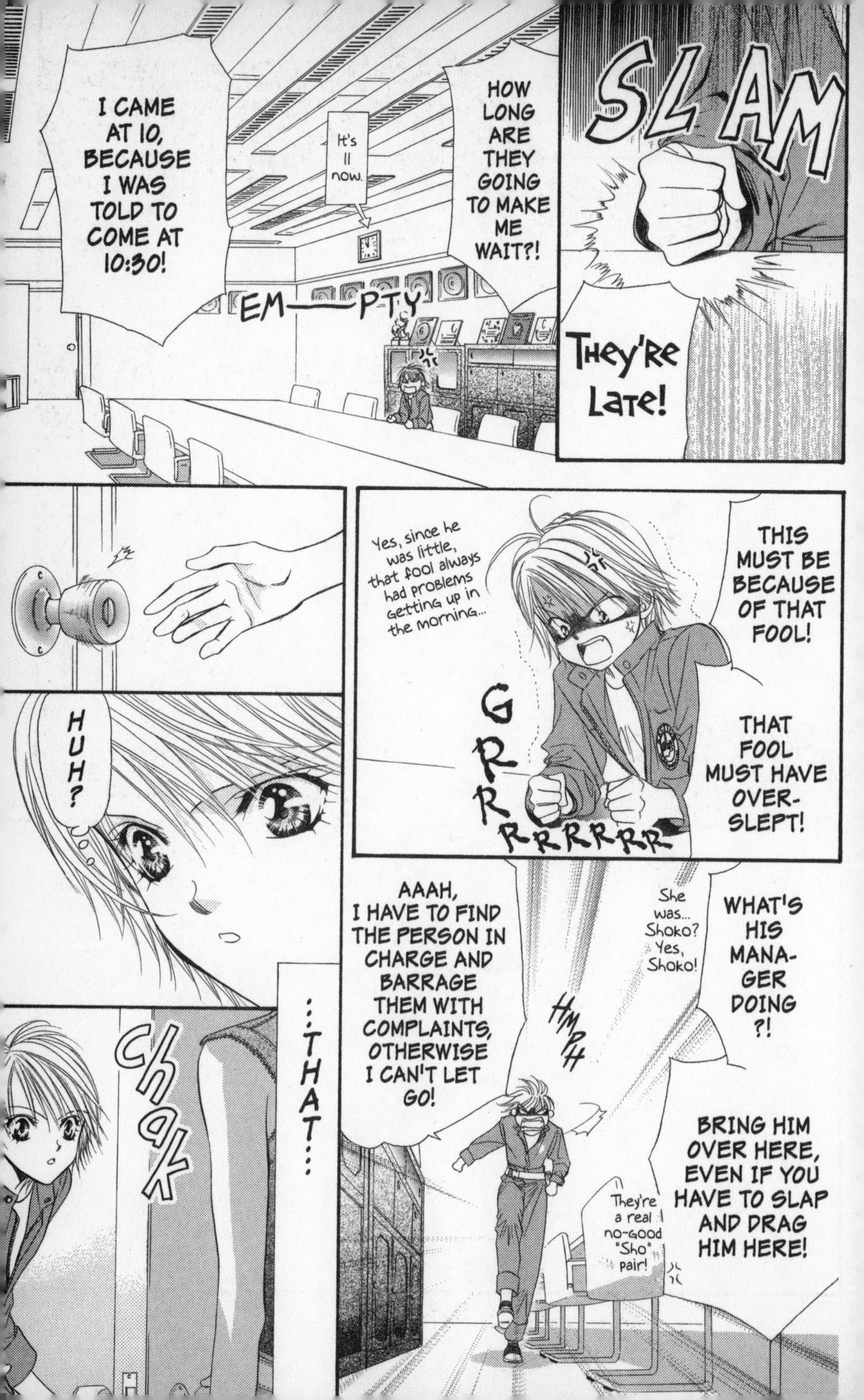
SLAM
They're Late!
HOW LONG ARE THEY GOING TO MAKE ME WAIT?!
It's 11 now.
I CAME AT 10, BECAUSE I WAS TOLD TO COME AT 10:30!
EM——PTY
THIS MUST BE BECAUSE OF THAT FOOL!
Yes, since he was little, that fool always had problems getting up in the morning...
THAT FOOL MUST HAVE OVER-SLEPT!
GRRRRRRRR
HUH?
WHAT'S HIS MANA-GER DOING?!
She was... Shoko? Yes, Shoko!
AAAH, I HAVE TO FIND THE PERSON IN CHARGE AND BARRAGE THEM WITH COMPLAINTS, OTHERWISE I CAN'T LET GO!
HMPH
BRING HIM OVER HERE, EVEN IF YOU HAVE TO SLAP AND DRAG HIM HERE!
They're a real no-good "Sho" pair!
...THAT...
Chak

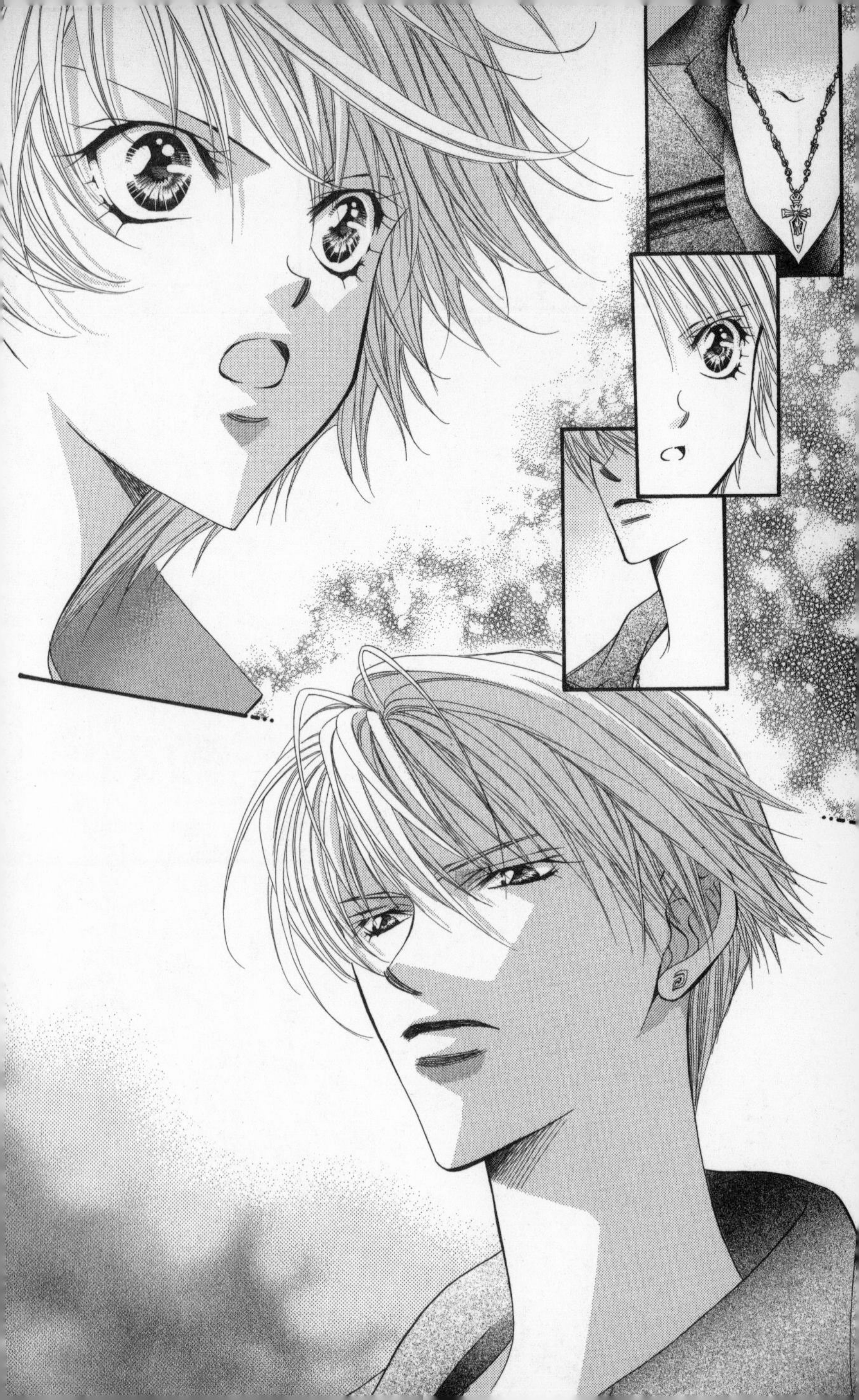

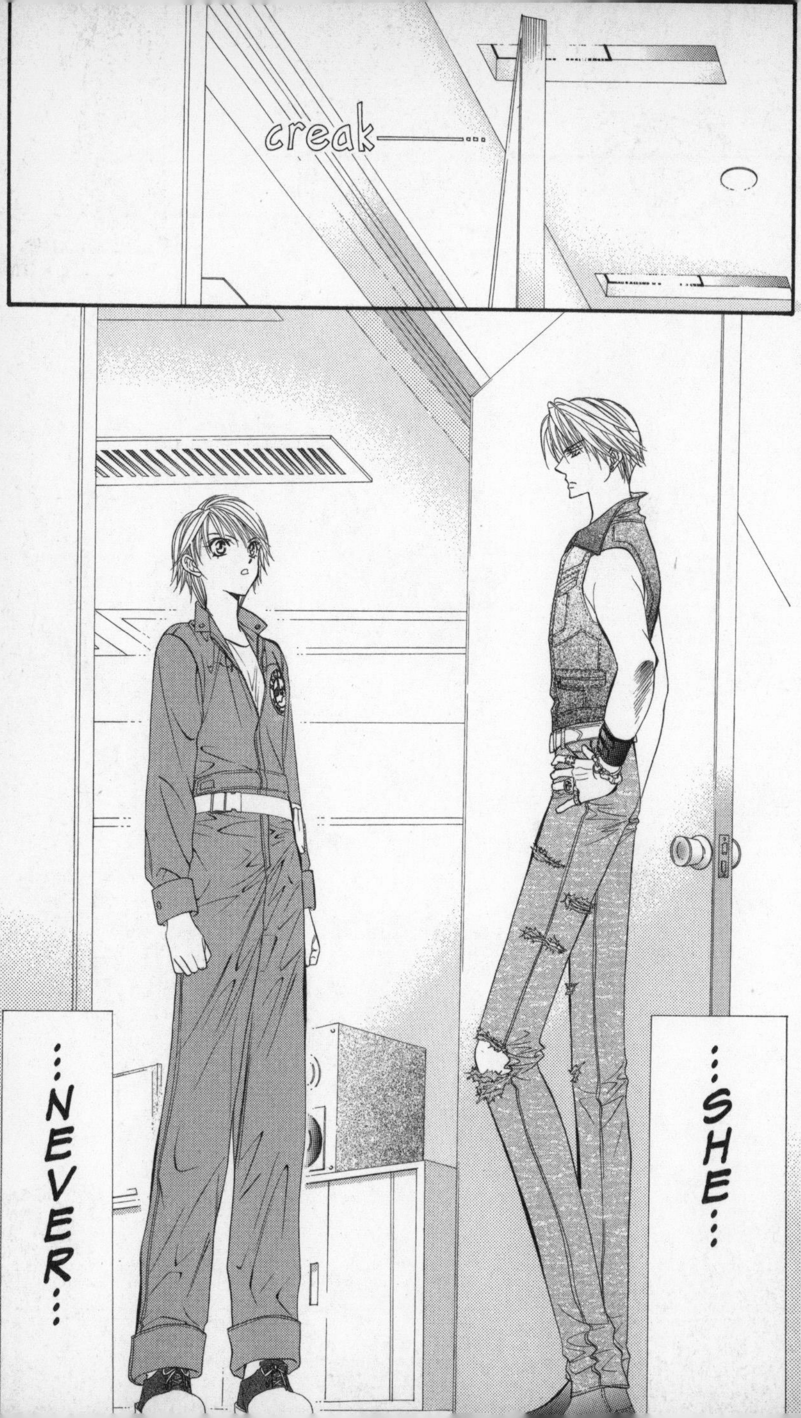
creak——....
...SHE...
...NEVER...

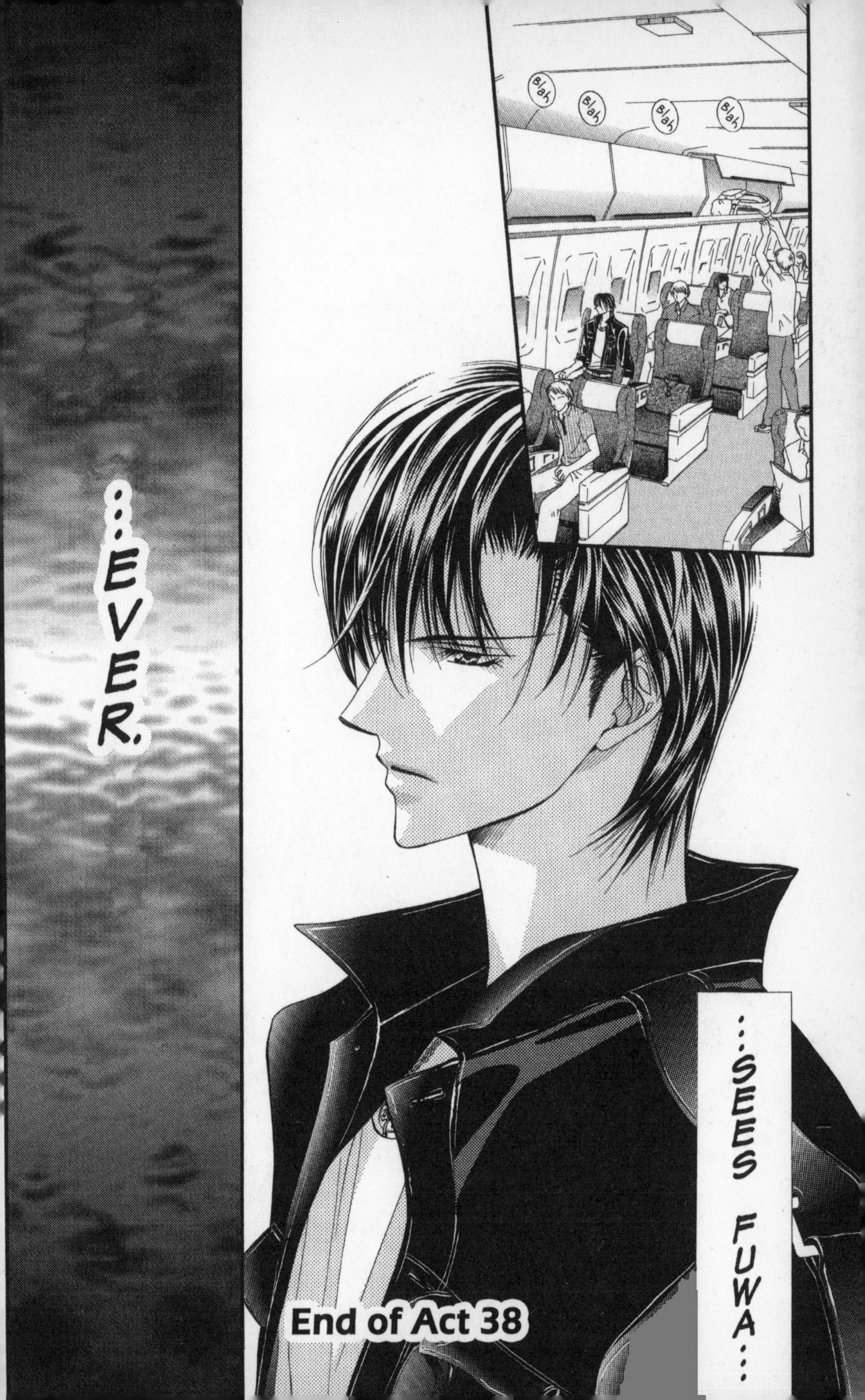
Blah
Blah
Blah
Blah
...SEES FUWA...
End of Act 38
...EVER.

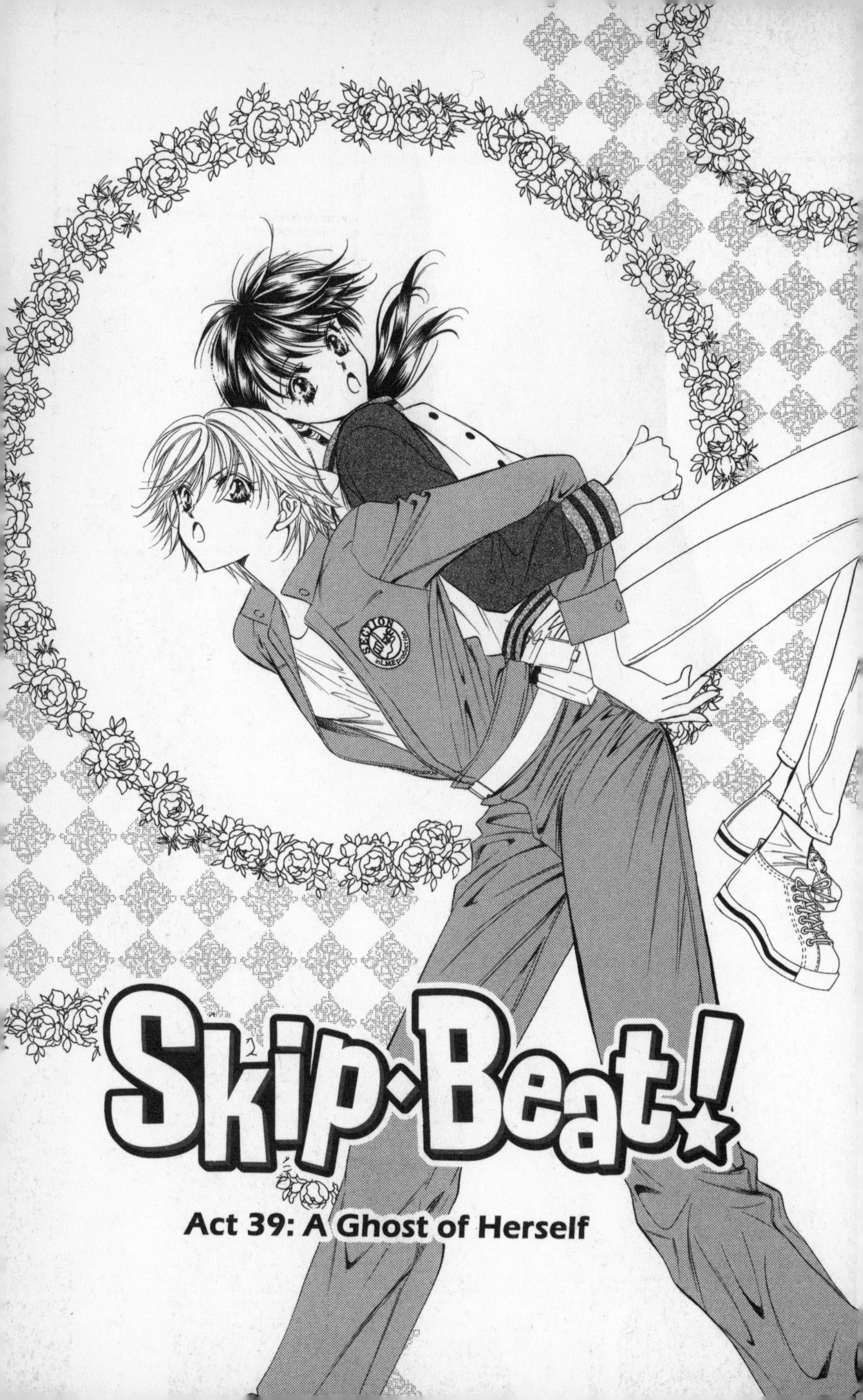
Skip·Beat!
SECTION

Act 39: A Ghost of Herself

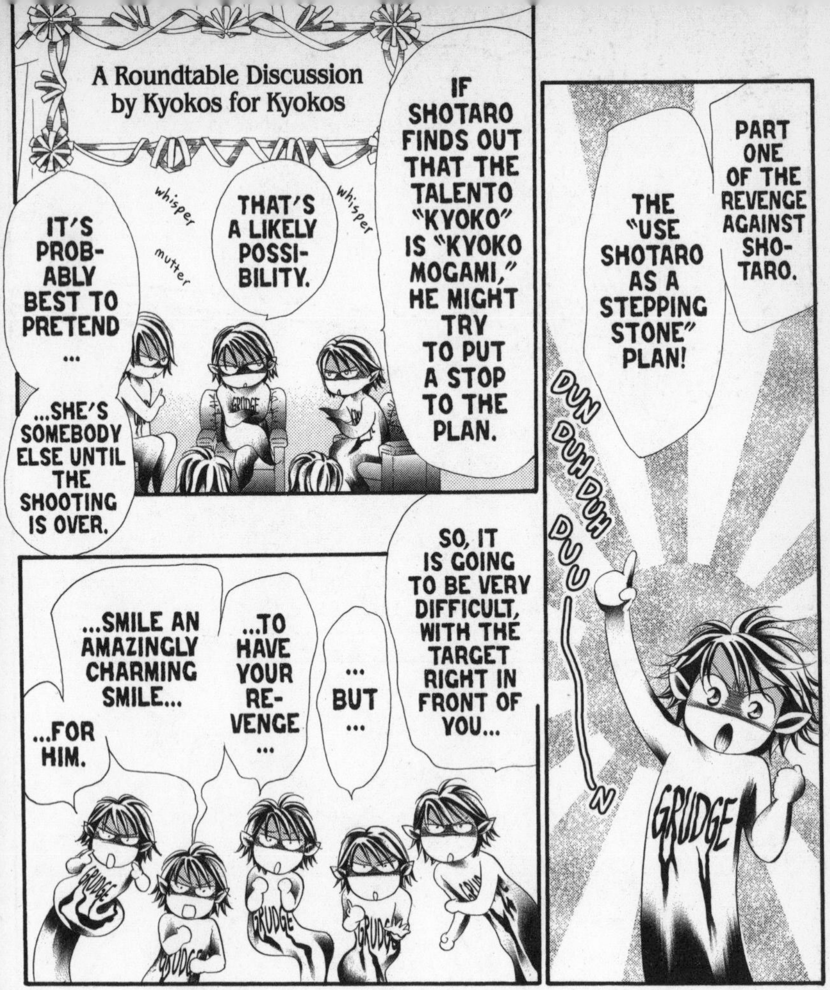
PART ONE OF THE REVENGE AGAINST SHOTARO.
THE "USE SHOTARO AS A STEPPING STONE" PLAN!
DUN DUH DUH DUUUN
A Roundtable Discussion by Kyokos for Kyokos
IF SHOTARO FINDS OUT THAT THE TALENTO "KYOKO" IS "KYOKO MOGAMI," HE MIGHT TRY TO PUT A STOP TO THE PLAN.
whisper
THAT'S A LIKELY POSSIBILITY.
whisper
mutter
IT'S PROBABLY BEST TO PRETEND ...
...SHE'S SOMEBODY ELSE UNTIL THE SHOOTING IS OVER.
GRUDGE
SO, IT IS GOING TO BE VERY DIFFICULT, WITH THE TARGET RIGHT IN FRONT OF YOU...
... BUT ...
...TO HAVE YOUR REVENGE ...
...SMILE AN AMAZINGLY CHARMING SMILE...
...FOR HIM.
GRUDGE

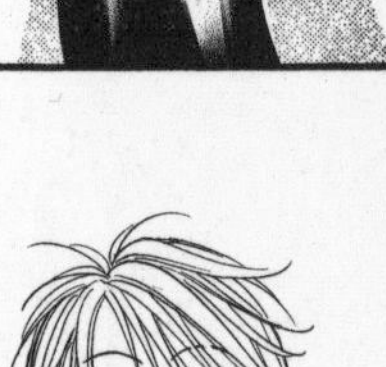

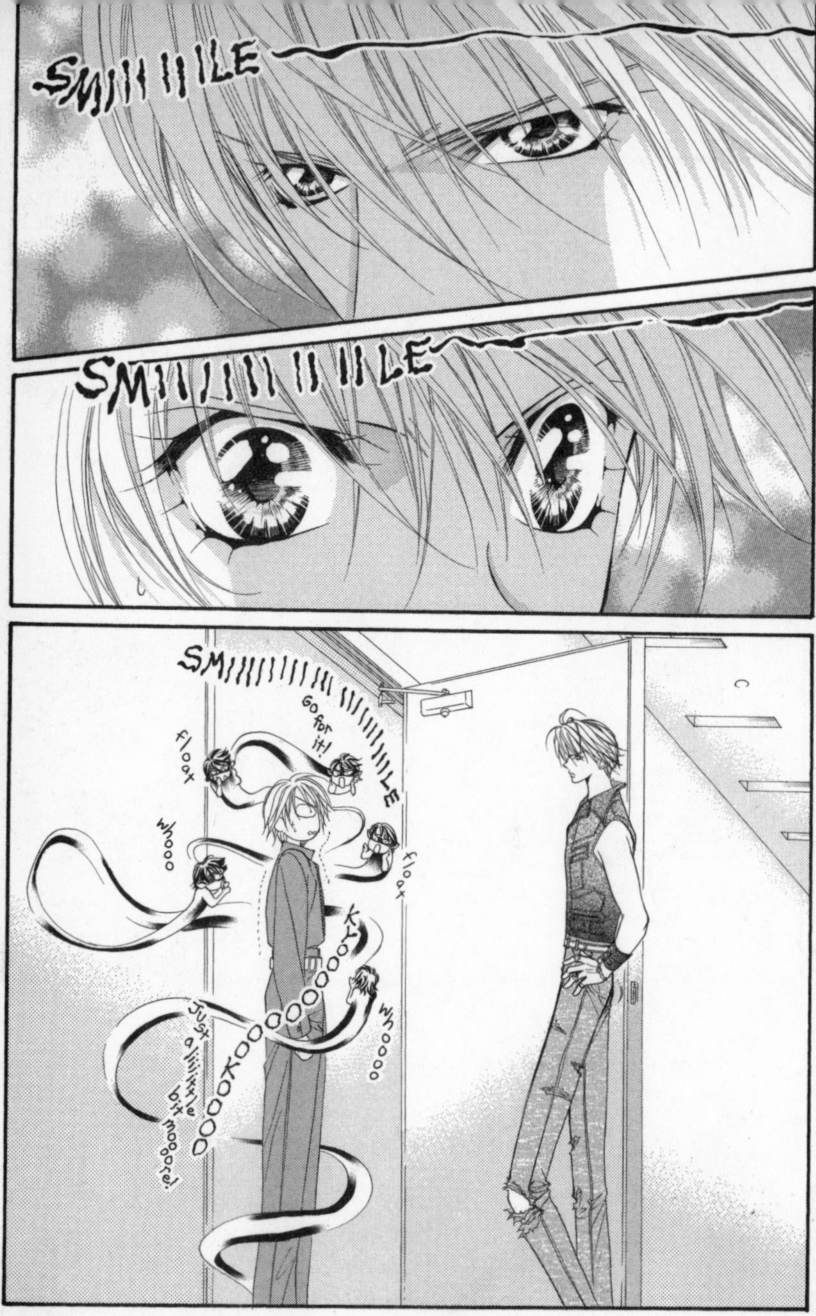
SMIIIIILE
SMIIIIIIIILE
SMIIIIIIIIIIIIIIIILE
Go for it!
float
float
whooo
KYOOOOOOOOOOOOOO
whoooo
Just a liiiiittle bit mooore!

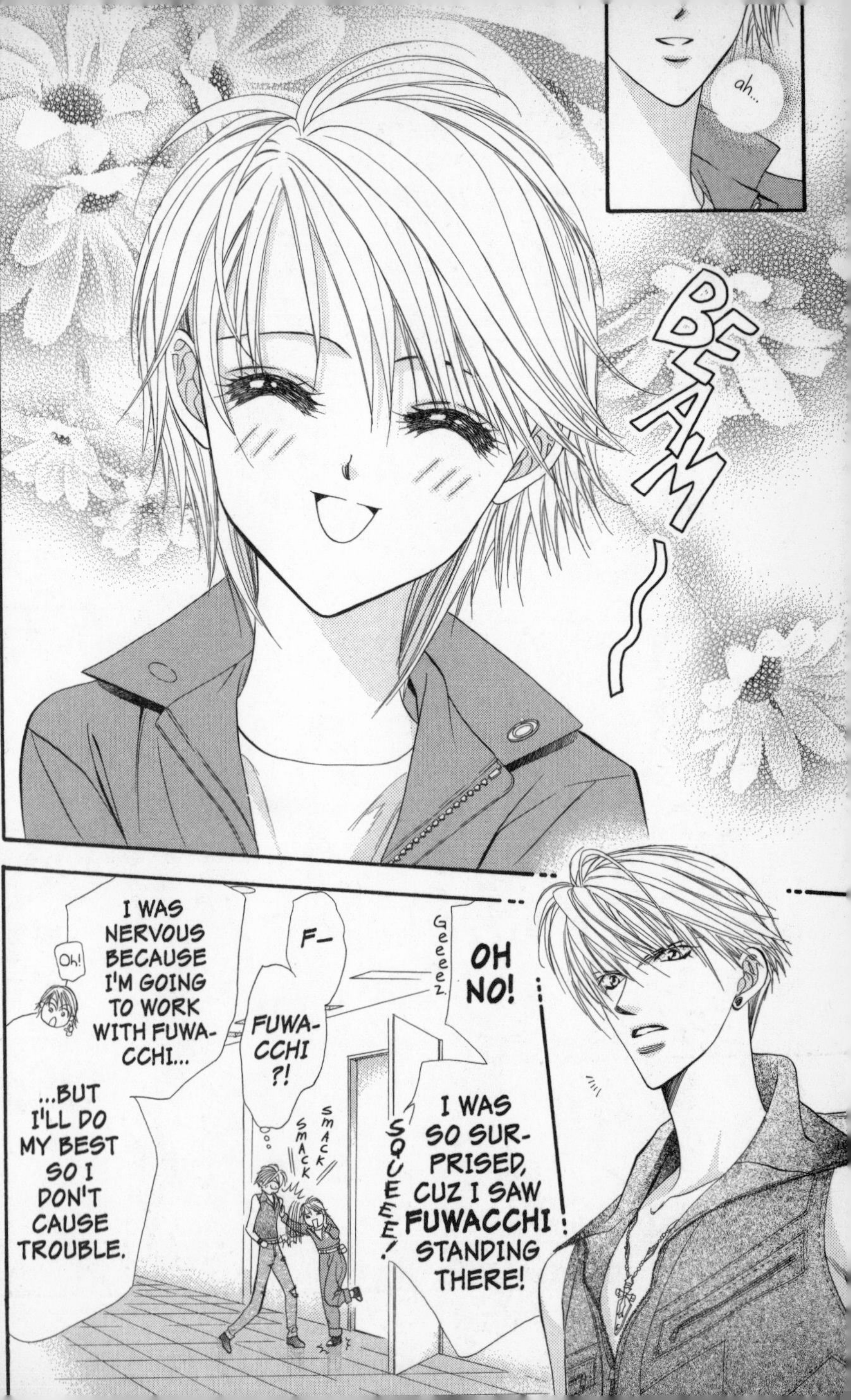
ah...
BEAM—
OH NO!
Geeeez
F—
FUWACCHI?!
I WAS NERVOUS BECAUSE I'M GOING TO WORK WITH FUWACCHI...
Oh!
I WAS SO SURPRISED, CUZ I SAW FUWACCHI STANDING THERE!
SQUEEEE!
SMACK
SMACK
...BUT I'LL DO MY BEST SO I DON'T CAUSE TROUBLE.

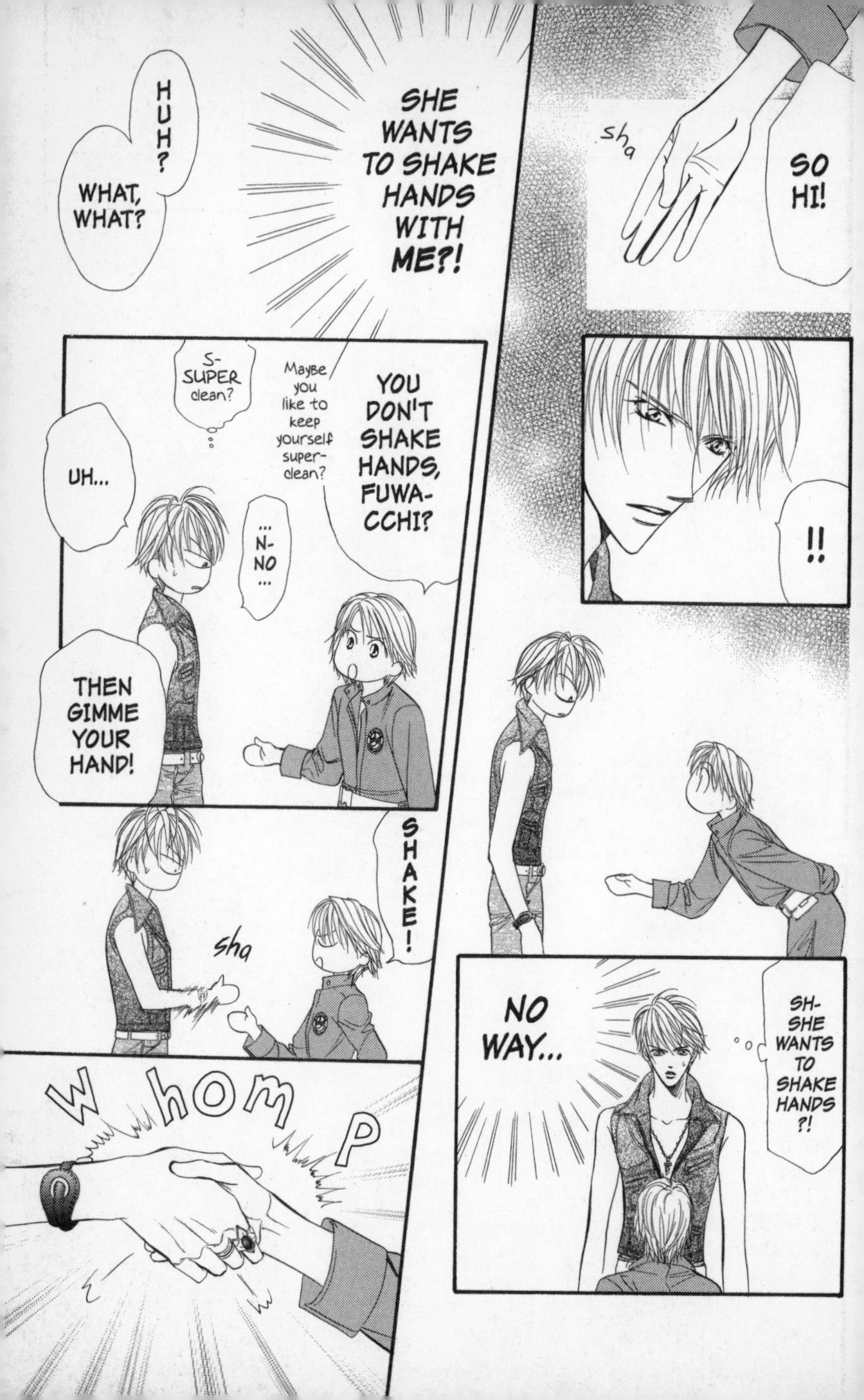
sha
SO HI!
!!
SH-SHE WANTS TO SHAKE HANDS?!
NO WAY...
SHE WANTS TO SHAKE HANDS WITH ME?!
HUH?
WHAT, WHAT?
YOU DON'T SHAKE HANDS, FUWA-CCHI?
Maybe you like to keep yourself super-clean?
S-SUPER clean?
UH...
... N-NO ...
THEN GIMME YOUR HAND!
SHAKE!
sha
WHOMP

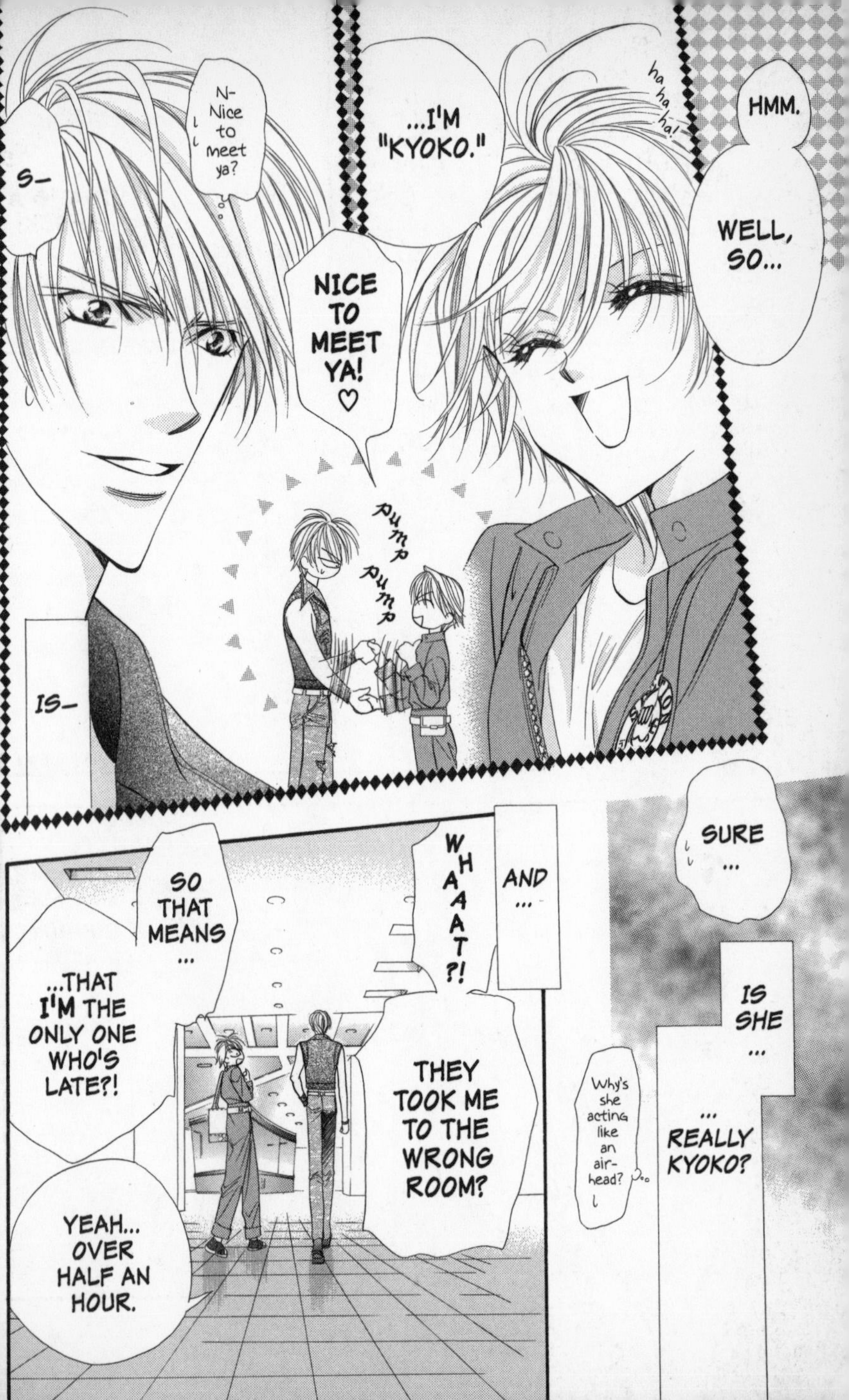
HMM.
WELL, SO...
ha ha ha!
...I'M "KYOKO."
NICE TO MEET YA! ♡
pump pump
N- Nice to meet ya?
S—
IS—
SURE...
IS SHE ... ...REALLY KYOKO?
Why's she acting like an air-head?
AND...
WHAAAT?!
SO THAT MEANS...
THEY TOOK ME TO THE WRONG ROOM?
...THAT I'M THE ONLY ONE WHO'S LATE?!
YEAH... OVER HALF AN HOUR.

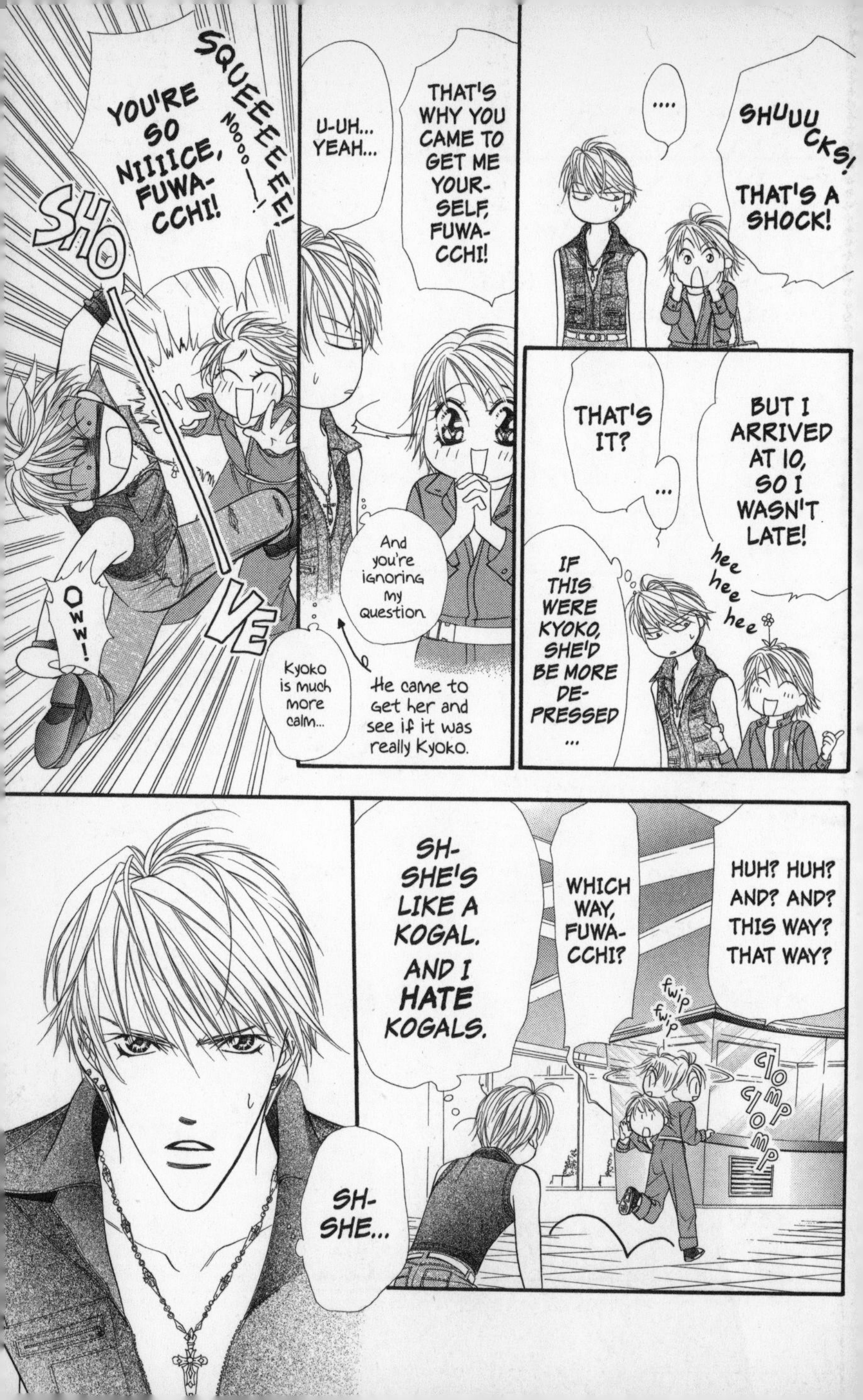
SHUUUCKS!
THAT'S A SHOCK!
....
BUT I ARRIVED AT 10, SO I WASN'T LATE!
hee hee hee
THAT'S IT?
...
IF THIS WERE KYOKO, SHE'D BE MORE DE-PRESSED ...
THAT'S WHY YOU CAME TO GET ME YOURSELF, FUWA-CCHI!
U-UH... YEAH...
And you're ignoring my question.
He came to get her and see if it was really Kyoko.
Kyoko is much more calm...
SQUEEEEEEE!
YOU'RE SO NIIIICE, FUWA-CCHI!
NOOOO—!
SHOVE
OWW!
HUH? HUH? AND? AND? THIS WAY? THAT WAY?
WHICH WAY, FUWA-CCHI?
SH-SHE'S LIKE A KOGAL.
AND I HATE KOGALS.
fwip fwip
CLOMP CLOMP CLOMP
SH-SHE...

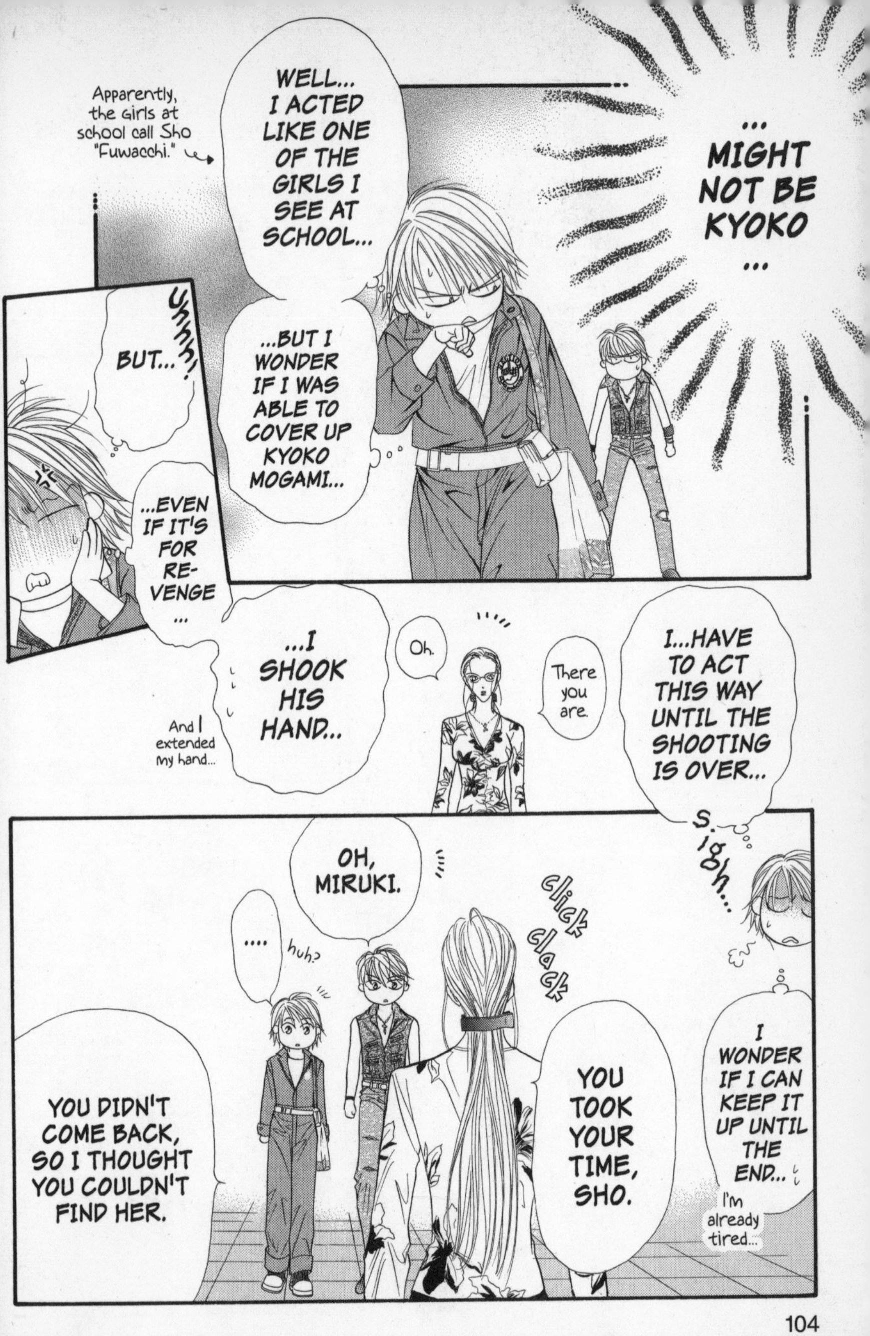
...MIGHT NOT BE KYOKO...
WELL... I ACTED LIKE ONE OF THE GIRLS I SEE AT SCHOOL...
Apparently, the girls at school call Sho "Fuwacchi."
...BUT I WONDER IF I WAS ABLE TO COVER UP KYOKO MOGAMI...
Uhhh!
BUT...
...EVEN IF IT'S FOR RE-VENGE...
...I SHOOK HIS HAND...
And I extended my hand...
I...HAVE TO ACT THIS WAY UNTIL THE SHOOTING IS OVER...
There you are.
Oh.
Sigh...
I WONDER IF I CAN KEEP IT UP UNTIL THE END...
I'm already tired...
YOU TOOK YOUR TIME, SHO.
click clack
OH, MIRUKI.
huh?
....
YOU DIDN'T COME BACK, SO I THOUGHT YOU COULDN'T FIND HER.

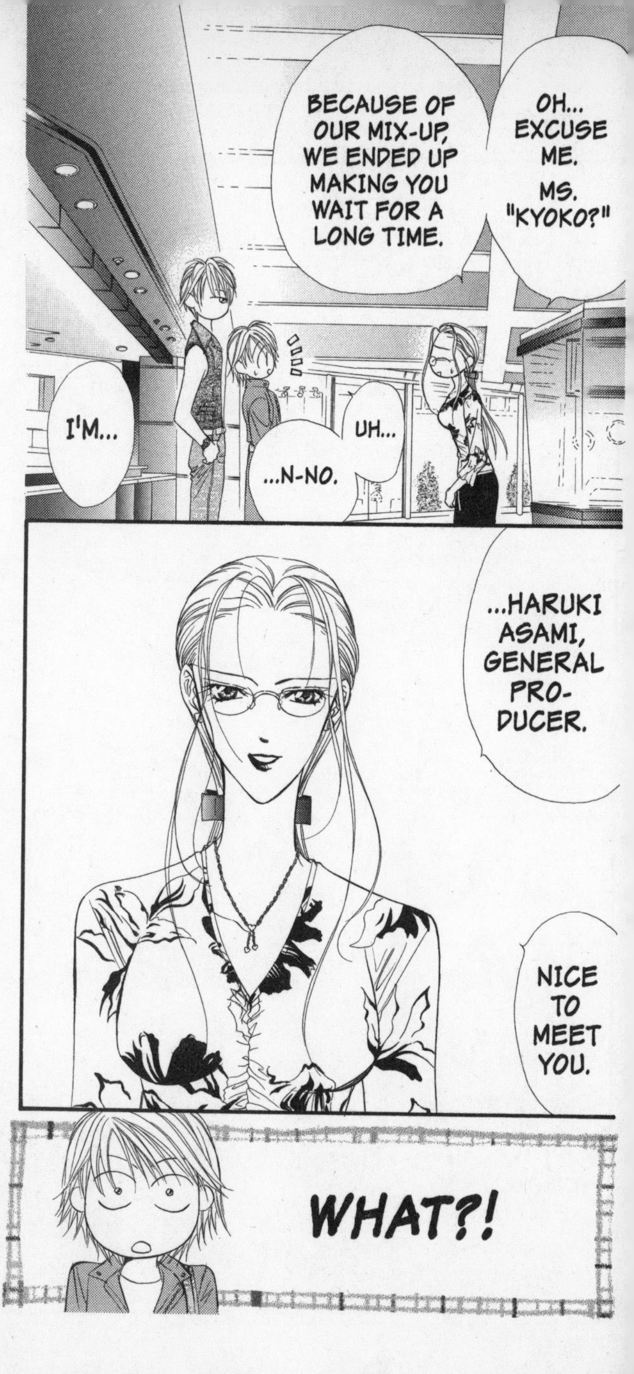
OH... EXCUSE ME. MS. "KYOKO?"
BECAUSE OF OUR MIX-UP, WE ENDED UP MAKING YOU WAIT FOR A LONG TIME.
UH...
...N-NO.
I'M...
...HARUKI ASAMI, GENERAL PRO-DUCER.
NICE TO MEET YOU.
WHAT?!
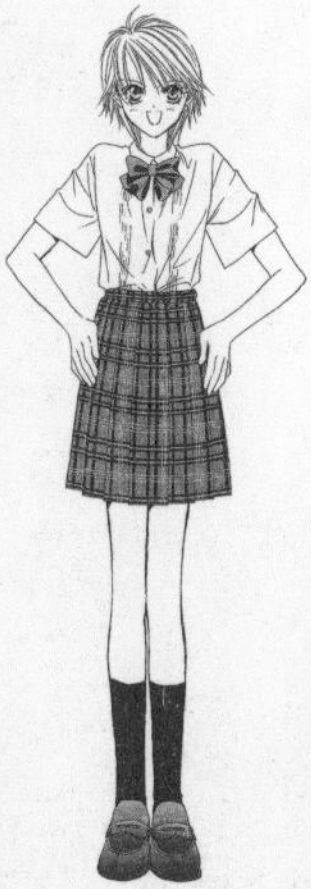

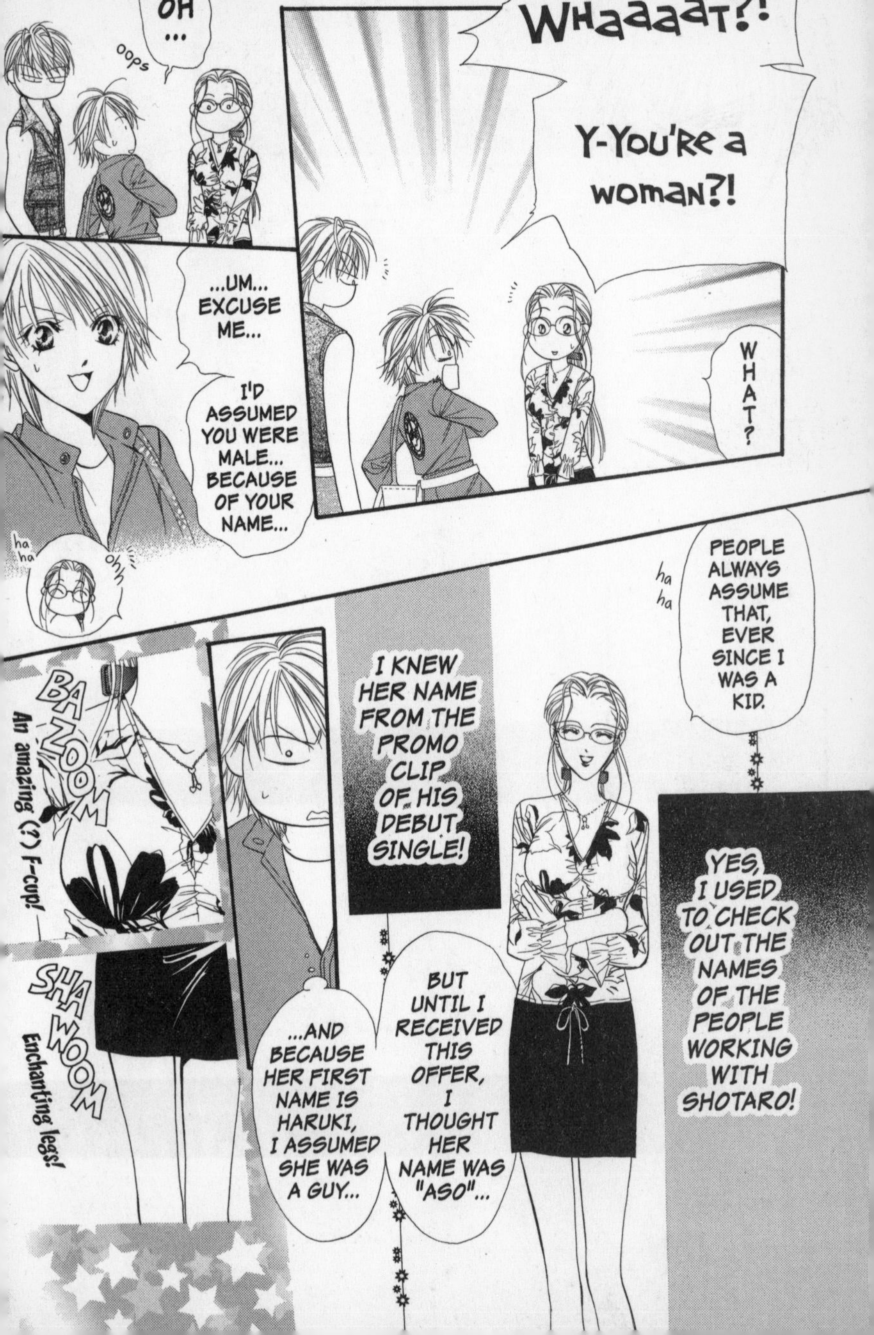

WHAAAAAT?!
Y-YOU'RE A WOMAN?!
WHAT?
OH ...
oops
...UM... EXCUSE ME...
I'D ASSUMED YOU WERE MALE... BECAUSE OF YOUR NAME...
ha ha
oh
PEOPLE ALWAYS ASSUME THAT, EVER SINCE I WAS A KID.
ha ha
YES, I USED TO CHECK OUT THE NAMES OF THE PEOPLE WORKING WITH SHOTARO!
I KNEW HER NAME FROM THE PROMO CLIP OF HIS DEBUT SINGLE!
BUT UNTIL I RECEIVED THIS OFFER, I THOUGHT HER NAME WAS "ASO"...
...AND BECAUSE HER FIRST NAME IS HARUKI, I ASSUMED SHE WAS A GUY...
BAZOOM
An amazing (?) F-cup!
SHAWOOM
Enchanting legs!

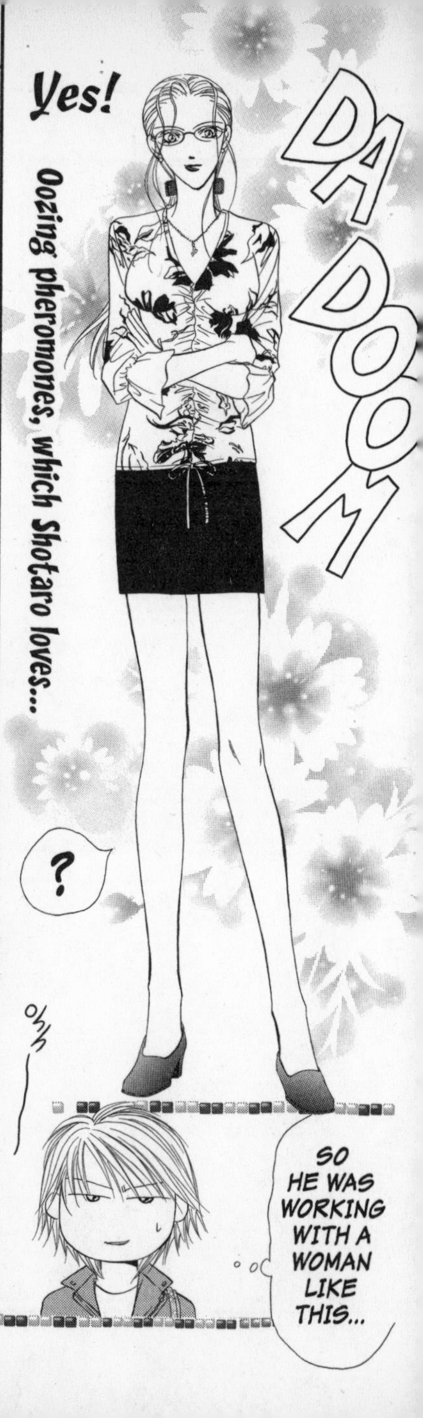
Yes!
Oozing pheromones, which Shotaro loves...
DA DOOM
?
Ohh
SO HE WAS WORKING WITH A WOMAN LIKE THIS...

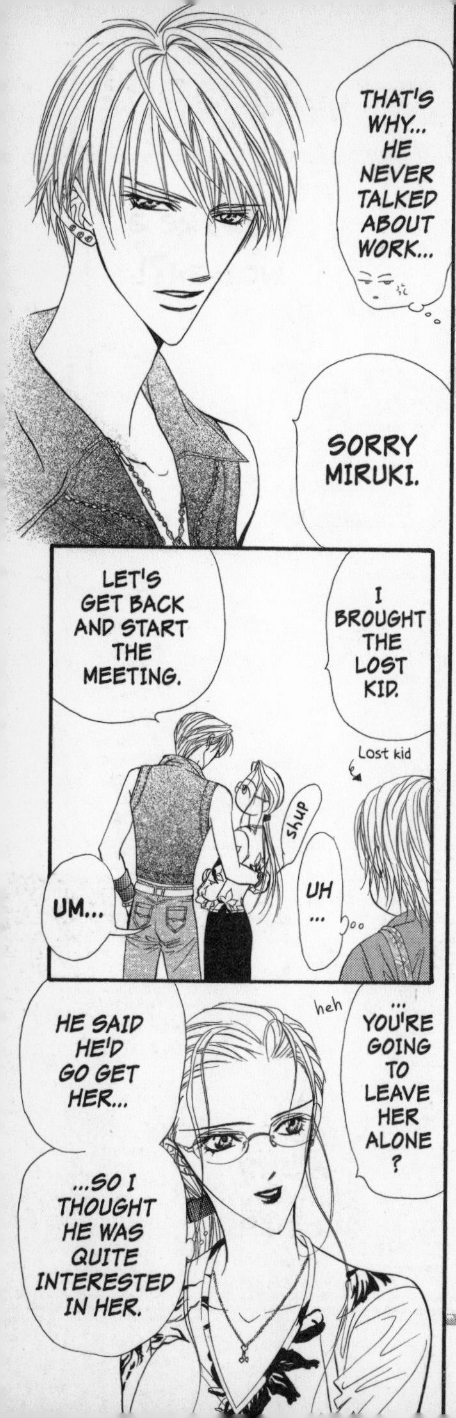
THAT'S WHY... HE NEVER TALKED ABOUT WORK...
SORRY MIRUKI.
I BROUGHT THE LOST KID.
Lost kid
LET'S GET BACK AND START THE MEETING.
shup
UH ...
UM...
heh
... YOU'RE GOING TO LEAVE HER ALONE?
HE SAID HE'D GO GET HER...
...SO I THOUGHT HE WAS QUITE INTERESTED IN HER.

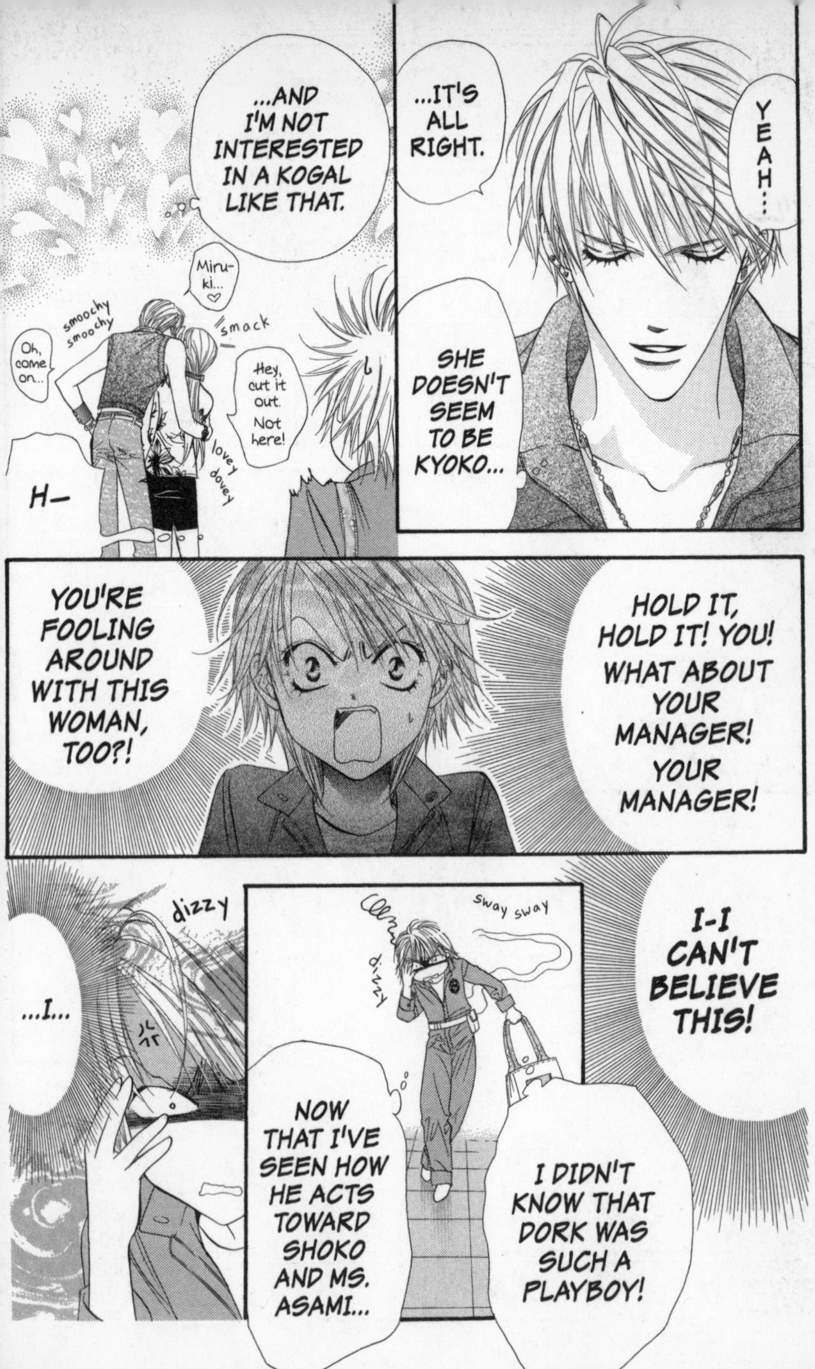
YEAH...
...IT'S ALL RIGHT.
SHE DOESN'T SEEM TO BE KYOKO...
...AND I'M NOT INTERESTED IN A KOGAL LIKE THAT.
Miru-ki... ♡
smack
Hey, cut it out. Not here!
smoochy smoochy
Oh, come on...
lovey dovey
H—
HOLD IT, HOLD IT! YOU! WHAT ABOUT YOUR MANAGER! YOUR MANAGER!
YOU'RE FOOLING AROUND WITH THIS WOMAN, TOO?!
I-I CAN'T BELIEVE THIS!
sway sway
dizzy
I DIDN'T KNOW THAT DORK WAS SUCH A PLAYBOY!
NOW THAT I'VE SEEN HOW HE ACTS TOWARD SHOKO AND MS. ASAMI...
dizzy
...I...

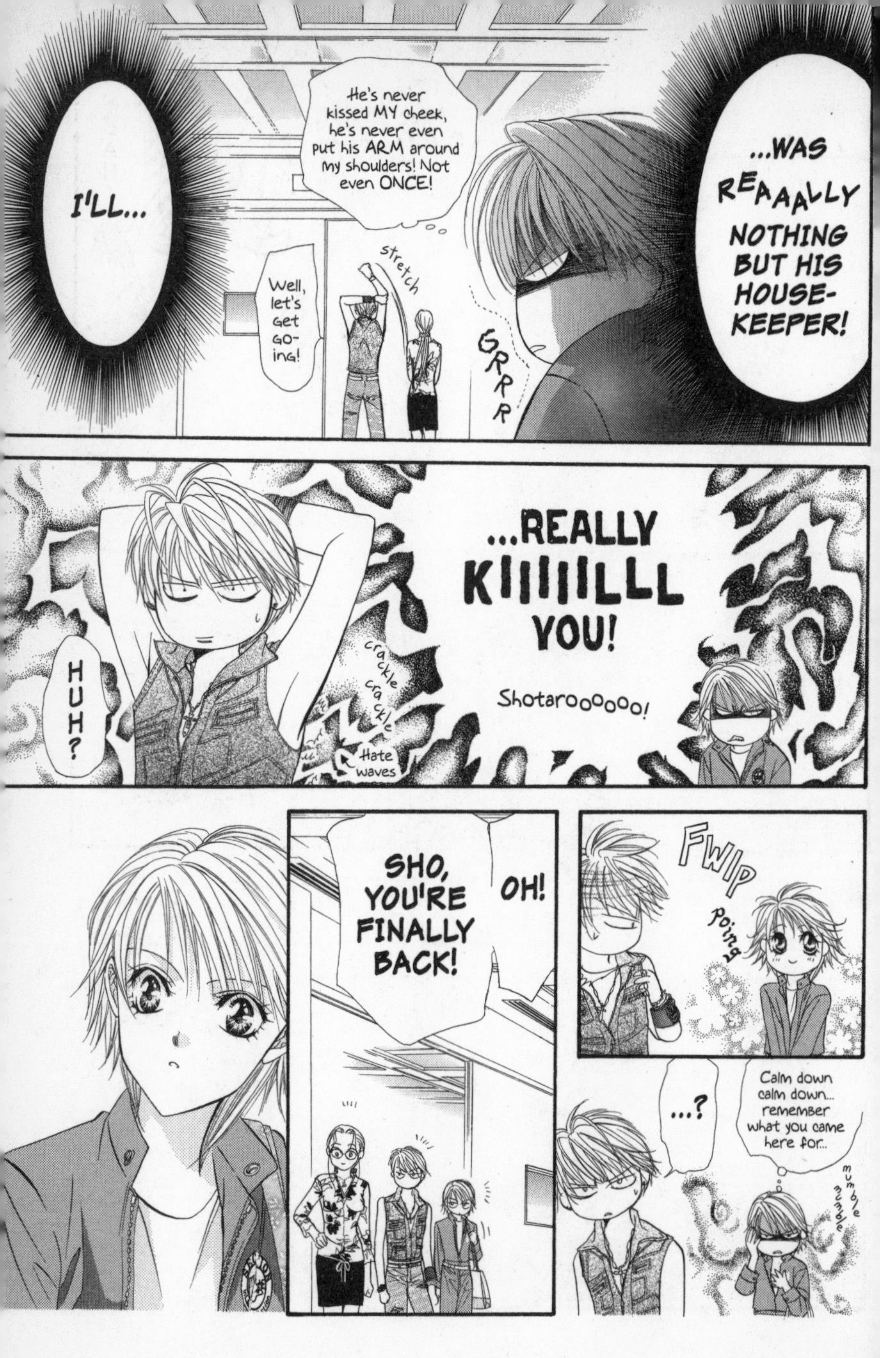
...WAS REAAAALLY NOTHING BUT HIS HOUSE-KEEPER!
He's never kissed MY cheek, he's never even put his ARM around my shoulders! Not even ONCE!
GRRR
stretch
Well, let's get go-ing!
I'LL...
...REALLY KIIIIILLL YOU!
Shotarooooooo!
crackle crackle
Hate waves
HUH?
FWIP
Poing
Calm down calm down... remember what you came here for..
mumble mumble
...?
OH!
SHO, YOU'RE FINALLY BACK!

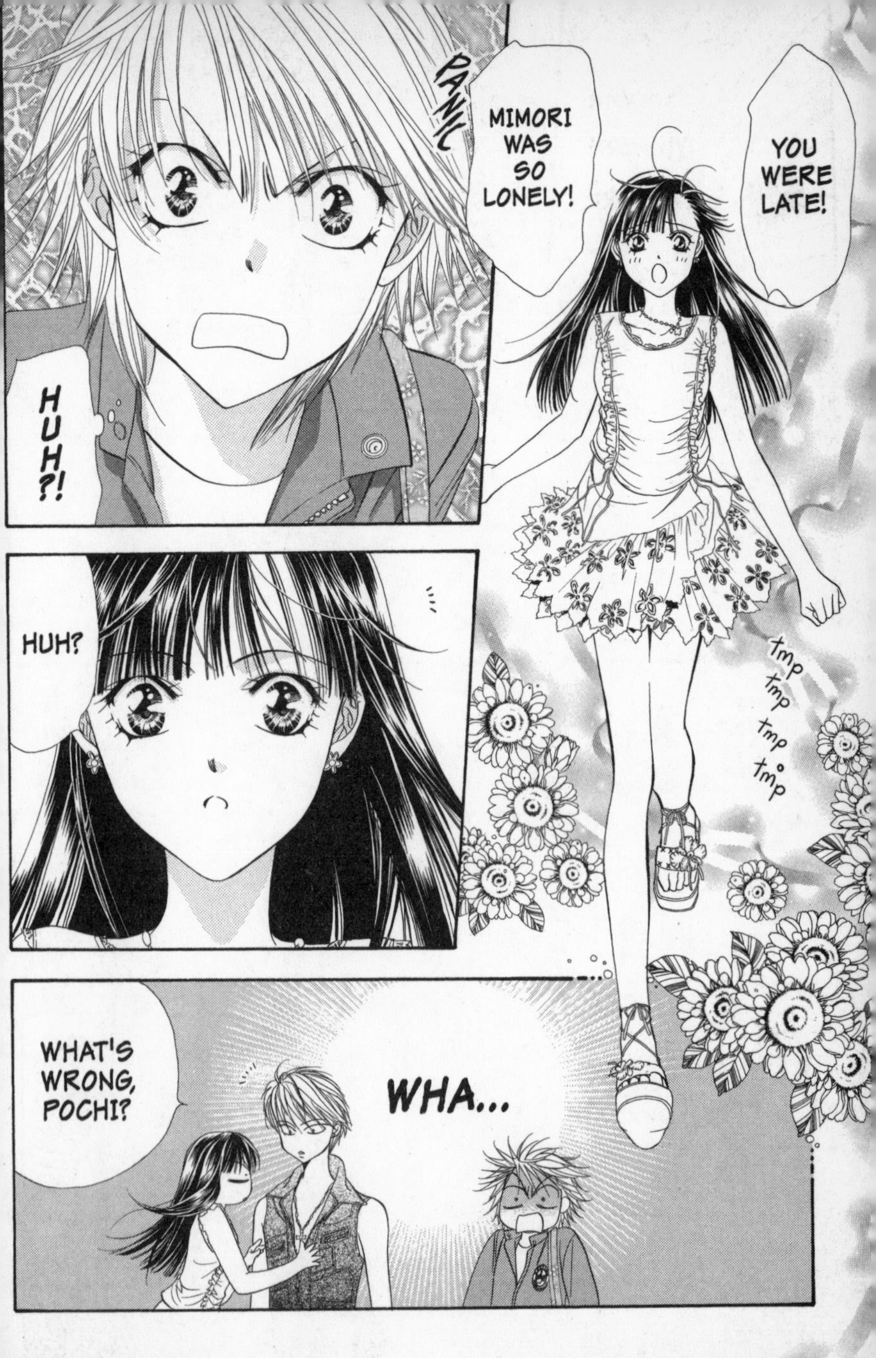
YOU WERE LATE!
MIMORI WAS SO LONELY!
tmp tmp tmp tmp
PANIC
HUH?!
HUH?
WHA...
WHAT'S WRONG, POCHI?

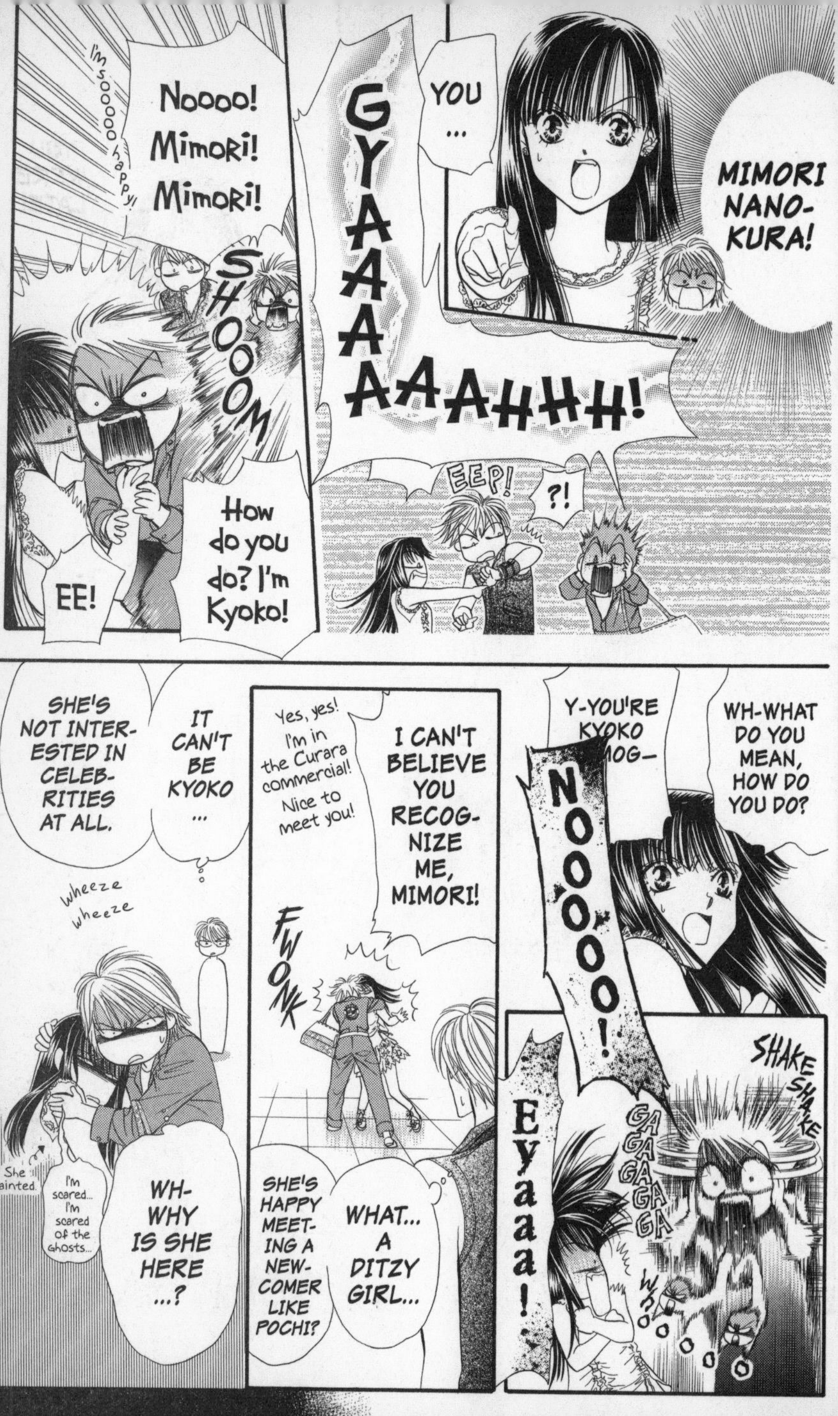
MIMORI NANO-KURA!
YOU ...
GYAAAAAAHHH!
EEP!
?!
Noooo! Mimori! Mimori!
I'm sooooo happy!
SHOOOOM
How do you do? I'm Kyoko!
EE!
WH-WHAT DO YOU MEAN, HOW DO YOU DO?
Y-YOU'RE KYOKO MOG—
NOOOOOO!
SHAKE SHAKE
GAGAGAGAGA
Whoooo
Eyaaa!
I CAN'T BELIEVE YOU RECOGNIZE ME, MIMORI!
Yes, yes! I'm in the Curara commercial! Nice to meet you!
FWONK
WHAT... A DITZY GIRL...
SHE'S HAPPY MEETING A NEWCOMER LIKE POCHI?
IT CAN'T BE KYOKO ...
SHE'S NOT INTERESTED IN CELEBRITIES AT ALL.
wheeze wheeze
WH-WHY IS SHE HERE ...?
I'm scared... I'm scared of the Ghosts...
She fainted.

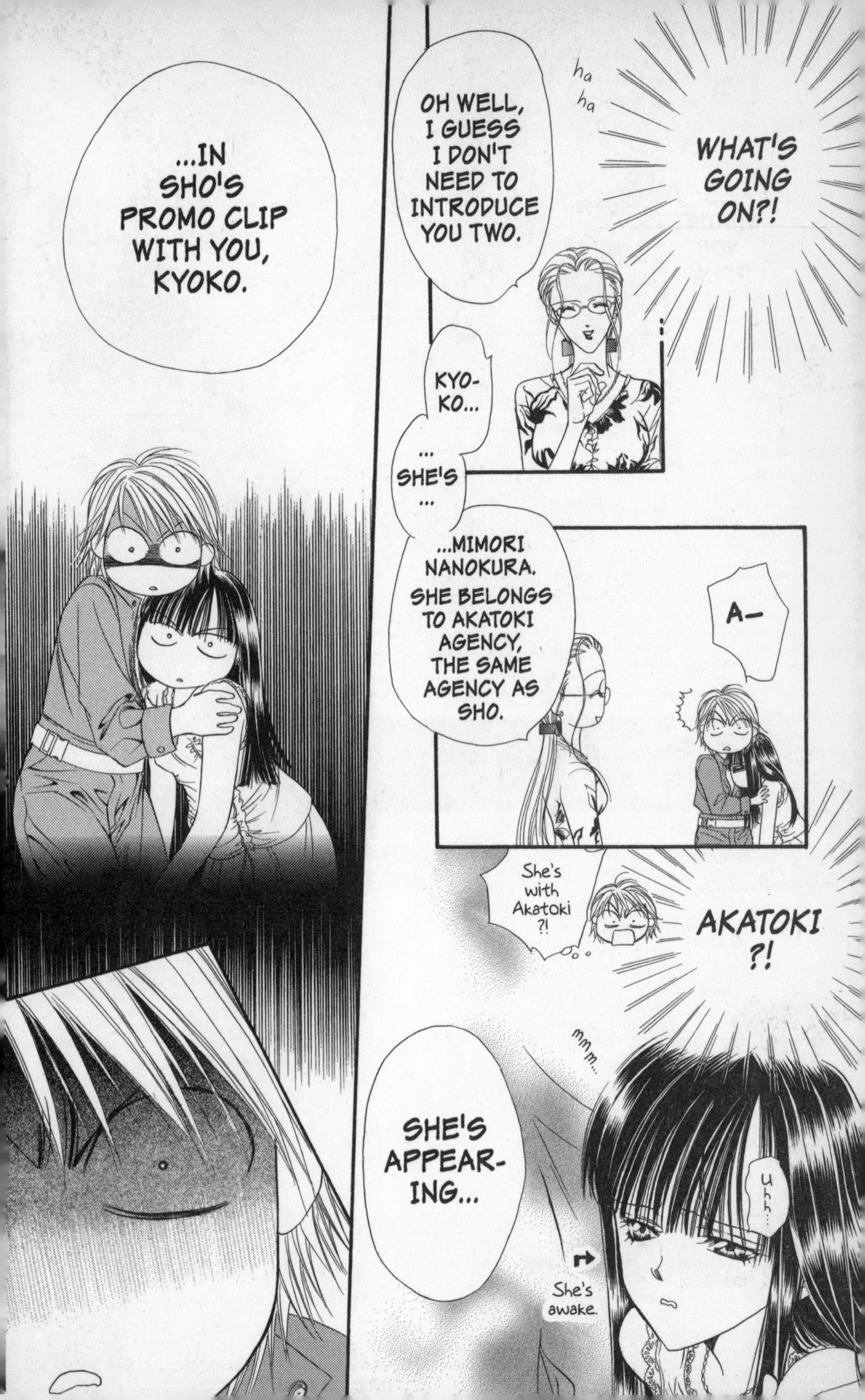
WHAT'S GOING ON?!
ha ha
OH WELL, I GUESS I DON'T NEED TO INTRODUCE YOU TWO.
KYO-KO...
... SHE'S ...
...MIMORI NANOKURA. SHE BELONGS TO AKATOKI AGENCY, THE SAME AGENCY AS SHO.
A–
AKATOKI ?!
She's with Akatoki ?!
mmm...
Uhh...
She's awake.
SHE'S APPEARING...
...IN SHO'S PROMO CLIP WITH YOU, KYOKO.

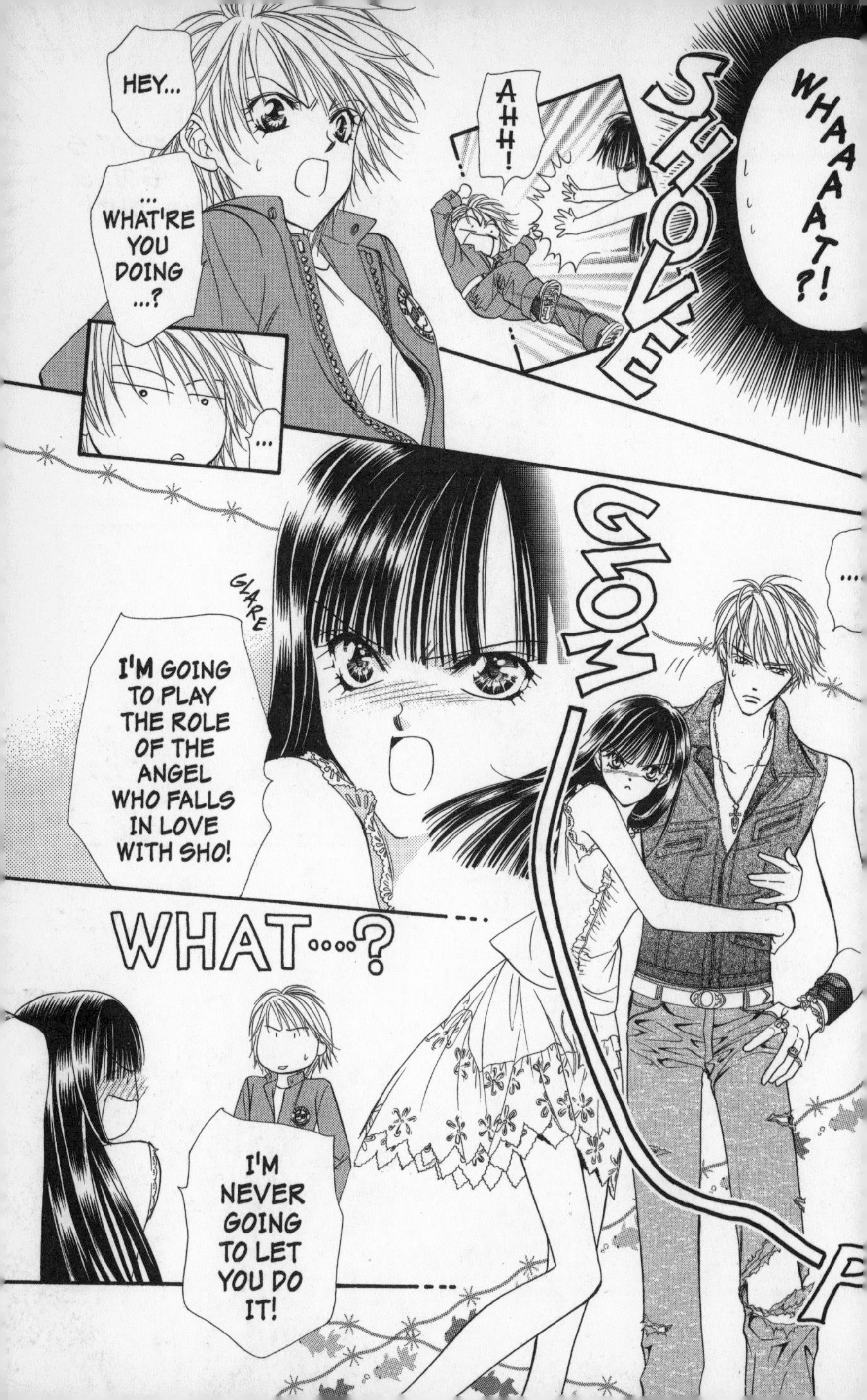
WHAAAAT?!
SHOVE
AHH!
HEY...
...WHAT'RE YOU DOING...?
...
...
GLOW
GLARE
I'M GOING TO PLAY THE ROLE OF THE ANGEL WHO FALLS IN LOVE WITH SHO!
WHAT....?
I'M NEVER GOING TO LET YOU DO IT!

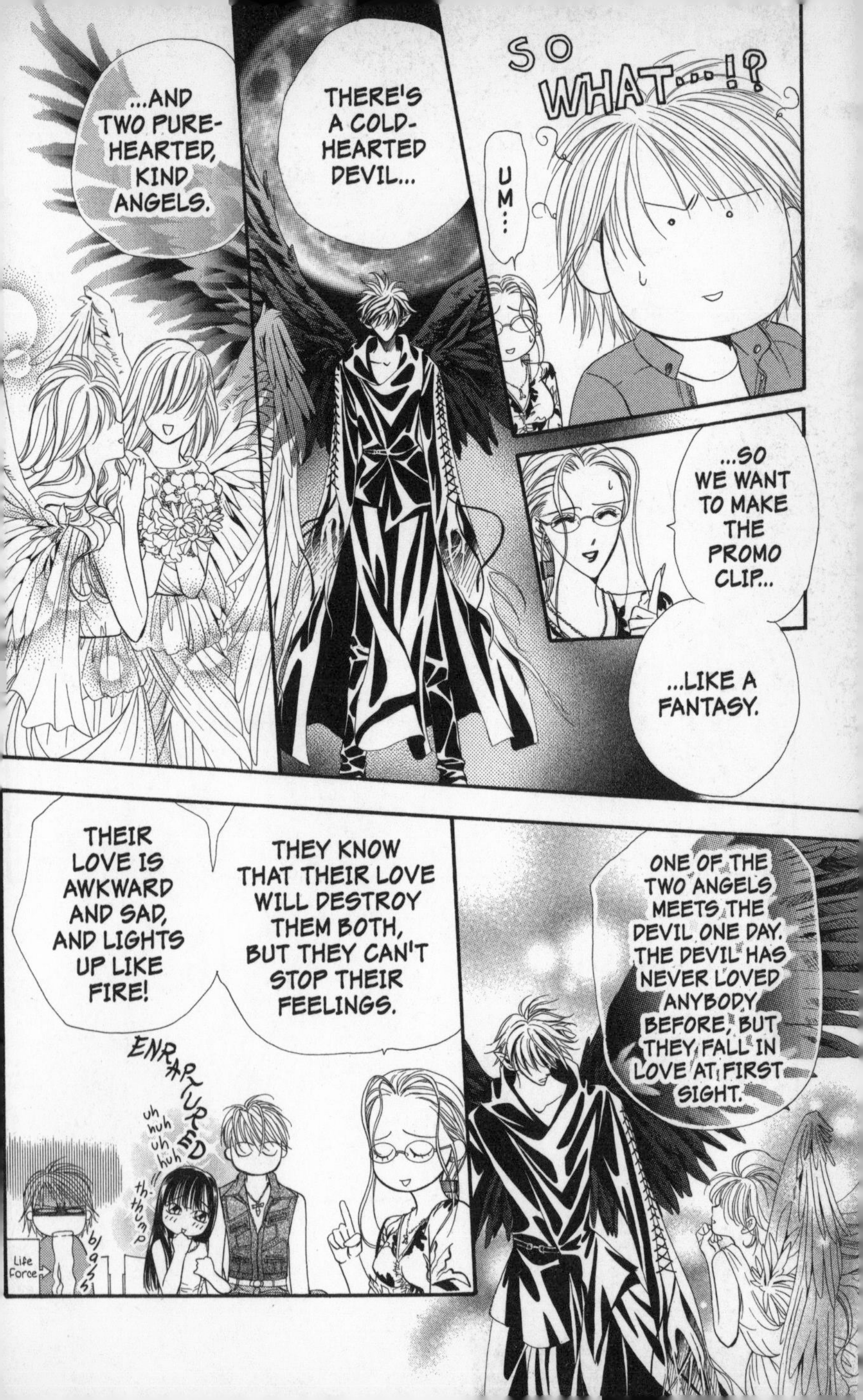
SO WHAT...!?
UM...
...SO WE WANT TO MAKE THE PROMO CLIP...
...LIKE A FANTASY.
THERE'S A COLD-HEARTED DEVIL...
...AND TWO PURE-HEARTED, KIND ANGELS.
ONE OF THE TWO ANGELS MEETS THE DEVIL ONE DAY. THE DEVIL HAS NEVER LOVED ANYBODY BEFORE, BUT THEY FALL IN LOVE AT FIRST SIGHT.
THEY KNOW THAT THEIR LOVE WILL DESTROY THEM BOTH, BUT THEY CAN'T STOP THEIR FEELINGS.
THEIR LOVE IS AWKWARD AND SAD, AND LIGHTS UP LIKE FIRE!
ENRAPTURED
uh huh uh huh
th-thump
Life Force

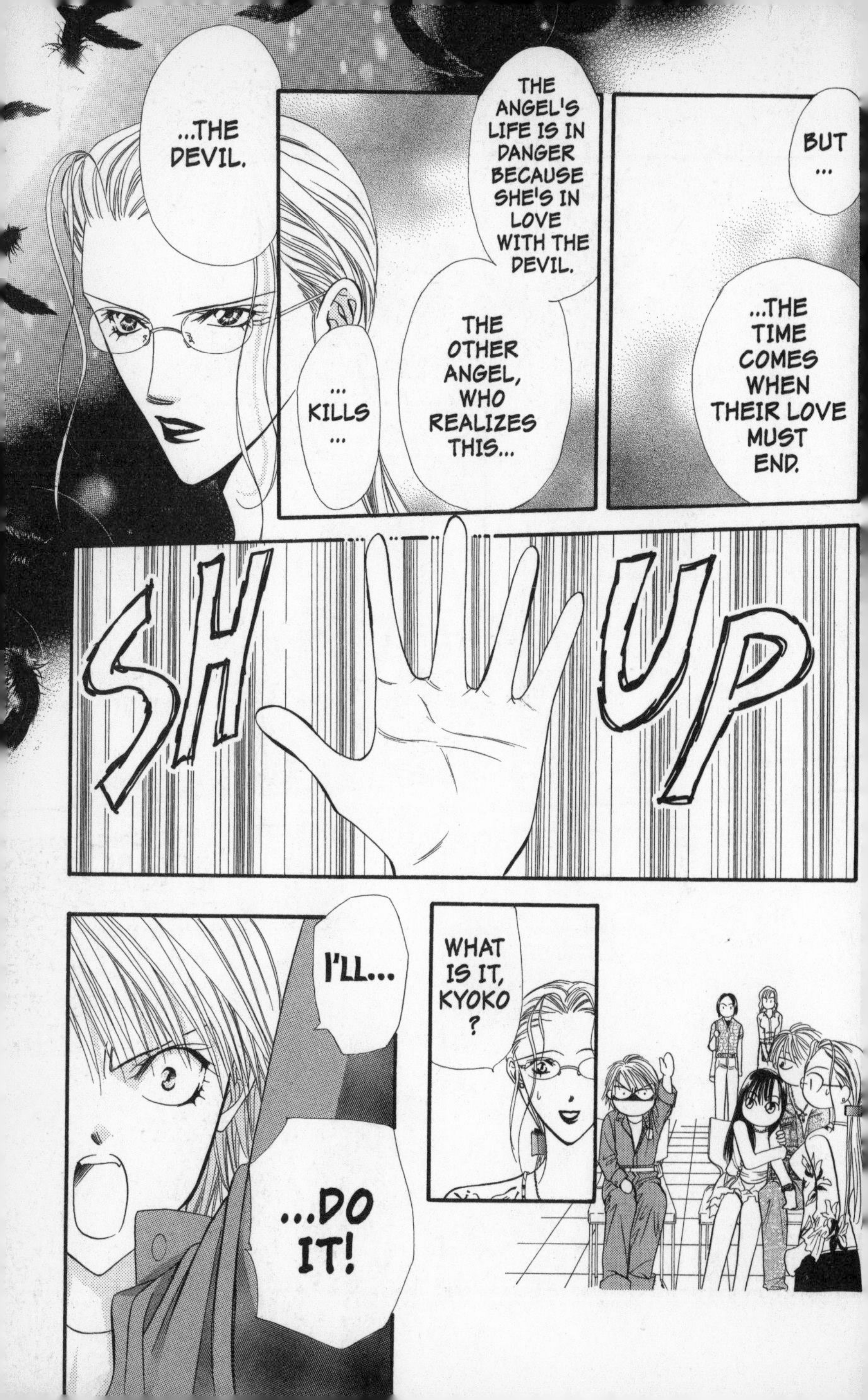
BUT ...
...THE TIME COMES WHEN THEIR LOVE MUST END.
THE ANGEL'S LIFE IS IN DANGER BECAUSE SHE'S IN LOVE WITH THE DEVIL.
THE OTHER ANGEL, WHO REALIZES THIS...
... KILLS ...
...THE DEVIL.
SHUT UP
WHAT IS IT, KYOKO?
I'LL...
...DO IT!

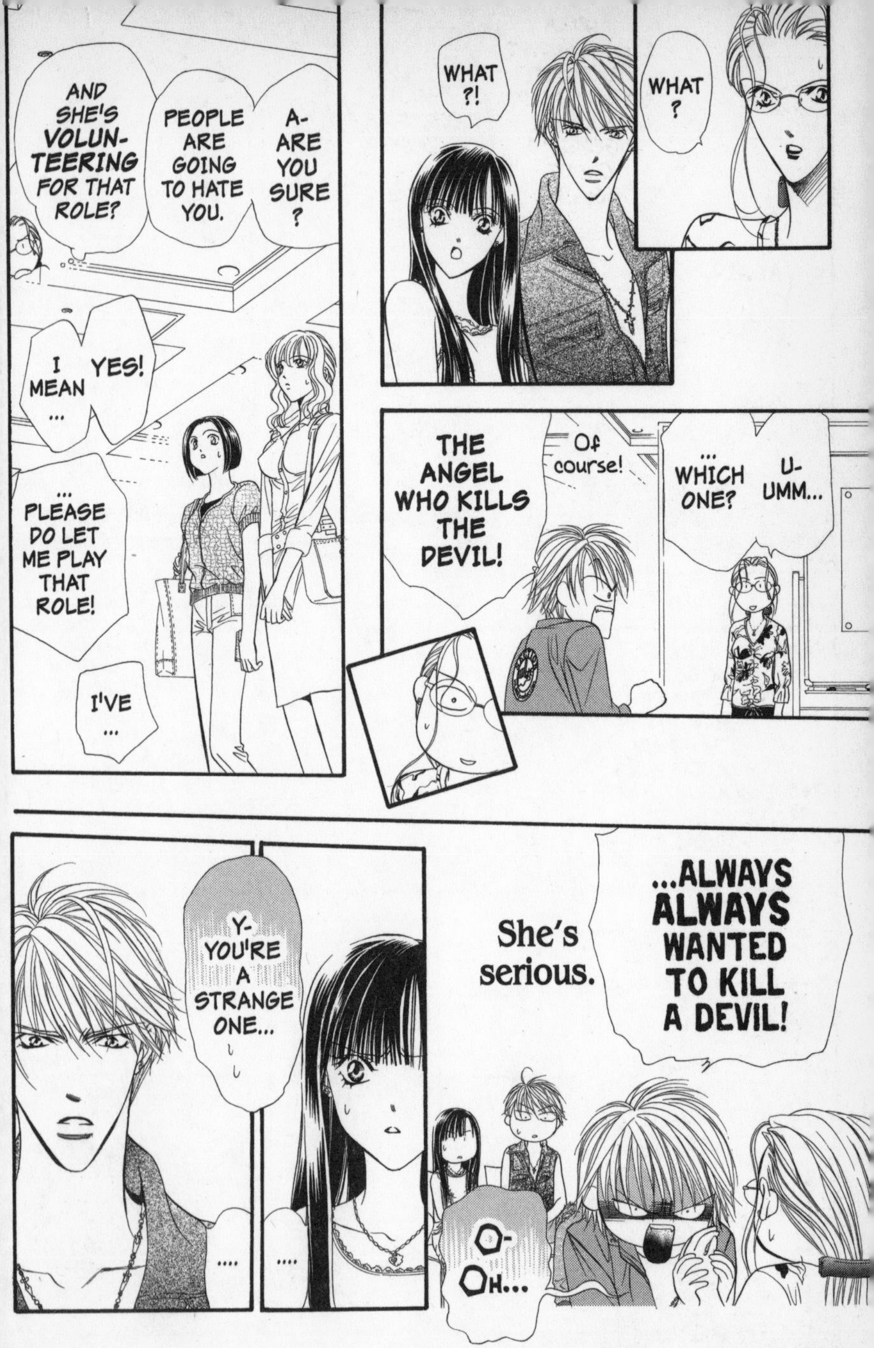
WHAT ?
WHAT ?!
U-UMM...
...WHICH ONE?
Of course!
THE ANGEL WHO KILLS THE DEVIL!
A-ARE YOU SURE ?
PEOPLE ARE GOING TO HATE YOU.
AND SHE'S VOLUNTEERING FOR THAT ROLE?
YES!
I MEAN ...
... PLEASE DO LET ME PLAY THAT ROLE!
I'VE ...
...ALWAYS ALWAYS WANTED TO KILL A DEVIL!
She's serious.
O-OH...
Y-YOU'RE A STRANGE ONE...
....
....

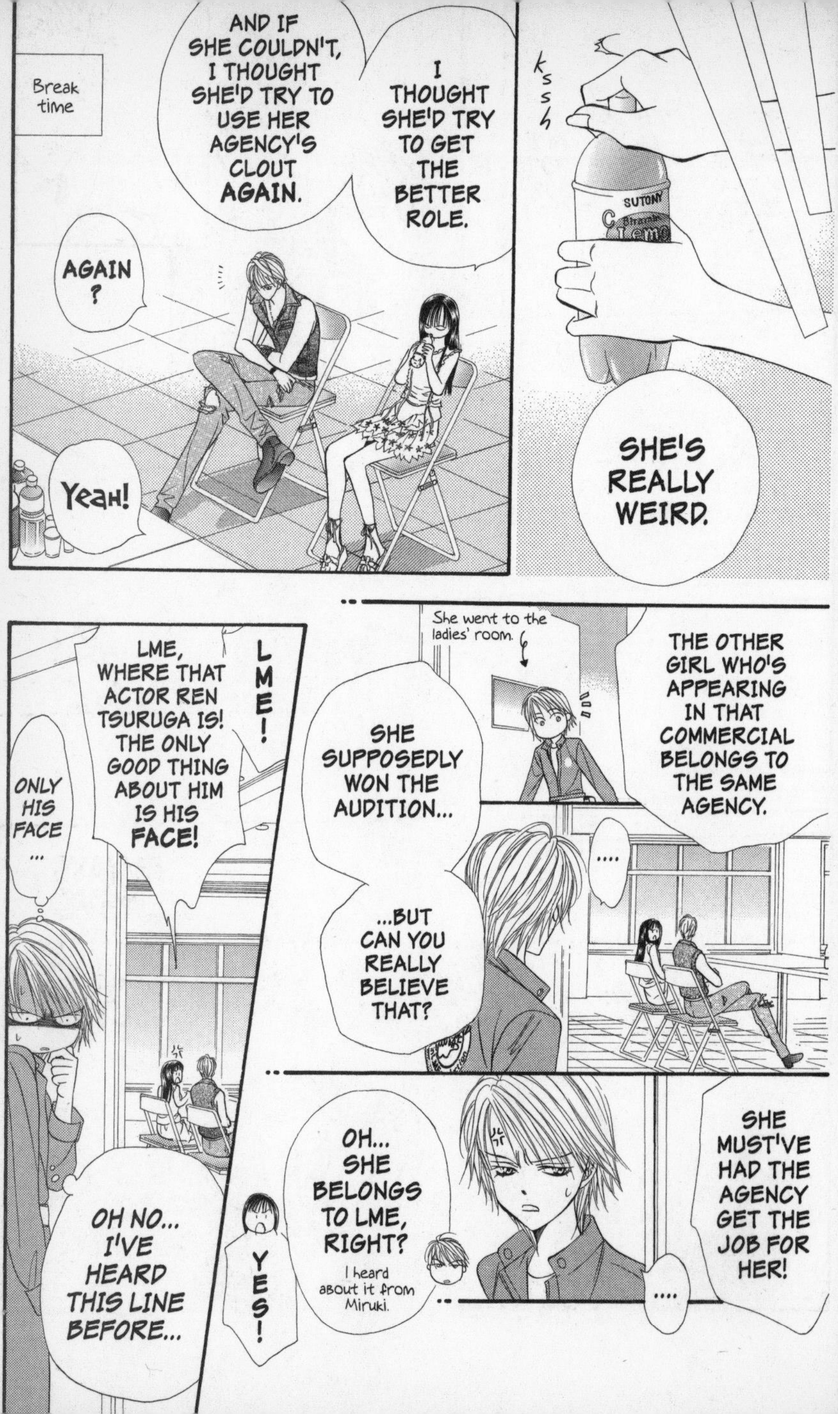
kssh
SHE'S REALLY WEIRD.
I THOUGHT SHE'D TRY TO GET THE BETTER ROLE.
AND IF SHE COULDN'T, I THOUGHT SHE'D TRY TO USE HER AGENCY'S CLOUT AGAIN.
Break time
AGAIN?
Yeah!
She went to the ladies' room.
THE OTHER GIRL WHO'S APPEARING IN THAT COMMERCIAL BELONGS TO THE SAME AGENCY.
....
SHE SUPPOSEDLY WON THE AUDITION...
...BUT CAN YOU REALLY BELIEVE THAT?
SHE MUST'VE HAD THE AGENCY GET THE JOB FOR HER!
....
OH... SHE BELONGS TO LME, RIGHT?
I heard about it from Miruki.
YES!
LME!
LME, WHERE THAT ACTOR REN TSURUGA IS! THE ONLY GOOD THING ABOUT HIM IS HIS FACE!
ONLY HIS FACE...
OH NO... I'VE HEARD THIS LINE BEFORE...

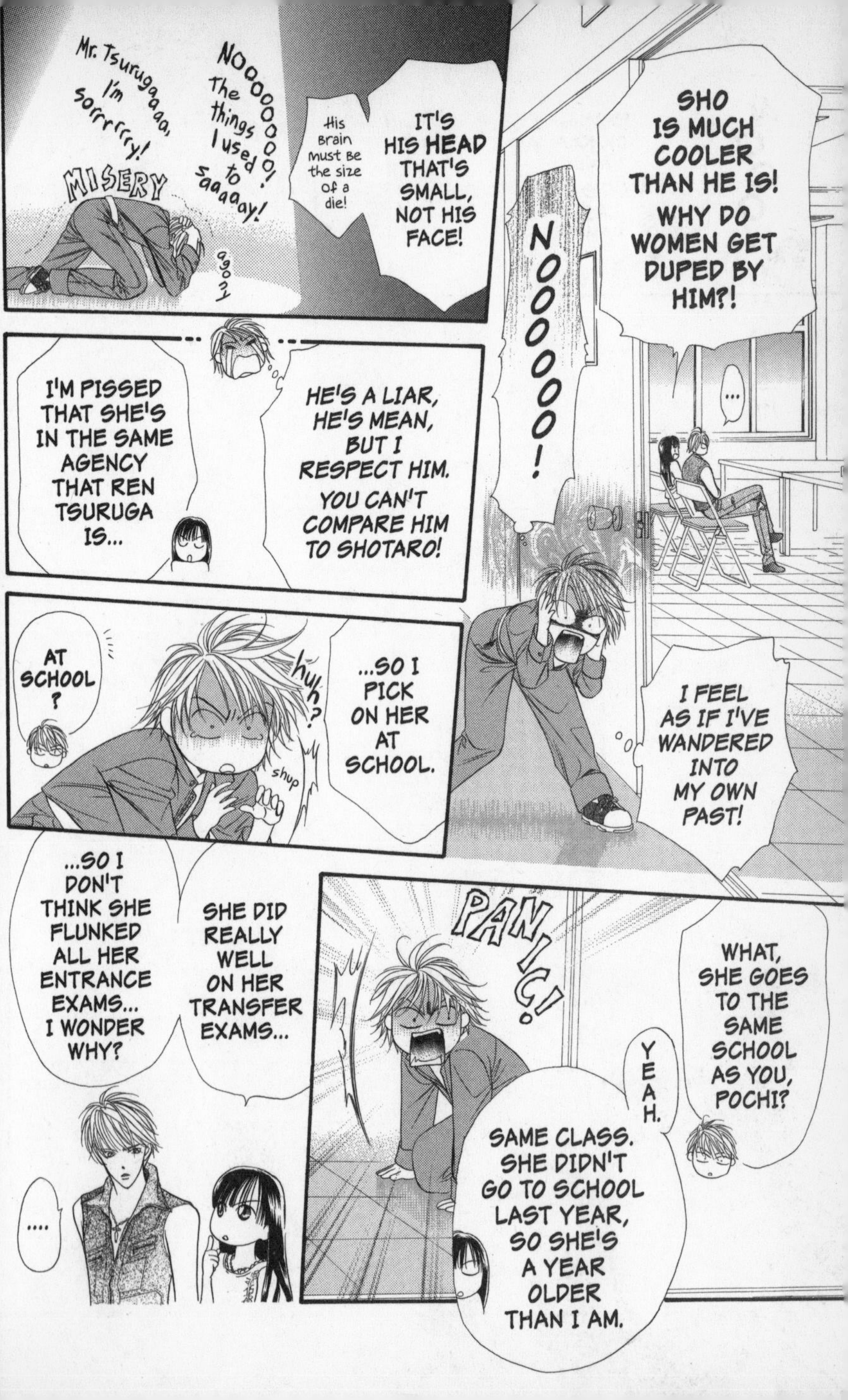
SHO IS MUCH COOLER THAN HE IS! WHY DO WOMEN GET DUPED BY HIM?!
NOOOOOOOO!
...
I FEEL AS IF I'VE WANDERED INTO MY OWN PAST!
IT'S HIS HEAD THAT'S SMALL, NOT HIS FACE!
His brain must be the size of a die!
Noooooooo! The things I used to saaaaay!
Mr. Tsurugaaaa, I'm sorrrrrry!
MISERY
agony
-- --
HE'S A LIAR, HE'S MEAN, BUT I RESPECT HIM. YOU CAN'T COMPARE HIM TO SHOTARO!
I'M PISSED THAT SHE'S IN THE SAME AGENCY THAT REN TSURUGA IS...
...SO I PICK ON HER AT SCHOOL.
huh?
shup
AT SCHOOL?
WHAT, SHE GOES TO THE SAME SCHOOL AS YOU, POCHI?
PANIC!
YEAH.
SAME CLASS. SHE DIDN'T GO TO SCHOOL LAST YEAR, SO SHE'S A YEAR OLDER THAN I AM.
SHE DID REALLY WELL ON HER TRANSFER EXAMS...
...SO I DON'T THINK SHE FLUNKED ALL HER ENTRANCE EXAMS... I WONDER WHY?
....

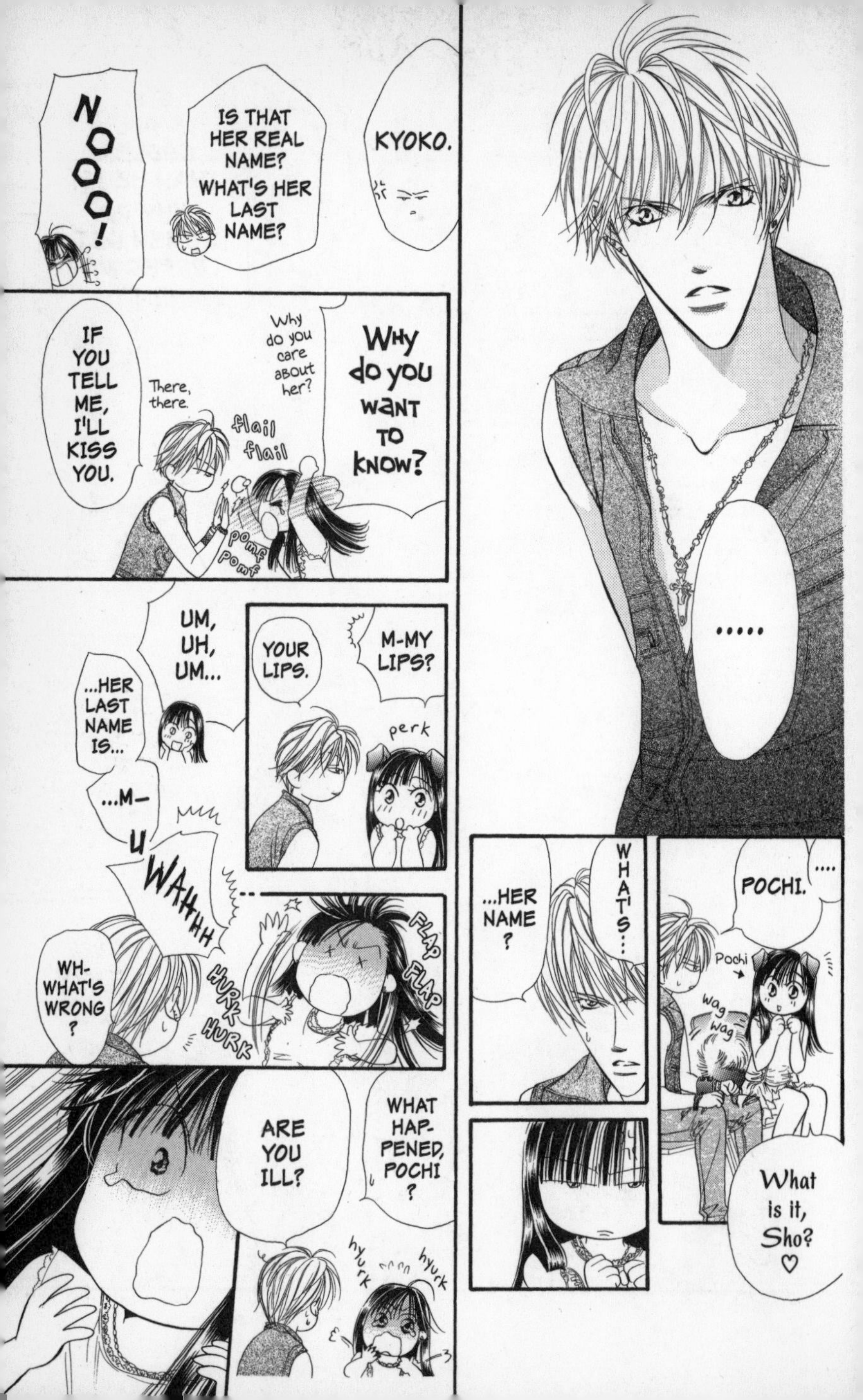
.....
....
POCHI.
Pochi
wag wag
What is it, Sho? ♡
WHAT'S...
...HER NAME ?
KYOKO.
IS THAT HER REAL NAME? WHAT'S HER LAST NAME?
NOOOO!
WHY do you WANT TO KNOW?
Why do you care about her?
flail flail
There, there.
IF YOU TELL ME, I'LL KISS YOU.
pomf pomf
M-MY LIPS?
YOUR LIPS.
perk
UM, UH, UM...
...HER LAST NAME IS...
...M-
U WAHHHH
FLAP FLAP
HURK HURK
WH-WHAT'S WRONG ?
WHAT HAP-PENED, POCHI ?
ARE YOU ILL?
hyurk hyurk

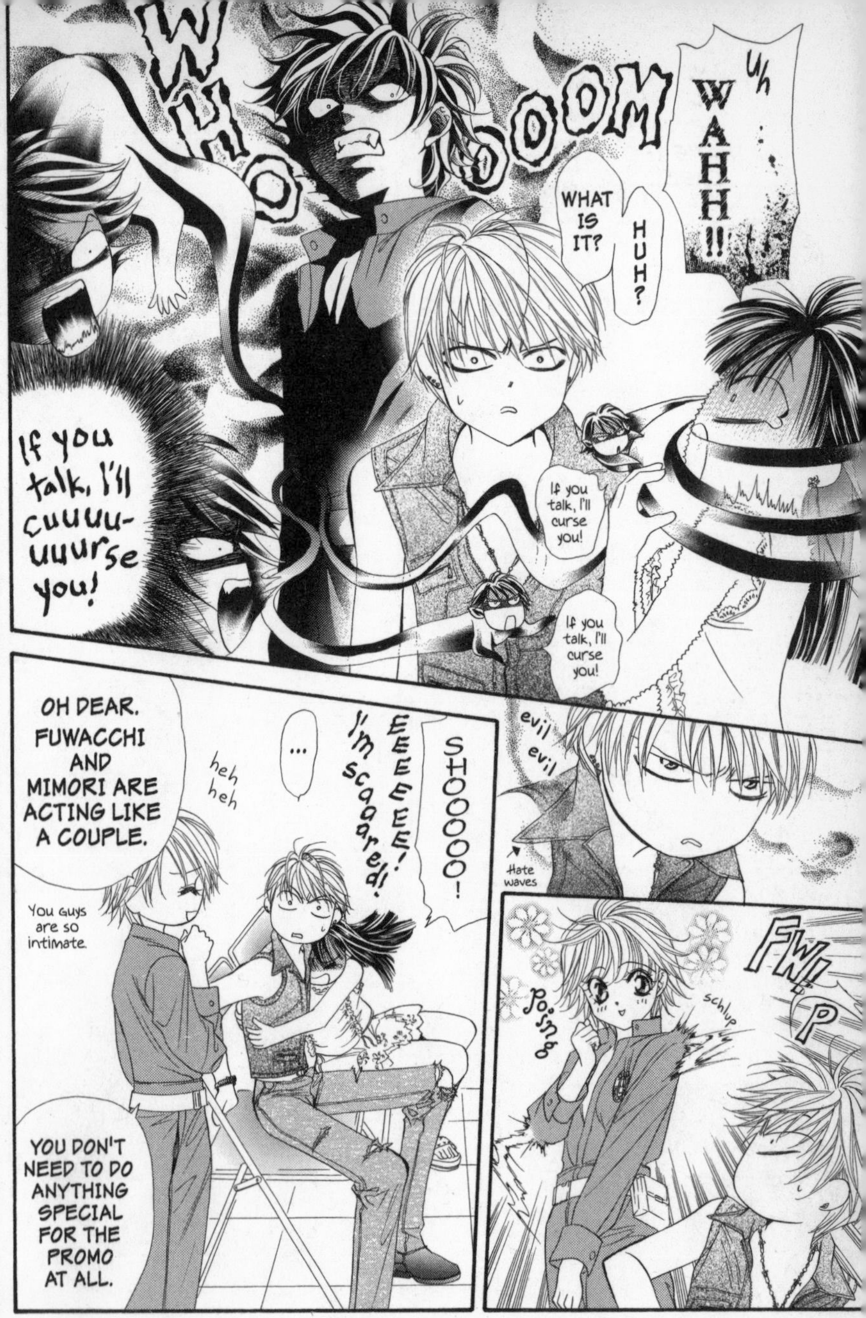
Uh WAHH!!
WHOOOOM
HUH?
WHAT IS IT?
If you talk, I'll curse you!
If you talk, I'll curse you!
If you talk, I'll cuuuu-uuurse you!
evil evil
Hate waves
FWIP
schlup
Posing
SHOOOOOO!
EEEEEE! I'm scaaared!
...
heh heh
OH DEAR. FUWACCHI AND MIMORI ARE ACTING LIKE A COUPLE.
You guys are so intimate.
YOU DON'T NEED TO DO ANYTHING SPECIAL FOR THE PROMO AT ALL.

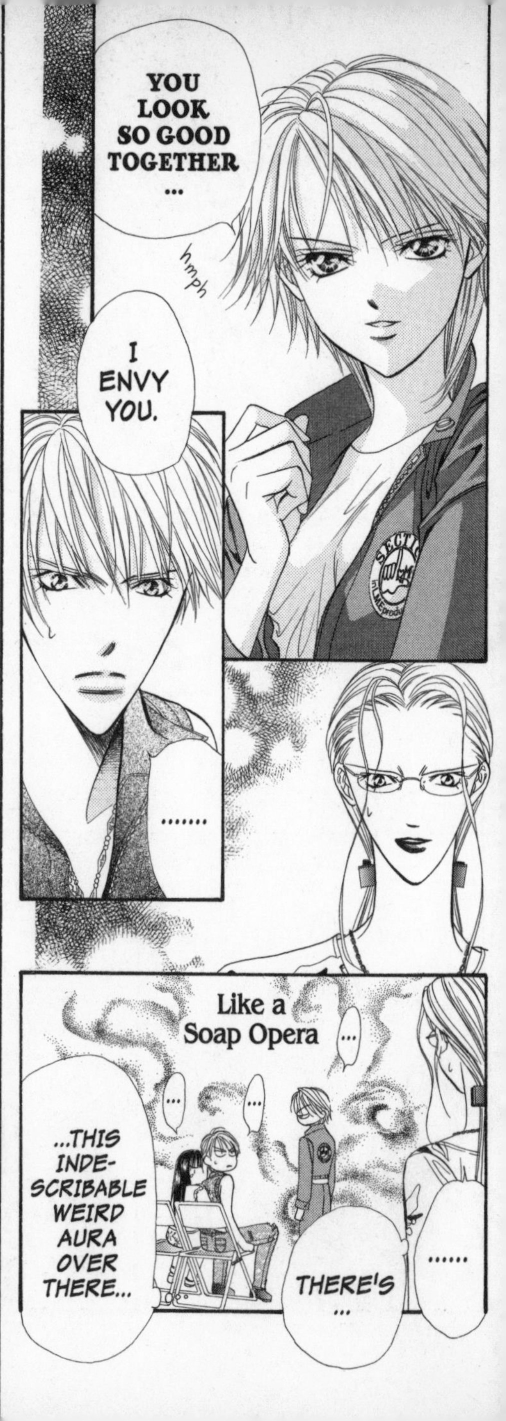
YOU LOOK SO GOOD TOGETHER ...
hmph
I ENVY YOU.
....
Like a Soap Opera
...
...
...
......
THERE'S ...
...THIS INDE-SCRIBABLE WEIRD AURA OVER THERE...
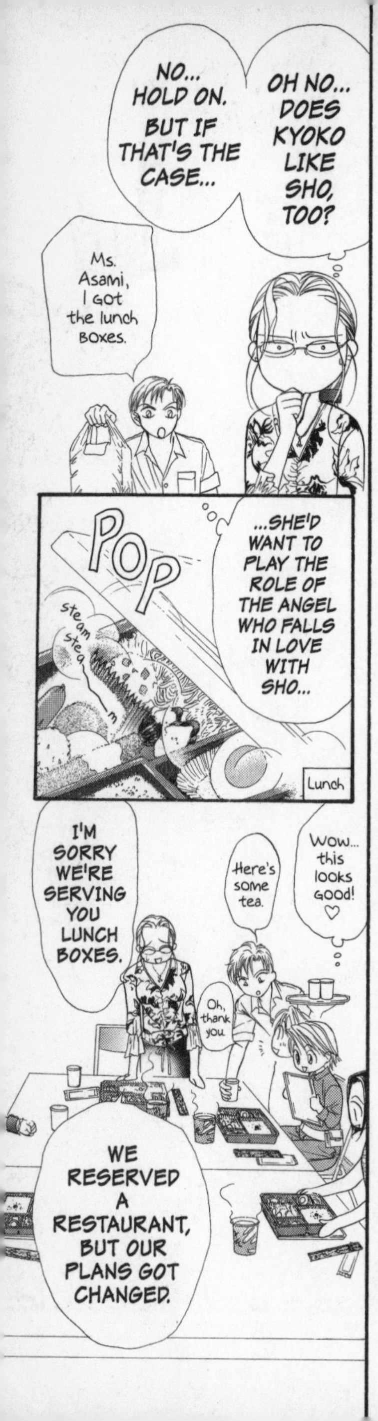
OH NO... DOES KYOKO LIKE SHO, TOO?
NO... HOLD ON. BUT IF THAT'S THE CASE...
Ms. Asami, I got the lunch boxes.
...SHE'D WANT TO PLAY THE ROLE OF THE ANGEL WHO FALLS IN LOVE WITH SHO...
POP
steam steam
Lunch
Wow... this looks good! ♡
Here's some tea.
I'M SORRY WE'RE SERVING YOU LUNCH BOXES.
Oh, thank you.
WE RESERVED A RESTAURANT, BUT OUR PLANS GOT CHANGED.

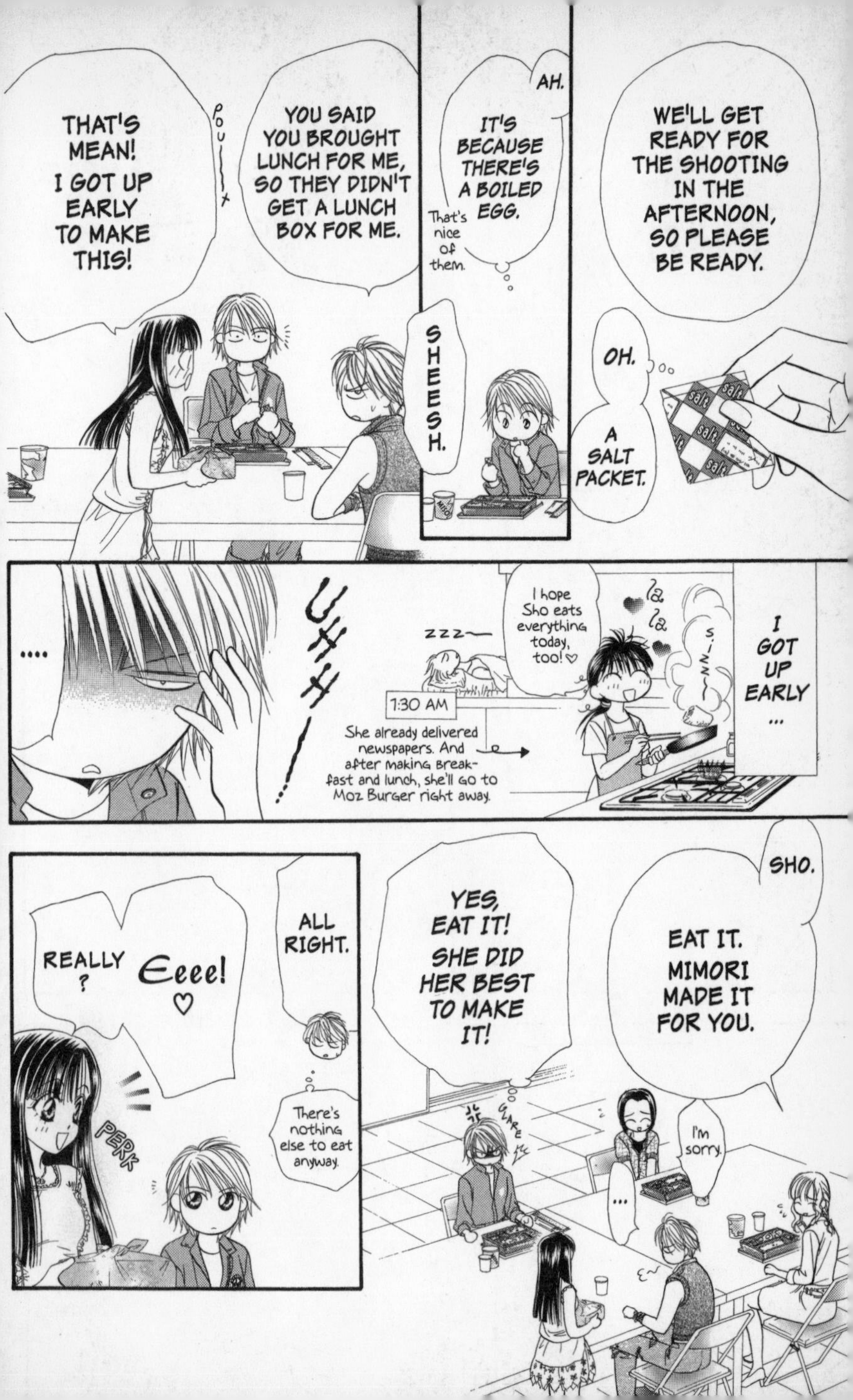
WE'LL GET READY FOR THE SHOOTING IN THE AFTERNOON, SO PLEASE BE READY.
OH.
A SALT PACKET.
salt
AH.
IT'S BECAUSE THERE'S A BOILED EGG.
That's nice of them.
YOU SAID YOU BROUGHT LUNCH FOR ME, SO THEY DIDN'T GET A LUNCH BOX FOR ME.
SHEESH.
POUT
THAT'S MEAN! I GOT UP EARLY TO MAKE THIS!
I GOT UP EARLY...
I hope Sho eats everything today, too! ♡
la la
SIZZ~
ZZZ~
1:30 AM
She already delivered newspapers. And after making break-fast and lunch, she'll go to Moz Burger right away.
UGH—!
....
SHO.
EAT IT. MIMORI MADE IT FOR YOU.
I'm sorry.
YES, EAT IT! SHE DID HER BEST TO MAKE IT!
GLARE
...
ALL RIGHT.
There's nothing else to eat anyway.
REALLY?
Eeee! ♡
PERK

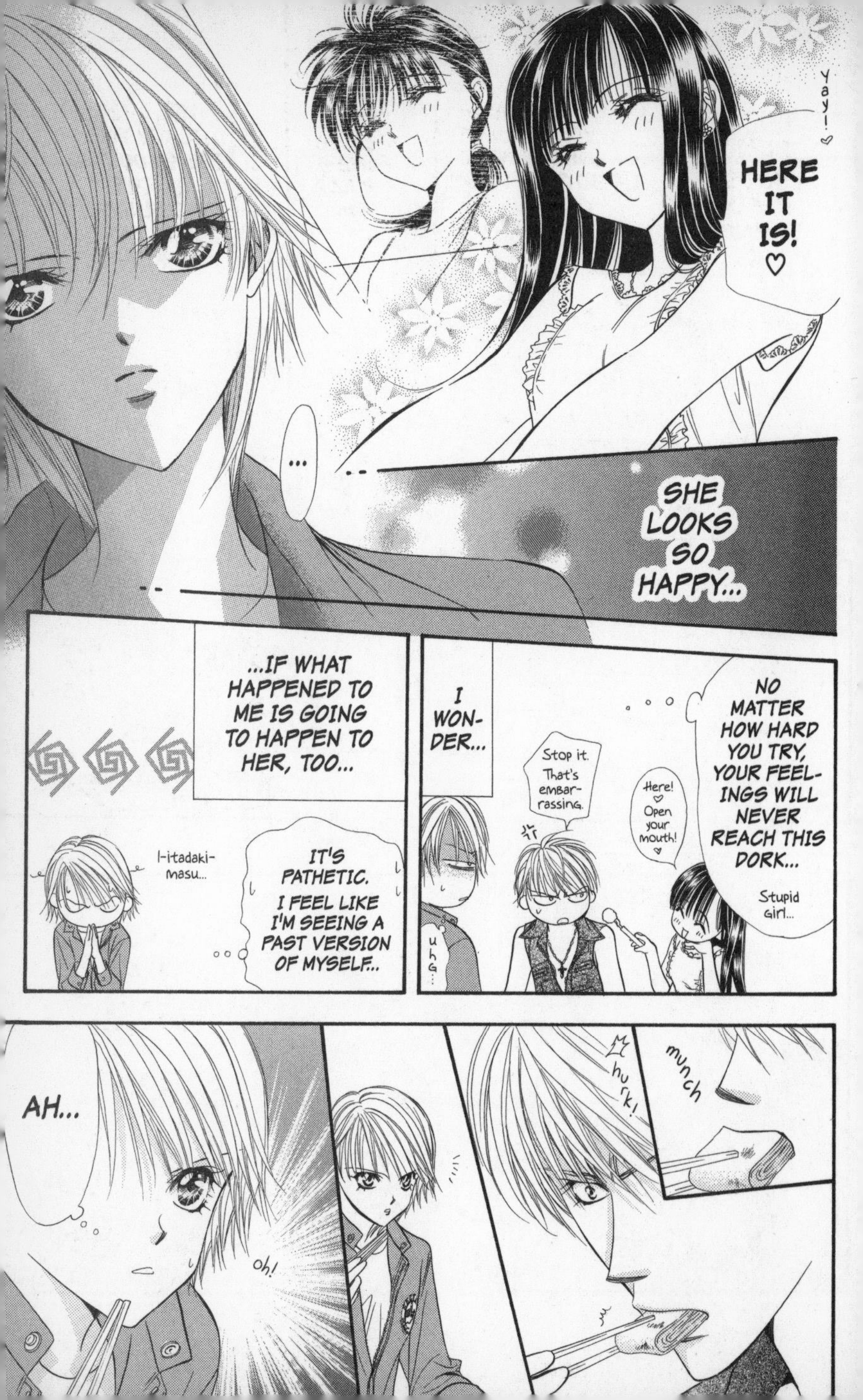
Yay! ♥
HERE IT IS! ♥
...
SHE LOOKS SO HAPPY...
NO MATTER HOW HARD YOU TRY, YOUR FEELINGS WILL NEVER REACH THIS DORK...
Stupid girl...
Here! ♥ Open your mouth! ♥
Stop it. That's embarrassing.
I WONDER...
uhg...
...IF WHAT HAPPENED TO ME IS GOING TO HAPPEN TO HER, TOO...
IT'S PATHETIC. I FEEL LIKE I'M SEEING A PAST VERSION OF MYSELF...
I-itadaki-masu...
munch
hurk!
AH...
oh!

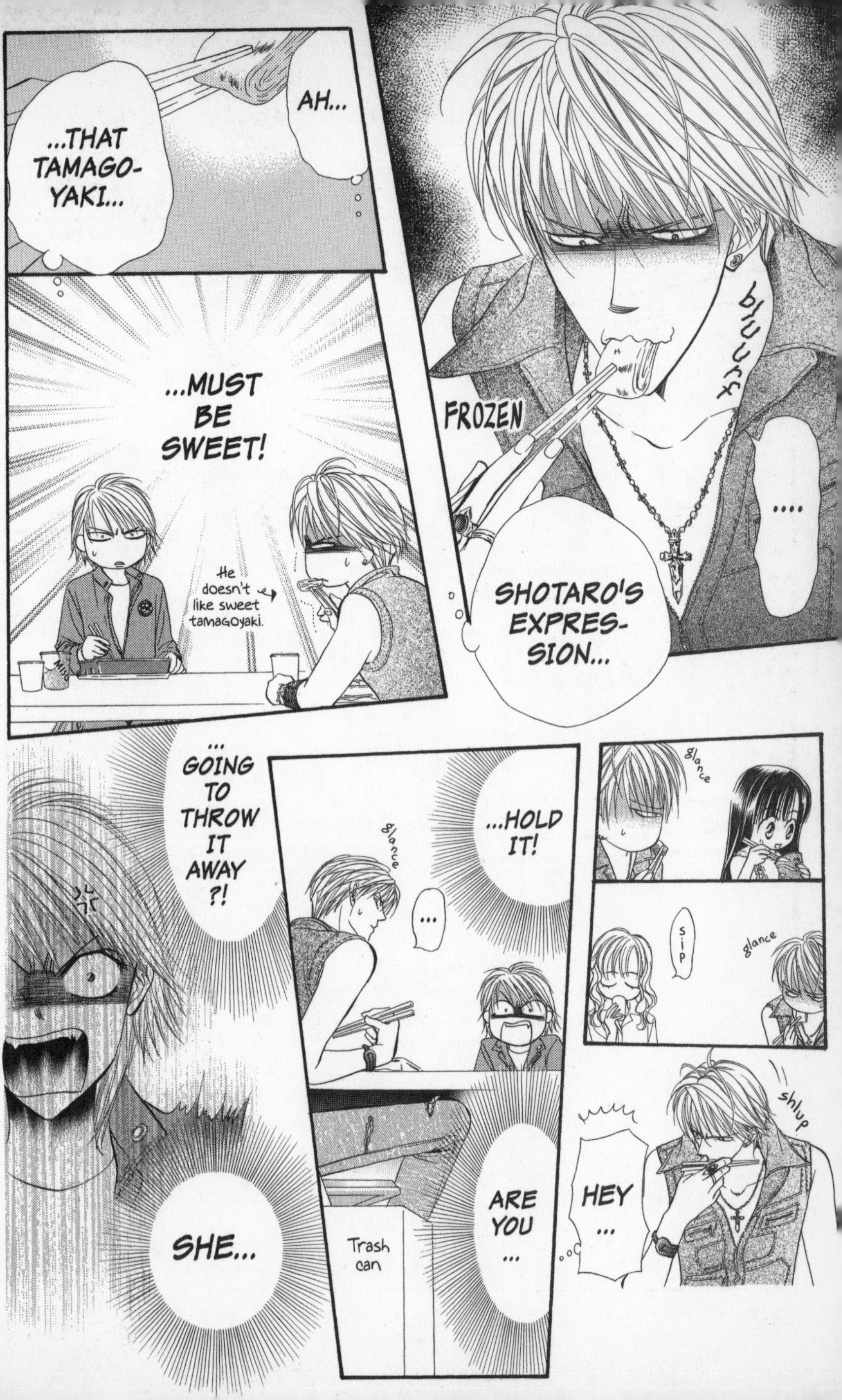
blurrf
....
FROZEN
SHOTARO'S EXPRES-SION...
AH...
...THAT TAMAGO-YAKI...
...MUST BE SWEET!
He doesn't like sweet tamagoyaki.
glance
sip
glance
shlup
HEY ...
...HOLD IT!
glance
...
ARE YOU ...
Trash can
... GOING TO THROW IT AWAY ?!
SHE...

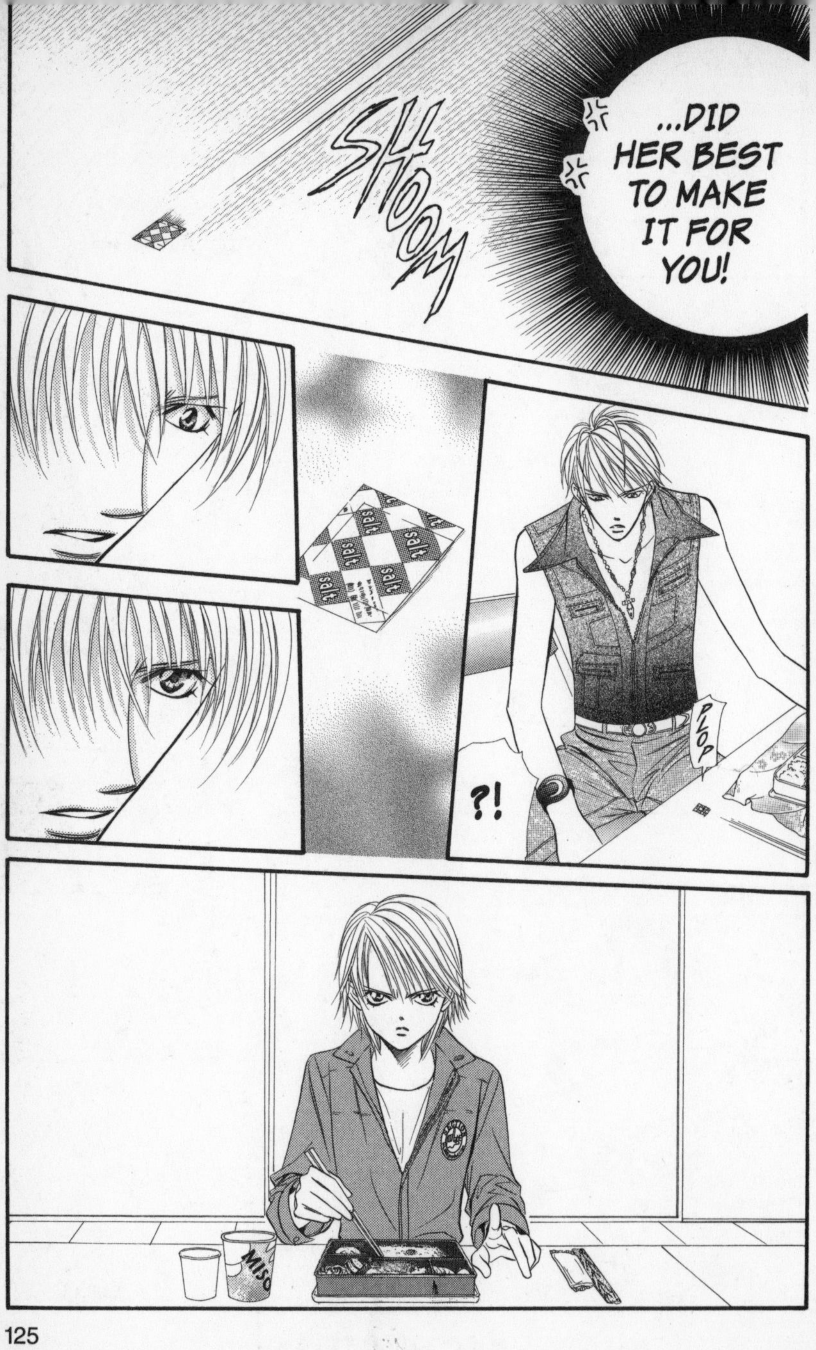
...DID HER BEST TO MAKE IT FOR YOU!
SHOOM
PLOP
?!
salt
MISO

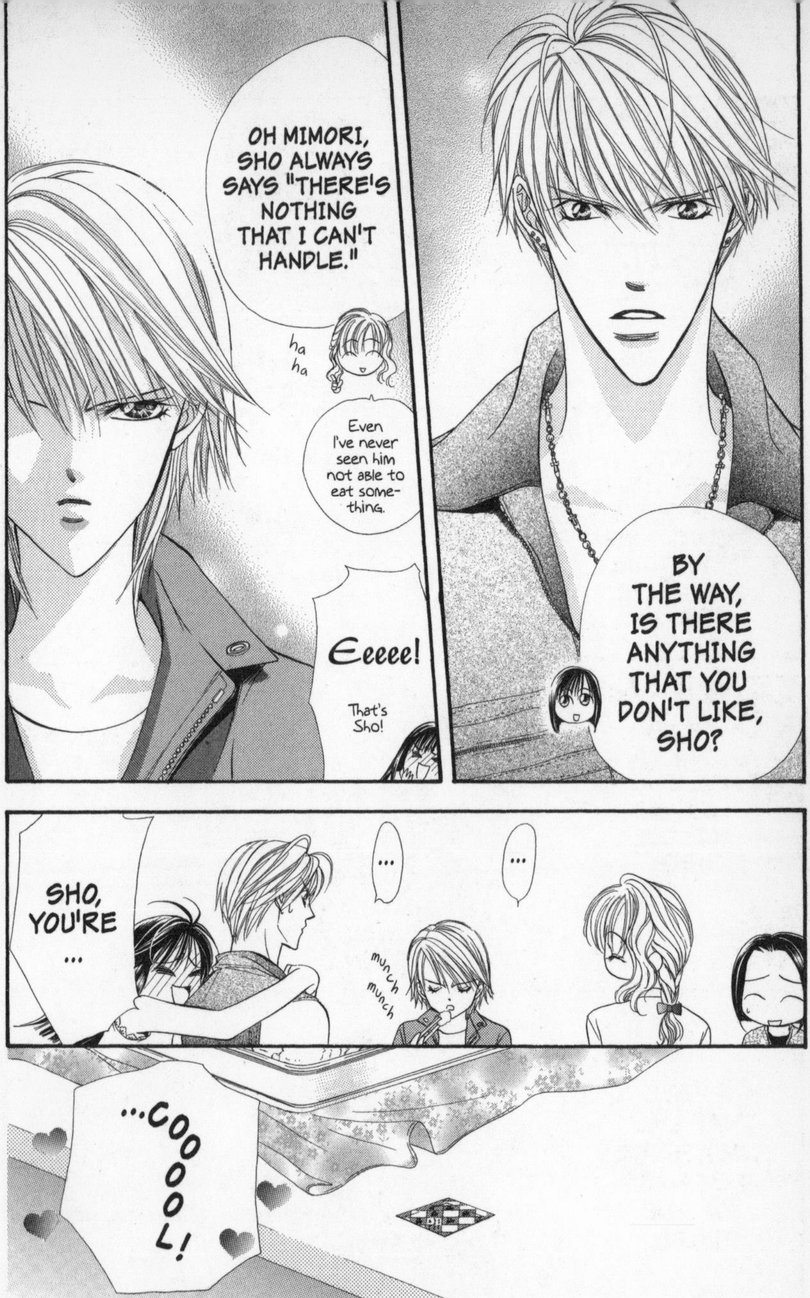
BY THE WAY, IS THERE ANYTHING THAT YOU DON'T LIKE, SHO?
OH MIMORI, SHO ALWAYS SAYS "THERE'S NOTHING THAT I CAN'T HANDLE."
ha ha
Even I've never seen him not able to eat some-thing.
Eeeee!
That's Sho!
...
...
SHO, YOU'RE ...
munch munch
...COOOOOL!

End of Act 39

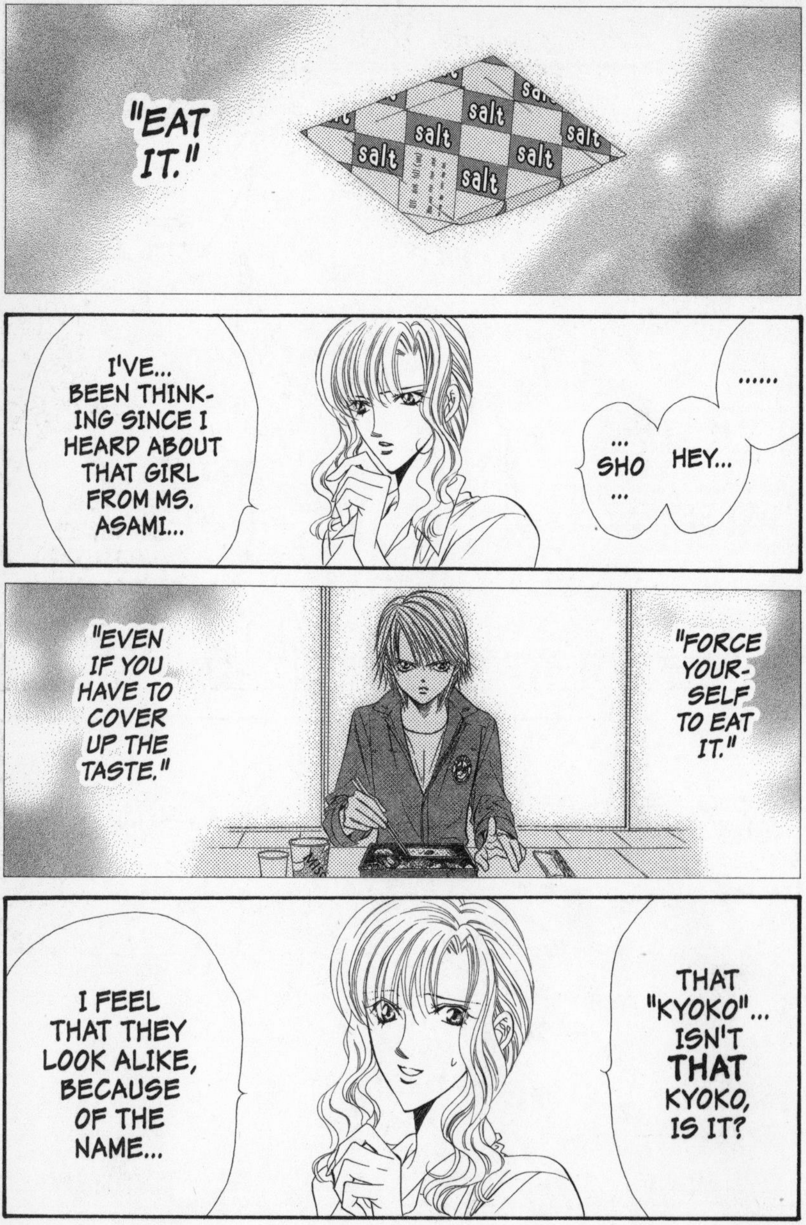
salt
"EAT IT."
......
HEY...
... SHO ...
I'VE... BEEN THINKING SINCE I HEARD ABOUT THAT GIRL FROM MS. ASAMI...
"FORCE YOURSELF TO EAT IT."
"EVEN IF YOU HAVE TO COVER UP THE TASTE."
THAT "KYOKO"... ISN'T **THAT** KYOKO, IS IT?
I FEEL THAT THEY LOOK ALIKE, BECAUSE OF THE NAME...

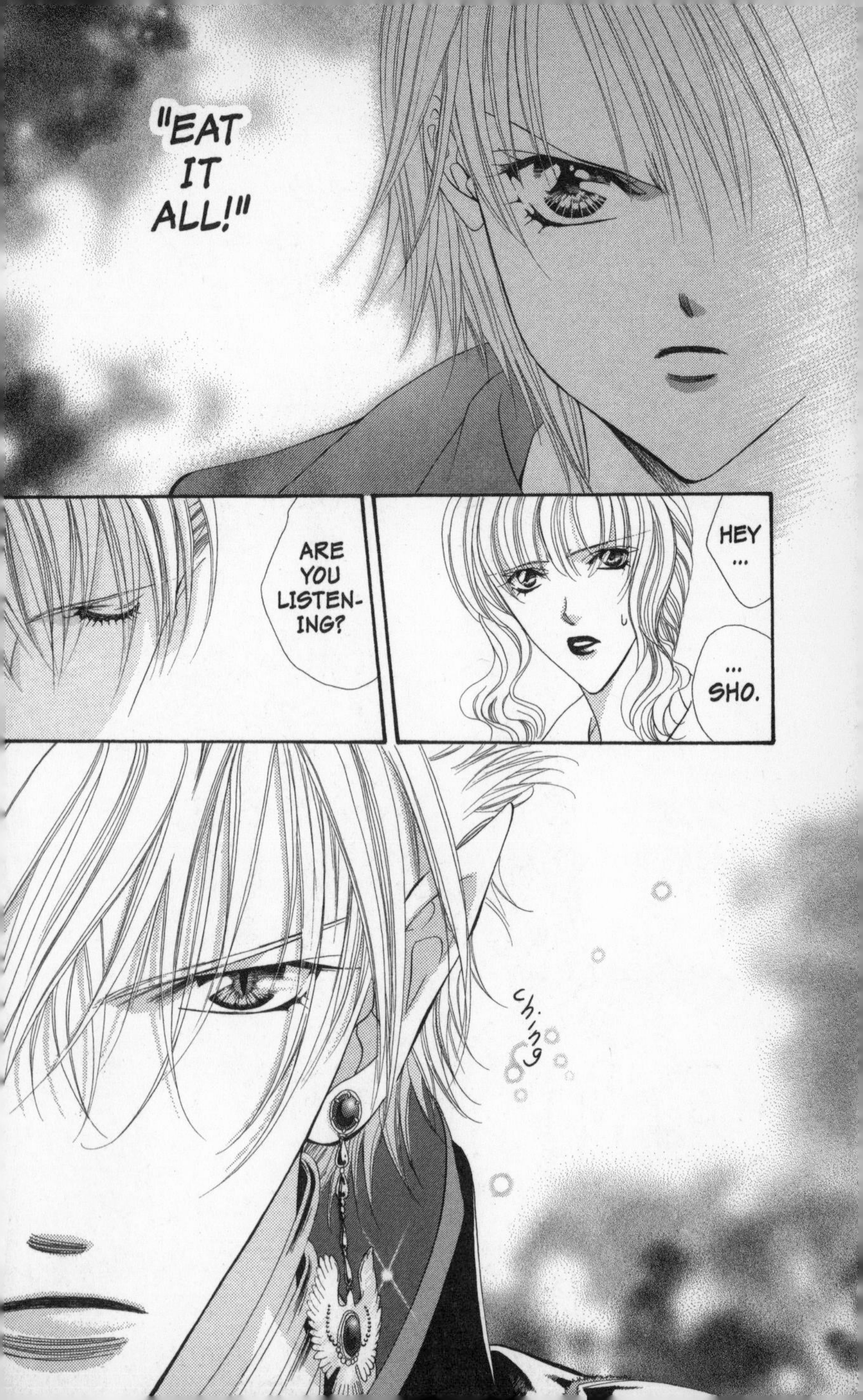
"EAT IT ALL!"
HEY ...
... SHO.
ARE YOU LISTEN-ING?
ching

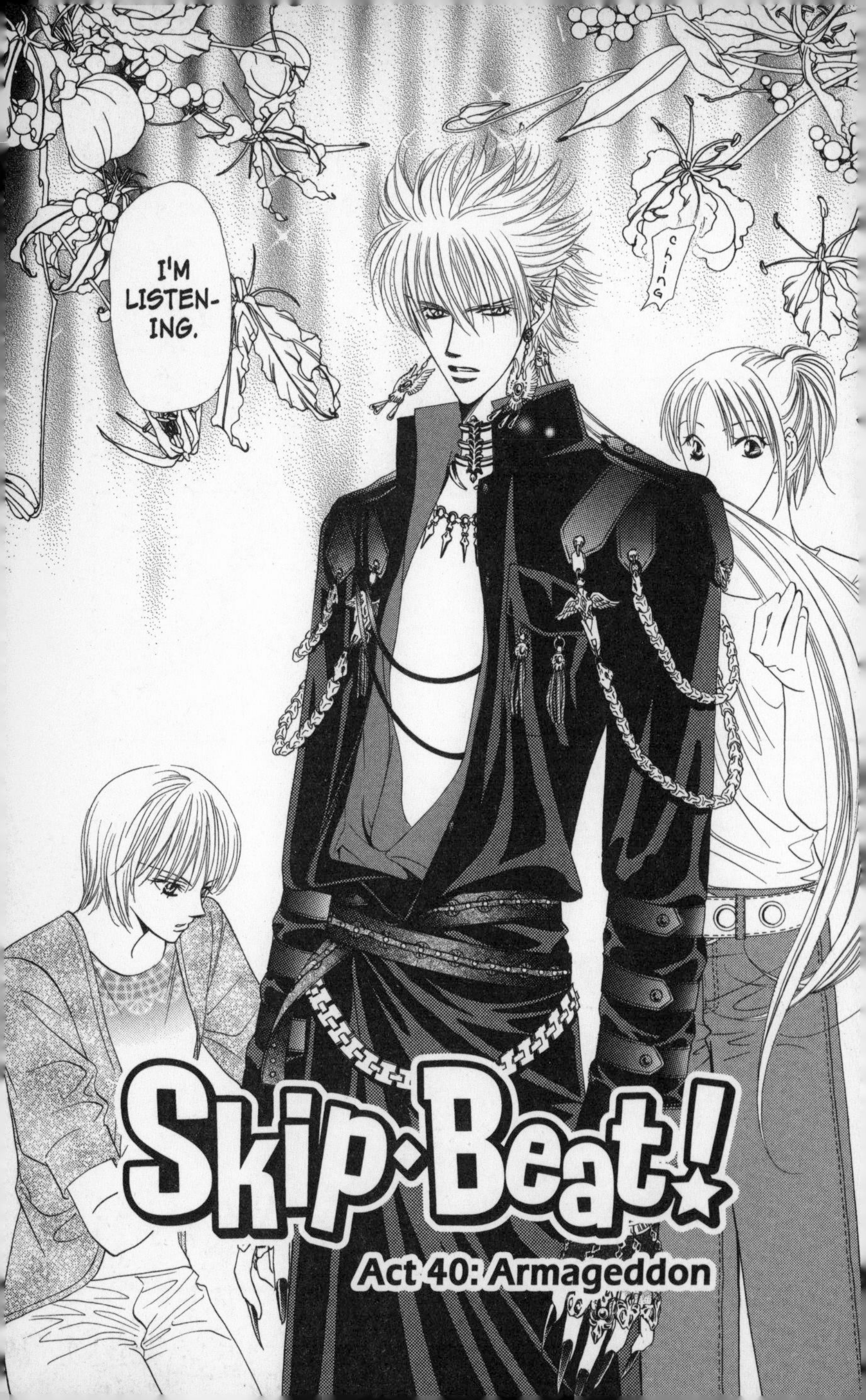

I'M LISTENING.
ching
Skip·Beat!
Act 40: Armageddon

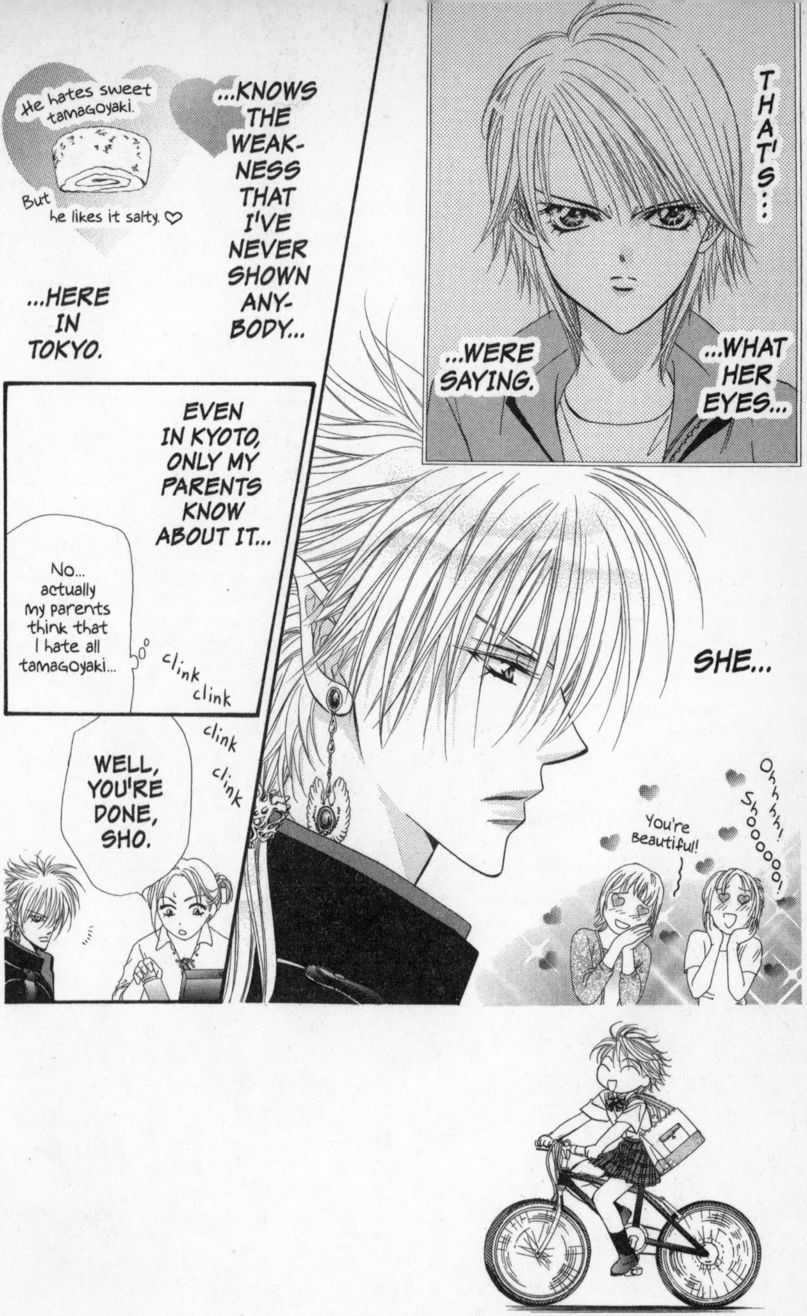
THAT'S...
...WHAT HER EYES...
...WERE SAYING.
SHE...
...KNOWS THE WEAK-NESS THAT I'VE NEVER SHOWN ANY-BODY...
...HERE IN TOKYO.
He hates sweet tamagoyaki.
But he likes it salty. ♡
Ohhhh! Shooooo!
You're Beautiful!
EVEN IN KYOTO, ONLY MY PARENTS KNOW ABOUT IT...
No... actually my parents think that I hate all tamagoyaki...
clink clink
clink clink
WELL, YOU'RE DONE, SHO.

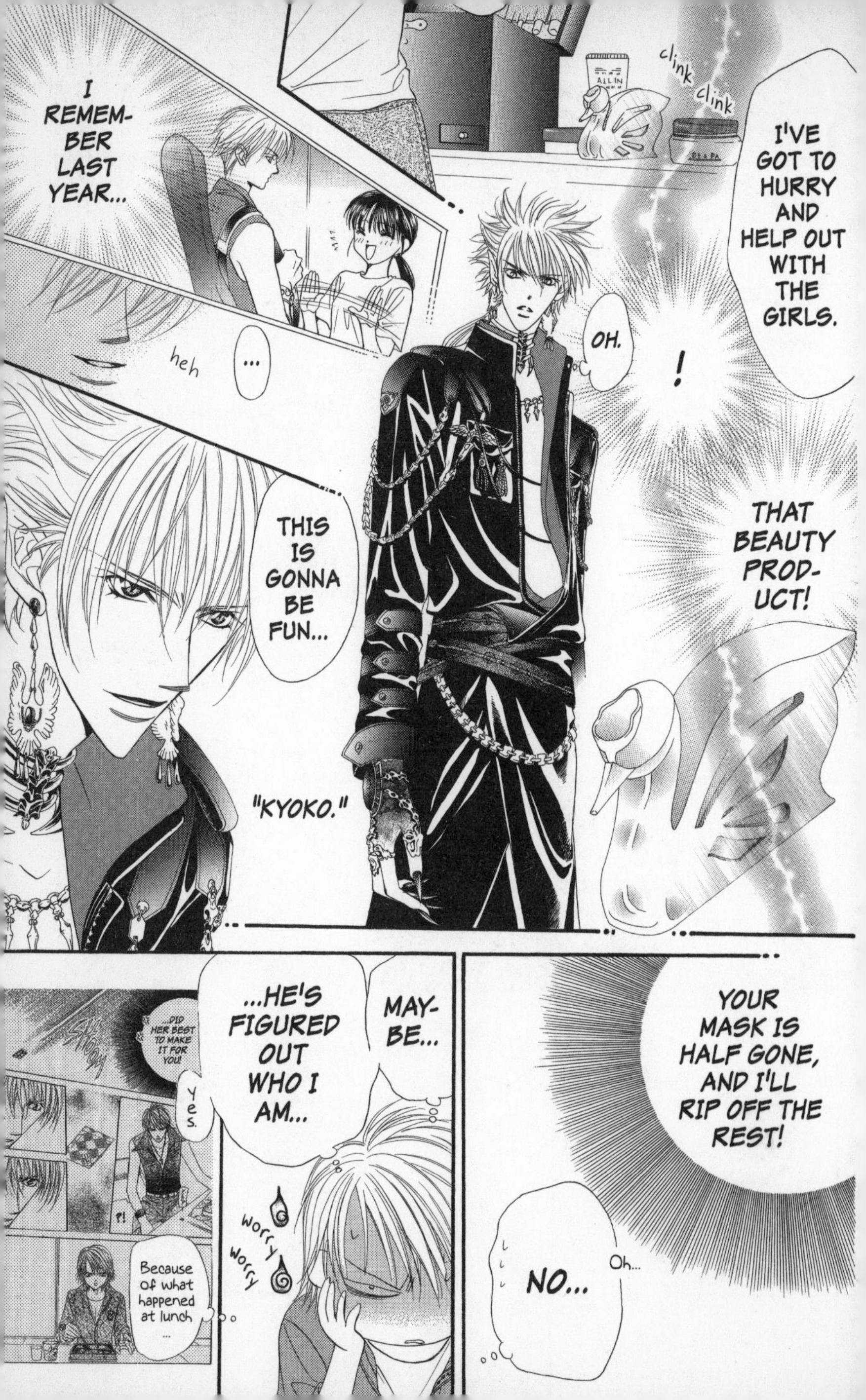
clink
clink
I'VE GOT TO HURRY AND HELP OUT WITH THE GIRLS.
!
OH.
THAT BEAUTY PROD-UCT!
I REMEM-BER LAST YEAR...
heh
...
THIS IS GONNA BE FUN...
"KYOKO."
YOUR MASK IS HALF GONE, AND I'LL RIP OFF THE REST!
Oh...
NO...
MAY-BE...
...HE'S FIGURED OUT WHO I AM...
worry
worry
Yes.
...DID HER BEST TO MAKE IT FOR YOU!
Because of what happened at lunch ...

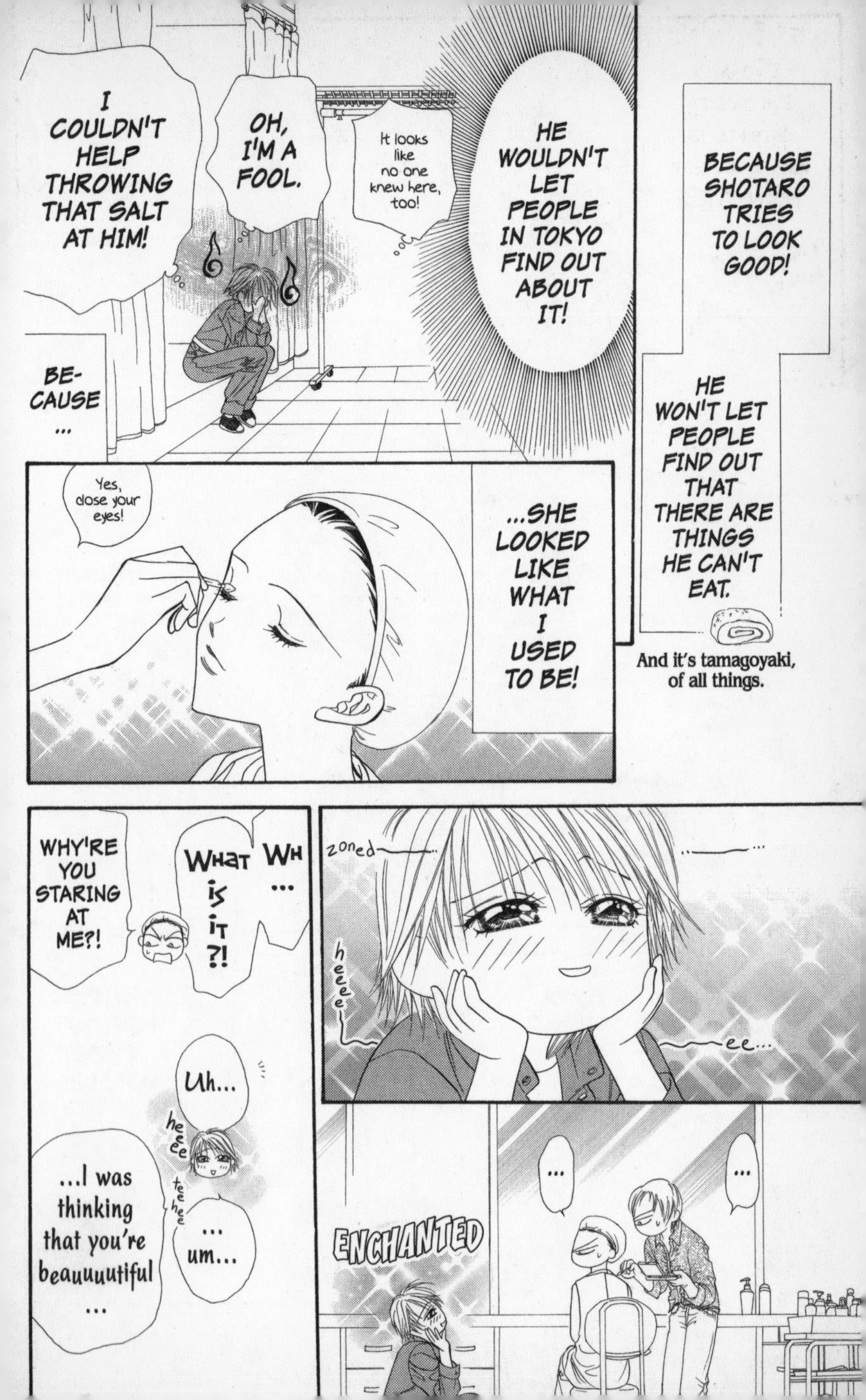

BECAUSE SHOTARO TRIES TO LOOK GOOD!
HE WON'T LET PEOPLE FIND OUT THAT THERE ARE THINGS HE CAN'T EAT.
And it's tamagoyaki, of all things.
HE WOULDN'T LET PEOPLE IN TOKYO FIND OUT ABOUT IT!
It looks like no one knew here, too!
OH, I'M A FOOL.
I COULDN'T HELP THROWING THAT SALT AT HIM!
BE-CAUSE ...
...SHE LOOKED LIKE WHAT I USED TO BE!
Yes, close your eyes!
...—...
zoned—
heeee—ee...
Wh ...
What is it?!
WHY'RE YOU STARING AT ME?!
...
...
ENCHANTED
Uh...
heeee
tee hee
... um...
...I was thinking that you're beauuuutiful ...

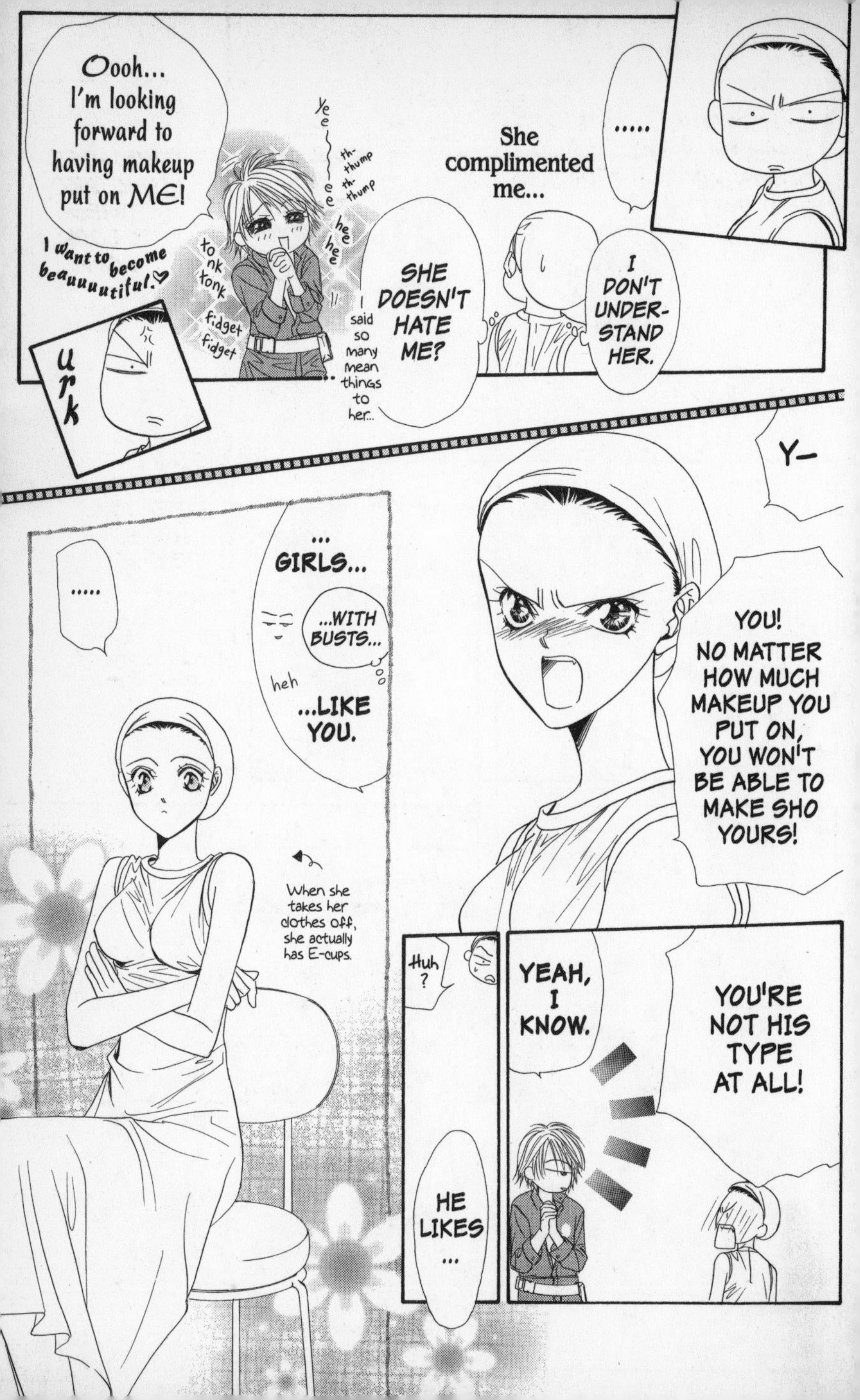
.....
She complimented me...
I DON'T UNDER-STAND HER.
SHE DOESN'T HATE ME?
I said so many mean things to her...
Oooh... I'm looking forward to having makeup put on ME!
Yee—eee
th-thump th-thump
hee hee
I want to become beauuuutiful.♡
tonk tonk
fidget fidget
Urk
Y—
YOU! NO MATTER HOW MUCH MAKEUP YOU PUT ON, YOU WON'T BE ABLE TO MAKE SHO YOURS!
YOU'RE NOT HIS TYPE AT ALL!
YEAH, I KNOW.
Huh?
HE LIKES ...
... GIRLS...
...WITH BUSTS...
heh
...LIKE YOU.
.....
When she takes her clothes off, she actually has E-cups.

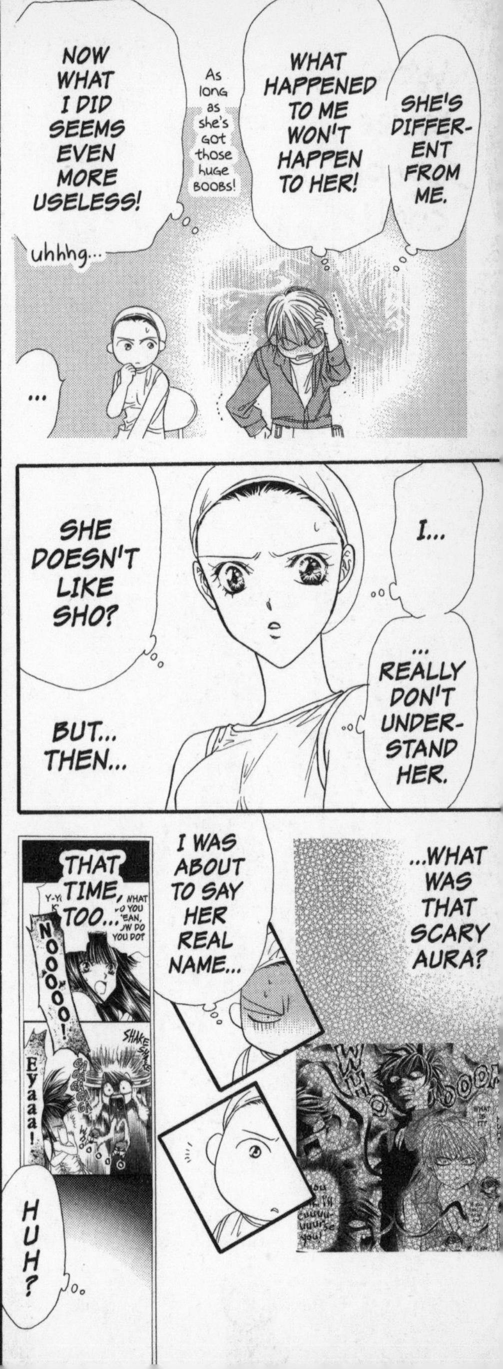
SHE'S DIFFERENT FROM ME.
WHAT HAPPENED TO ME WON'T HAPPEN TO HER!
As long as she's got those huge BOOBS!
NOW WHAT I DID SEEMS EVEN MORE USELESS!
uhhhg...
...
I...
...REALLY DON'T UNDERSTAND HER.
SHE DOESN'T LIKE SHO?
BUT... THEN...
...WHAT WAS THAT SCARY AURA?
I WAS ABOUT TO SAY HER REAL NAME...
THAT TIME, TOO...
NOOOOOO!
SHAKE
Eyaaa!
HUH?
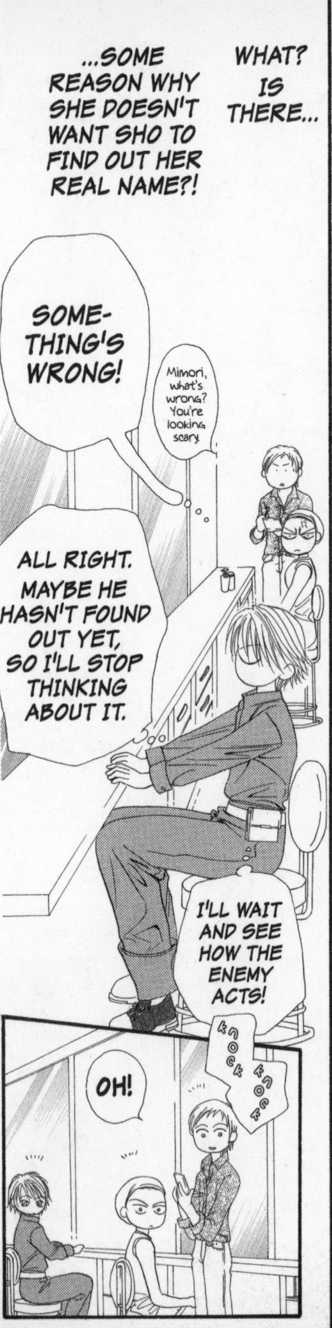
WHAT? IS THERE...
...SOME REASON WHY SHE DOESN'T WANT SHO TO FIND OUT HER REAL NAME?!
SOMETHING'S WRONG!
Mimori, what's wrong? You're looking scary.
ALL RIGHT. MAYBE HE HASN'T FOUND OUT YET, SO I'LL STOP THINKING ABOUT IT.
I'LL WAIT AND SEE HOW THE ENEMY ACTS!
knock knock
OH!

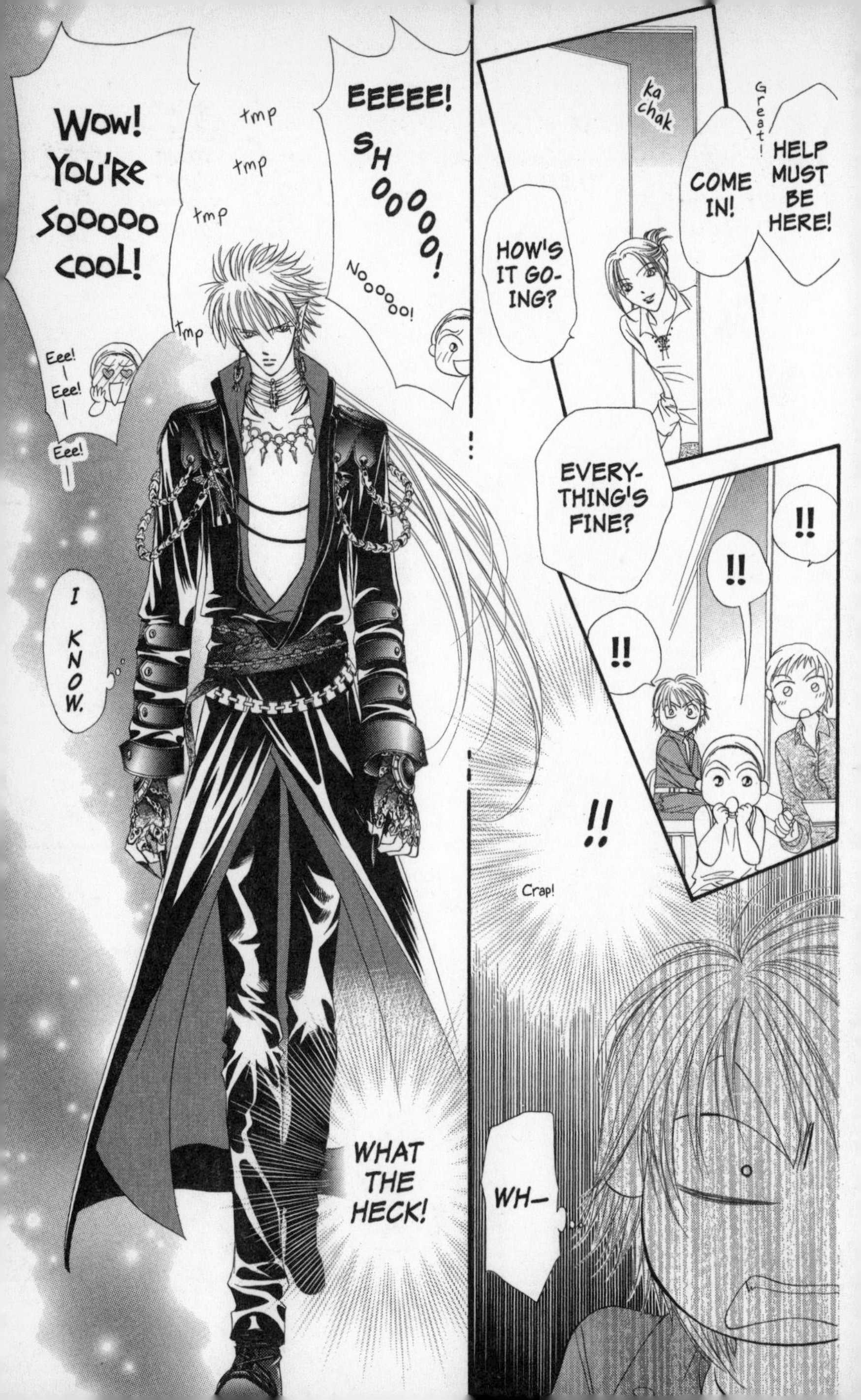
Great!
HELP MUST BE HERE!
COME IN!
ka chak
HOW'S IT GOING?
EVERY-THING'S FINE?
!!
!!
!!
!!
Crap!
WH—
EEEEE!
SHOOOOOO!
Noooooo!
tmp
tmp
tmp
tmp
WOW! YOU'RE SOOOOO COOL!
Eee! Eee! Eee!
I KNOW.
WHAT THE HECK!

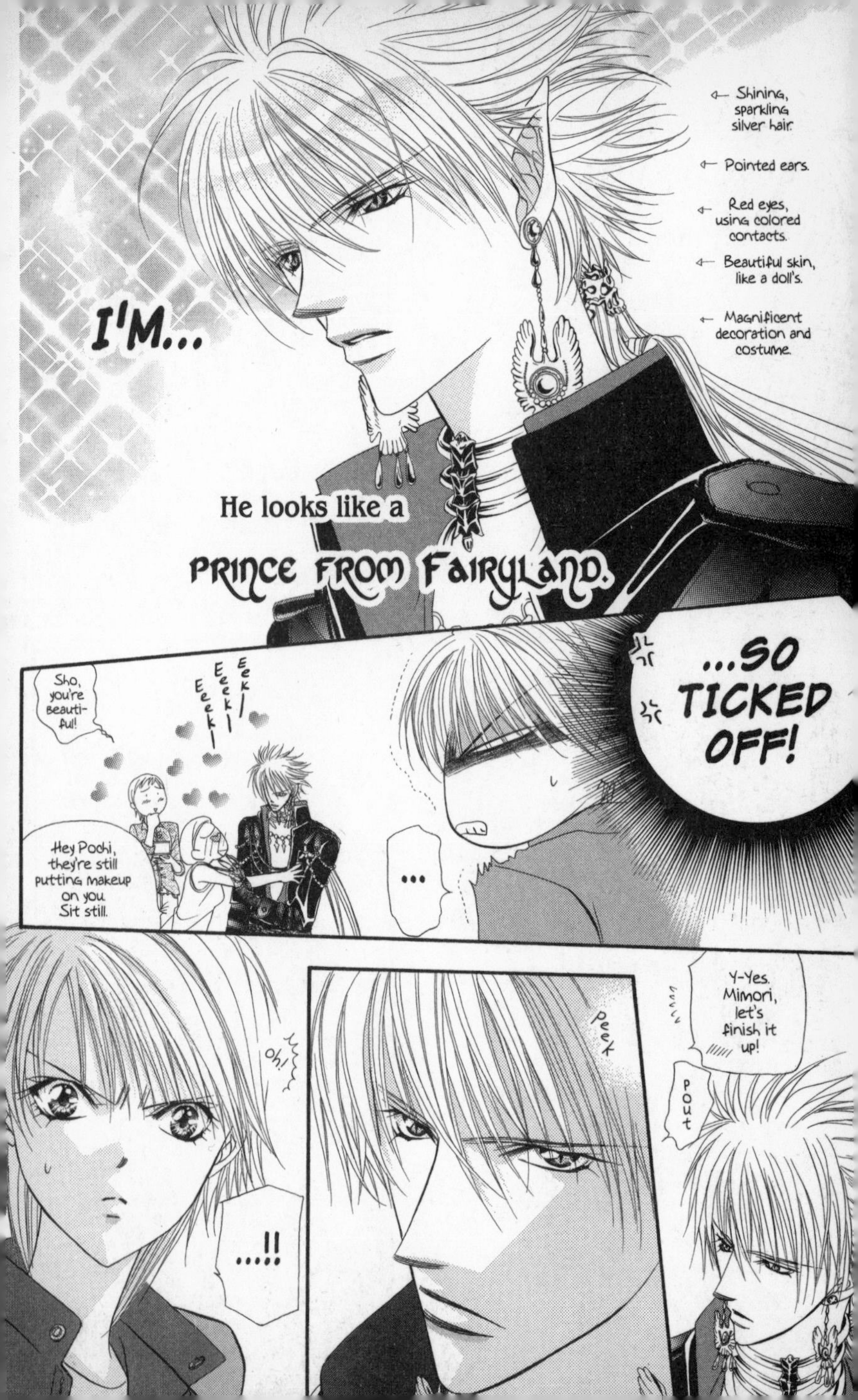

Shining, sparkling silver hair.
Pointed ears.
Red eyes, using colored contacts.
Beautiful skin, like a doll's.
Magnificent decoration and costume.
I'M...
He looks like a
PRINCE FROM FAIRYLAND.
...SO TICKED OFF!
...
Eeek! Eeek! Eeek!
Sho, you're beauti-ful!
Hey Pochi, they're still putting makeup on you. Sit still.
Y-Yes. Mimori, let's finish it up!
Pout
Peek
Oh!
...!!

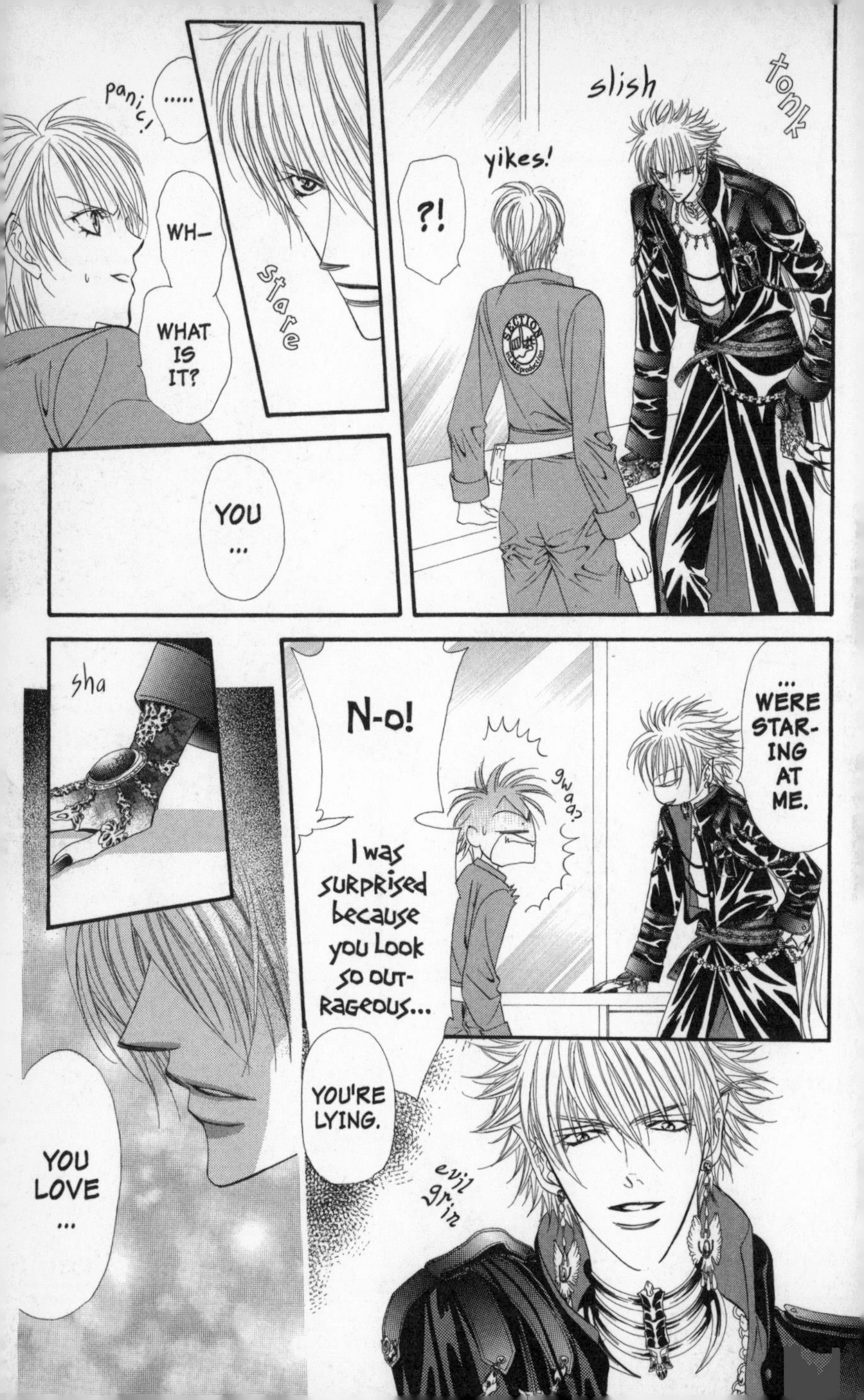
tonk
slish
yikes!
?!
stare
.....
panic!
WH–
WHAT IS IT?
YOU ...
... WERE STAR-ING AT ME.
N-o!
gwaa?
I was surprised because you look so out-rageous...
sha
YOU'RE LYING.
evil grin
YOU LOVE ...

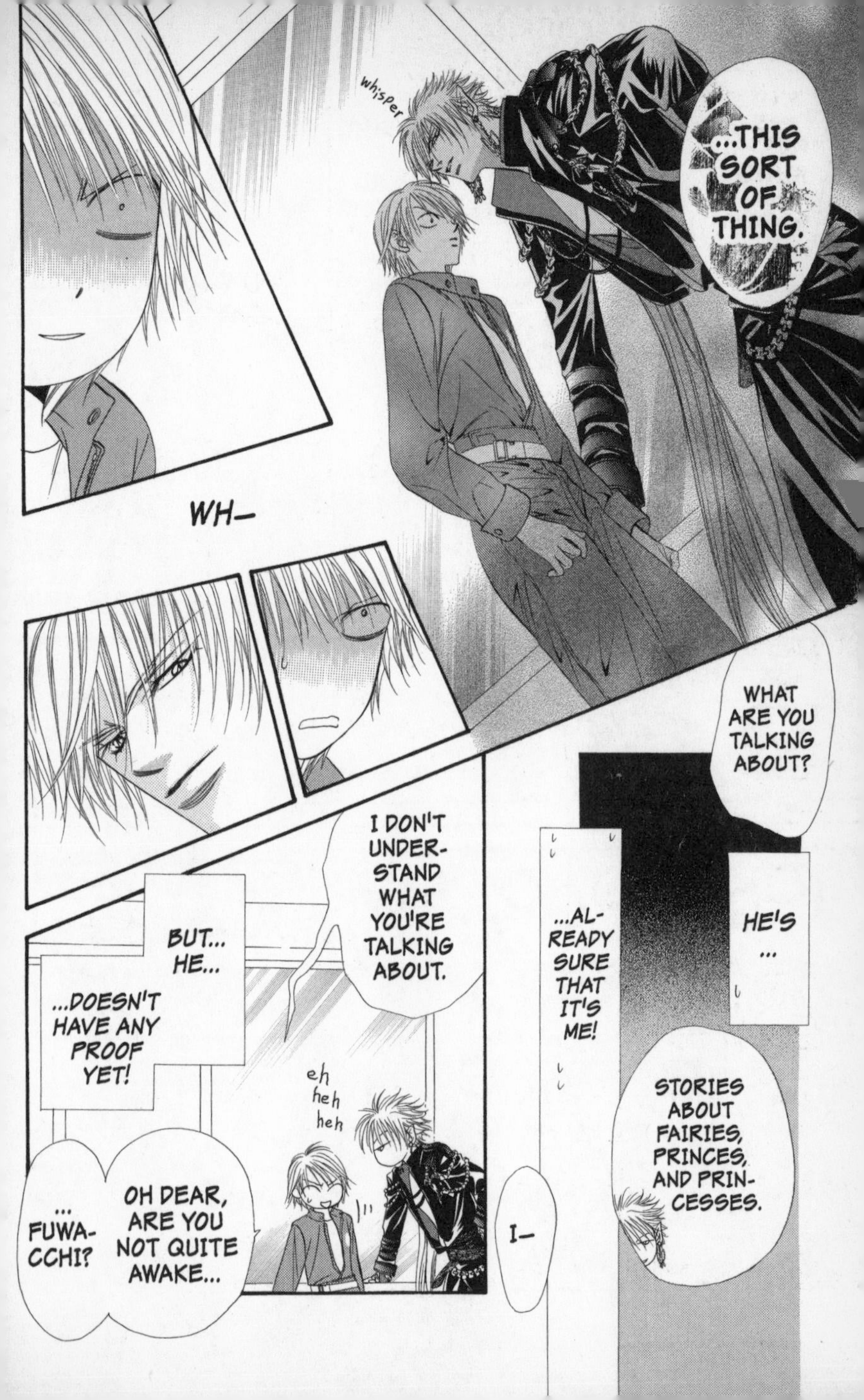
whisper
...THIS SORT OF THING.
WH—
WHAT ARE YOU TALKING ABOUT?
HE'S ...
...ALREADY SURE THAT IT'S ME!
STORIES ABOUT FAIRIES, PRINCES, AND PRINCESSES.
I—
I DON'T UNDERSTAND WHAT YOU'RE TALKING ABOUT.
BUT... HE...
...DOESN'T HAVE ANY PROOF YET!
eh heh heh
OH DEAR, ARE YOU NOT QUITE AWAKE...
...FUWACCHI?

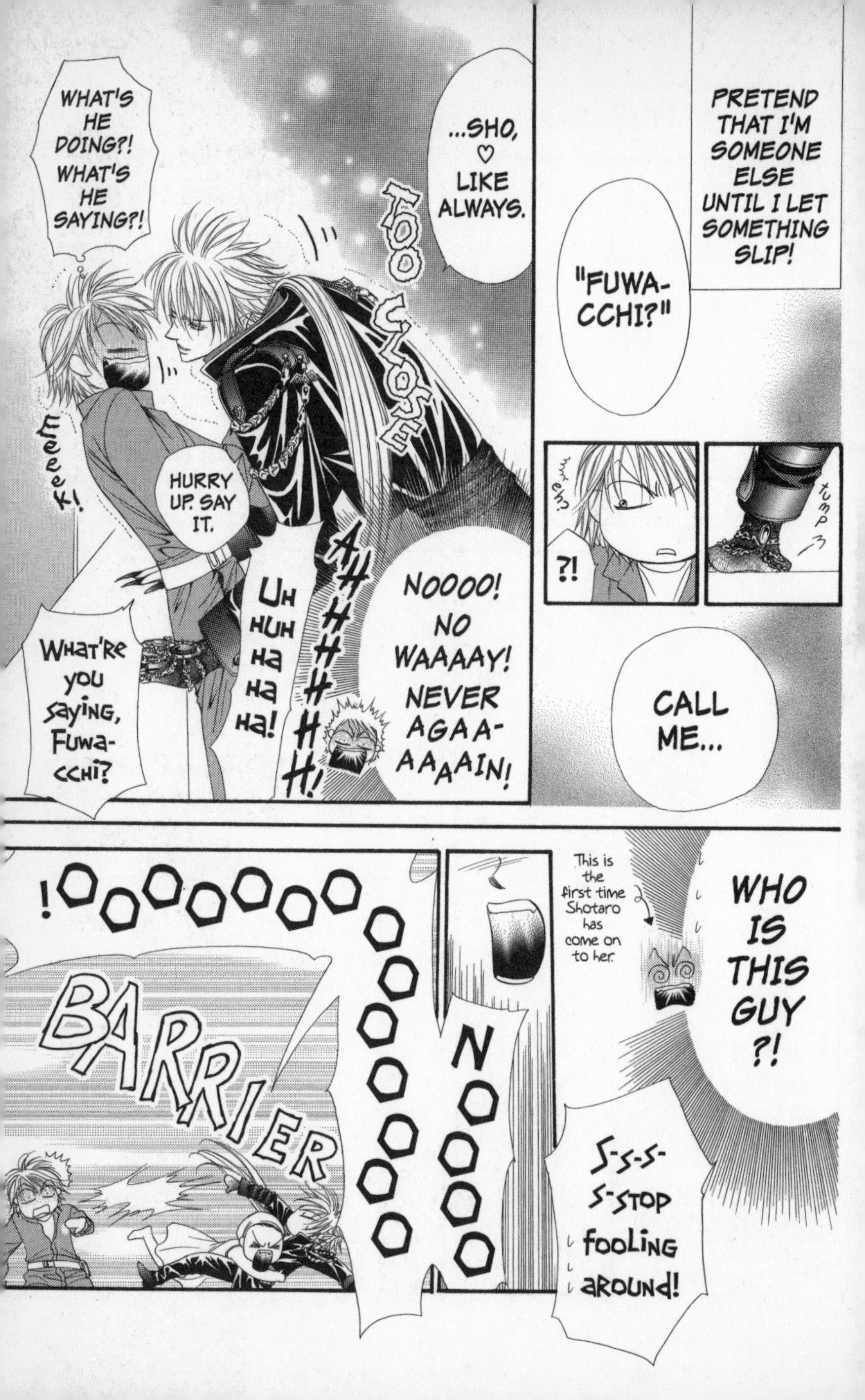
PRETEND THAT I'M SOMEONE ELSE UNTIL I LET SOMETHING SLIP!
"FUWA-CCHI?"
eh?
?!
tump
CALL ME...
...SHO, ♡ LIKE ALWAYS.
TOO CLOSE
WHAT'S HE DOING?! WHAT'S HE SAYING?!
HURRY UP. SAY IT.
Eeeek!
NOOOO! NO WAAAAY! NEVER AGAA-AAAAIN!
AHHHHHHH!
UH HUH HA HA HA!
What're you saying, Fuwa-cchi?
WHO IS THIS GUY?!
This is the first time Shotaro has come on to her.
S-S-S-S-STOP fooling around!
NOOOOOOOOOOOOOOOOOOO!
BARRIER

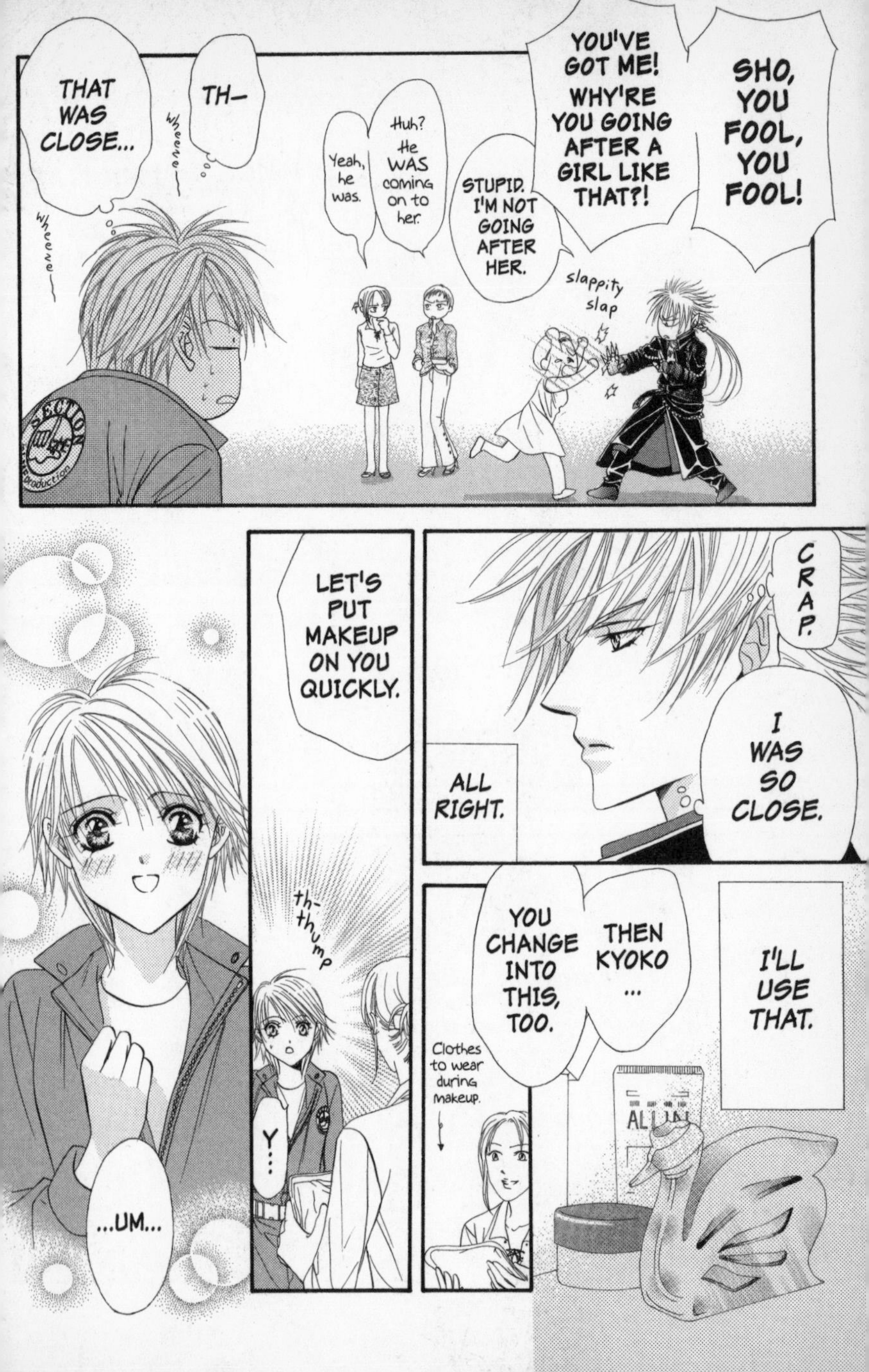
SHO, YOU FOOL, YOU FOOL!
YOU'VE GOT ME! WHY'RE YOU GOING AFTER A GIRL LIKE THAT?!
STUPID. I'M NOT GOING AFTER HER.
slappity slap
Huh? He WAS coming on to her.
Yeah, he was.
TH—
wheeze
THAT WAS CLOSE...
wheeze
CRAP.
I WAS SO CLOSE.
ALL RIGHT.
LET'S PUT MAKEUP ON YOU QUICKLY.
I'LL USE THAT.
THEN KYOKO...
YOU CHANGE INTO THIS, TOO.
Clothes to wear during makeup.
th-thump
Y...
...UM...

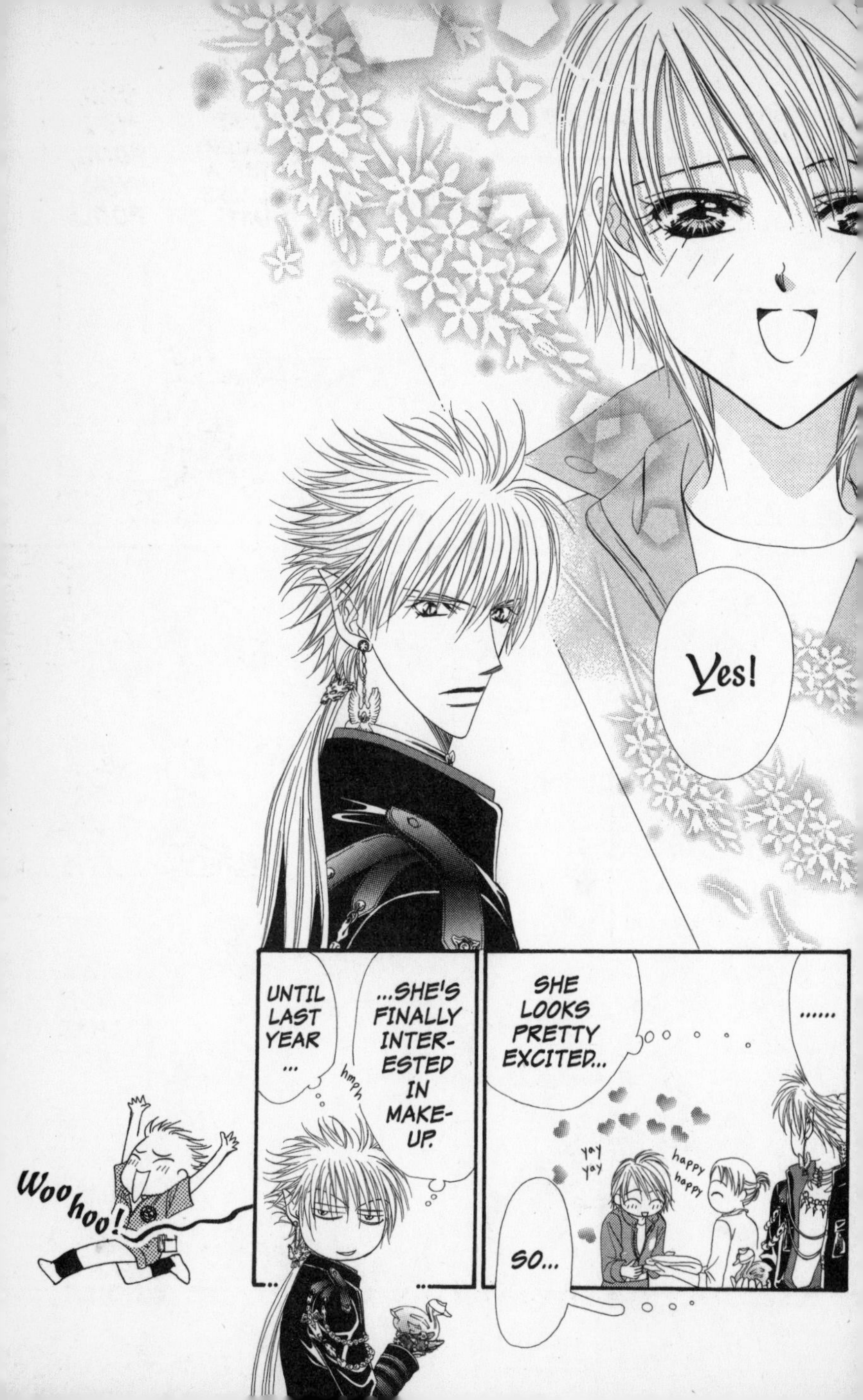
Yes!
......
SHE LOOKS PRETTY EXCITED...
happy happy
yay yay
SO...
UNTIL LAST YEAR...
...SHE'S FINALLY INTERESTED IN MAKE-UP.
hmph
Woo hoo!

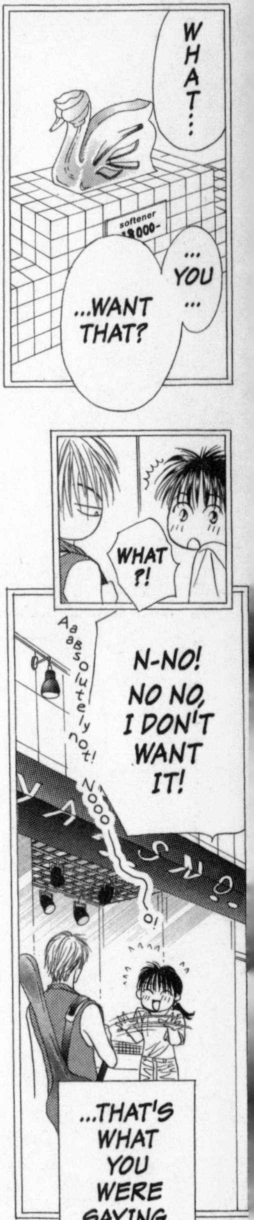
WHAT...
... YOU ...
...WANT THAT?
softener
WHAT ?!
N-NO! NO NO, I DON'T WANT IT!
Aa absolutely not!
Nooooo!
...THAT'S WHAT YOU WERE SAYING.

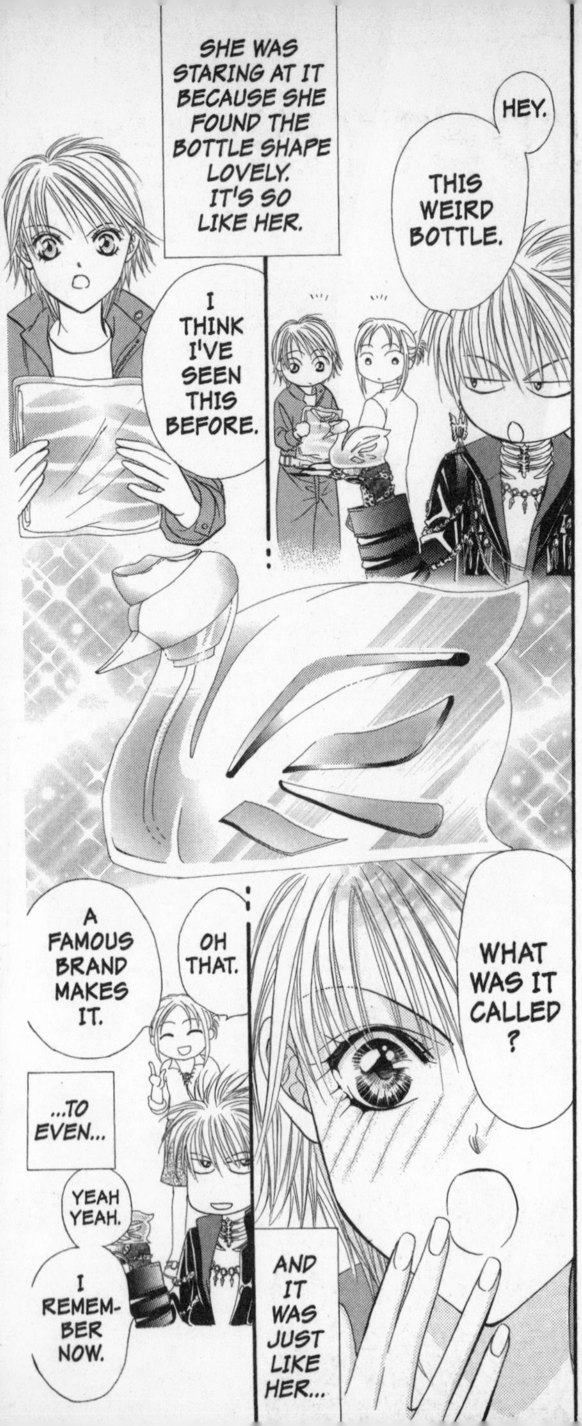
HEY.
THIS WEIRD BOTTLE.
SHE WAS STARING AT IT BECAUSE SHE FOUND THE BOTTLE SHAPE LOVELY. IT'S SO LIKE HER.
I THINK I'VE SEEN THIS BEFORE.
WHAT WAS IT CALLED ?
AND IT WAS JUST LIKE HER...
OH THAT.
A FAMOUS BRAND MAKES IT.
...TO EVEN...
YEAH YEAH.
I REMEMBER NOW.

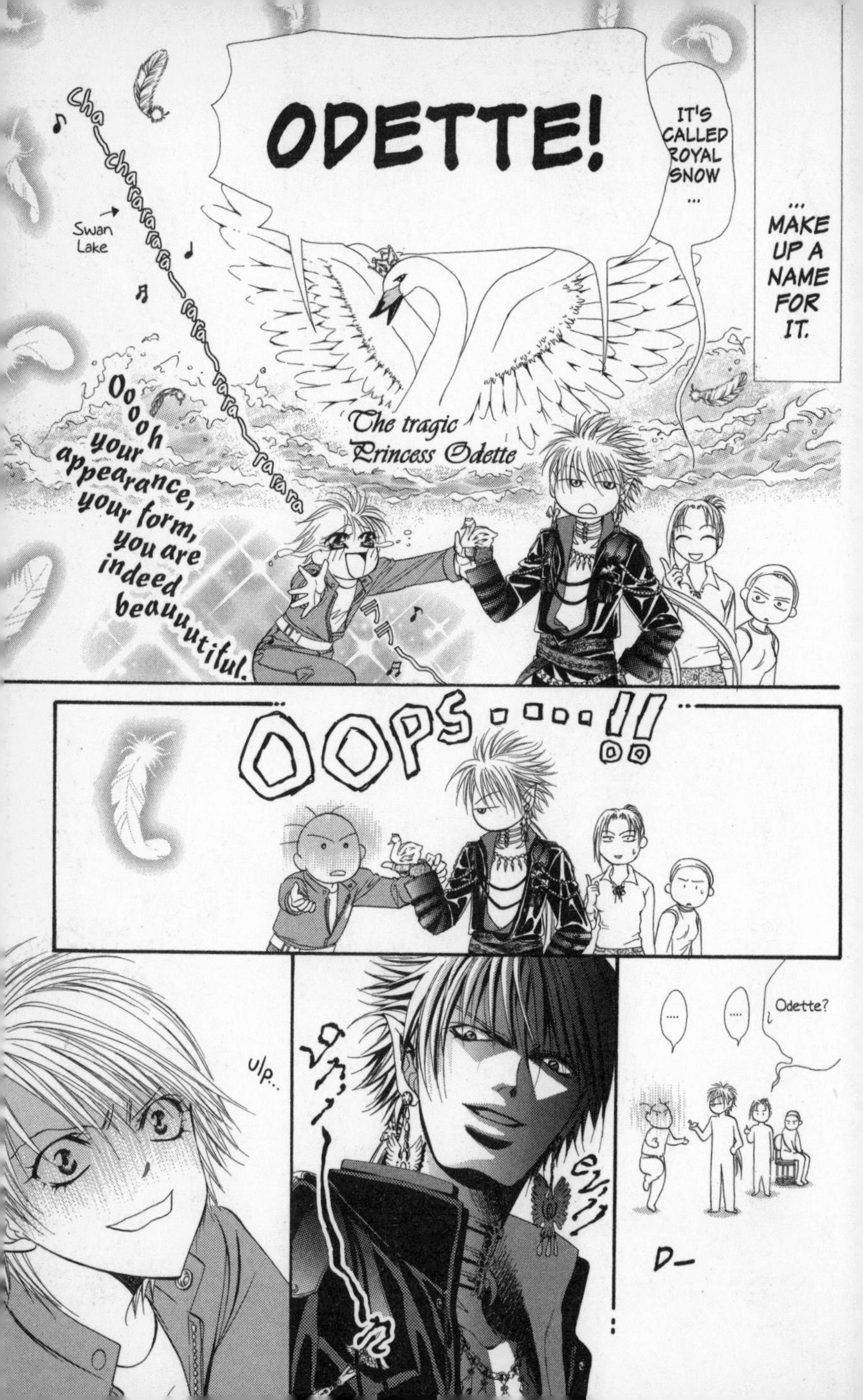
... MAKE UP A NAME FOR IT.
IT'S CALLED ROYAL SNOW ...
ODETTE!
Cha—chararara—rara—rara—rarara
Swan Lake
The tragic Princess Odette
Ooooh your appearance, your form, you are indeed beauuutiful.
OOPS....!!
Odette?
....
....
D—
evil!
ulp...

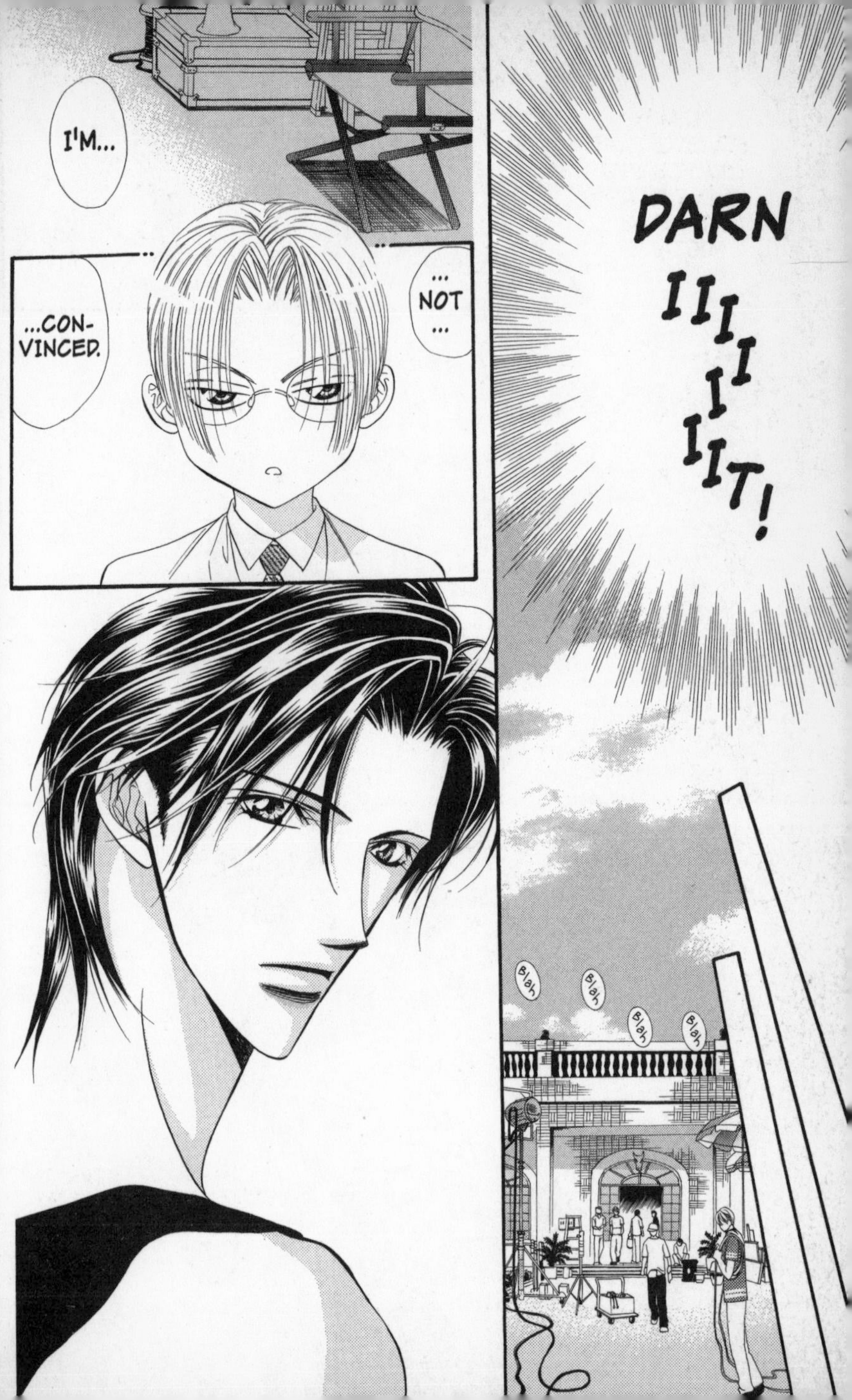
DARN IIIIIT!
Blah
Blah
Blah
Blah
I'M...
... NOT ...
...CON-VINCED.

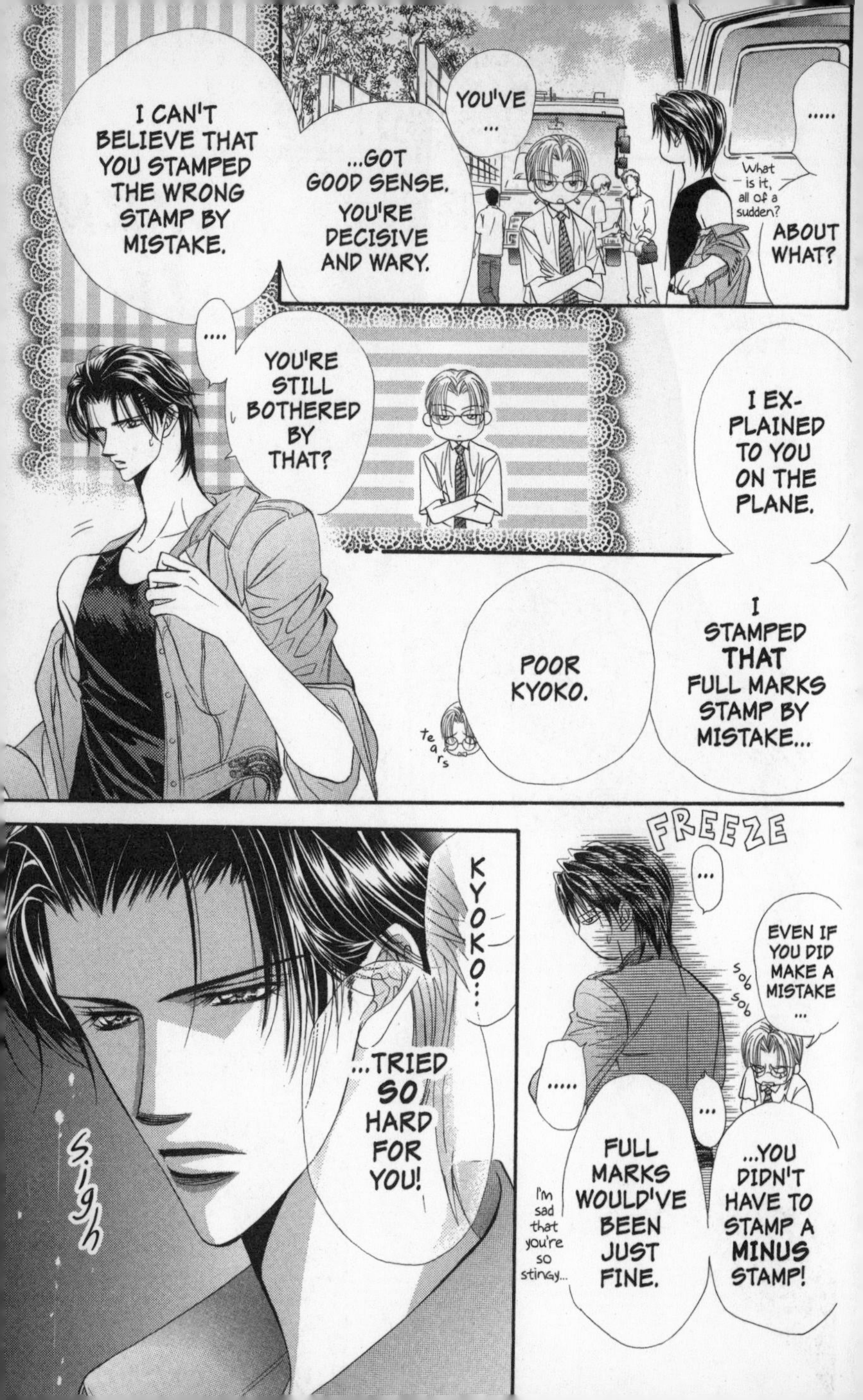
.....
What is it, all of a sudden?
ABOUT WHAT?
YOU'VE ...
...GOT GOOD SENSE. YOU'RE DECISIVE AND WARY.
I CAN'T BELIEVE THAT YOU STAMPED THE WRONG STAMP BY MISTAKE.
I EX-PLAINED TO YOU ON THE PLANE.
I STAMPED THAT FULL MARKS STAMP BY MISTAKE...
POOR KYOKO.
tears
....
YOU'RE STILL BOTHERED BY THAT?
FREEZE
...
EVEN IF YOU DID MAKE A MISTAKE ...
sob sob
...
...YOU DIDN'T HAVE TO STAMP A MINUS STAMP!
.....
FULL MARKS WOULD'VE BEEN JUST FINE.
I'm sad that you're so stingy...
KYOKO...
...TRIED SO HARD FOR YOU!
Sigh

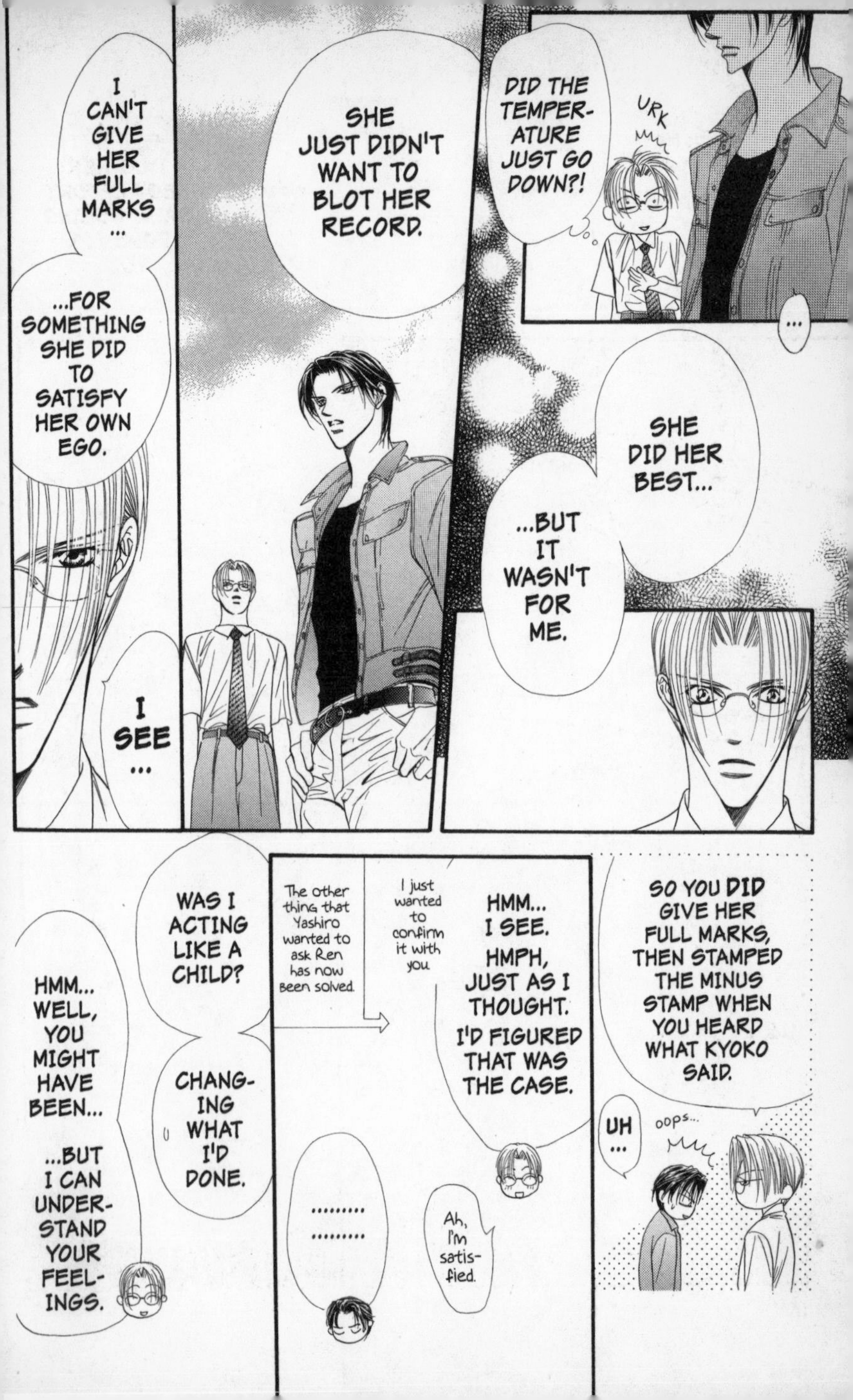
DID THE TEMPER-ATURE JUST GO DOWN?!
URK
...
SHE DID HER BEST...
...BUT IT WASN'T FOR ME.
SHE JUST DIDN'T WANT TO BLOT HER RECORD.
I CAN'T GIVE HER FULL MARKS...
...FOR SOMETHING SHE DID TO SATISFY HER OWN EGO.
I SEE...
SO YOU DID GIVE HER FULL MARKS, THEN STAMPED THE MINUS STAMP WHEN YOU HEARD WHAT KYOKO SAID.
UH...
oops...
HMM... I SEE. HMPH, JUST AS I THOUGHT. I'D FIGURED THAT WAS THE CASE.
I just wanted to confirm it with you
The other thing that Yashiro wanted to ask Ren has now been solved.
Ah, I'm satis-fied.
....
....
WAS I ACTING LIKE A CHILD?
CHANGING WHAT I'D DONE.
HMM... WELL, YOU MIGHT HAVE BEEN...
...BUT I CAN UNDER-STAND YOUR FEEL-INGS.

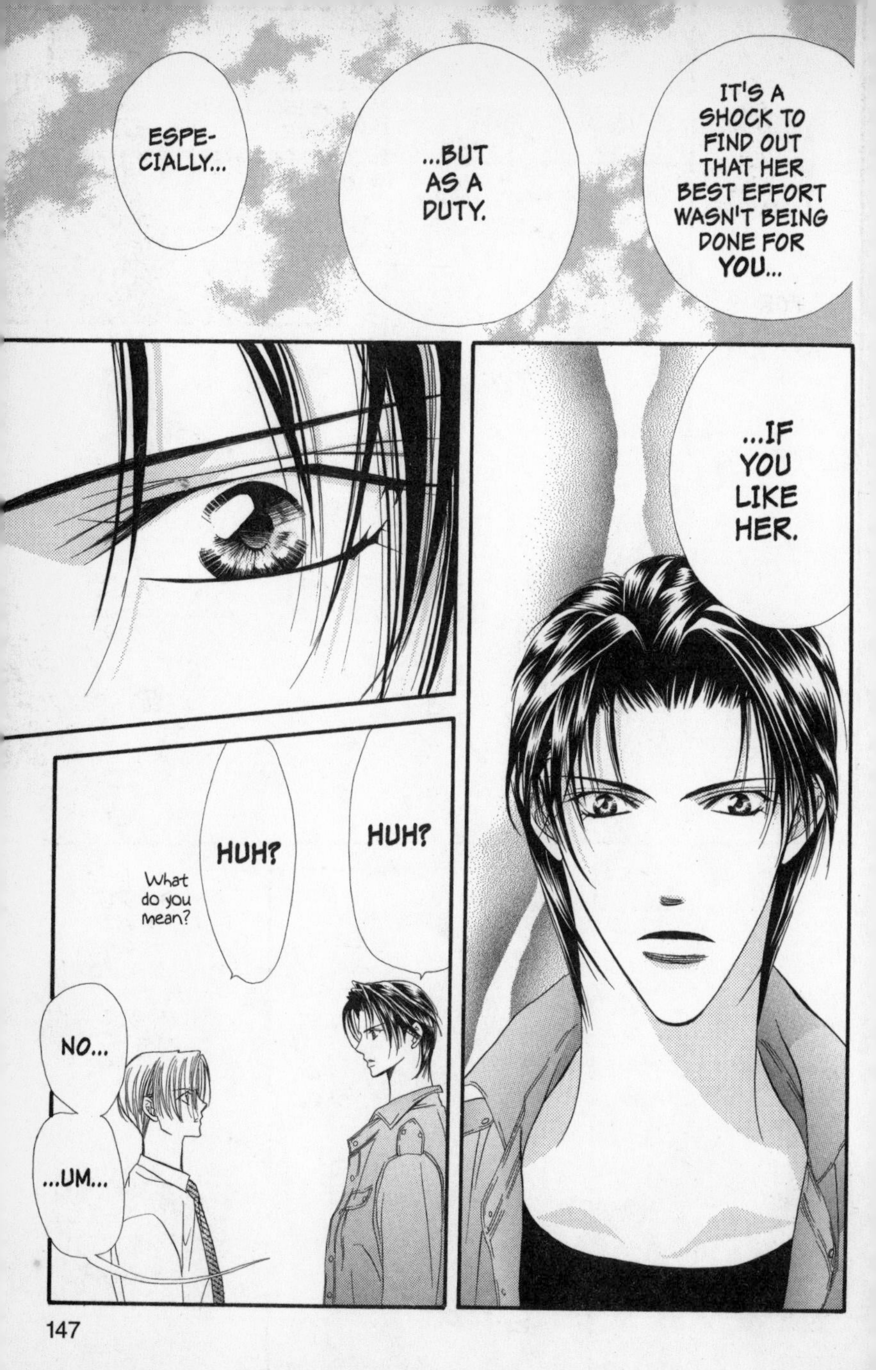
IT'S A SHOCK TO FIND OUT THAT HER BEST EFFORT WASN'T BEING DONE FOR **YOU**...
...BUT AS A DUTY.
ESPE-CIALLY...
...IF YOU LIKE HER.
HUH?
HUH?
What do you mean?
NO...
...UM...

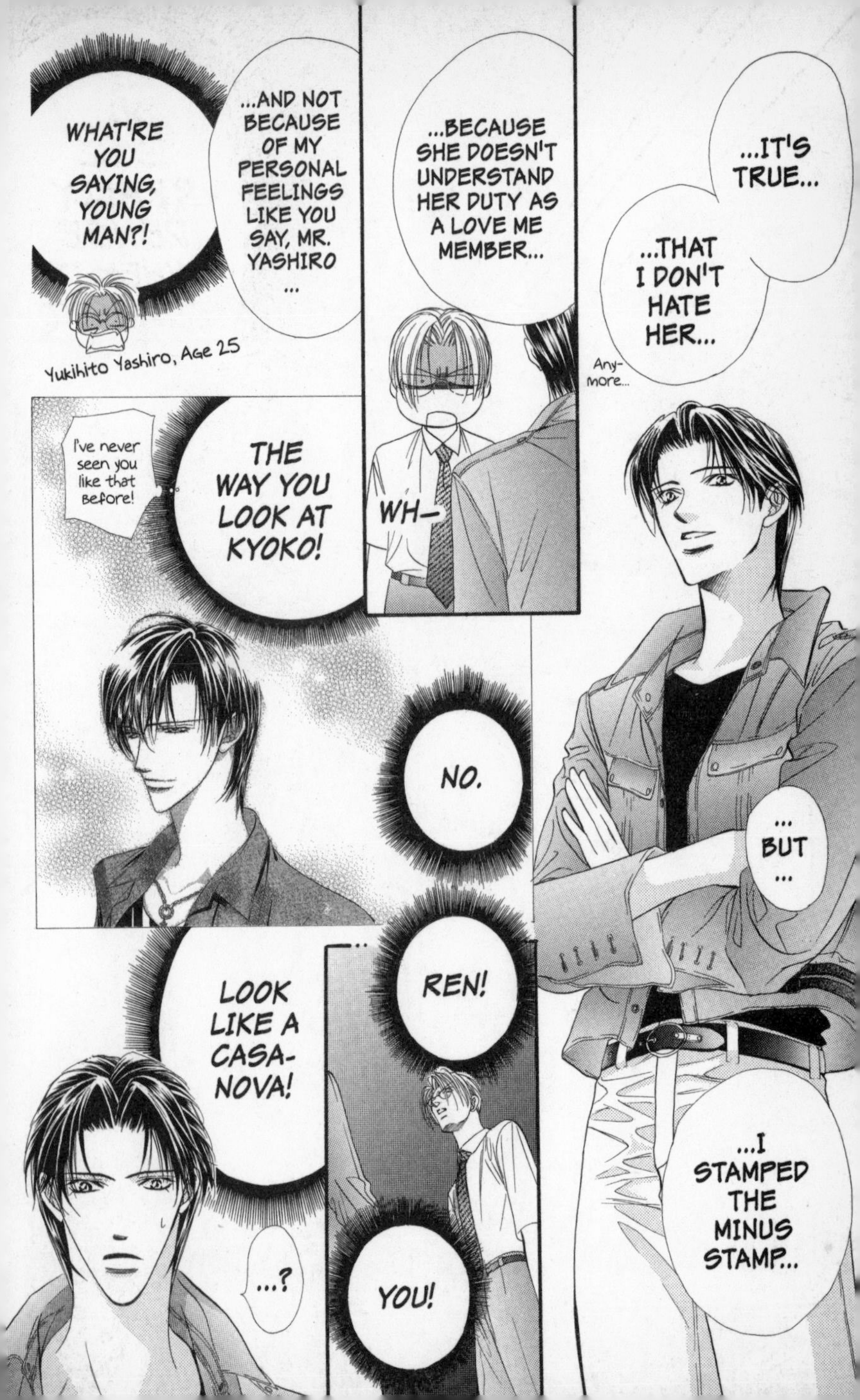

...IT'S TRUE...
...THAT I DON'T HATE HER...
Any-more...
...BUT...
...I STAMPED THE MINUS STAMP...
...BECAUSE SHE DOESN'T UNDERSTAND HER DUTY AS A LOVE ME MEMBER...
...AND NOT BECAUSE OF MY PERSONAL FEELINGS LIKE YOU SAY, MR. YASHIRO...
WHAT'RE YOU SAYING, YOUNG MAN?!
Yukihito Yashiro, Age 25
WH—
THE WAY YOU LOOK AT KYOKO!
I've never seen you like that before!
NO.
REN!
YOU!
LOOK LIKE A CASA-NOVA!
...?

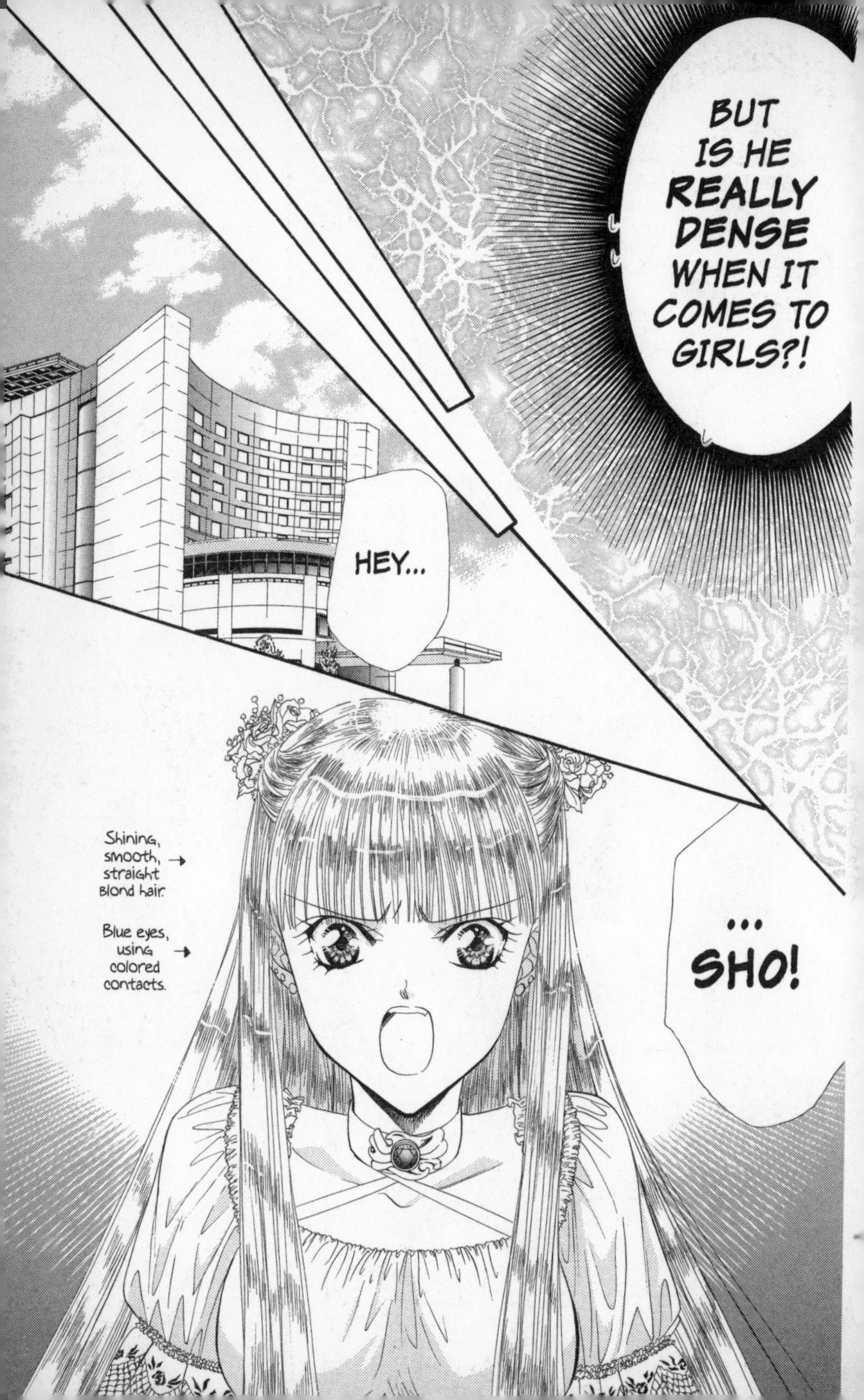
BUT IS HE REALLY DENSE WHEN IT COMES TO GIRLS?!
HEY...
...SHO!
Shining, smooth, straight blond hair.
Blue eyes, using colored contacts.

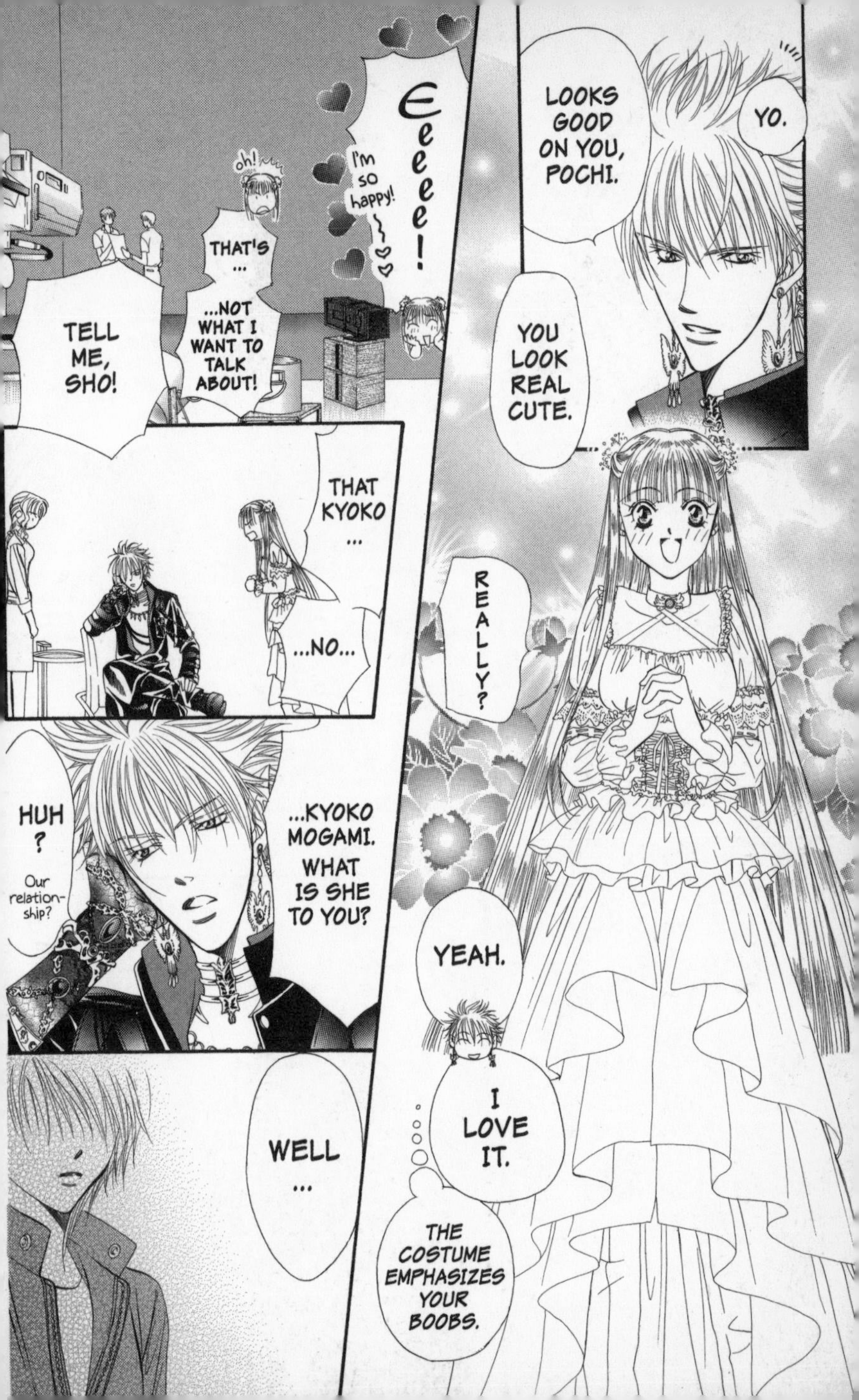
YO.
LOOKS GOOD ON YOU, POCHI.
YOU LOOK REAL CUTE.
REALLY?
YEAH.
I LOVE IT.
THE COSTUME EMPHASIZES YOUR BOOBS.
Eeeee!
I'm so happy! ~♡♡
oh!
THAT'S...
...NOT WHAT I WANT TO TALK ABOUT!
TELL ME, SHO!
THAT KYOKO...
...NO...
...KYOKO MOGAMI. WHAT IS SHE TO YOU?
HUH?
Our relationship?
WELL...

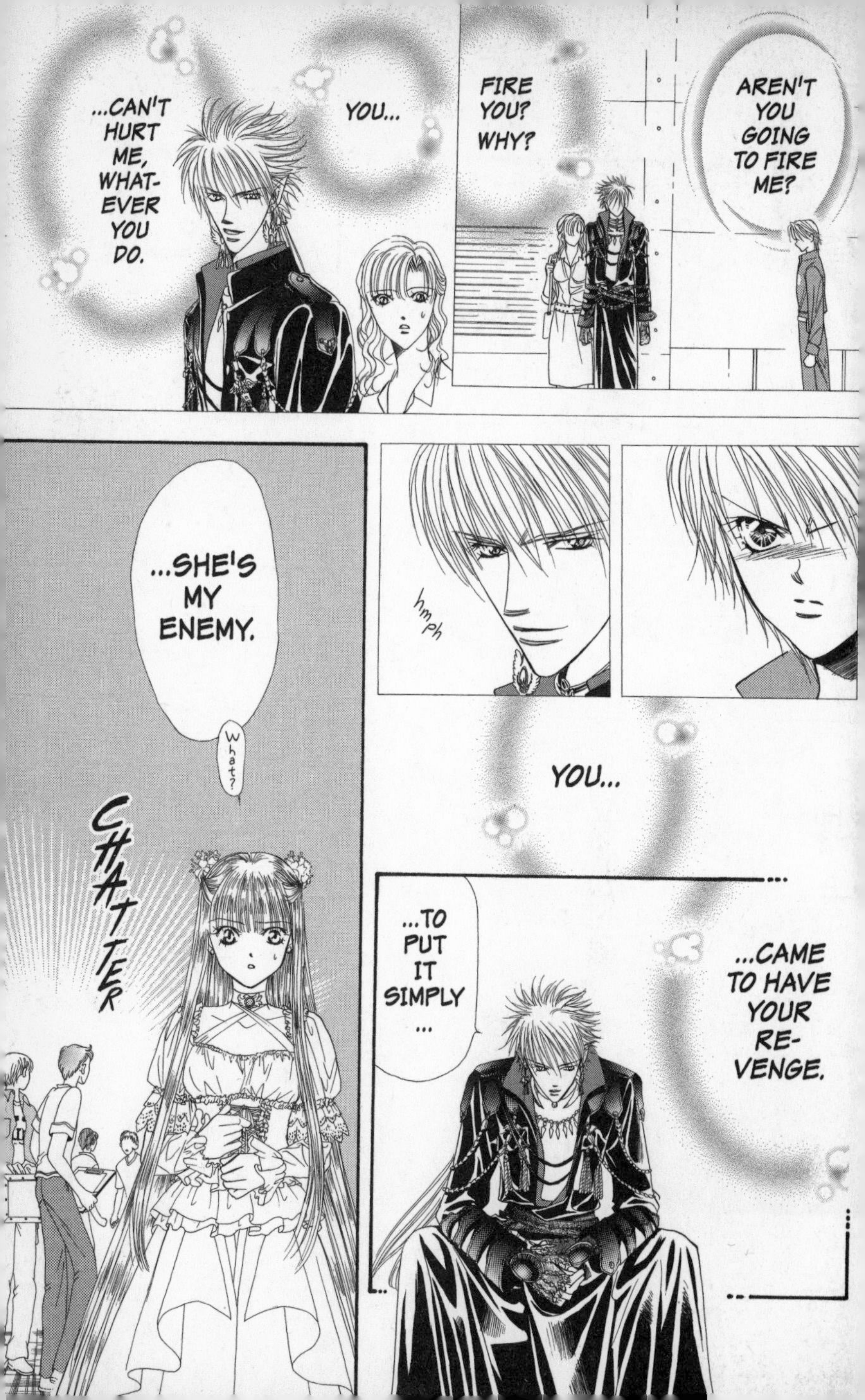
AREN'T YOU GOING TO FIRE ME?
FIRE YOU? WHY?
YOU...
...CAN'T HURT ME, WHATEVER YOU DO.
hmph
YOU...
...CAME TO HAVE YOUR REVENGE.
...TO PUT IT SIMPLY...
...SHE'S MY ENEMY.
What?
CHATTER

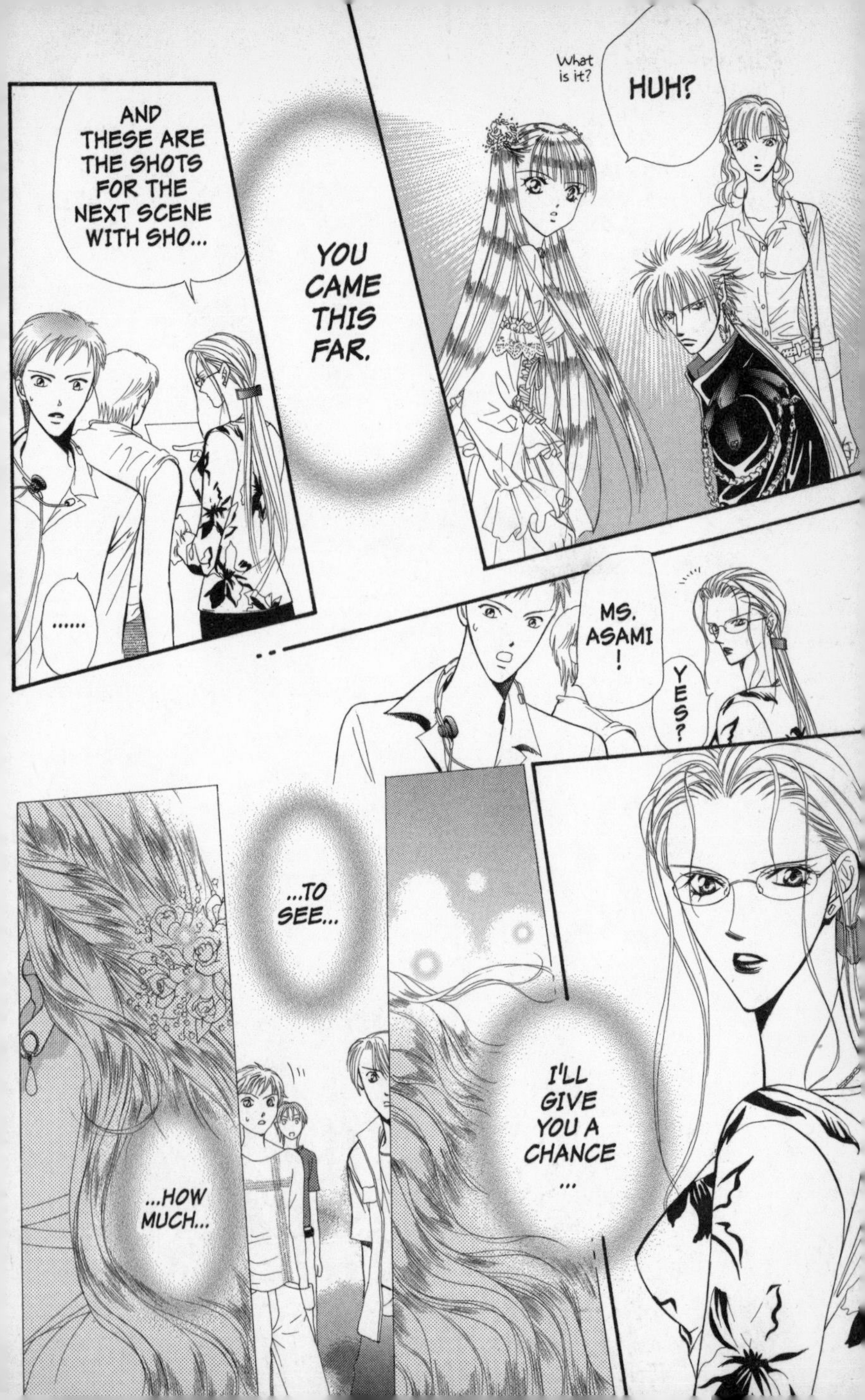
HUH?
What is it?
YOU CAME THIS FAR.
AND THESE ARE THE SHOTS FOR THE NEXT SCENE WITH SHO...
......
MS. ASAMI!
YES?
I'LL GIVE YOU A CHANCE...
...TO SEE...
...HOW MUCH...

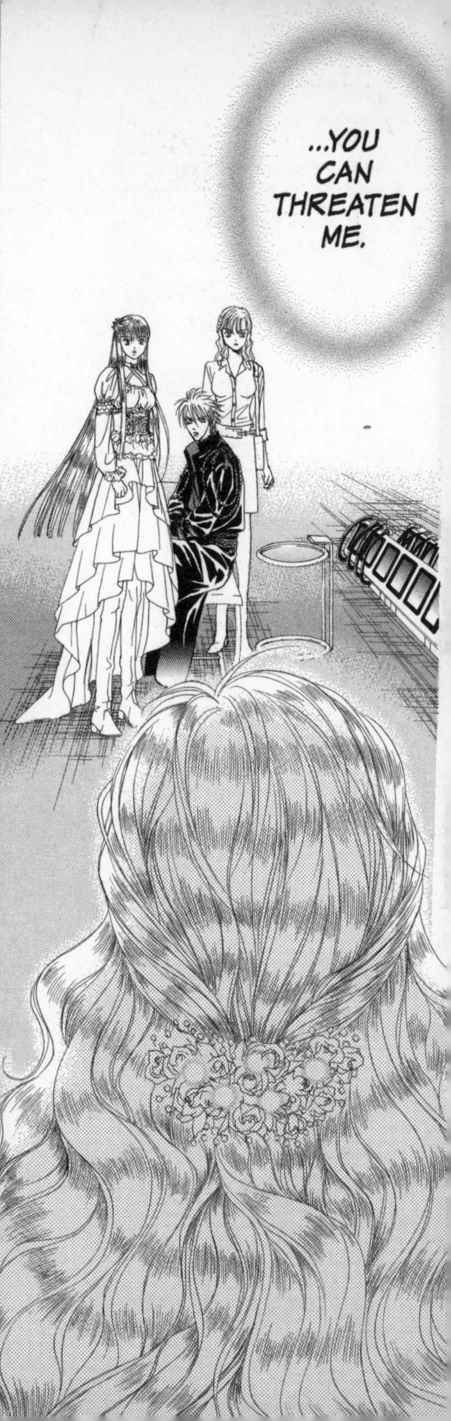
...YOU CAN THREATEN ME.

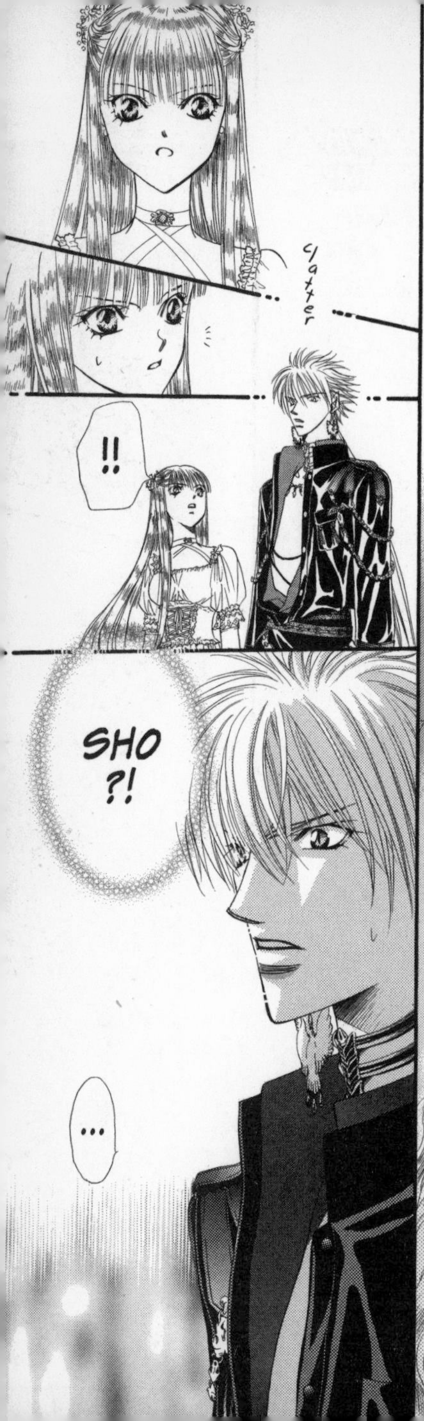
clatter
!!
SHO ?!
...

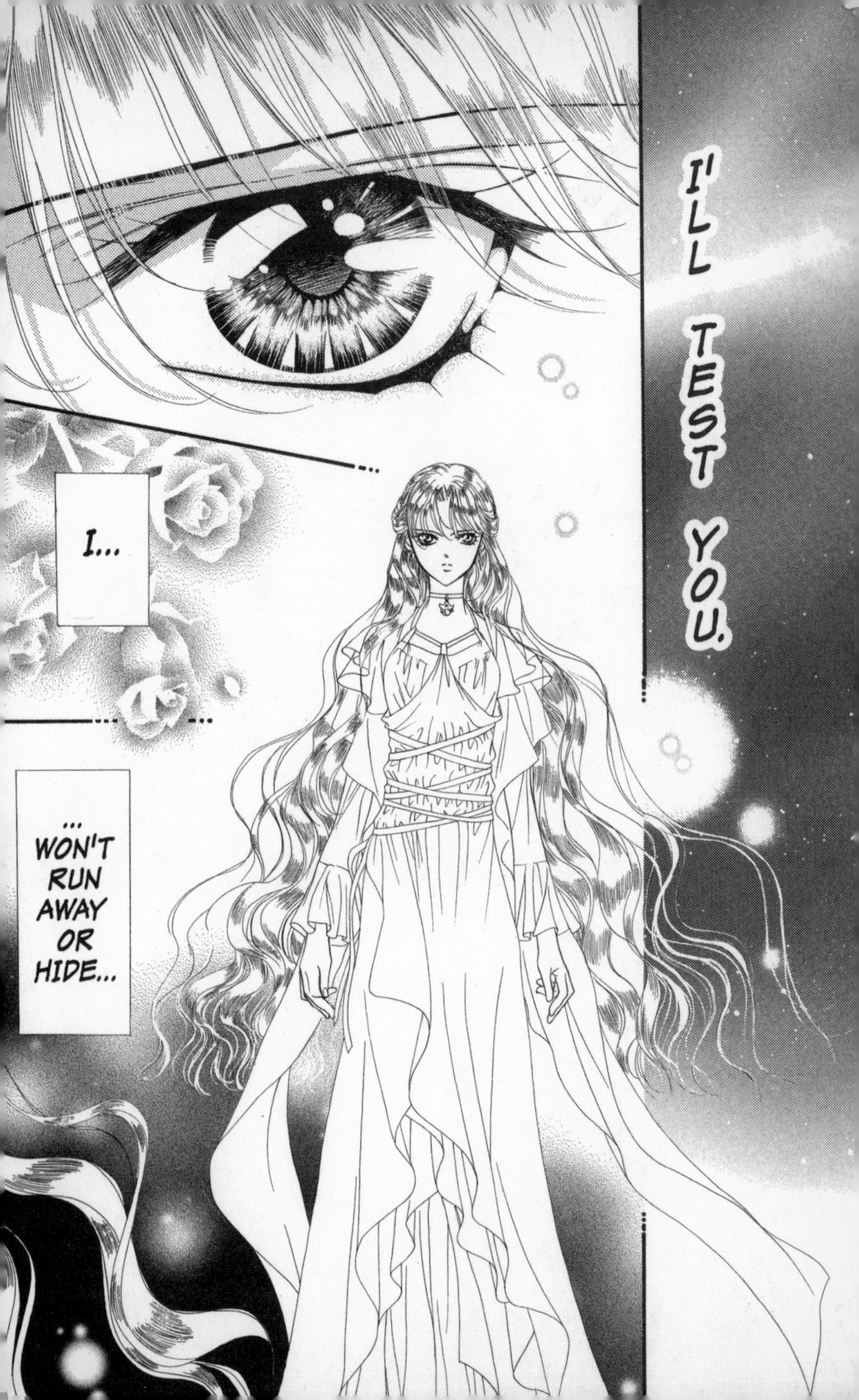
I'LL TEST YOU.
I...
... WON'T RUN AWAY OR HIDE...

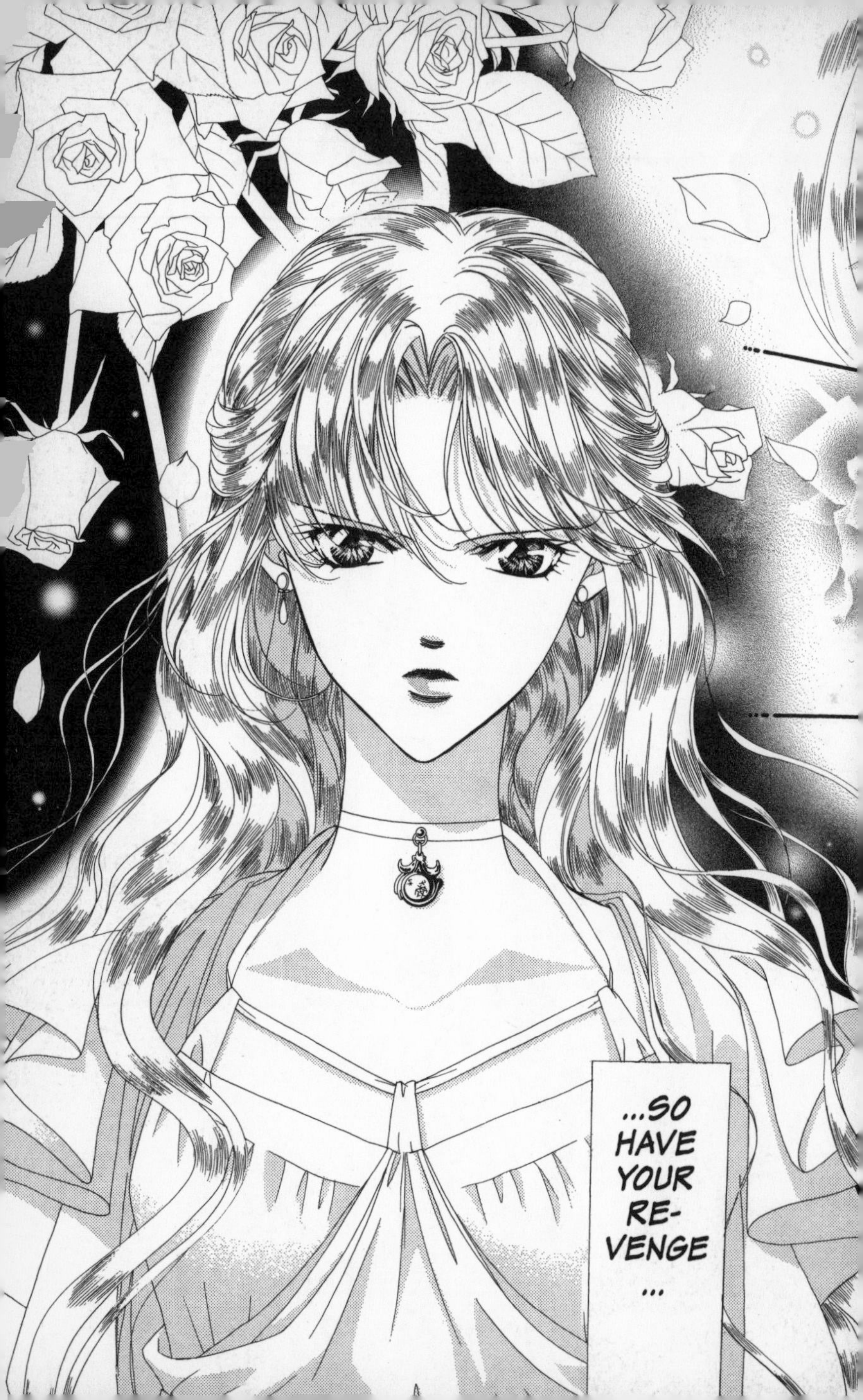
...SO HAVE YOUR RE- VENGE ...

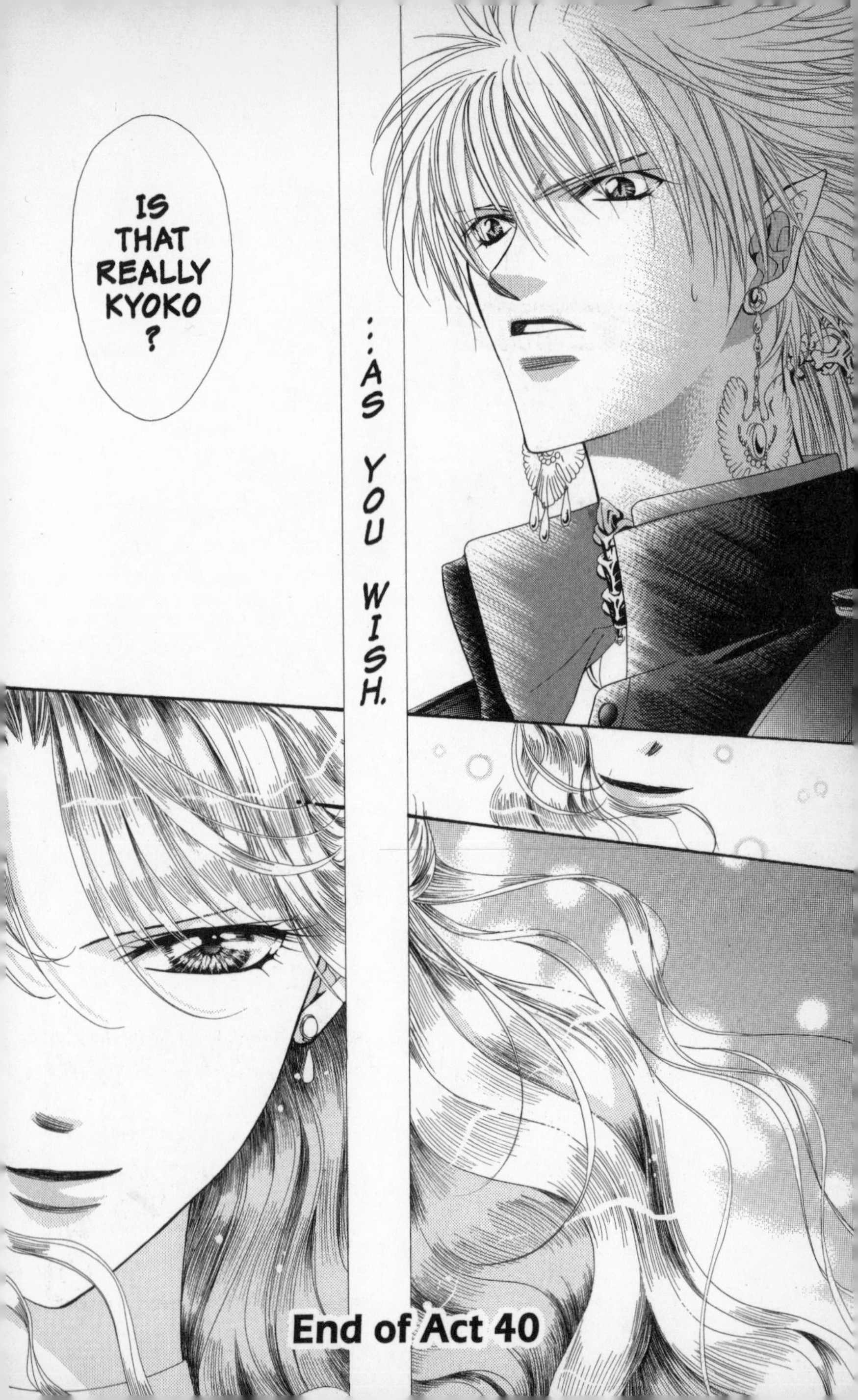
...AS YOU WISH.
IS THAT REALLY KYOKO?
End of Act 40

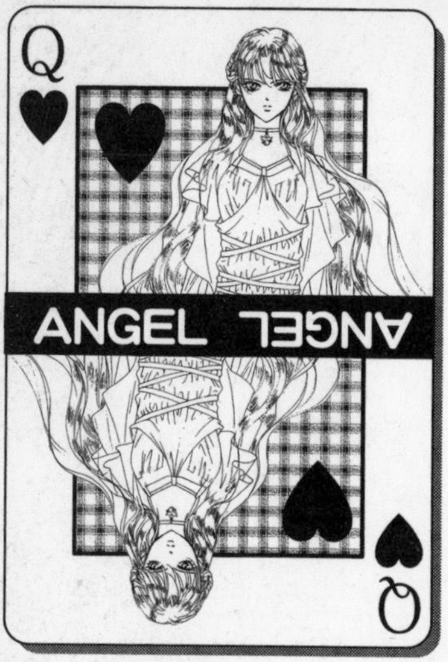
Q
ANGEL
ANGEL
Q
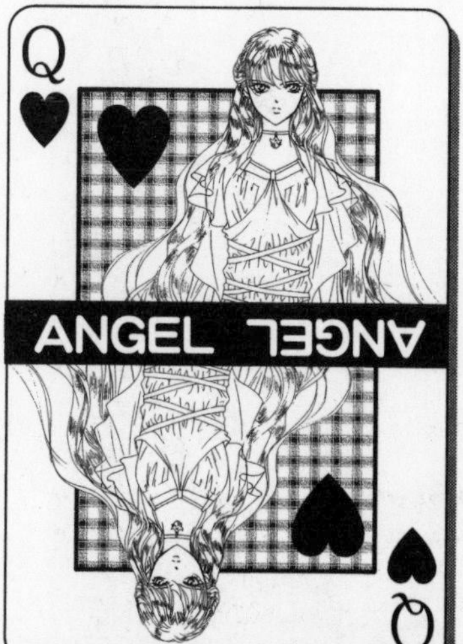
Q
ANGEL
ANGEL
Q

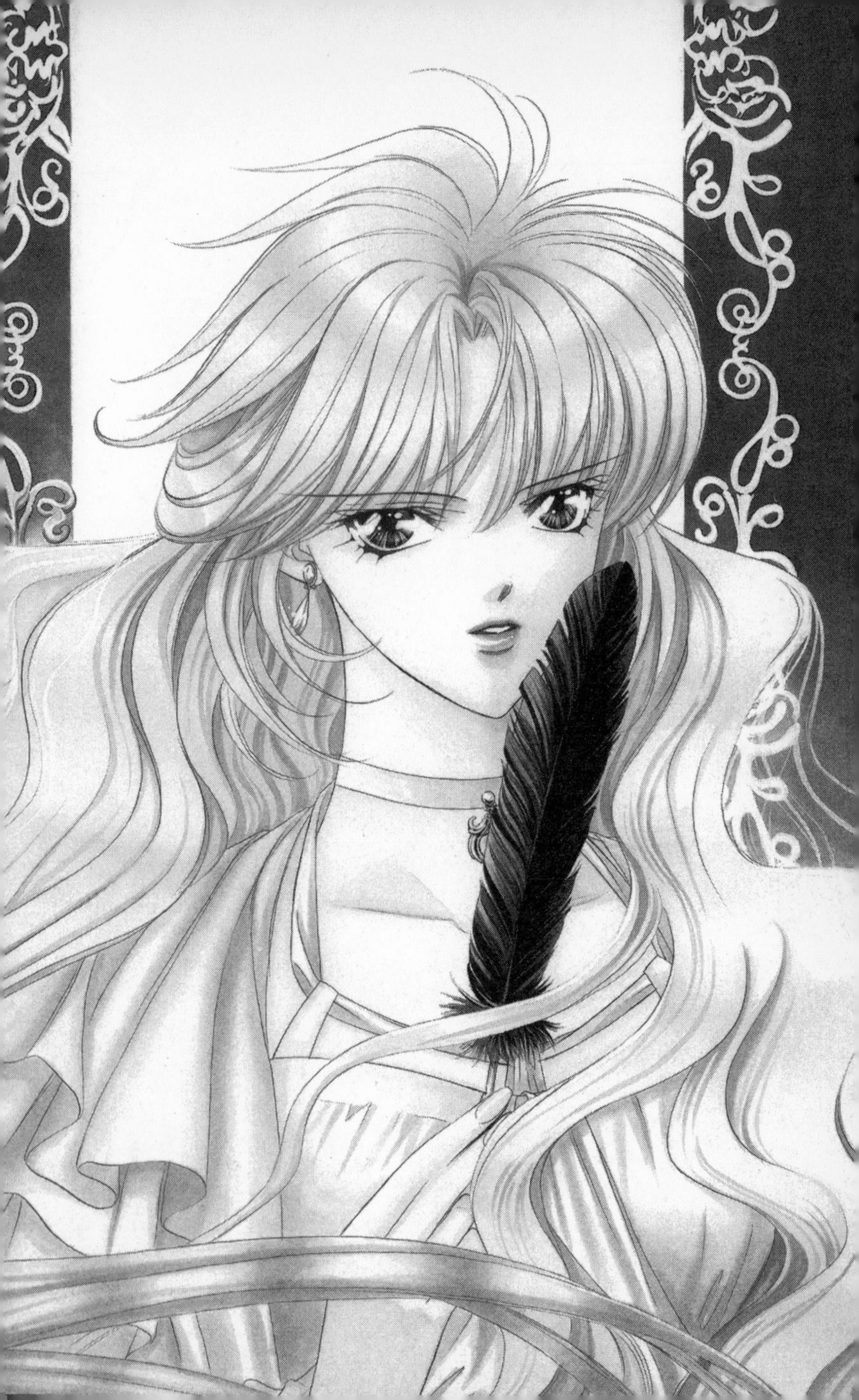

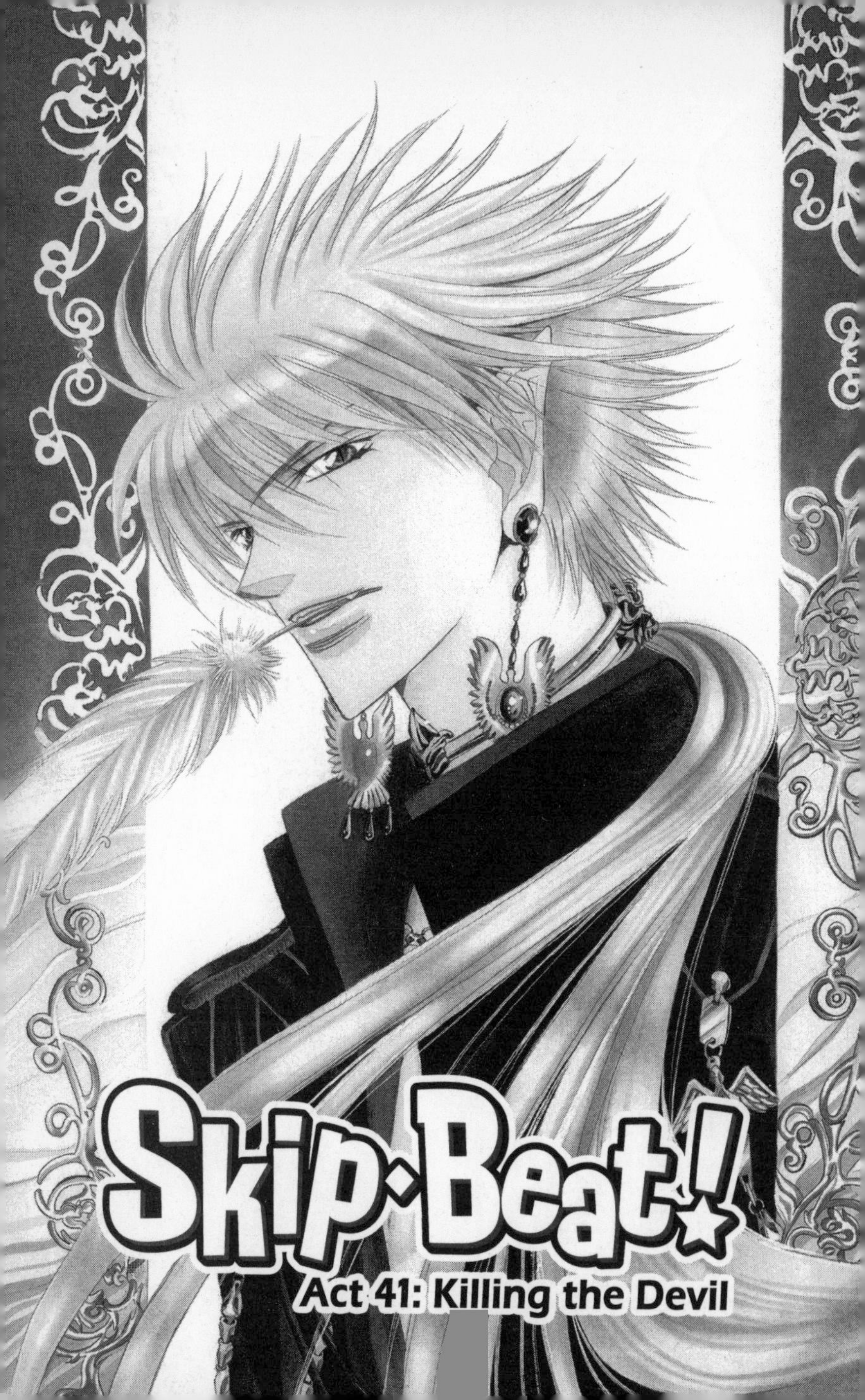
Skip·Beat!
Act 41: Killing the Devil

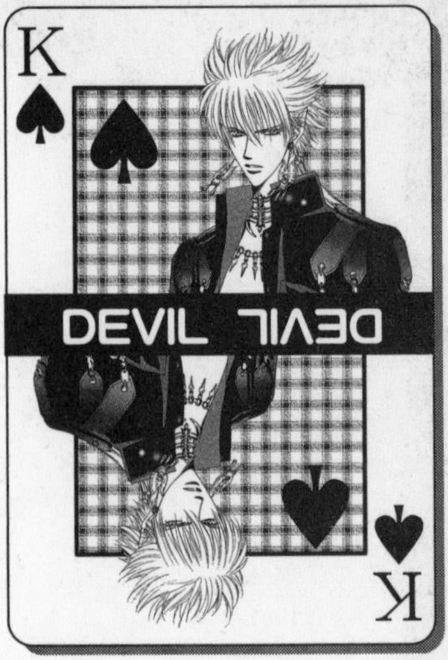
K
DEVIL
DEVIL
K
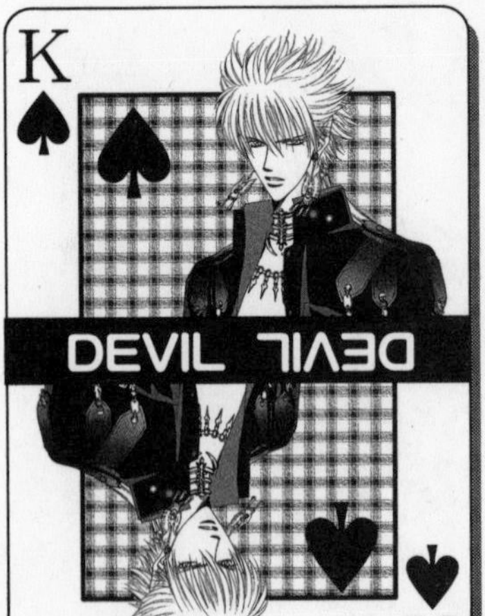
K
DEVIL
DEVIL
K

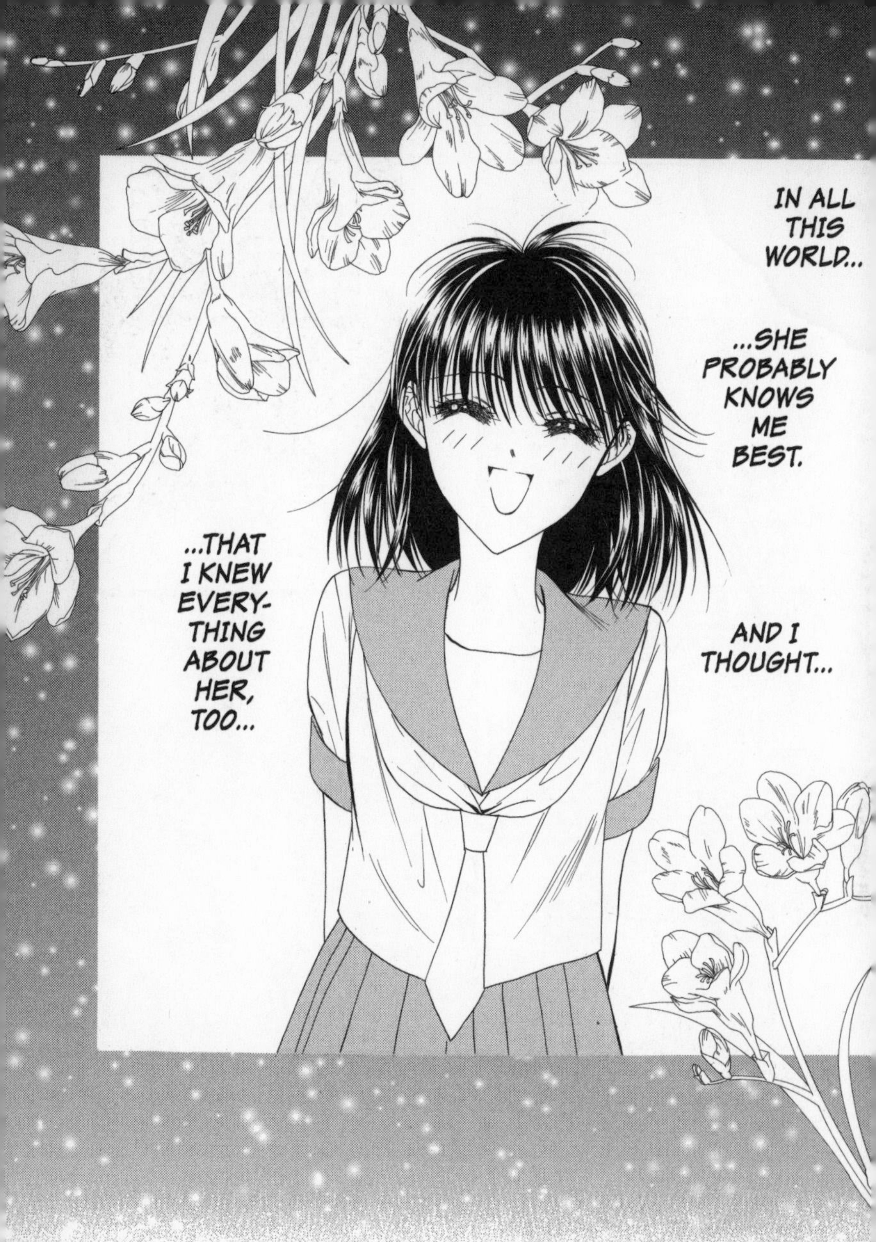
IN ALL THIS WORLD...
...SHE PROBABLY KNOWS ME BEST.
AND I THOUGHT...
...THAT I KNEW EVERY-THING ABOUT HER, TOO...

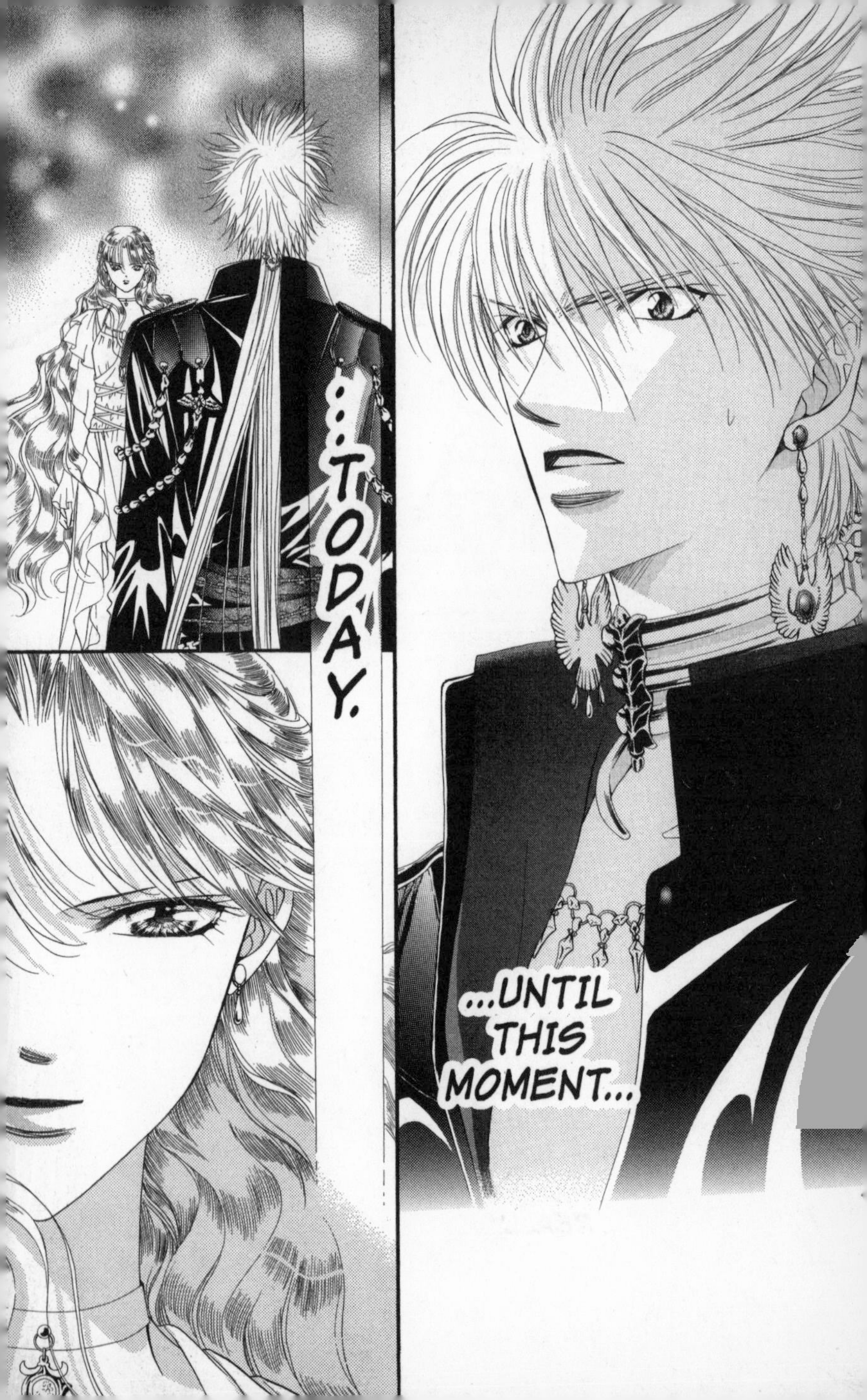
...UNTIL THIS MOMENT...
...TODAY.

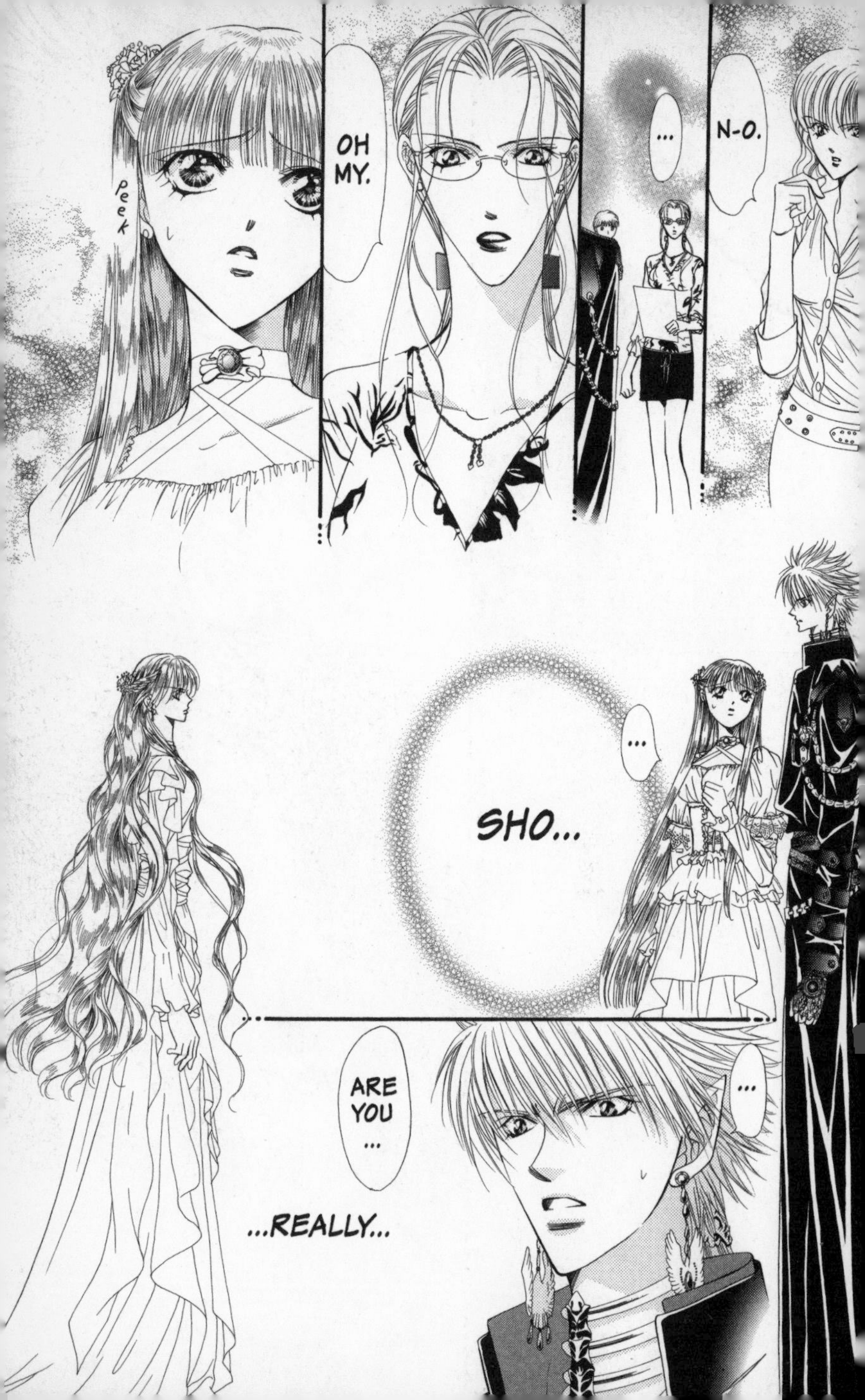
N-O.
...
OH MY.
Peek
...
SHO...
...
ARE YOU ...
...REALLY...

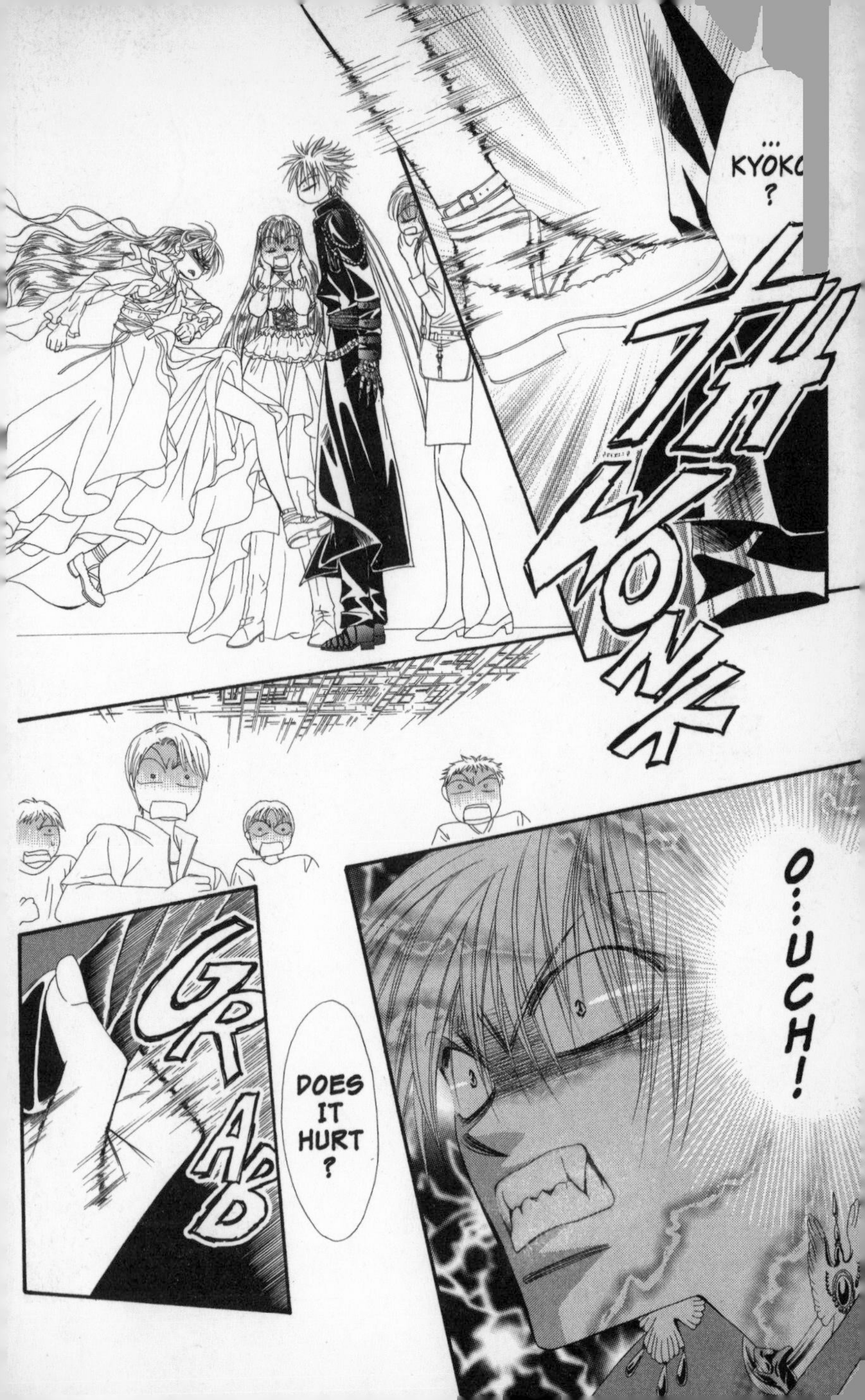
...KYOKO?
THWONK
O...UCH!
DOES IT HURT?
GRAB

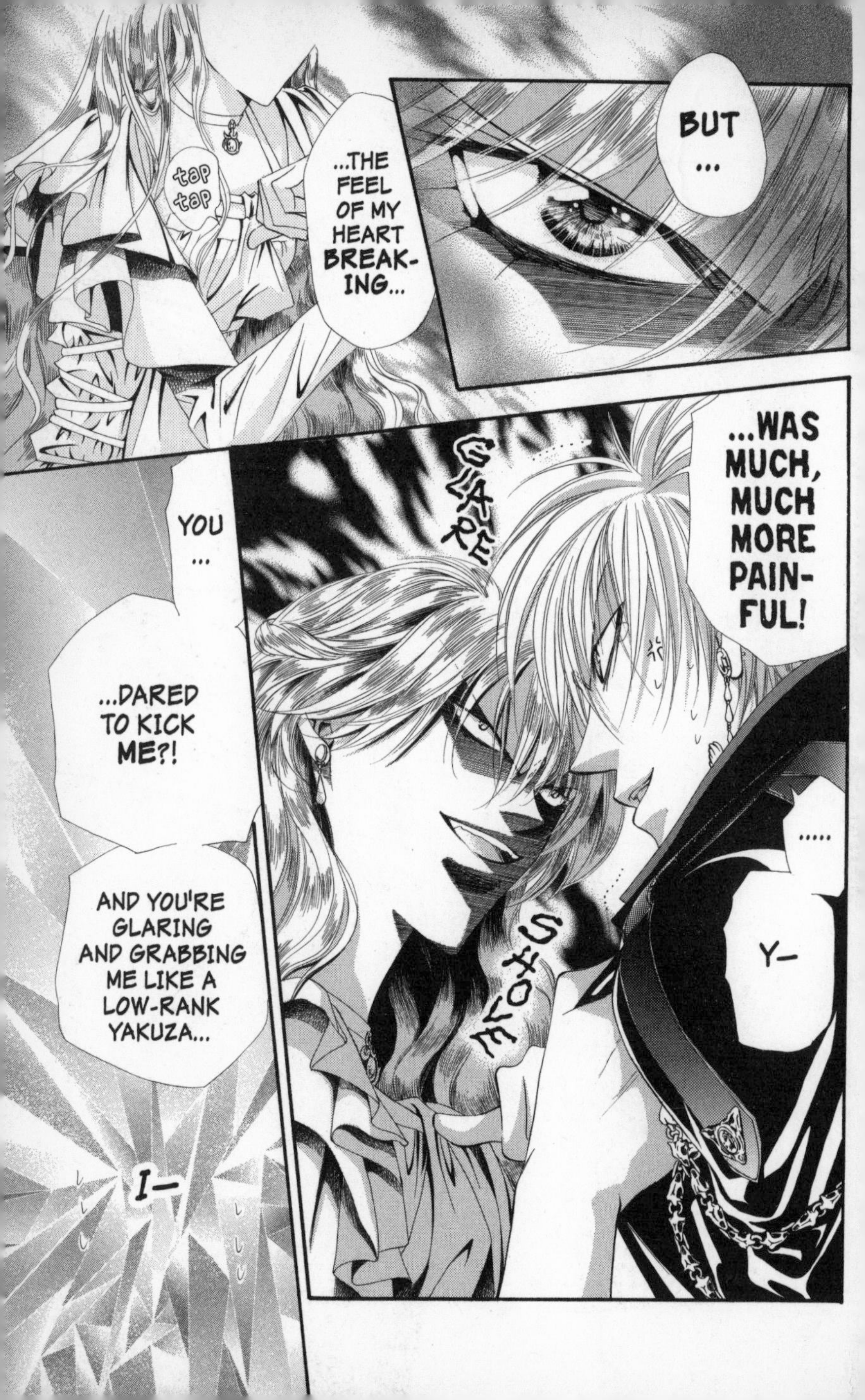
BUT ...
tap tap
...THE FEEL OF MY HEART BREAKING...
...WAS MUCH, MUCH MORE PAIN-FUL!
GLARE
.....
Y—
SHOVE
YOU ...
...DARED TO KICK ME?!
AND YOU'RE GLARING AND GRABBING ME LIKE A LOW-RANK YAKUZA...
I—

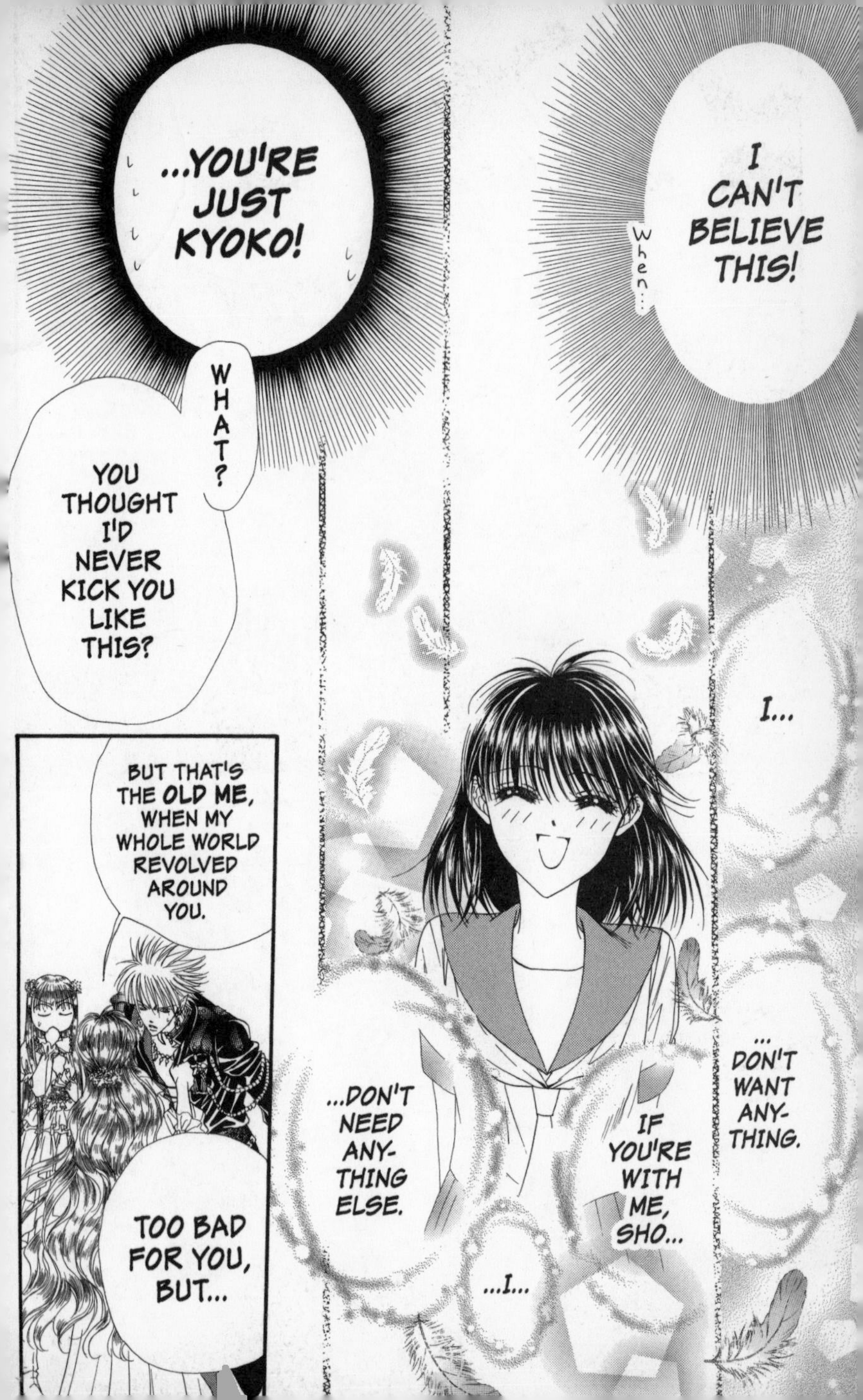
When...
I CAN'T BELIEVE THIS!
I...
...DON'T WANT ANYTHING.
IF YOU'RE WITH ME, SHO...
...I...
...DON'T NEED ANYTHING ELSE.
...YOU'RE JUST KYOKO!
WHAT?
YOU THOUGHT I'D NEVER KICK YOU LIKE THIS?
BUT THAT'S THE OLD ME, WHEN MY WHOLE WORLD REVOLVED AROUND YOU.
TOO BAD FOR YOU, BUT...

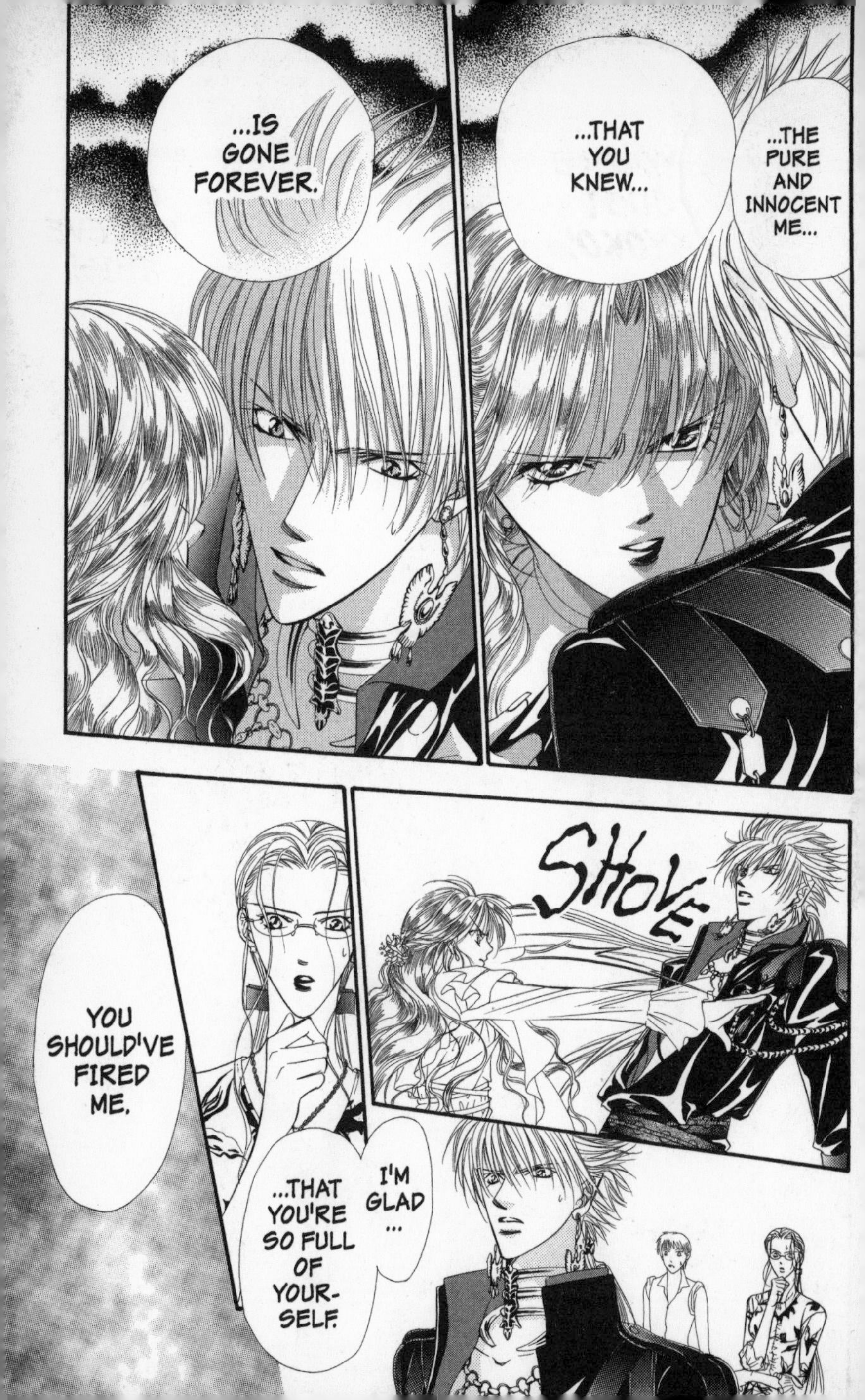
...THE PURE AND INNOCENT ME...
...THAT YOU KNEW...
...IS GONE FOREVER.
SHOVE
YOU SHOULD'VE FIRED ME.
I'M GLAD ...
...THAT YOU'RE SO FULL OF YOUR-SELF.

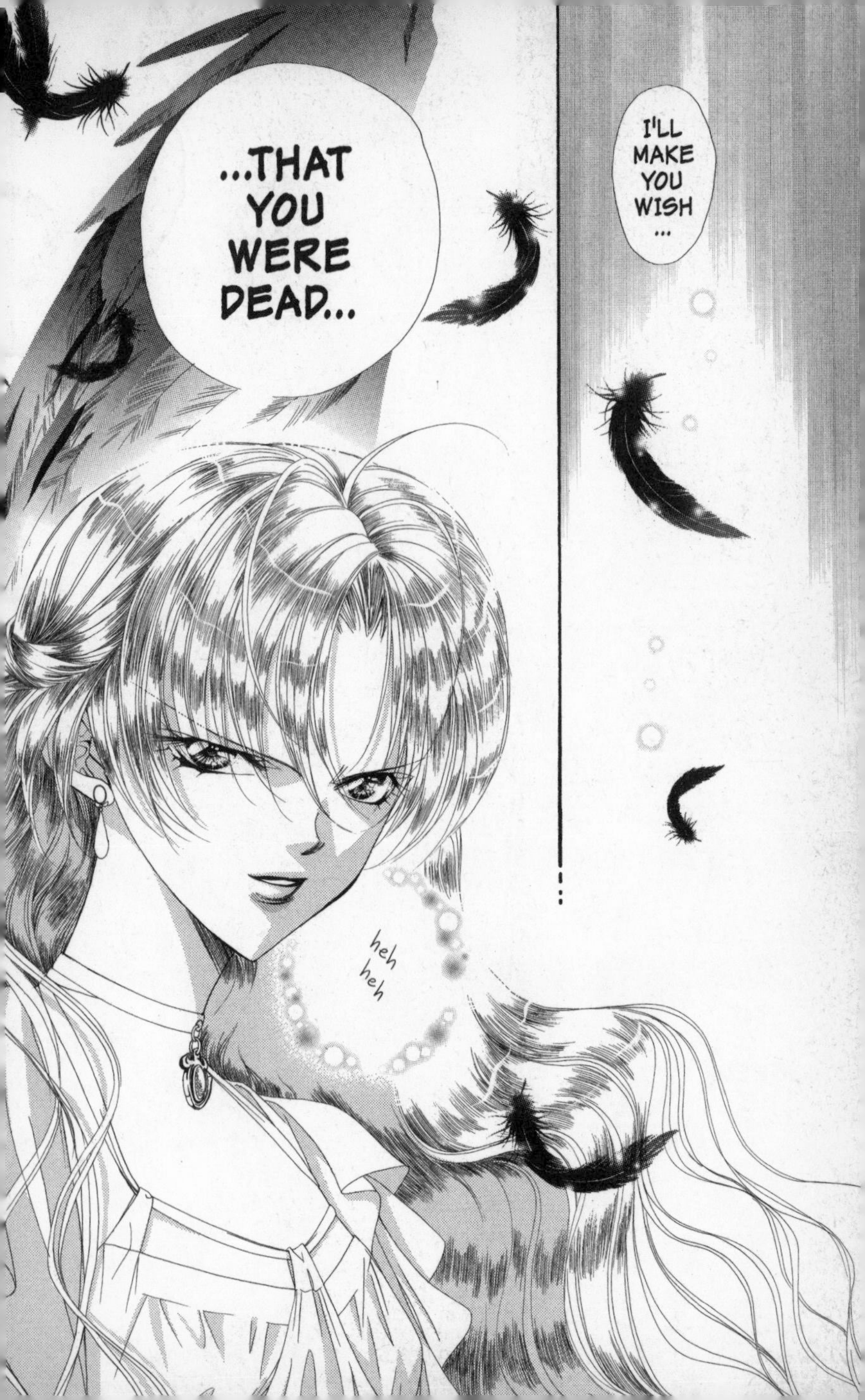
I'LL MAKE YOU WISH ...
...THAT YOU WERE DEAD...
heh heh

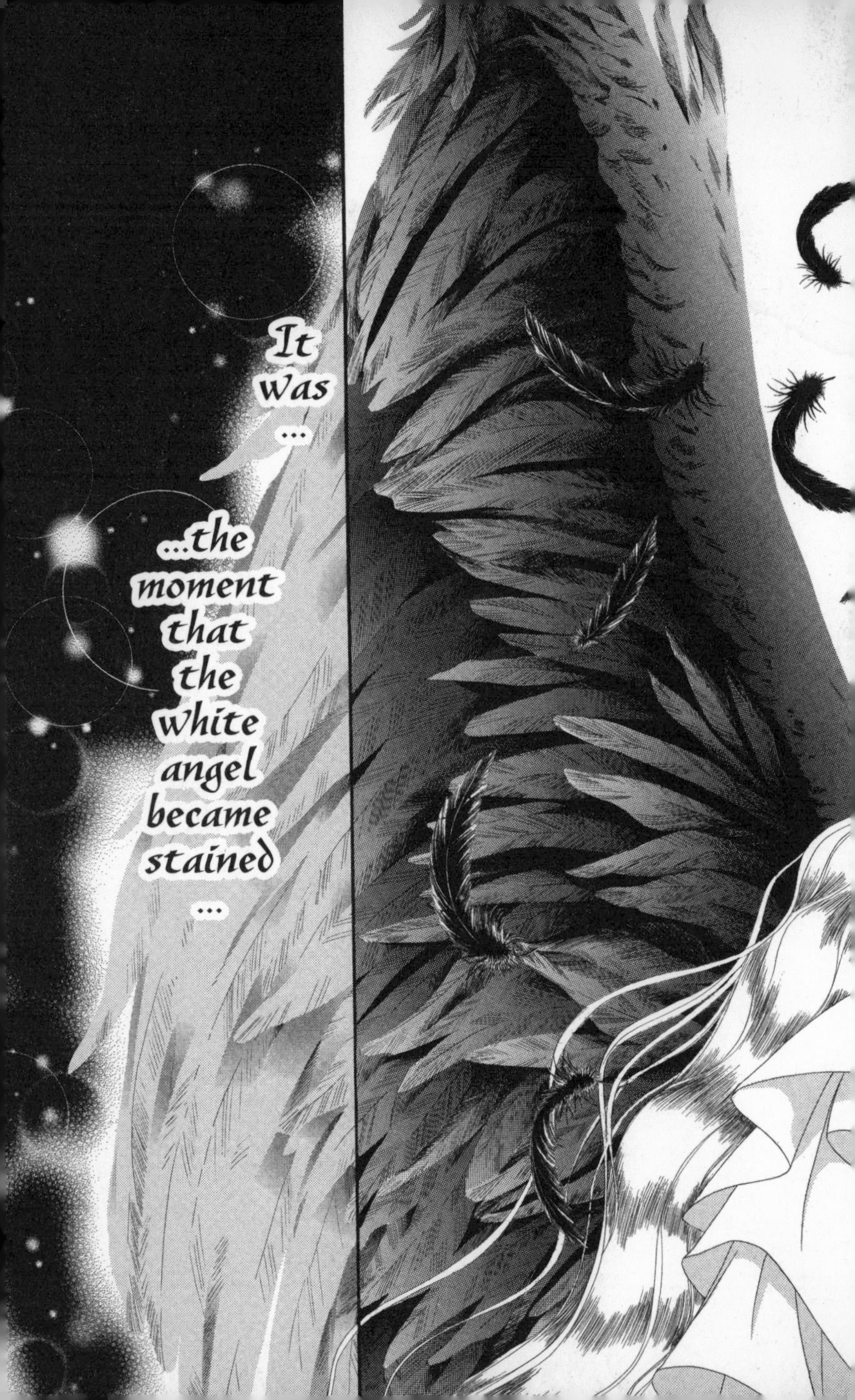
It was ...
...the moment that the white angel became stained ...

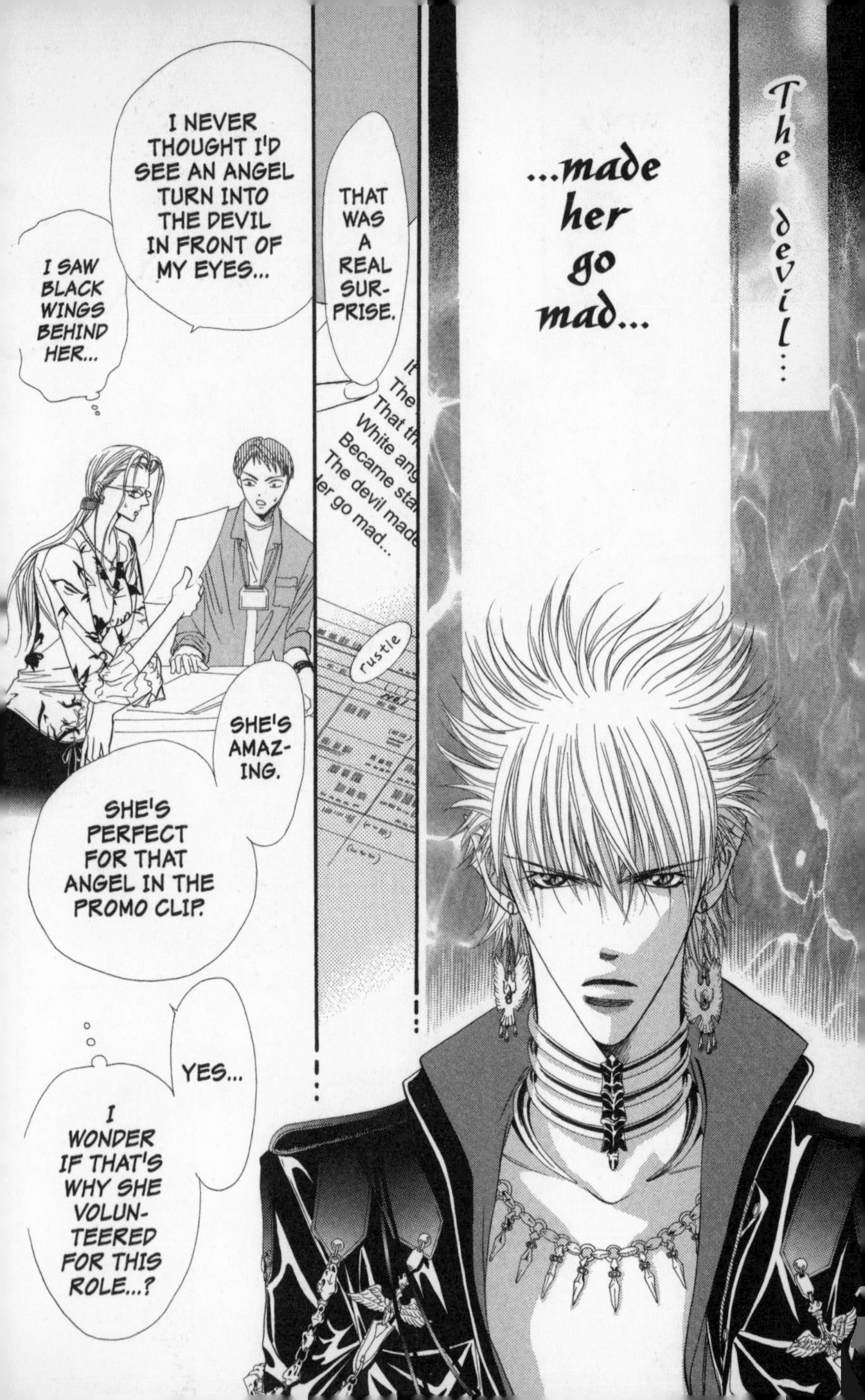
The devil...
...made her go mad...
THAT WAS A REAL SURPRISE.
I NEVER THOUGHT I'D SEE AN ANGEL TURN INTO THE DEVIL IN FRONT OF MY EYES...
I SAW BLACK WINGS BEHIND HER...
rustle
SHE'S AMAZING.
SHE'S PERFECT FOR THAT ANGEL IN THE PROMO CLIP.
YES...
I WONDER IF THAT'S WHY SHE VOLUNTEERED FOR THIS ROLE...?

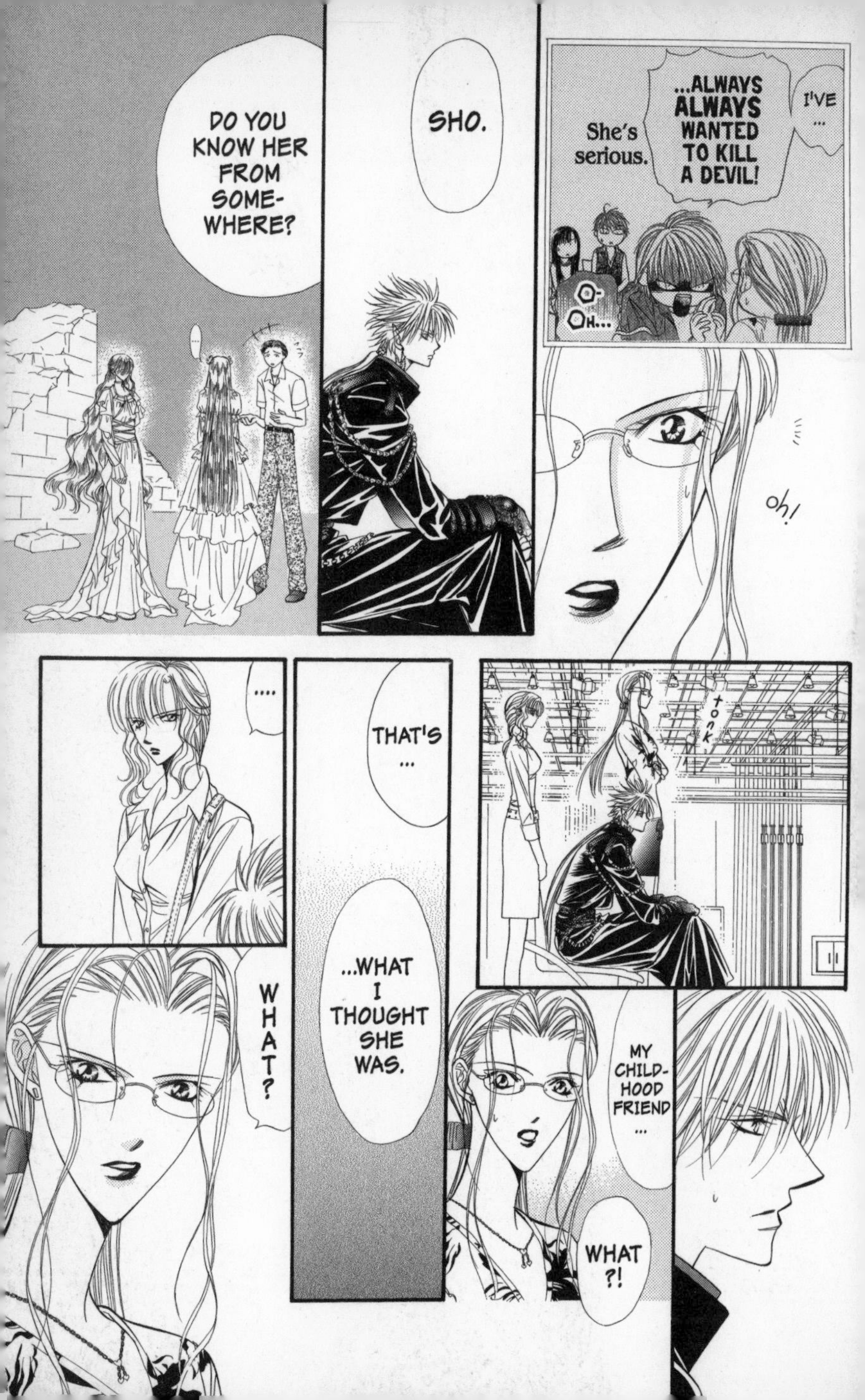
I'VE ...
...ALWAYS ALWAYS WANTED TO KILL A DEVIL!
She's serious.
O-OH...
oh!
SHO.
DO YOU KNOW HER FROM SOME-WHERE?
...
tonk
MY CHILDHOOD FRIEND ...
WHAT ?!
THAT'S ...
...WHAT I THOUGHT SHE WAS.
....
WHAT?

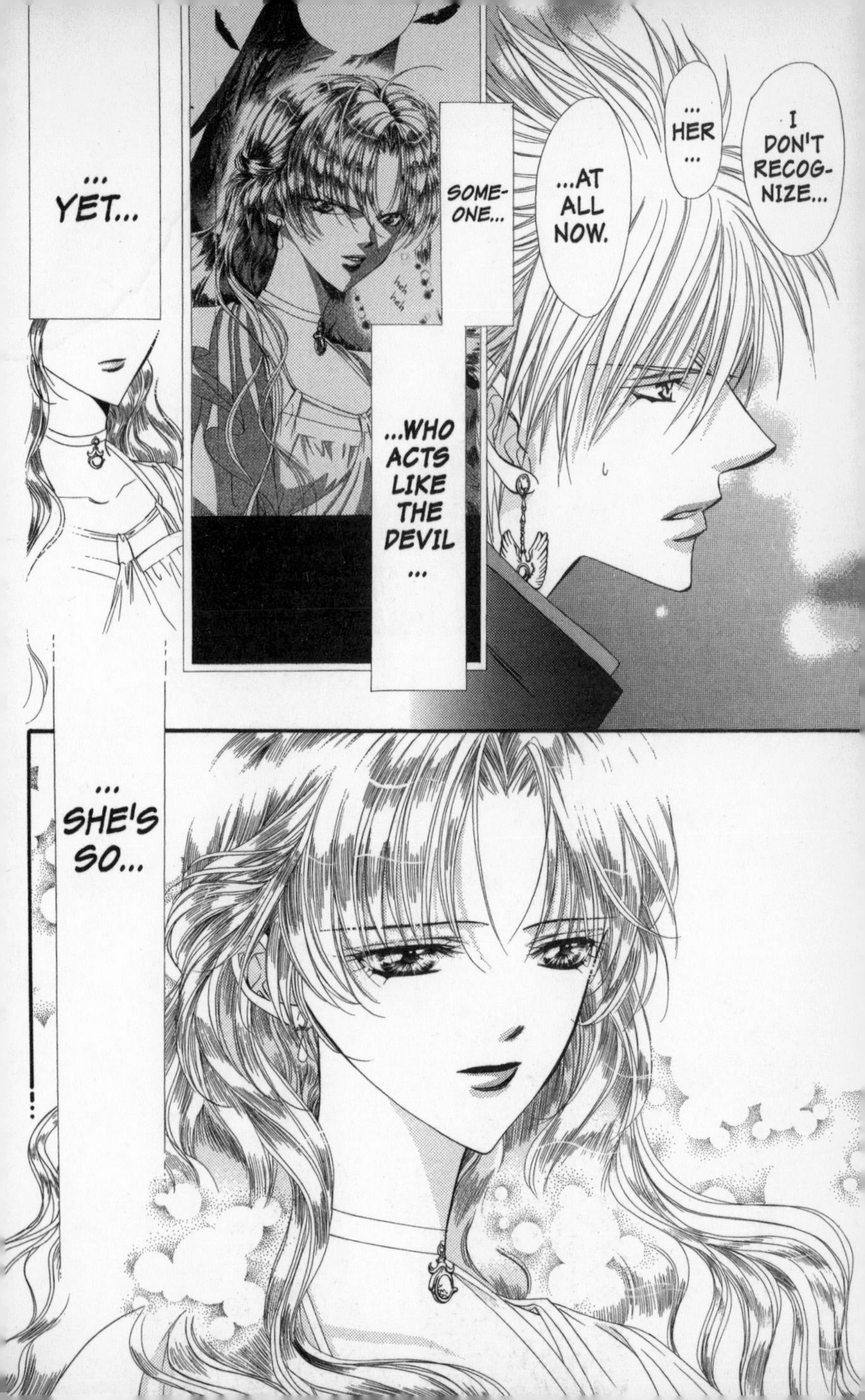
I DON'T RECOGNIZE...
...HER...
...AT ALL NOW.
SOMEONE...
...WHO ACTS LIKE THE DEVIL...
...YET...
...SHE'S SO...

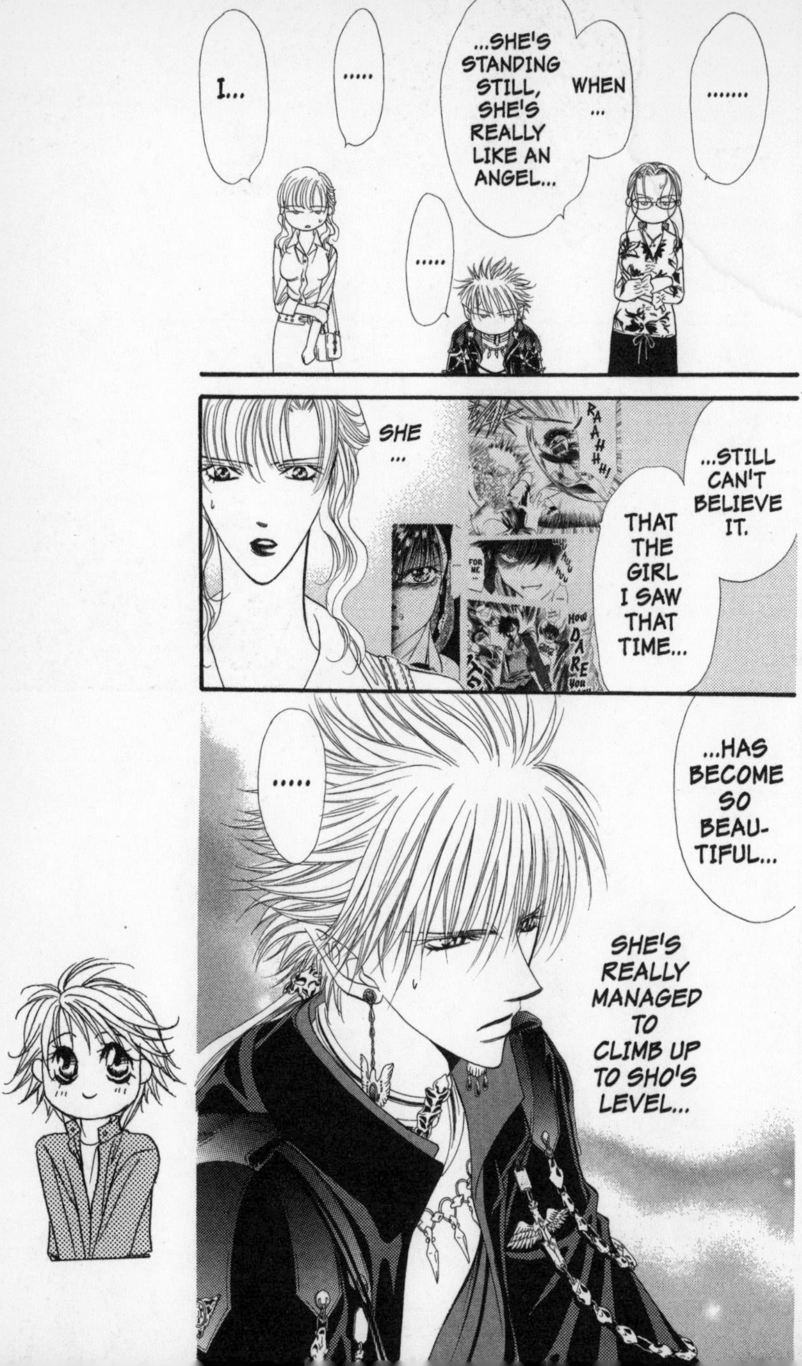
....
WHEN ...
...SHE'S STANDING STILL, SHE'S REALLY LIKE AN ANGEL...
.....
......
I...
...STILL CAN'T BELIEVE IT.
THAT THE GIRL I SAW THAT TIME...
RAAHHH!
HOW DARE YOU
SHE ...
...HAS BECOME SO BEAU-TIFUL...
SHE'S REALLY MANAGED TO CLIMB UP TO SHO'S LEVEL...
.....

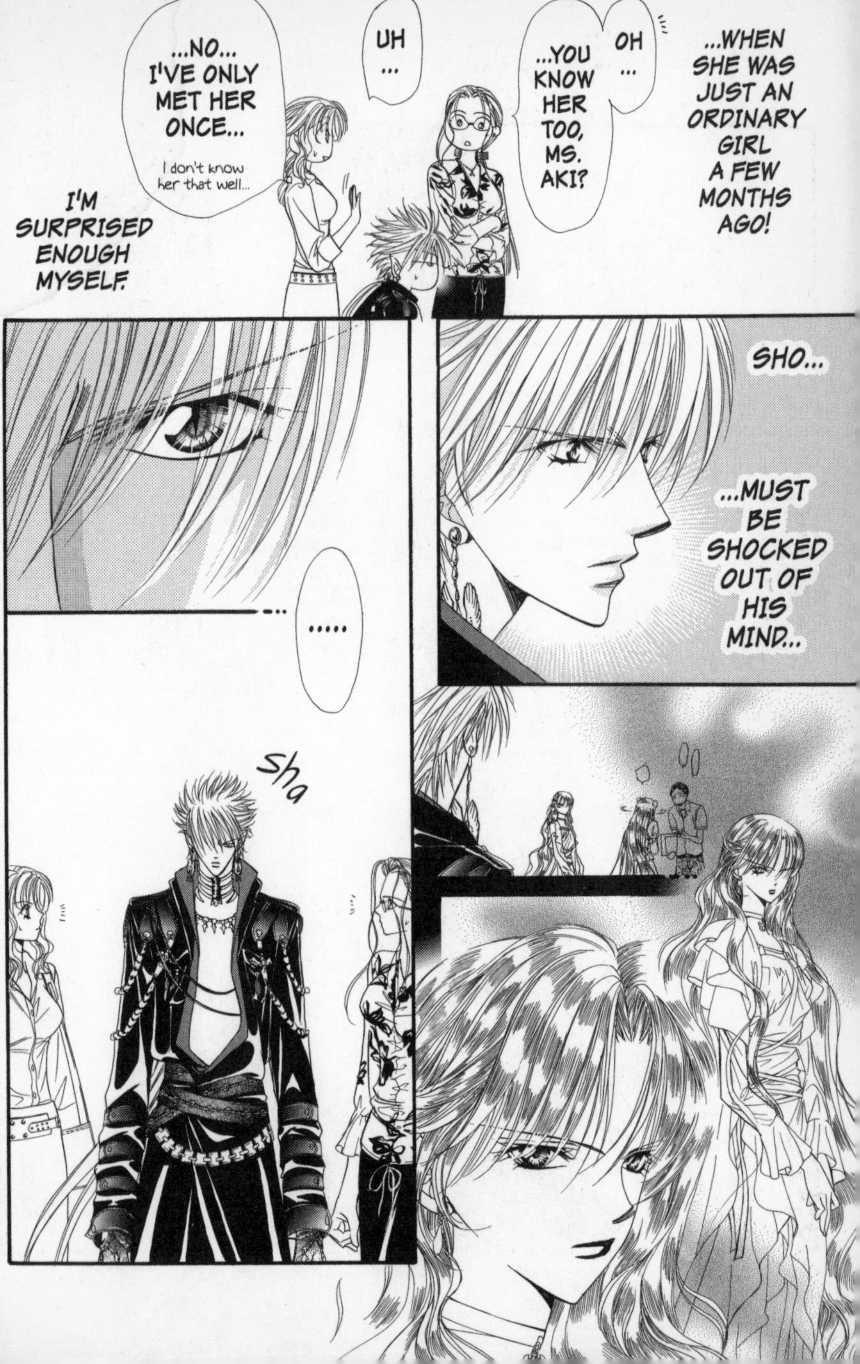
...WHEN SHE WAS JUST AN ORDINARY GIRL A FEW MONTHS AGO!
OH ...
...YOU KNOW HER TOO, MS. AKI?
UH ...
...NO... I'VE ONLY MET HER ONCE...
I don't know her that well...
I'M SURPRISED ENOUGH MYSELF.
SHO...
...MUST BE SHOCKED OUT OF HIS MIND...
.....
Sha

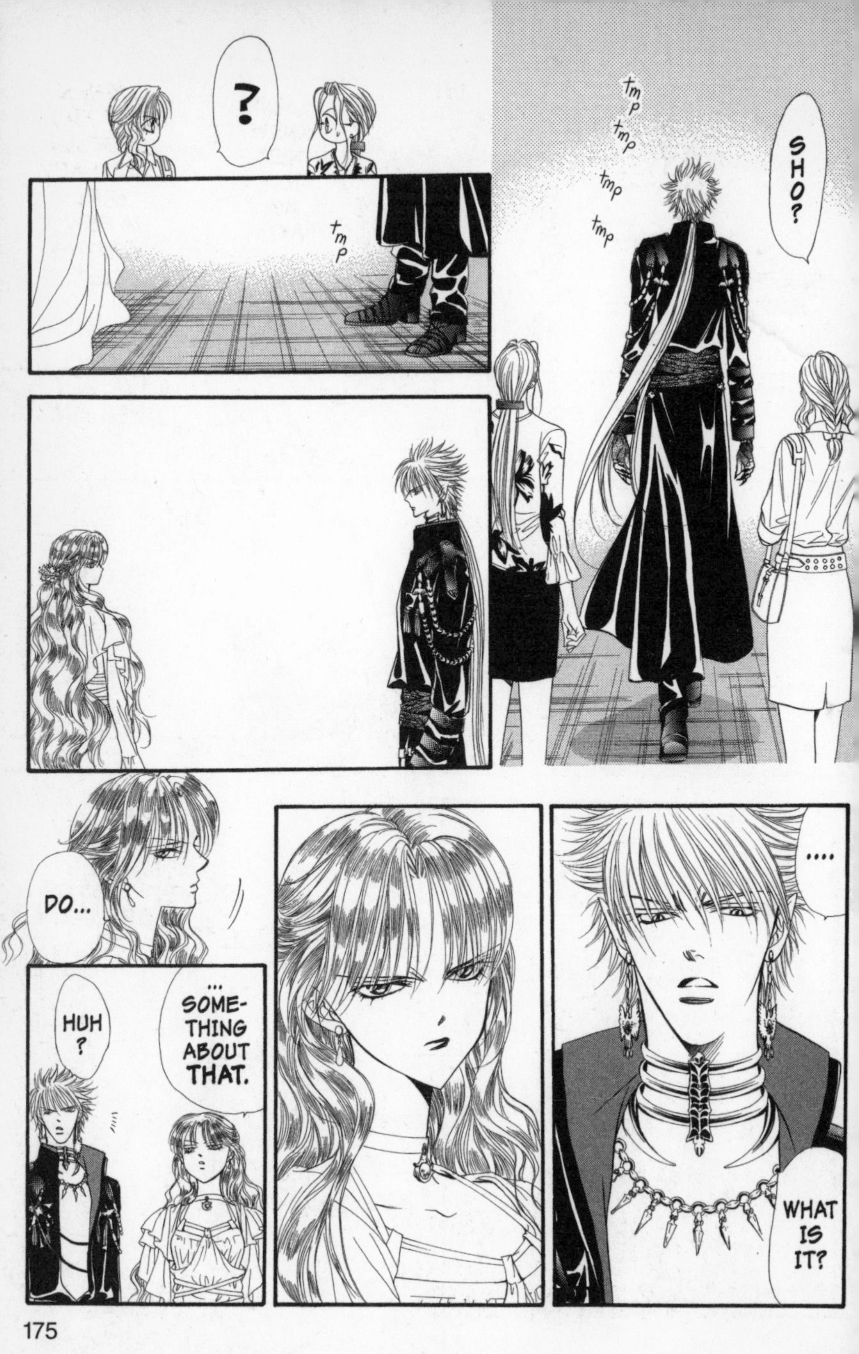

SHO?
tmp
tmp
tmp
tmp
?
tmp
....
WHAT IS IT?
DO...
... SOME-THING ABOUT THAT.
HUH?

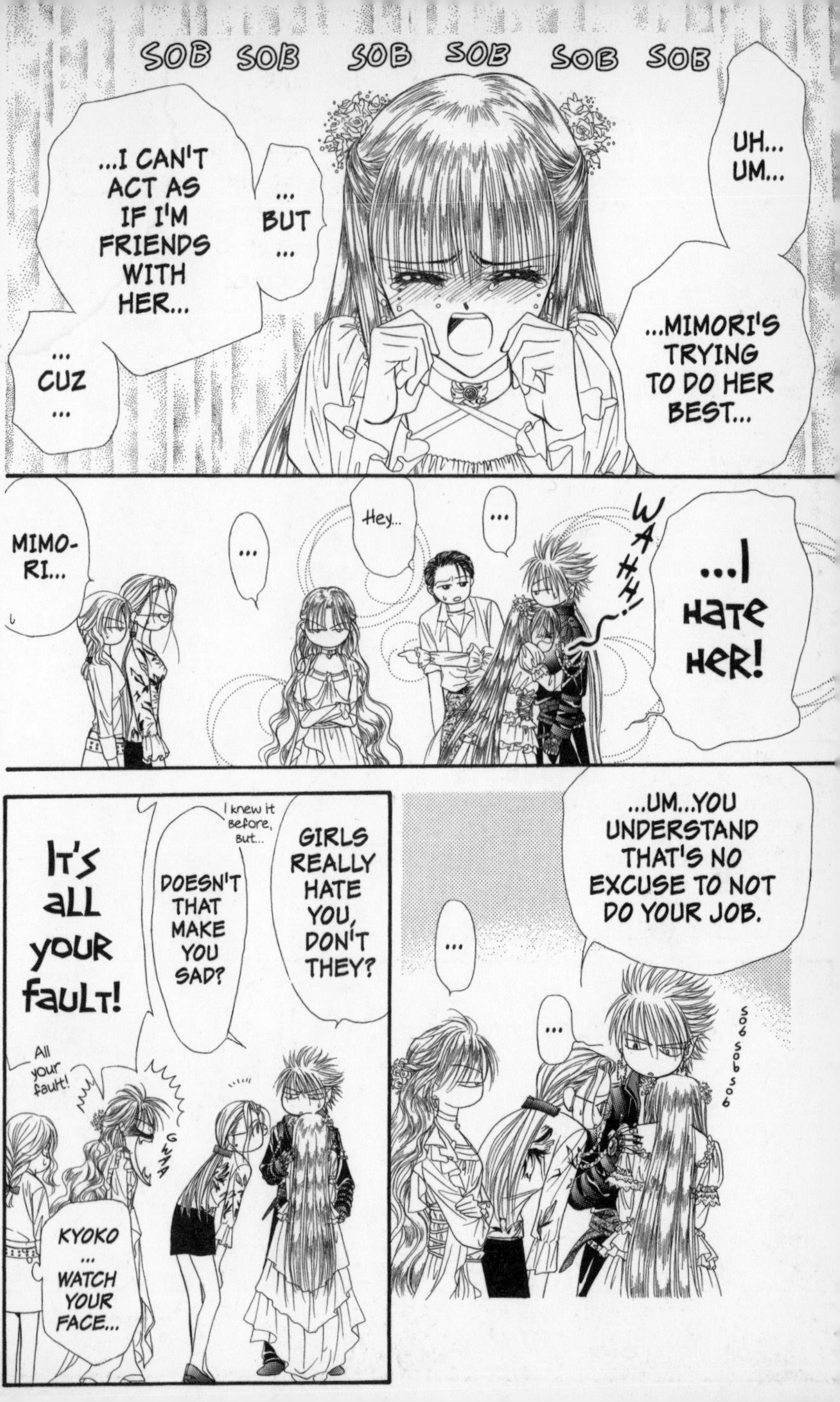
SOB SOB SOB SOB SOB SOB
UH... UM...
...MIMORI'S TRYING TO DO HER BEST...
... BUT ...
...I CAN'T ACT AS IF I'M FRIENDS WITH HER...
... CUZ ...
...I HATE HER!
WAHH!
...
Hey...
...
MIMO-RI...
...UM...YOU UNDERSTAND THAT'S NO EXCUSE TO NOT DO YOUR JOB.
SOB SOB SOB
...
...
GIRLS REALLY HATE YOU, DON'T THEY?
I knew it before, but...
DOESN'T THAT MAKE YOU SAD?
It's all your fault!
All your fault!
GWAA
KYOKO ... WATCH YOUR FACE...

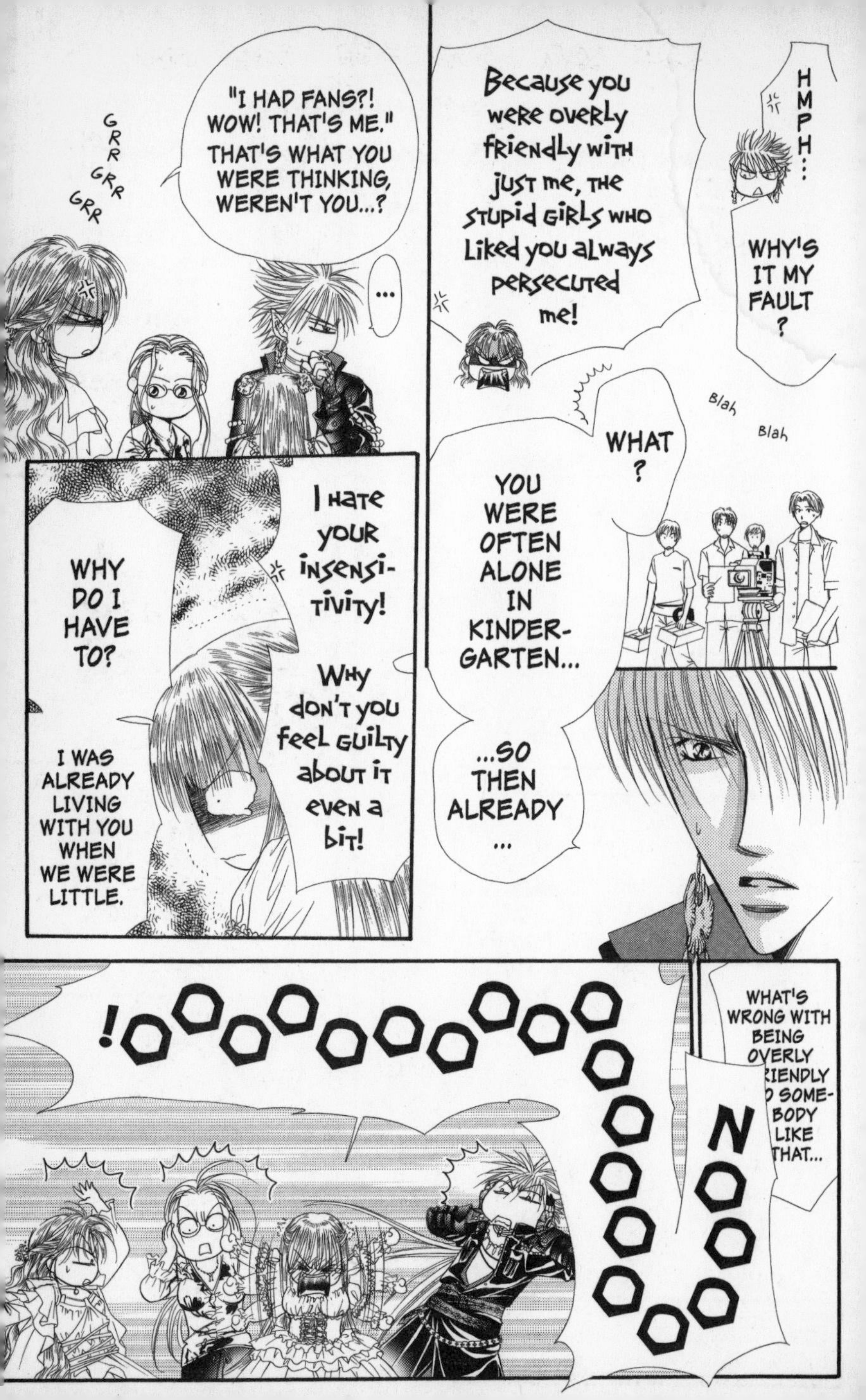
HMPH...
Because you were overly friendly with just me, the stupid girls who liked you always persecuted me!
WHY'S IT MY FAULT?
Blah
Blah
WHAT?
YOU WERE OFTEN ALONE IN KINDERGARTEN...
...SO THEN ALREADY...
"I HAD FANS?! WOW! THAT'S ME." THAT'S WHAT YOU WERE THINKING, WEREN'T YOU...?
GRR GRR GRR
...
I hate your insensitivity!
Why don't you feel guilty about it even a bit!
WHY DO I HAVE TO?
I WAS ALREADY LIVING WITH YOU WHEN WE WERE LITTLE.
WHAT'S WRONG WITH BEING OVERLY RIENDLY O SOME-BODY LIKE THAT...
NOOOOOOOOOOOOOOOOOOOOOOOO!

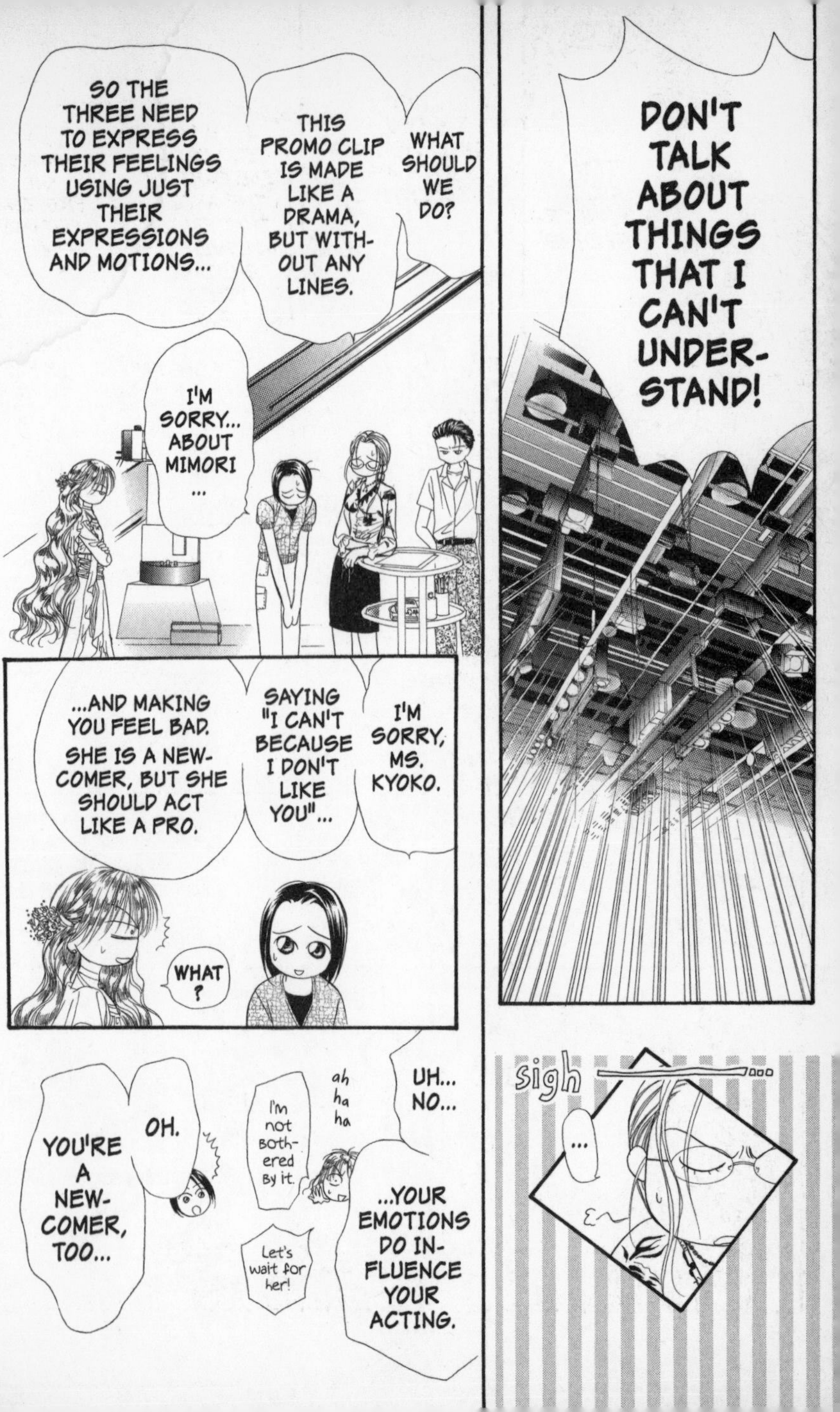
DON'T TALK ABOUT THINGS THAT I CAN'T UNDER-STAND!
WHAT SHOULD WE DO?
THIS PROMO CLIP IS MADE LIKE A DRAMA, BUT WITH-OUT ANY LINES.
SO THE THREE NEED TO EXPRESS THEIR FEELINGS USING JUST THEIR EXPRESSIONS AND MOTIONS...
I'M SORRY... ABOUT MIMORI ...
I'M SORRY, MS. KYOKO.
SAYING "I CAN'T BECAUSE I DON'T LIKE YOU"...
...AND MAKING YOU FEEL BAD.
SHE IS A NEW-COMER, BUT SHE SHOULD ACT LIKE A PRO.
WHAT ?
sigh
...
UH... NO...
ah ha ha
I'm not Both-ered By it.
...YOUR EMOTIONS DO IN-FLUENCE YOUR ACTING.
Let's wait for her!
OH.
YOU'RE A NEW-COMER, TOO...

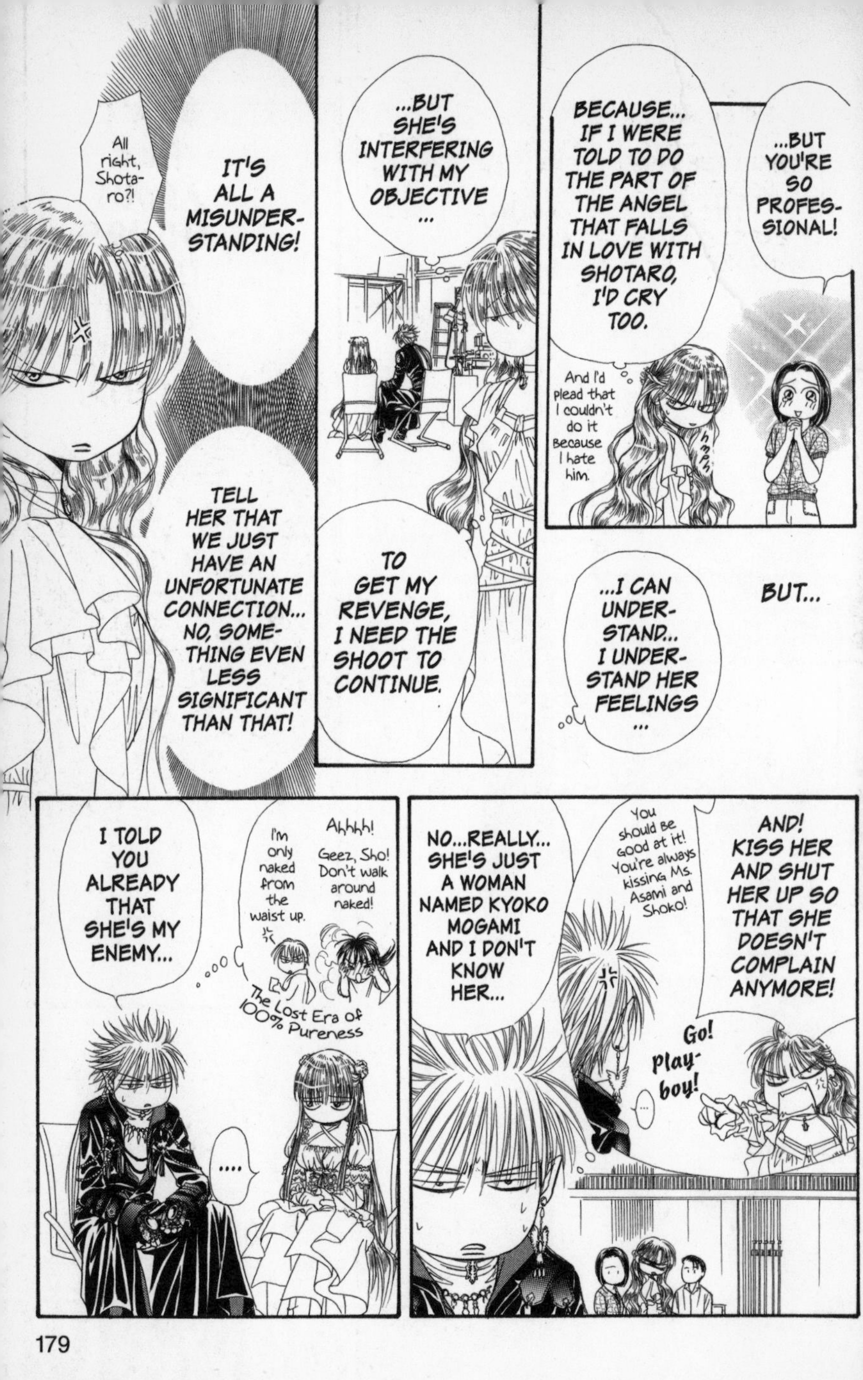
...BUT YOU'RE SO PROFESSIONAL!
BECAUSE... IF I WERE TOLD TO DO THE PART OF THE ANGEL THAT FALLS IN LOVE WITH SHOTARO, I'D CRY TOO.
And I'd plead that I couldn't do it Because I hate him.
hmph
BUT...
...I CAN UNDERSTAND... I UNDERSTAND HER FEELINGS ...
...BUT SHE'S INTERFERING WITH MY OBJECTIVE ...
TO GET MY REVENGE, I NEED THE SHOOT TO CONTINUE.
IT'S ALL A MISUNDERSTANDING!
All right, Shotaro?!
TELL HER THAT WE JUST HAVE AN UNFORTUNATE CONNECTION... NO, SOMETHING EVEN LESS SIGNIFICANT THAN THAT!
AND! KISS HER AND SHUT HER UP SO THAT SHE DOESN'T COMPLAIN ANYMORE!
You should Be good at it! You're always kissing Ms. Asami and Shoko!
NO...REALLY... SHE'S JUST A WOMAN NAMED KYOKO MOGAMI AND I DON'T KNOW HER...
Go! Playboy!
...
Ahhhh! Geez, Sho! Don't walk around naked!
I'm only naked from the waist up.
I TOLD YOU ALREADY THAT SHE'S MY ENEMY...
The Lost Era of 100% Pureness
....

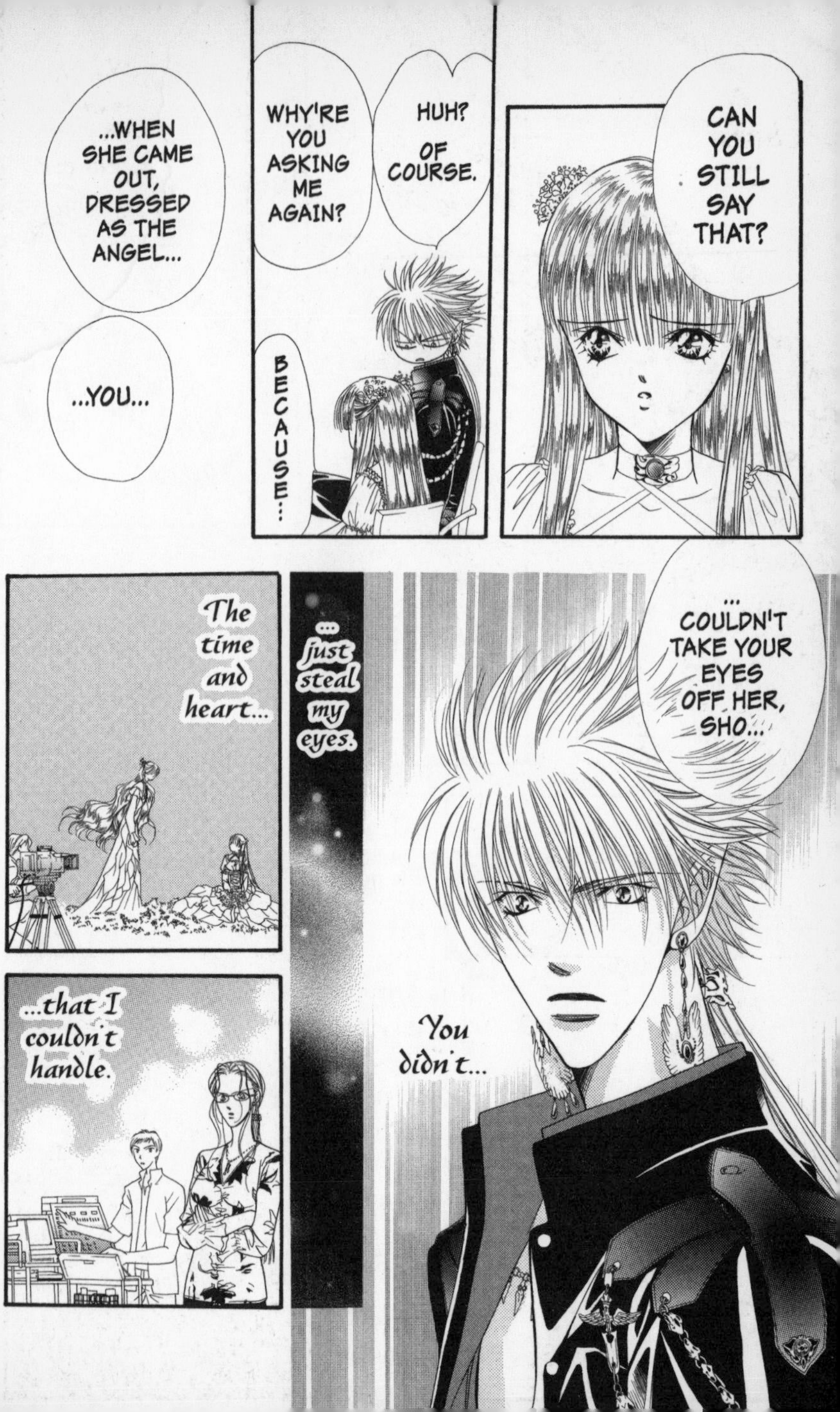
CAN YOU STILL SAY THAT?
HUH? OF COURSE.
WHY'RE YOU ASKING ME AGAIN?
BECAUSE...
...WHEN SHE CAME OUT, DRESSED AS THE ANGEL...
...YOU...
...COULDN'T TAKE YOUR EYES OFF HER, SHO...
You didn't...
...just steal my eyes.
The time and heart...
...that I couldn't handle.

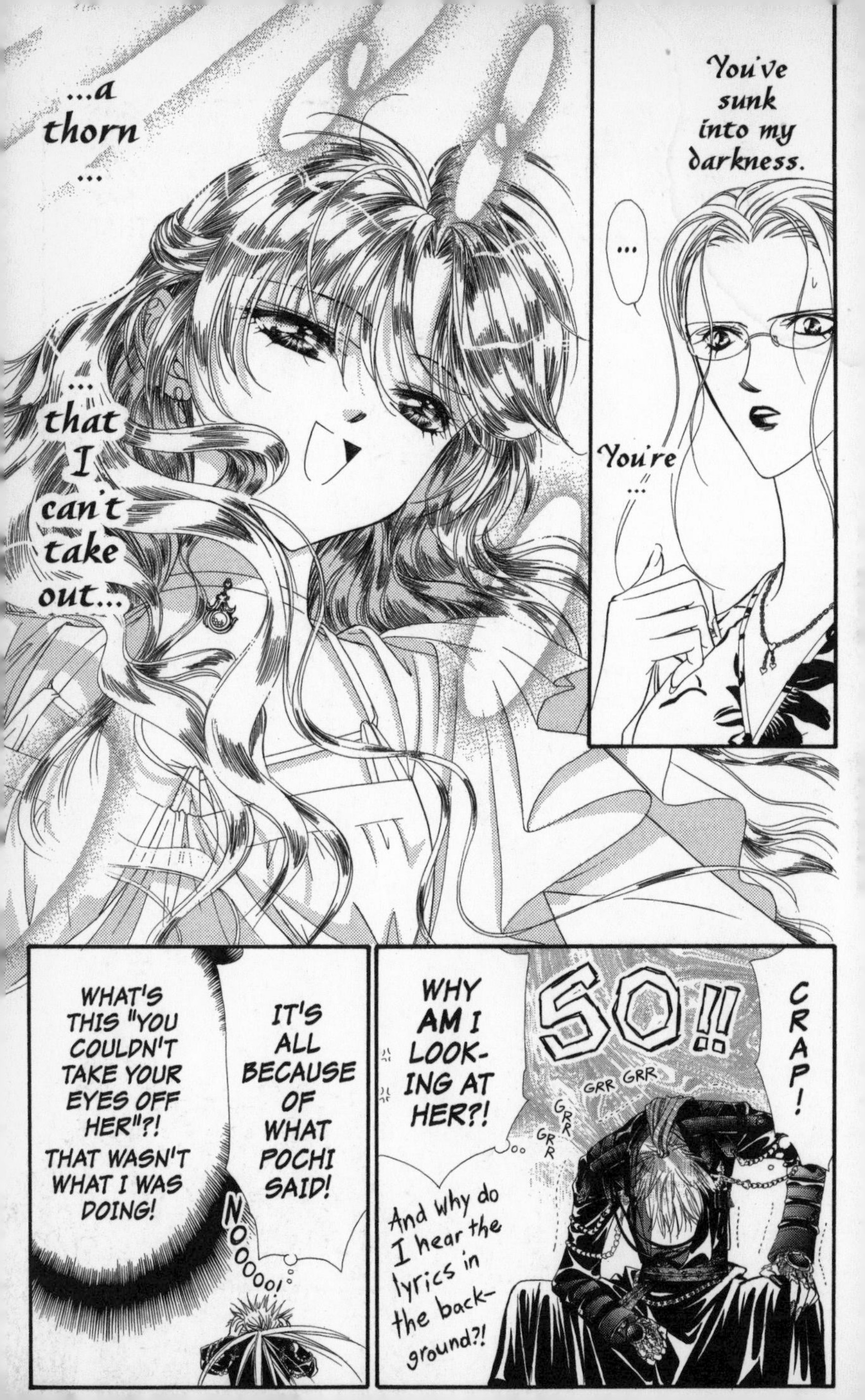
You've sunk into my darkness.
...
You're ...
...a thorn ...
... that I can't take out...
WHY AM I LOOKING AT HER?!
And why do I hear the lyrics in the background?!
SO!!
CRAP!
GRR GRR
GRR GRR
WHAT'S THIS "YOU COULDN'T TAKE YOUR EYES OFF HER"?! THAT WASN'T WHAT I WAS DOING!
IT'S ALL BECAUSE OF WHAT POCHI SAID!
NOOOOO!

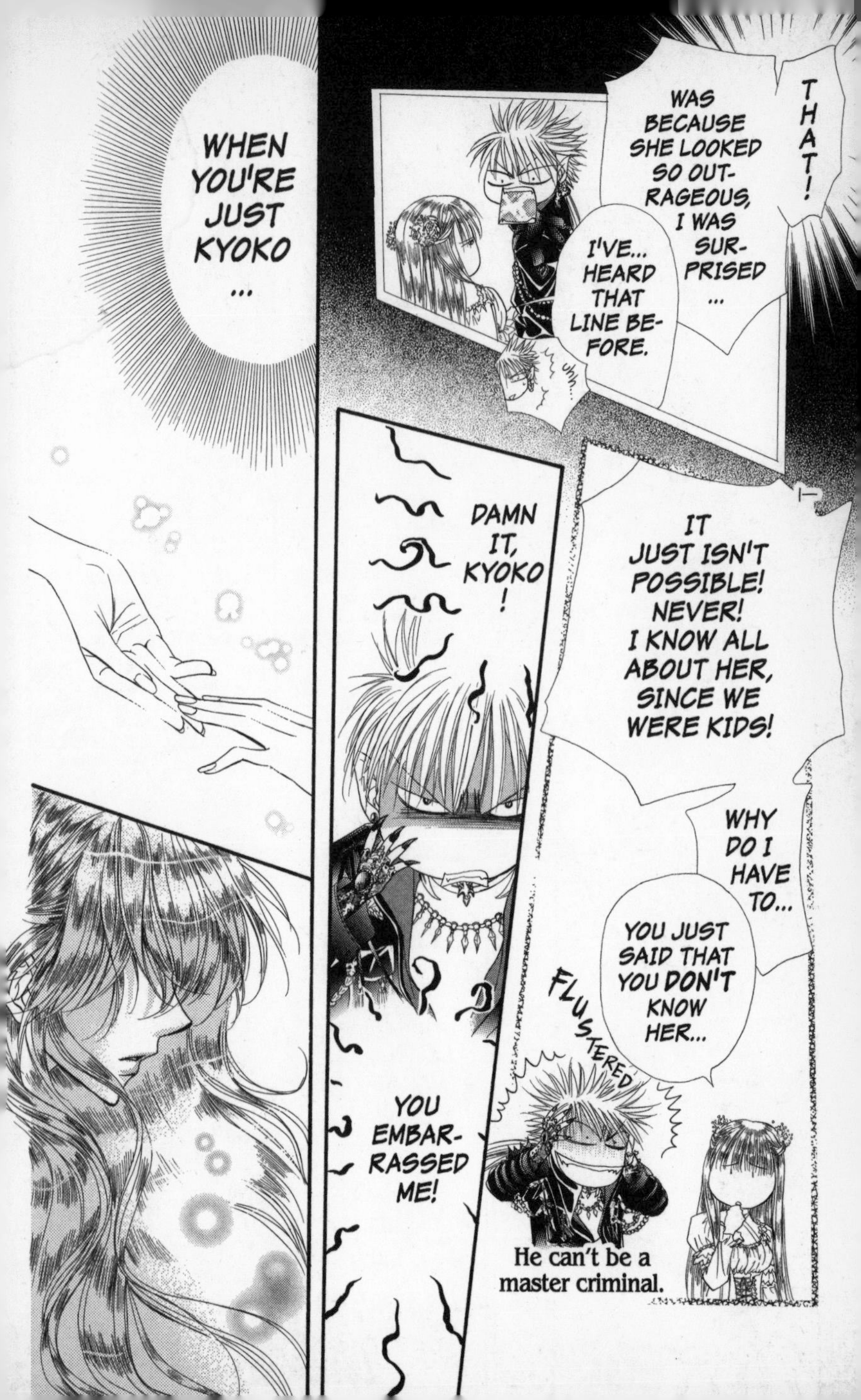
THAT!
WAS BECAUSE SHE LOOKED SO OUT-RAGEOUS, I WAS SUR-PRISED...
I'VE... HEARD THAT LINE BE-FORE.
IT JUST ISN'T POSSIBLE! NEVER! I KNOW ALL ABOUT HER, SINCE WE WERE KIDS!
WHY DO I HAVE TO...
YOU JUST SAID THAT YOU DON'T KNOW HER...
FLUSTERED
He can't be a master criminal.
DAMN IT, KYOKO!
YOU EMBAR-RASSED ME!
WHEN YOU'RE JUST KYOKO...

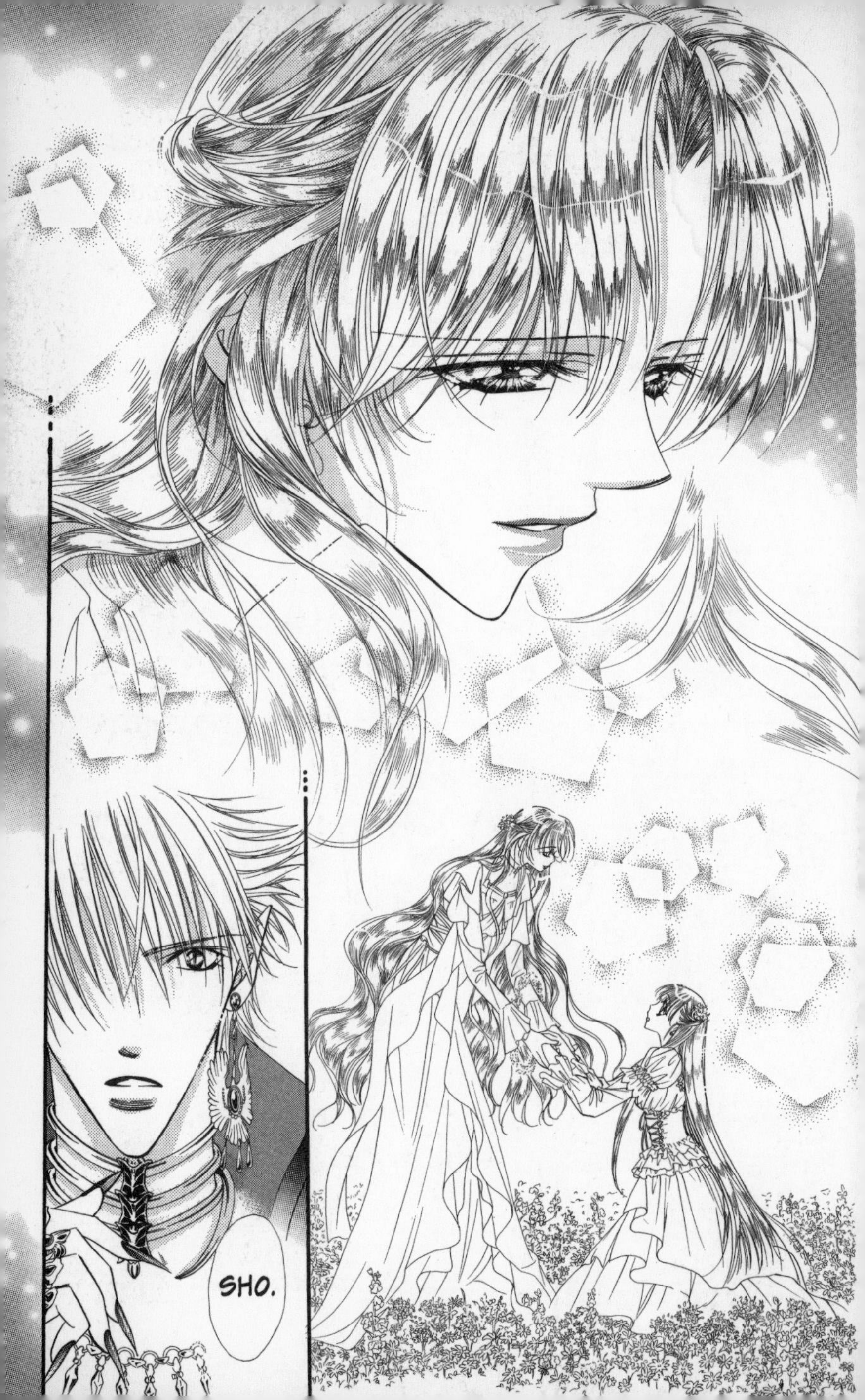
SHO.

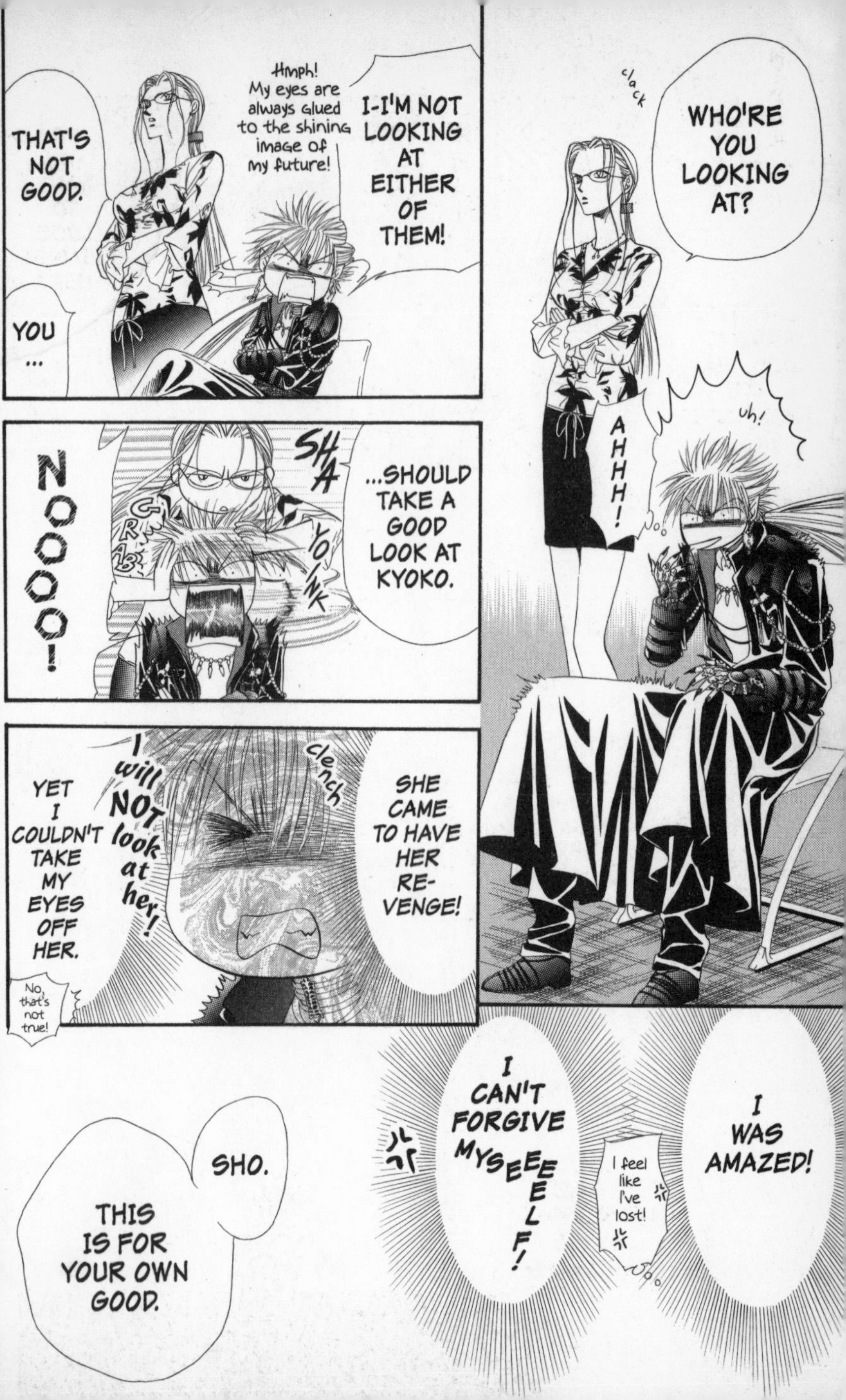
clack
WHO'RE YOU LOOKING AT?
uh!
AHHHH!
I-I'M NOT LOOKING AT EITHER OF THEM!
Hmph! My eyes are always glued to the shining image of my future!
THAT'S NOT GOOD.
YOU ...
...SHOULD TAKE A GOOD LOOK AT KYOKO.
SHA
YOINK
GRAB
NOOOOO!
SHE CAME TO HAVE HER RE-VENGE!
clench
I will NOT look at her!
YET I COULDN'T TAKE MY EYES OFF HER.
No, that's not true!
I WAS AMAZED!
I feel like I've lost!
I CAN'T FORGIVE MYSEEEELF!
SHO.
THIS IS FOR YOUR OWN GOOD.

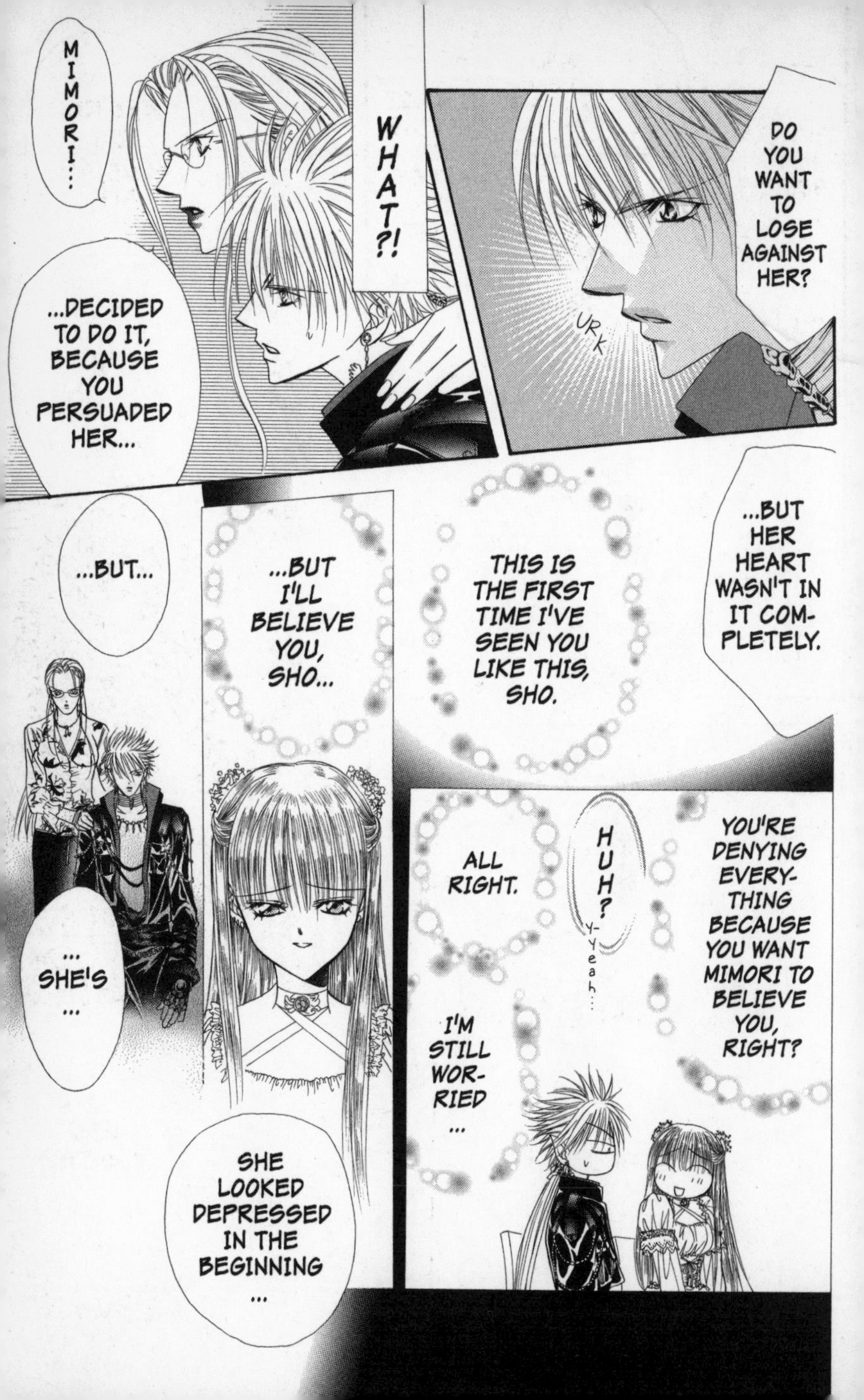
DO YOU WANT TO LOSE AGAINST HER?
URK
WHAT?!
MIMORI...
...DECIDED TO DO IT, BECAUSE YOU PERSUADED HER...
...BUT HER HEART WASN'T IN IT COMPLETELY.
THIS IS THE FIRST TIME I'VE SEEN YOU LIKE THIS, SHO.
YOU'RE DENYING EVERYTHING BECAUSE YOU WANT MIMORI TO BELIEVE YOU, RIGHT?
HUH?
Y-Yeah...
ALL RIGHT.
I'M STILL WORRIED ...
...BUT I'LL BELIEVE YOU, SHO...
...BUT...
... SHE'S ...
SHE LOOKED DEPRESSED IN THE BEGINNING ...

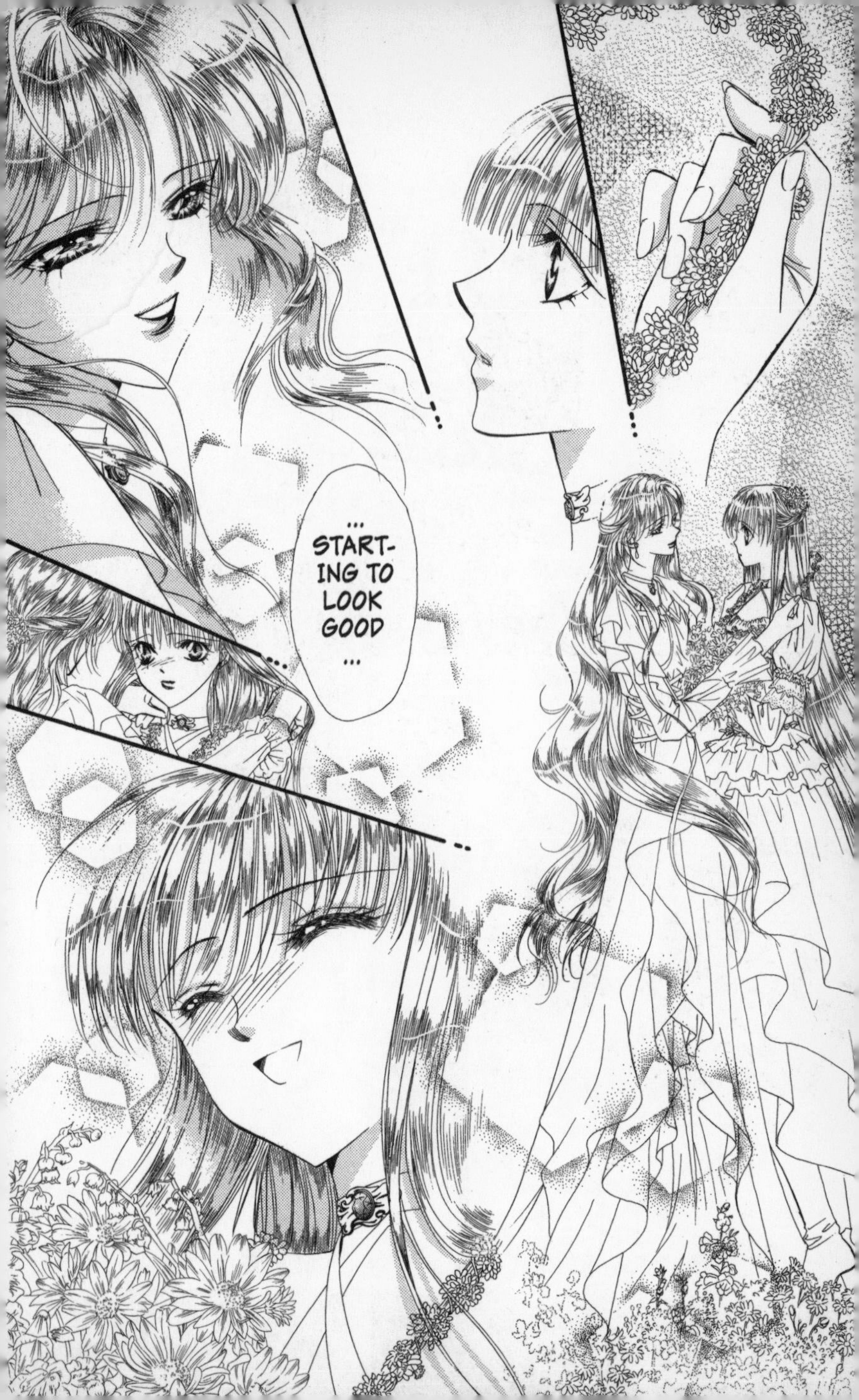
... STARTING TO LOOK GOOD ...

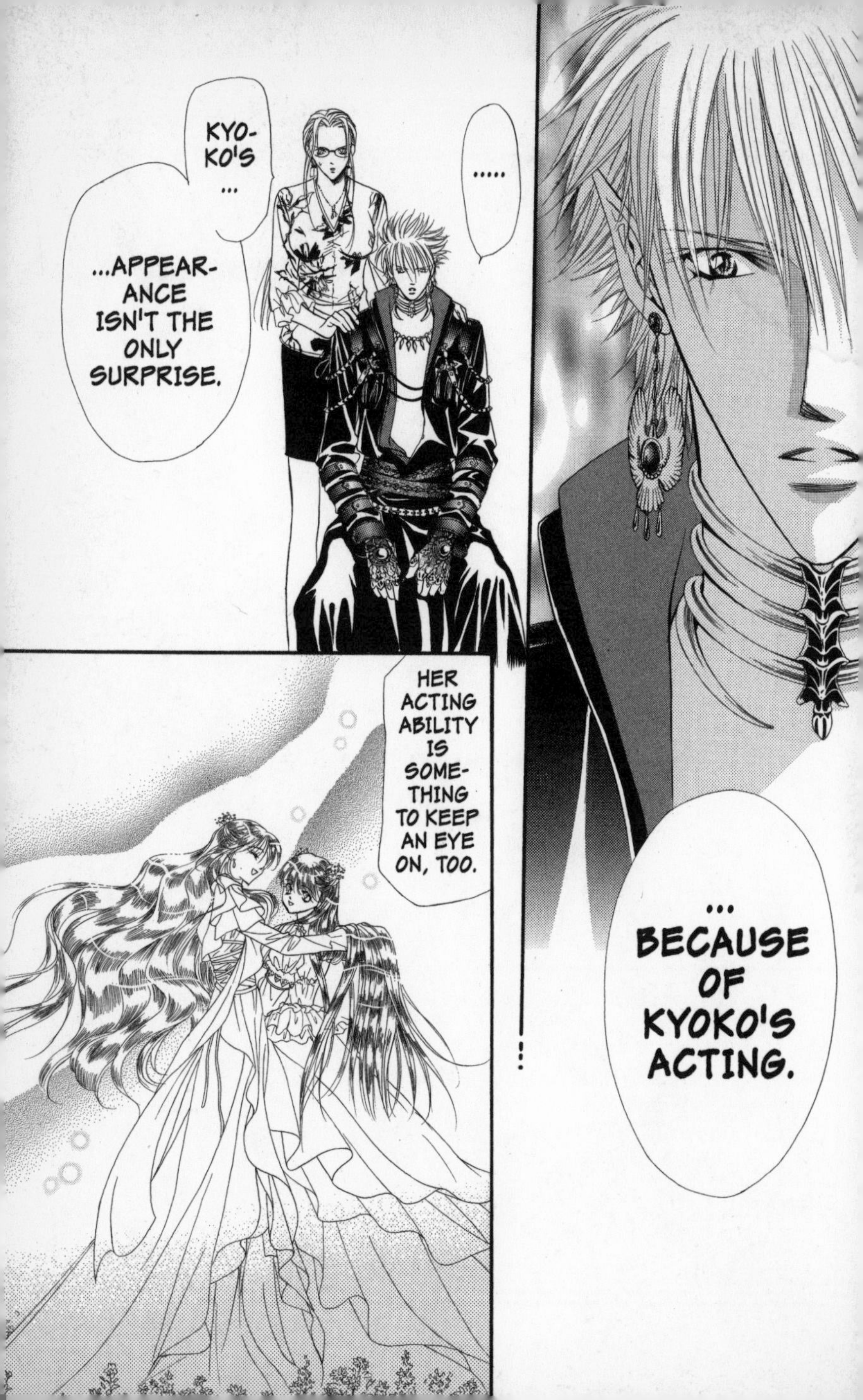
...BECAUSE OF KYOKO'S ACTING.
KYO-KO'S ...
.....
...APPEAR-ANCE ISN'T THE ONLY SURPRISE.
HER ACTING ABILITY IS SOME-THING TO KEEP AN EYE ON, TOO.

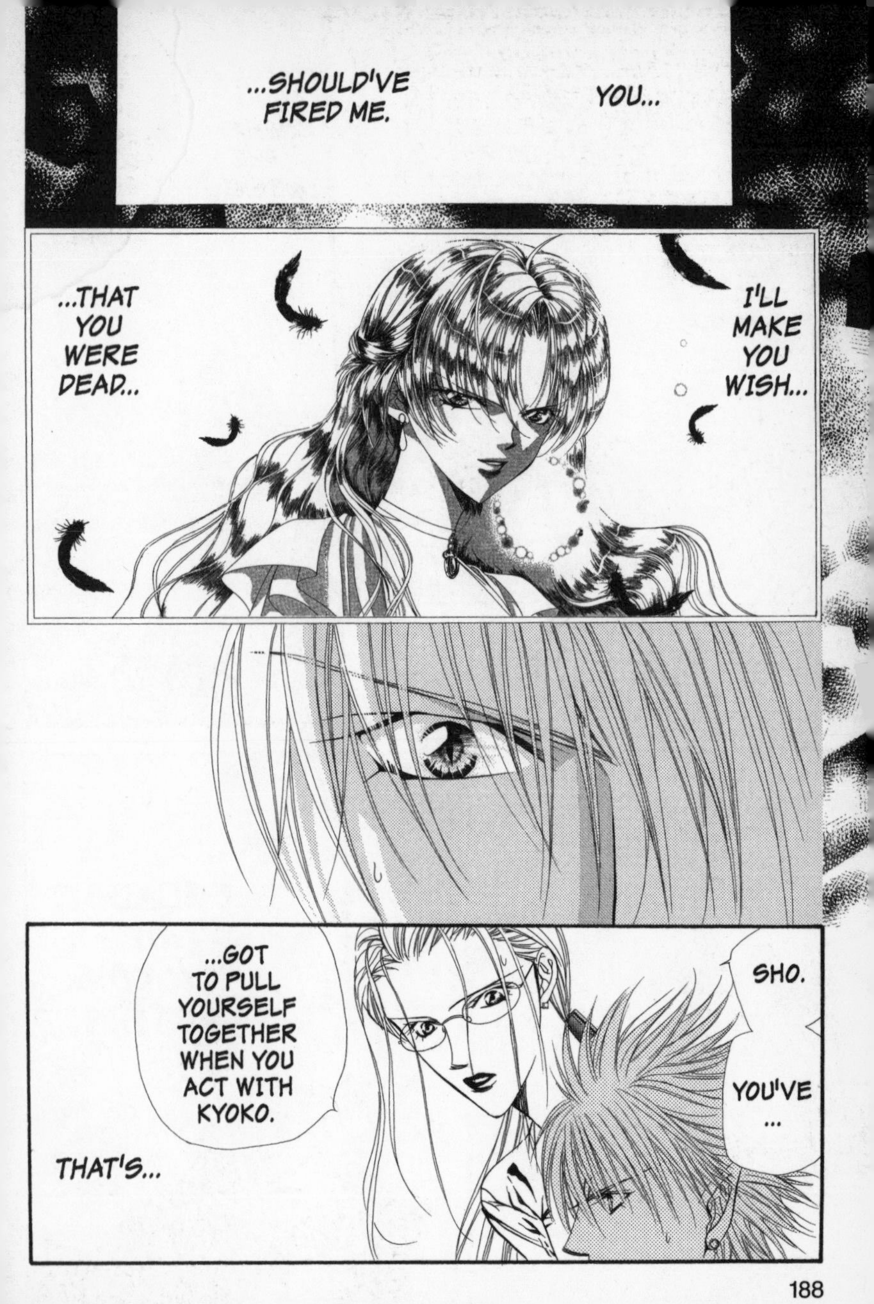
YOU...
...SHOULD'VE FIRED ME.
I'LL MAKE YOU WISH...
...THAT YOU WERE DEAD...
SHO.
YOU'VE ...
...GOT TO PULL YOURSELF TOGETHER WHEN YOU ACT WITH KYOKO.
THAT'S...

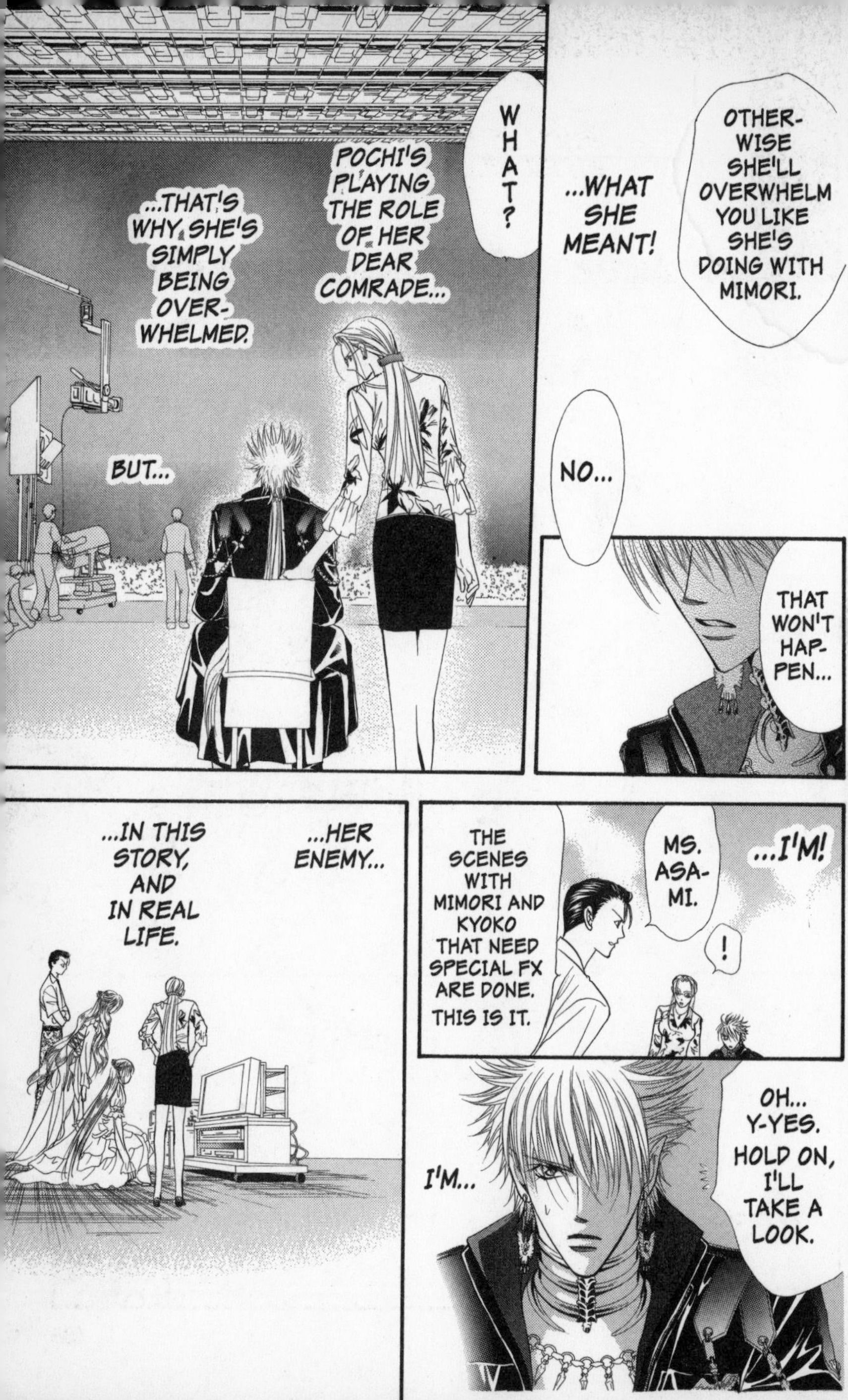
OTHER-WISE SHE'LL OVERWHELM YOU LIKE SHE'S DOING WITH MIMORI.
...WHAT SHE MEANT!
NO...
THAT WON'T HAP-PEN...
WHAT?
POCHI'S PLAYING THE ROLE OF HER DEAR COMRADE...
...THAT'S WHY SHE'S SIMPLY BEING OVER-WHELMED.
BUT...
...I'M!
MS. ASA-MI.
!
THE SCENES WITH MIMORI AND KYOKO THAT NEED SPECIAL FX ARE DONE.
THIS IS IT.
OH... Y-YES. HOLD ON, I'LL TAKE A LOOK.
I'M...
...HER ENEMY...
...IN THIS STORY, AND IN REAL LIFE.

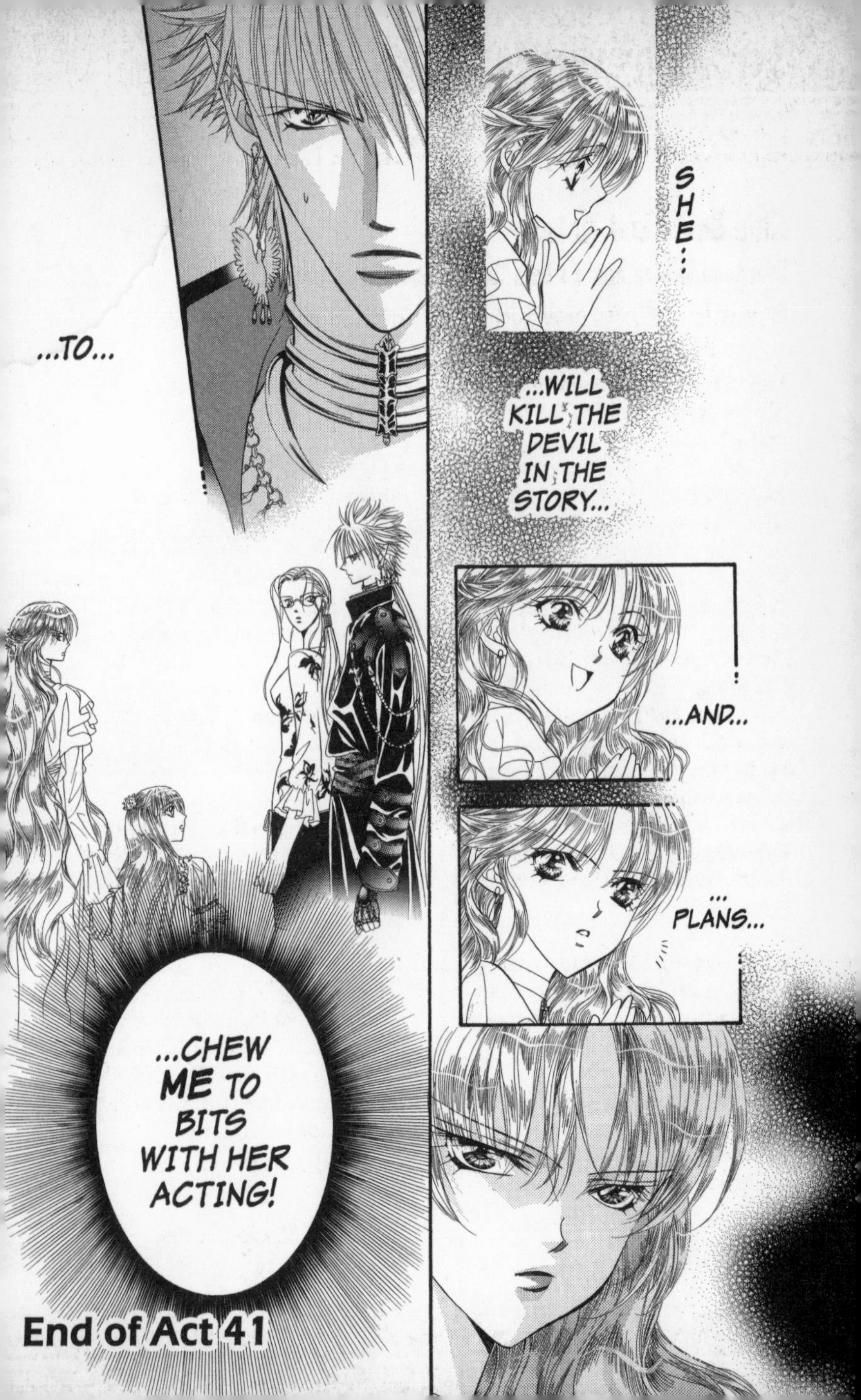
SHE...
...WILL KILL THE DEVIL IN THE STORY...
...AND...
... PLANS...
...TO...
...CHEW ME TO BITS WITH HER ACTING!

End of Act 41

Skip·Beat! End Notes
Everyone knows how to be a fan, but sometimes cool things from other cultures need a little help crossing the language barrier.

Page 28, panel 6: _Godfather_ Theme
This song is typically used by motorbike gangs.

Page 39, panel 3: Taisho
Kyoko's boss and landlord. In traditional Japanese restaurants, the boss is called Taisho by employees and customers alike.

Page 39, panel 3: Okamisan
The Taisho's wife. In Japan, the _okami_ acts as the face of the restaurant while her husband stays in the background to deal with cooking or managerial duties.

Page 43, panel 3: Itadakimasu
A little blessing or thank you before you eat.

Page 71, panel 3: Good Morning
Saying good morning regardless of the time is a custom in Japanese showbiz.

Page 73, panel 1: 2-hour drama
Two-hour dramas are the one-shots of the drama world. Many of them are mysteries, based on popular novels.

Page 82, panel 2: Pochi
Pochi is a popular name for dogs in Japan.

Page 103, panel 5: Kogal
Kogals are bleach-blonde, overly-bronzed girls who wear lots of makeup and accessories. They are similar to California Valley Girls in their use of slang and airhead personas.

Page 106, panel 4: Aso
The kanji for Asami can be read as Aso.

Page 124, panel 2: Tamagoyaki
A Japanese rolled omelet, sometimes called dashimaki. It's very popular in bento boxes, and can be either sweet or salty.

Page 132, panel 2: Throwing salt
The original Japanese is from the expression "To send the enemy salt," which is literally what Kyoko did, but also has the meaning of aiding the enemy.

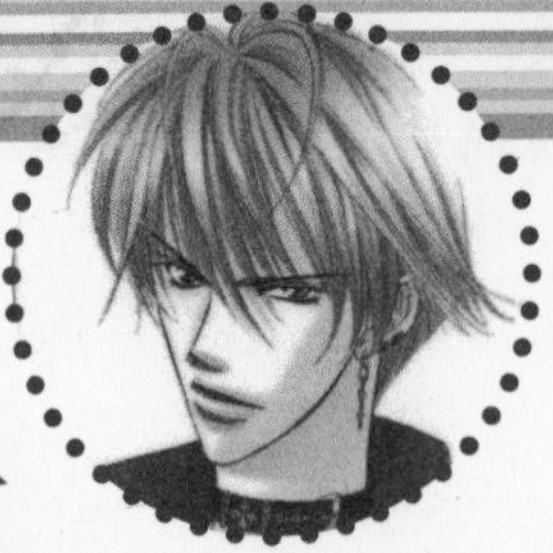

Yoshiki Nakamura is originally from Tokushima prefecture. She started drawing manga in elementary school, which eventually led to her 1993 debut of *Yume de Au yori Suteki* (Better than Seeing in a Dream) in *Hana to Yume* magazine. Her other works include the basketball series *Saint Love*, *MVP wa Yuzurenai* (Can't Give Up MVP), *Blue Wars*, and *Tokyo Crazy Paradise*, a series about a female bodyguard in 2020 Tokyo.

SKIP·BEAT!
Vol. 7
The Shojo Beat Manga Edition

STORY AND ART BY YOSHIKI NAKAMURA

English Translation & Adaptation/Tomo Kimura
Touch-up Art & Lettering/Sabrina Heep
Design/Yukiko Whitley
Editor/Pancha Diaz

Editor in Chief, Books/Alvin Lu
Editor in Chief, Magazines/Marc Weidenbaum
VP, Publishing Licensing/Rika Inouye
VP, Sales & Product Marketing/Gonzalo Ferreyra
VP, Creative/Linda Espinosa
Publisher/Hyoe Narita

Printed in Canada

Published by VIZ Media, LLC
P.O. Box 77010
San Francisco, CA 94107

Shojo Beat Manga Edition
10 9 8 7 6 5 4 3
First printing, July 2007
Third printing, December 2008

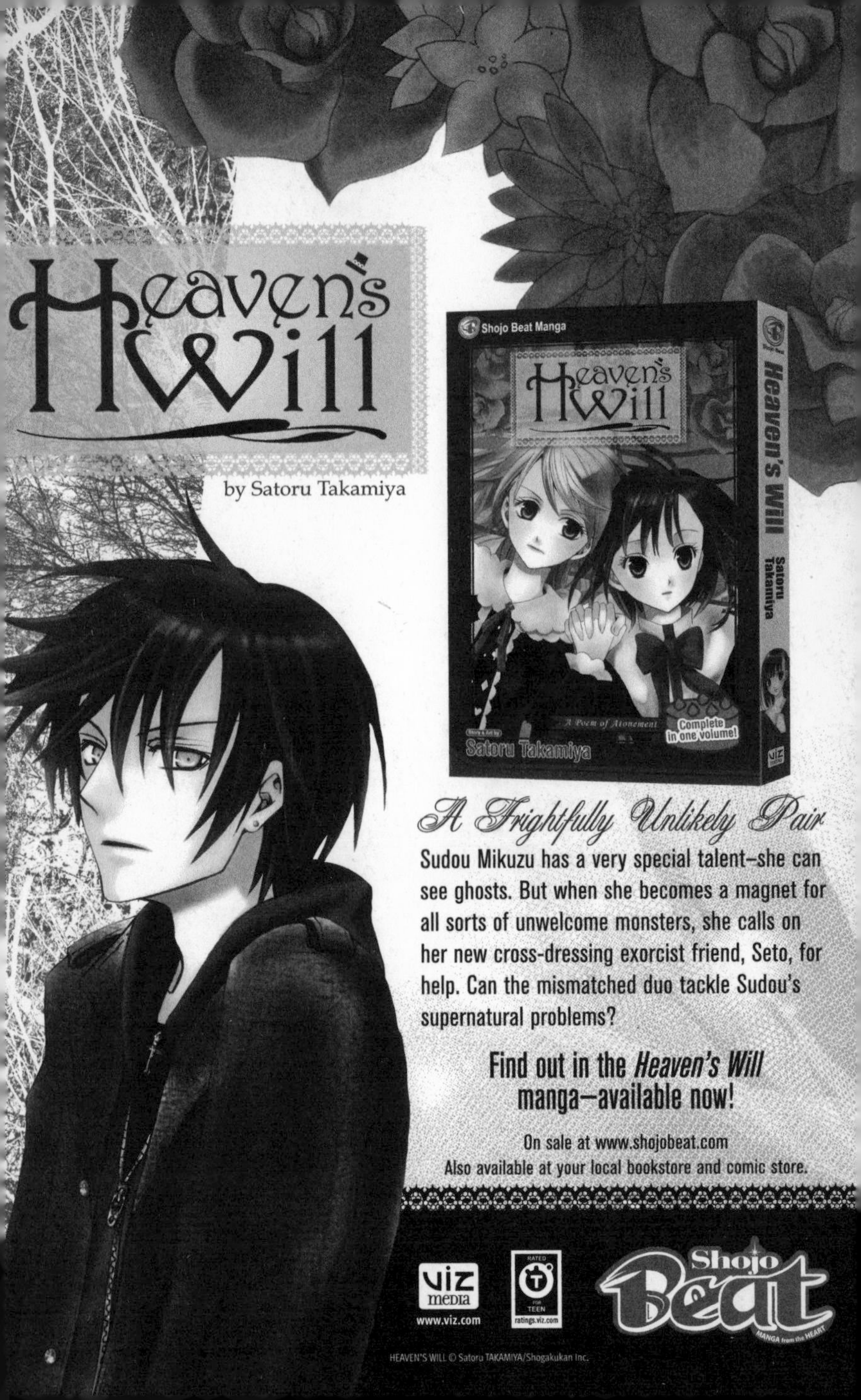
Heaven's Will
by Satoru Takamiya
Shojo Beat Manga
Heaven's Will
A Poem of Atonement
Story & Art by
Satoru Takamiya
Complete in one volume!
Heaven's Will
Satoru Takamiya
A Frightfully Unlikely Pair
Sudou Mikuzu has a very special talent—she can see ghosts. But when she becomes a magnet for all sorts of unwelcome monsters, she calls on her new cross-dressing exorcist friend, Seto, for help. Can the mismatched duo tackle Sudou's supernatural problems?
Find out in the Heaven's Will manga—available now!
On sale at www.shojobeat.com
Also available at your local bookstore and comic store.
VIZ MEDIA
www.viz.com
RATED T FOR TEEN
ratings.viz.com
Shojo Beat
MANGA from the HEART
HEAVEN'S WILL © Satoru TAKAMIYA/Shogakukan Inc.

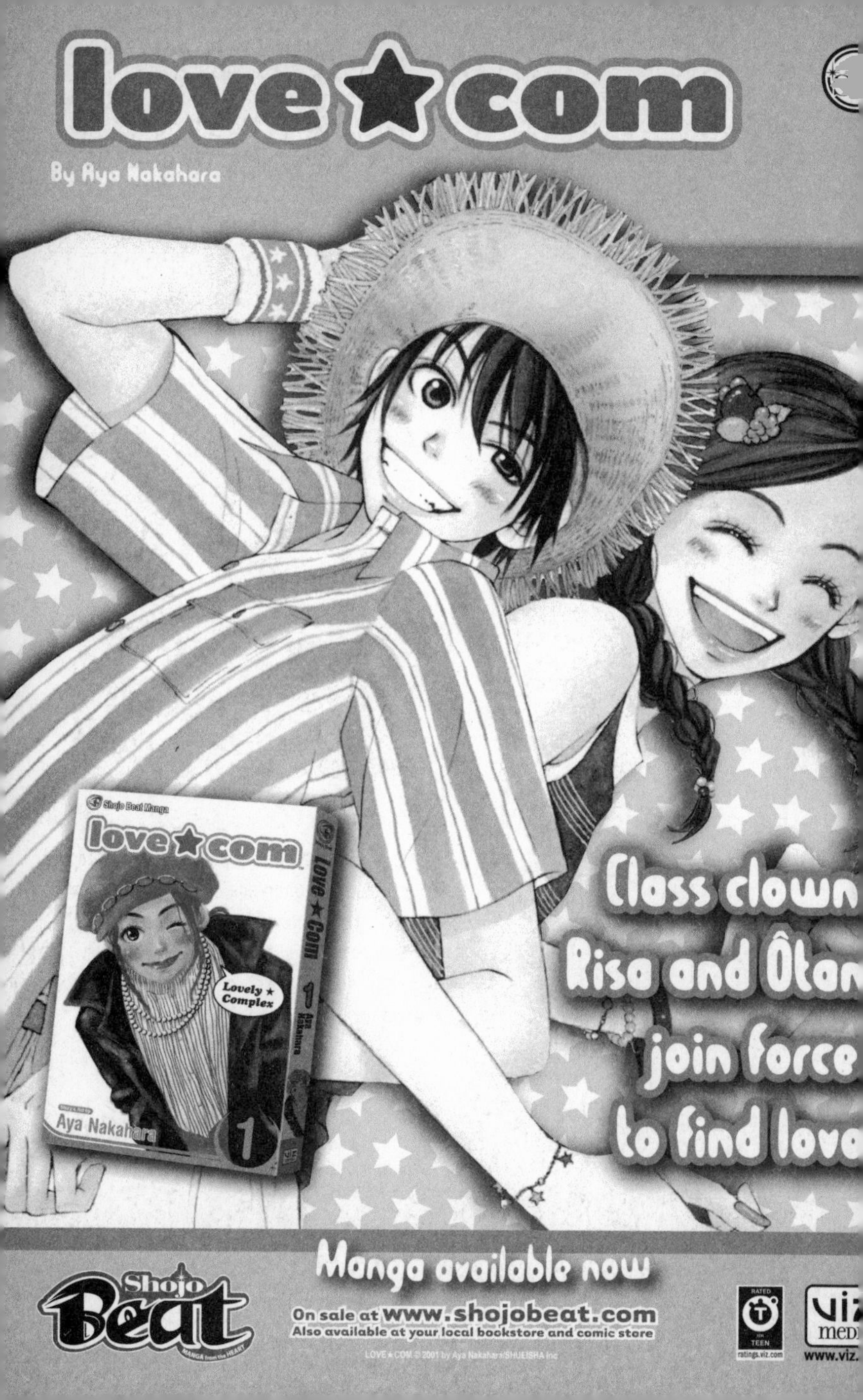

love★com
By Aya Nakahara
Shojo Beat Manga
love★com
Love★Com
Lovely★Complex
1
Aya Nakahara
Class clown
Risa and Ôtan
join force
to find love
Manga available now
Shojo Beat
On sale at www.shojobeat.com
Also available at your local bookstore and comic store
LOVE★COM © 2001 by Aya Nakahara/SHUEISHA Inc.
RATED T TEEN
ratings.viz.com

Love and Leftovers

Mixed Vegetables

by Ayumi Komura

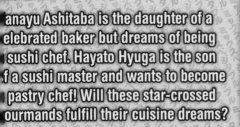

anayu Ashitaba is the daughter of a elebrated baker but dreams of being sushi chef. Hayato Hyuga is the son f a sushi master and wants to become pastry chef! Will these star-crossed ourmands fulfill their cuisine dreams?

ind out in *Mixed Vegetables*— nanga available now!

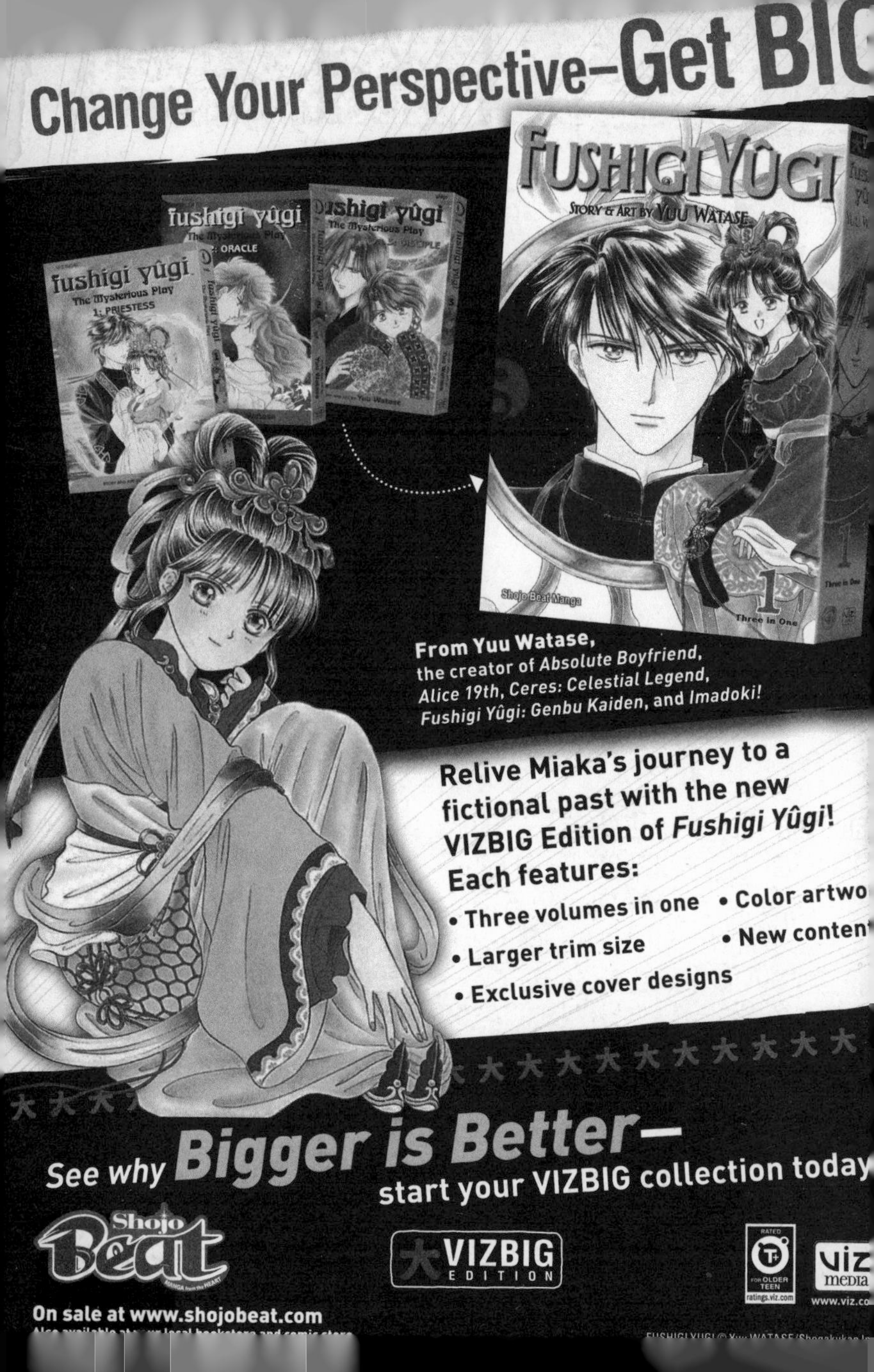

Change Your Perspective–Get BIG
fushigi yûgi
The Mysterious Play
1: PRIESTESS
fushigi yûgi
The Mysterious Play
ORACLE
fushigi yûgi
The Mysterious Play
DISCIPLE
Yuu Watase
FUSHIGI YÛGI
STORY & ART BY YUU WATASE
Shojo Beat Manga
1
Three in One
From Yuu Watase,
the creator of Absolute Boyfriend, Alice 19th, Ceres: Celestial Legend, Fushigi Yûgi: Genbu Kaiden, and Imadoki!
Relive Miaka's journey to a fictional past with the new VIZBIG Edition of Fushigi Yûgi!
Each features:
• Three volumes in one
• Color artwo
• Larger trim size
• New conten
• Exclusive cover designs
See why Bigger is Better—
start your VIZBIG collection today
Shojo Beat
MANGA from the HEART
VIZBIG EDITION
RATED T+ FOR OLDER TEEN
ratings.viz.com
VIZ media
www.viz.co
On sale at www.shojobeat.com

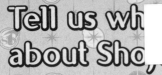

Tell us what you think
about Shojo Beat manga!

Our survey is now
available online. Go to:

shojobeat.com/mangasurvey

Help us make our
product offerings
better!

THE REAL
DRAMA BEGINS
IN...

Shojo
Beat

MANGA from the HEART